Public Sp

Public Sp

P

PUBLIC SPEECH AND THE CULTURE OF PUBLIC LIFE IN THE AGE OF GLADSTONE

Gladstone on the hustings in the 1870's

Public Speech and the Culture of Public Life in the Age of Gladstone

Joseph S. Meisel

COLUMBIA UNIVERSITY PRESS, NEW YORK

COLUMBIA UNIVERSITY PRESS

Publishers Since 1893

New York Chichester, West Sussex

Library of Congress

Cataloging-in-Publication Data

Meisel, Joseph S.

Public speech and the culture of public

life in the Age of Gladstone /

Joseph S. Meisel.

p. cm.

Based on the author's doctoral dissertation.

Includes bibliographical references and index.

ISBN 0–231–12144–X (cloth)

1. Political oratory—Great Britain—History—19th century.

2. Gladstone, W. E. (William Ewart), 1809–1898—Oratory.

3. Great Britain—Politics and government—1837–1901.

4. Oratory—Great Britain—History—19th century.

5. Great Britain—Civilization—19th century. I. Title

DA560 .M45 2001

941.081—dc21 2001028834

Casebound editions of Columbia University Press books

are printed on permanent and durable acid-free paper.

Printed in the United States of America

Designed by Audrey Smith

c 10 9 8 7 6 5 4 3 2 1

For Felice

CONTENTS

LIST OF TABLES ix

LIST OF ILLUSTRATIONS xi

ACKNOWLEDGMENTS xiii

Introduction 1

CHAPTER ONE
Schools for Public Speaking 11

CHAPTER TWO
The House of Commons 51

CHAPTER THREE
Religion 107

CHAPTER FOUR
Law 167

CHAPTER FIVE
The Platform 223

Conclusion 275

NOTES 291

BIBLIOGRAPHY 341

INDEX 365

TABLES

TABLE 1.1
Cambridge and Oxford Union Presidents by Career Category 36

TABLE 1.2
Union Presidents in the Dictionary of National Biography 38

TABLE 1.3
Union Presidents in the Dictionary of National Biography by Career Category 39

TABLE 1.4
Union Presidents Who Attained Judicial, Cabinet, or Episcopal Rank 40

TABLE 2.1
Contributions to House of Commons Debates 75

TABLE 4.1
Some Provincial Courthouses Constructed Between 1830 and 1900 178

TABLE 4.2
MPs Chiefly Associated with the Legal Profession 209

LIST OF ILLUSTRATIONS

COVER
"Mr. Gladstone's Campaign: The Meeting in the Music Hall at Edinburgh" (*The Graphic*, July 9, 1892)

FRONTISPIECE
Gladstone on the hustings at Greenwich (Greenwich Local History Library)

Following page 166

FIGURE 1
"A Debate in the Oxford Union" (*The Graphic*, May 31, 1873)

FIGURE 2
"The House of Commons in 1793: Mr. Pitt Addressing the House" [after Hickel] (Supplement to *The Illustrated London News*, November 28, 1885)

FIGURE 3
"The House Rule Debate in the House of Commons—Mr. Gladstone's Peroration" (*The Graphic*, April 17, 1886)

FIGURE 4
"The Reporters' Gallery, House of Commons" (*The Illustrated London News*, March 23, 1867)

FIGURE 5
Archibald Campbell Tait (by courtesy of the National Portrait Gallery, London).

FIGURE 6
Charles Haddon Spurgeon (by courtesy of the National Portrait Gallery, London).

FIGURE 7
"The Late Canon Liddon Preaching in St. Paul's Cathedral" (*The Illustrated News of the World*, October 4, 1890)

FIGURE 8
"The Tichborne Trial: Sketch in Court" (*The Illustrated London News*, July 8, 1871)

FIGURE 9
"Mr. Gladstone's Visit to Greenwich—In Front of the Hustings" (*The Graphic*, November 11, 1871)

FIGURE 10
"The General Election: Mr. Gladstone Addressing the Electors of Greenwich on Blackheath" (*The Illustrated London News*, February 7, 1874)

ACKNOWLEDGMENTS

Research for this book was conducted at, and many thanks are due to the staffs of: the Bodleian Library, Oxford; the British Library; the Burke Library of Union Theological Seminary; Cambridge University Library; Columbia University Libraries (especially Avery Art and Architectural Library, Butler Library, Diamond Law Library, the Rare Books and Manuscripts Library, and the Inter-Library Loan office); Dr. Williams's Library, London; the Greenwich Local History Library; Holker Library, Gray's Inn; Inner Temple Library; Lambeth Palace Library, London; Lincoln's Inn Library; Middle Temple Library; the New York Public Library; Newnham College Library, Cambridge; the Oxford Union Society Library; the Pierpont Morgan Library, New York; Pusey House Library, Oxford; St. Deiniol's Library, Hawarden (which generously furnished me with a residential scholarship); and Spurgeon's College Library, London.

For permission to quote from or incorporate material, I need to thank: the Bodleian Library; the Cambridge Union Society; Sir William Gladstone, Bt.; the Institute of Historical Research and Blackwell Publishers (for portions of chapter 4); the Monad Press (for portions of chapter 3); the Principal and Chapter of Pusey House; Spurgeon's College; and the Trustees of Dr. Williams's Library.

The doctoral dissertation on which this book is based was supervised by David Cannadine, to whom I owe an enormous scholarly debt. At different points, it was read by David Armitage, Robert Ferguson, Allan Silver, and Deborah Valenze; by Mark Kishlansky and Susan Pedersen; and by two anonymous readers for Columbia University Press. From each I received many useful suggestions, not all of which I could ultimately follow. Additionally, all manner of advice and assistance have been furnished by: Walter Arnstein, Steve Bates (who photographed most of the illustrations), David Bebbington, Eugenio Biagini (who generously read a draft of chapter 5), Marcus Collins, István Deák, Conrad Dehn QC, Nick Harding, Gwen Hyman, Philippa Levine, Peter Lindseth, Jennifer McBride, Julie Peters, Joyce Pedersen, John Rosenberg, John Seaman, Chris Stray (who generously read a draft of chapter 2), and Dan Unowsky. The late Colin Matthew provided early inspiration and much guidance. With all this high-powered help, it should go without saying that any remaining errors of fact and interpretation are the author's own. At Columbia University Press, many thanks are due to my editor, Kate Wittenberg, Leslie Bialler, and the rest of the editorial team.

My scholarly pursuits have been underpinned by the most supportive and generous employers: Jon Rosenhein at Columbia University; and Harriet Zuckerman and Bill Bowen at The Andrew W. Mellon Foundation.

My deepest personal gratitude begins, as did I, with my parents, Martin and Martha. It culminates with my wife, Felice, to whom this book could not but be dedicated with all my love.

PUBLIC SPEECH AND THE CULTURE OF PUBLIC LIFE IN THE AGE OF GLADSTONE

Introduction

I have very strong opinions on the subject of speechification, and hold that there is everywhere a vast amount too much of it. — *Charles Dickens, 1869*[1]

VERBOSITY IS A QUALITY we commonly associate with the Victorians, and for very good reasons. For the most part, our general feeling for life in Victorian Britain has been shaped by the great and prolific novelists of the period like Dickens, Eliot, Thackeray, and Trollope. In their works, characters and narrators alike can take pages of text to express their thoughts. As a result, we tend to think of Victorian speech as a product of the Circumlocution Office. Beyond the novelists' general prolixity, their works also regularly depict characters engaged in various kinds of public speaking. To take just a few notable examples from Trollope, we find the statesman Plantagenet Palliser addressing Parliament on decimalizing the currency with a fifth farthing, the Rev. Mr. Slope delivering a scandalous sermon in Barchester Cathedral, and the barrister Mr. Chaffanbrass employing all the tricks of courtroom rhetoric to get his clients (the guilty along with the innocent) acquitted.

In the context of the novels, it is natural that these characters should be speaking in public, because public speaking of one kind or another is what is supposed to happen in Parliament, in the pulpit, and in the courtroom. But the matter cannot simply be left there, for the novelistic evidence suggests that public speech enjoyed a particular heyday in nineteenth-century Britain. Eighteenth- and twentieth-century novelists do not depict public speaking with nearly as much frequency or with as much significance for the plot. In nineteenth-century novels, characters are revealed through acts of public speech. The literature of the period shows centrality of public speech in both the conception and the perception of Victorian public life.

If we can admit that the literary sources have something to say about how contemporaries understood and experienced their own times, then the prominence of oratory in nineteenth-century novels strongly suggests that public speaking deserves to be treated as a historical subject in its own right. But one does not need to rely upon literary sources alone to justify such an inquiry. The importance of speech-making in nineteenth-century Britain also comes across clearly from non-fictional observers such as Walter Bagehot, who wrote that "England is a country governed mainly by labour and by speech." [2] Beyond contemporary commentary, there is the historian's reliance upon various sorts of orations to understand the people, the events, and the "character" of nineteenth-century Britain. As one historian has written: "It may be possible to recover something of the atmosphere in which men lived, and for this purpose there may exist evidence which reveals something even about those who have left no trace. . . . If what they said is lost, the speeches to which they listened with applause may still be on record." [3]

In spite of the importance attached to public speech by contemporaries, and the utility of public speeches for historical analyses, the ways in which public speaking was central to the thought and practice of public life in nineteenth-century Britain has largely eluded historians. In general, what public speech was, what it meant, and what it accomplished have all been taken for granted. The orations themselves typically serve to illustrate or document a given historian's principal subject of inquiry. In recent years, speeches have been used to evidence the "discourse" of events, but too few scholars have paid attention to the historical developments that encouraged oratory and what public speaking of various kinds meant to both speakers and hearers. The evident prominence of oratory in Victorian public life must not only be recovered, but also explained. To this end, this work focuses on what were arguably the most pervasively influential areas of public life: politics, religion, and law. Speech-making was essential to the practices of each area and for all came to be the ultimate expression of their publicness in the nineteenth century.

This work breaks new ground by approaching both the history of British public life and the historical significance of oratory through the structures, practices, and contexts of public speaking. In the modern period, the historical study of public speaking has taken a variety of forms. There is, for example, a long tradition of celebrating the "great speech." This approach—a mixture of antiquarianism, reportage, and anecdote—is embodied in the numerous anthologies that collect the "jewels" of oratory through history for the edification of the present and future generations. The sensibility behind the "great speeches" approach is, in fact, far more literary (in a belletristic sense) than historical. Readers are meant to be uplifted by the noble sentiments and eternal verities articulated in the powerful phrases of the orators. Although it was more common in the past, such collections (now audio as well as print) continue to be assembled on a regular basis.

Great speeches are also at the heart of scholarship that analyzes orations based upon how they fulfilled or departed from the formal prescriptions of classical and modern theories of rhetoric. In recent years, some scholars of communications have written "rhetorical histories" seeking to place close speech analysis at the intersection of rhetorical processes and historical events. Robert Oliver, for example, looks at great speeches to argue that the "shaping of democracy was guided, supported, and hastened by public speakers of great persuasive ability."[4] Rhetorical histories also offer new views of particular individuals and events, like Karen Musolf's account of Nancy Astor's 1919 election campaign.[5] Although this kind of scholarship can be extremely interesting and informative in its own terms, it typically does not lend itself to deeper historical understanding of the period in which the speeches were spoken. By seeking to show how speeches helped to shape events, rhetorical histories tend to pass over the more significant historical question of how the times shaped the speech-making.

I by no means wish to argue that admiring and analyzing the excellent qualities of the selected best parliamentary, pulpit, courtroom, or platform orations is without utility for the study of history. Great speeches can provide some feel for what could be termed the "mouth" of the era. Yet, while they may serve as outstanding examples of rhetoric and argumentation, furnish a wealth of finely turned phrases, or articulate important themes, great speeches alone tell us little more than what the great speaker said (very well, as it happens) on a given occasion. Further, to the extent that great speeches give some sense of the mouth of a period, they are mute with respect to the "ear" that heard them or the "eye" that witnessed the event. What John Morley wrote about speech-making in politics also holds for other areas of public life:

> The statesman who makes or dominates a crisis, who has to rouse and mould the mind of senate or nation, has something else to think about than the production of literary masterpieces. The great polit-

> ical speech, which for that matter is a sort of drama, is not made by passages for elegant extract or anthologies, but by personality, movement, climax, spectacle, and the action of time.[6]

Therefore, this work will not perform close analyses of particular "representative" speeches or sermons. As important and useful as this kind of work can be, the following chapters will describe and dissect public speaking, not the speeches themselves.

Another approach to the study of speech in history (one nearly opposite to that of the rhetorical historians) is to find in the "languages" used by contemporaries to discuss their world the signs and significance, and even the engines of social change. As one of the most notable exponents of this approach, Gareth Stedman Jones, has written:

> There is an intimate connection between what is said and to whom. Yet it cannot be said that such a connection can be conceived in terms of a recognition of the pre-existence of the common social properties of the addressees. It should rather be thought of as the construction, successful or unsuccessful, of a possible representation of what such common properties might be. . . . The attempted relationship is prefigurative, not reflective.[7]

Other historians have broadened this approach by employing an expanded definition of "language" that includes various forms of symbolic communication along with the written and the oral. Patrick Joyce, for example, has made an important contribution to how we understand class and class formation by demonstrating the ways in which this broad band of communication was instrumental in creating what he terms "political constituencies, or collective political subjects."[8] Yet, even in Joyce's account, not all forms of communication are equal. As he states, the period from the middle of the nineteenth century to the beginning of the twentieth century "was the age of oratory and of the speech."[9] Nevertheless, speeches and oratory are the forms of communication to which he pays the least attention.

What Stedman Jones, Joyce, and others who have followed a similar approach do not help us to understand is how the domain of public speaking expanded so remarkably in the nineteenth century and what were the effects of this expansion on political culture generally. While the various "languages" with which certain concepts were articulated or (in another approach) the changing usages of certain "key words" [10] are historical evidence to be sifted and interpreted, the ways in which public speech was produced and consumed in nineteenth-century Britain are historical evidence of a more concrete, and perhaps even more eloquent, variety.

Scholars in disciplines other than rhetoric and history have also made important claims about the development of public communication in nineteenth-century Britain. The sociologist Jürgen Habermas, for example, posited that the "public sphere," which emerged in eighteenth-century Britain as a means of influencing state action through collecting and communicating bourgeois public opinion, was transformed in the nineteenth century through the advent of the mass circulation press and mass politics. As the political parties organized to integrate the mass electorate, the nature of public discourse changed to "something like modern propaganda ... with the Janus face of enlightenment and control; of information and advertising; of pedagogy and manipulation."[11] Aspects of my study tend to support Habermas's general scheme, but his account is premised on "a public sphere whose decisive mark was the written word."[12] As I will argue, the oratorical, at least as much as the written, lay at the core of the structural transformation of public institutions and their relationship to society.

In the field of historical linguistics, Walter Ong has shown how the nineteenth century was the pivotal period in Britain's shift from oral culture to written culture, even despite the tenacious survival of the old orality in the face of advancing literacy.[13] What Ong overlooks is the novel functionality that public speech acquired in nineteenth-century public culture, as well as the connected and mutually reinforcing nature of the new orality and the new literacy. Oral culture did not merely survive in the nineteenth century; it flourished. As this study will demonstrate, the practices of public speaking as they developed in nineteenth-century Britain were a *new* formulation strongly connected to a host of other modernizing trends in the period.

Speech is an inherently ephemeral phenomenon. Even with the benefit of modern audiovisual recording technologies, it is impossible to capture the full experience of what it was like to hear a speech at the time of its original delivery. We cannot play back context. For the historian of nineteenth-century Britain, the record of speeches is even more imperfect. Published texts of speeches range from near verbatim to remote approximation. (Even the published debates of Parliament were not verbatim reports until the early twentieth century.) The reminiscences of those who recall certain notable speeches or speakers are filtered through the veils of memory, opinion, and self-interest. While these are valuable and necessary sources, in order to understand why public speech generally became so prominent in the second half of the nineteenth century, I must look beyond the trace of the speeches themselves.

Accordingly, I have focused as far as possible on the *material* and *structural* factors involved in both the production and consumption of oratory. Very little work of this kind has been done for nineteenth-century Britain. The most notable example is the late Colin Matthew's brief study of how trends in the style, content, and performance of political speeches were tied into a number of historical developments such as extensions of the voting franchise and the rise of the popular press.[14] Following the lines suggested by Matthew's work, each of the following chapters will in one way or another explore the education and oratorical training of public speakers (both groups and individuals), the traditions (invented or otherwise) and genealogies of different genres of public speech, the relationship between oratory and its physical surroundings (that is, between the ephemeral and the durable), the printing and reading of public speeches, and the experience of both speaking and hearing. Some of these elements have been considered, to a greater or lesser extent, by other scholars, while others have been almost wholly neglected.

This book is the first time that an analysis of speech-making in nineteenth-century Britain has moved across the broad front of politics, religion, and law, while at the same time encompassing education, tradition, space, print, and experience.[15] Although oratorical production was already an established element of political, religious, and legal practice by the turn of the nineteenth century,[16] it was in the mid- and late Victorian period that public speech became both central and essential to the transaction of the business of public life. A variety of developments in public life caused an increasing volume of speech to be devoted to getting things done. Consequently, speech became an ever more important aspect of success in public life. As never before, legislating, saving souls, obtaining a verdict necessitated making speeches. Both cause and consequence of this, getting elected, filling pews, acquiring briefs necessitated speaking well.

Chapter 1 begins this study by describing the broad popularity and wide range of debating institutions established by people wishing to train themselves for oratorical performance. From the debating societies established at the elite schools and universities (particularly the Union Societies at

Oxford and Cambridge) in the 1810s and 1820s, to the popular local parliaments of the 1880s and 1890s, these organizations reflected, embodied, and promoted a new conception of public life that centered on public speaking.

Chapter 2 moves from mock parliaments to the mother of parliaments and examines the broader cultural significance ascribed to the changing stylistic conventions and functionality of MPs' speeches from the later eighteenth-century "golden age" of parliamentary oratory to the era of Gladstone and Disraeli. As Chapter 2 also shows, developments in the practices of parliamentary speaking occurred alongside and were intertwined with the minor obsession of contemporaries with what they perceived to be the declining quality of speech-making in the House of Commons.

Too often, histories of nineteenth-century culture and politics hold religion at arm's length, while histories of religion are too seldom connected to the concerns and events of the secular world. Chapter 3 seeks to avoid the habitual segregation of the sacred from the profane by describing the great growth of durable mass preaching celebrity in the second half of the nineteenth century and some of the ways in which the great preachers conditioned the broader political culture. Further, the struggle of the oratorically lackluster Church of England to improve the quality of its preaching reveals how the new public speaking demands of the age served to shake up national institutions. In many ways, the oratorical expansion of the nineteenth century had its roots in the transformation of worship. Ironically, however, the practices of Victorian religious oratory were indicative of a broader secularizing tendency.

Chapter 4 explores a parallel institutionalization of speech-making in the law. Among the many other structural changes wrought by nineteenth-century legal reforms, procedural legislation enlarged the oratorical functions of barristers in the courtroom. This had a variety consequences: the creation of debating societies for law students, heightened anxieties over the morality of barristerial speech, and the increased popularity of the Victorian courtroom as a kind of "oratorical theater." Chapter 4 also revisits the parliamentary context to examine the oratorical contributions of the increasing number of barristers in the House of Commons.

Chapter 5 analyzes the development, techniques, and experience of extra-parliamentary speech-making. The adoption of the platform as a vehicle of mainstream politics in the later nineteenth century resulted from a longer-term learning process in British political culture that forged a particular set of relationships and expectations between speakers and audiences. By the time Gladstone launched into his legendary barnstorming Midlothian campaigns of 1879 and 1880, a system of structures and conventions had been progressively established in the political arena by the experience of popular radical demonstrations in the first half of the century, the effects of franchise extensions and party organization on hustings oratory, and the variety of semi-private and public gatherings at which political leaders increasingly spoke. These structures and conventions were also connected to the developments in religious practices described in chapter 3. By the last quarter of the century, the combination of these various strands made the platform the major locus for the delivery of important political addresses in the nineteenth century as well as a major arena for political combat.

The Conclusion attempts to draw together the various nineteenth-century developments and explain how the importance of public speaking in public life came to be significantly diminished in the changed circumstances of the twentieth century.

Over the years that I have been working on this project, friends, colleagues, critics, and sheer obviousness suggested many chapters that could be, and perhaps ought to have been, added: public lecturing, professional organizations, the theater, and the House of Lords to name only a few. I have tried at least to acknowledge these and other possible avenues of inquiry along the way. Broad as the present study is, I neither pretend to have exhausted the subject of public speaking in nineteenth-century Britain, nor do I claim to have the last word even in those areas with which I have dealt. In the course of my research, I was struck by (what seemed to me) a prefigurative critique of the scope of this study in an 1827 essay "On Eloquence" by none other than the young William Gladstone:

> It has been usual in this country to divide this great art into three portions only: and to reduce all under the heads of the Senate, the Pulpit, and the Bar. Further investigation will suggest to an inquiring mind many additional subdivisions: which, though they may not assume so lofty a character, nor boast so widely-extended an influence, have a legitimate claim to be considered by him who undertakes to descant on this subject.[17]

Among the less-celebrated, but historically fascinating kinds of speech to which the Eton schoolboy pointed were auctioneers' eloquence, advertising eloquence, bill-sticking eloquence, shopkeeping eloquence, and the eloquence of beggars. By studying politics, religion, and law, I have admittedly proceeded along lines more horizontally broad than vertically deep. But one aim of this study is to make new connections among historical developments in areas of public life that are most often dealt with separately. The shared "lofty" character of politics, religion, and law facilitates such connections.

Compared to the accumulating body of important historical scholarship that has sought to throw off the dead weight of Anglocentricism and give the interconnected developments in Scotland, Wales, and Ireland their due emphasis, the actions and events discussed in the following chapters take place for the most part in England. Nevertheless, I consider this work to be a contribution to *British* history in the sense that, as Keith Robbins has written: "It was, indeed, in England that the blending of Britain reached its height."[18] This study bears out Robbins's contention: the orators discussed here may have been speaking in London and other parts of England, but they came from all parts of the British Isles. For example, as one legal historian has written, "The Scots as a whole . . . were magnificent in their qualities of mind and endurance—a race particularly adept at conquering the English Bar."[19] It would also have been instructive to examine related developments in other European countries and the Empire; but I hope that I have at least provided a useful model for future scholarship in these areas.

At a time when historians make great efforts to bring the regional and particular to the fore, much of the action described in the following chapters takes place in and around the Metropolis. But London was where official national public life was based, and the place where almost all of the leading oratorical talent from the provinces came to speak at one point or another and often remained. Additionally, with a resident population that comprised roughly one-tenth of all Britons, further enlarged by vast numbers of tourists, London was the nation's greatest supplier of audience. Even so, this study will show that some places outside the Metropolitan world—Birmingham, for example—proved to be particularly notable nurseries of orators.

Most of the people who appear on these pages were among the most prominent politicians, preachers, and lawyers of their time. When one's subject is the official, national public life of nineteenth-century Britain, and when one is concerned with those individuals whose speaking brought them most before the public, it is impossible to avoid the "great men."

Women do appear in the following pages but, as was the case in official, national public life, they appear for the most part in supporting, rather than leading roles. In this connection, one cannot overlook the fact that the most important public woman, Queen Victoria, ceased making speeches from the throne after the death of Albert in 1861,[20] precisely when public speaking was becoming central to the practice of public life. Despite the familiarity of most of the figures that appear in the following chapters, far more important are the material and structural factors that encouraged the growth of oratory within public life. The cast of characters discussed here consists of those individuals who succeeded within that context.

As indicated by its title, however, this study does take a special interest in one individual. Gladstone's long and active life spanned practically the whole of the nineteenth century, but I use "the age of Gladstone" to mean essentially the century's second half. It was in this period that Gladstone became not only Britain's most prominent public figure, but also its most prolific and captivating public speaker. While the following chapters in no way constitute a systematic analysis of Gladstone's life or career, he is, if not quite the protagonist, at least the most often-recurring character. As Lytton Strachey observed, "speech was the fibre of his being."[21] More famously, Gladstone's great political rival, Benjamin Disraeli, mocked him in 1878 as "a sophistical rhetorician inebriated with the exuberance of his own verbosity."[22] Yet the same could be said for many of the public speakers that appear in the following chapters. Thus, Gladstone is not only the focal person for the period I cover, but also the greatest single example of the developments I discuss. But beyond the man himself, the age of Gladstone, as I intend to demonstrate, was the period in which public speech—by virtue of its valuation, its utility, and its openness to experimentation—enjoyed its heyday in British public life.

CHAPTER ONE

Schools for Public Speaking

ON OCTOBER 22, 1873, around 400 men gathered for a banquet at the Oxford Corn Exchange. For those traveling from London, the Great Western Railway Company had arranged special trains to convey them to and from the banquet. One hundred and fifty additional gentlemen joined the 400 for dessert, and a gallery was provided for a large number of ladies. Presiding was the Lord Chancellor, Roundell Palmer, Earl of Selborne. The guest list was a veritable *Who's Who.* Absent invitees included the Prince of Wales and his youngest brother Leopold, Prime Minister William Ewart Gladstone, and Chancellor of the Exchequer Robert Lowe. Yet, even without these stellar figures, those assembled were a phenomenally brilliant constellation of Victorian pubic life—cabinet ministers, statesmen, MPs, Lords, bishops, judges and scholars. Among the most notable of those present were the Marquis of Salisbury, Earl Stanhope, Earl Beauchamp, Archbishop of Canterbury Tait, Archbishop (later Cardinal) Manning, Attorney General (later Lord Chief Justice) Coleridge, and Matthew Arnold. This impressive assemblage of notables had come together to celebrate the jubilee of their alma mater—not their college, nor the University itself, but rather an institution to which they owed at least equal loyalty: the Oxford Union Society.[1]

The founding of the Union Societies at Cambridge (1815) and Oxford (1823) anticipated the wide popularity that debating societies would attain in nineteenth-century Britain. This is not to say that debating societies were a new idea. Small, private or semi-private discussion groups were not uncommon by the late eighteenth century. In London during the 1780s, numbers of these fora were transformed into large-scale, commercial debating societies whose proceedings were well advertised in the popular London dailies. By 1800, however, these societies had almost disappeared under measures of wartime suppression.[2] A resurgence of debating societies began in the immediate postwar years, the university Unions being among the earliest and most significant instances. In the early years of this resurgence—as evidenced by the history of the Unions—debating societies often met with setbacks and official discouragement (not the least of which being the infamous "Six Acts" of 1819). By the 1830s, however, the movement progressed more or less unchecked.

The Union Societies

The Cambridge and Oxford Unions were (and remain today) debating societies where university students learned and practiced the arts of public speaking. Although they are fixtures of student life, the Unions are private organizations and not a formal part of the Universities. The Oxford Union achieved particular distinction and over the years it has been called "toy parliament," "nursery of statesmen," and "playground of power."[3] Clearly, to judge by those who celebrated its fiftieth anniversary, the Oxford Union was an institution whose members went on to hold the highest offices of Victorian public life—an institution that they all credited with playing a deeply significant if not indispensable role in their *bildung.* Therefore, the Oxford Union, and its counterpart at Cambridge, are appropriate places to begin an examination of Victorian public life through its public speech.

ORIGINS AND DEVELOPMENT

At the beginning of the nineteenth century, the young men who formed the Union Societies at Cambridge and Oxford (as well as many future members) were able to draw upon the oratorical experience they had gained in debating groups at their schools and university colleges. At the great public schools, for example, speech activities were a natural outgrowth of a curriculum in which students read classical authorities on rhetoric, and educational methods that stressed recitation. Speech activities at school could turn into semi-public events, as when Charles James Fox requested his father's presence at Eton in 1763 to hear him declaim a speech from Cicero.[4] In 1811, a group of Eton's famously self-governing students created the prototypical public school student debating society: the Eton Society, or "Pop."

The rules of the Eton Society forbade discussion of the politics of the past fifty years, although debates over earlier history admitted many references by analogy to current events. At first, Eton boys viewed Pop with suspicion. In 1827, while still at Eton, Gladstone wrote that the Society had been faced with ridicule, contempt, and prejudice.[5] The eventual success of Pop in the life of the school can be measured in its elitist forms. One had to be "a good sort" to gain acceptance. Aspirants were elected (or blackballed) by the membership, and members set themselves apart from the rest of the student body with fancy waistcoats. The members of Pop also enjoyed their own exclusive space within the school. As the future Lord Chief Justice, John Duke Coleridge (President of the Oxford Union, 1843), wrote to his father in the early 1830s on being elected to the Society: "I am now writing from the Room in which we hold our Debates, and use as a lounging-room for reading, writing, or warming oneself during the remainder of the week."[6]

For the most part, Pop's achievements as a debating society were limited—even in the eyes of some of its fondest alumni. During a banquet to celebrate the centenary of the Eton Society in 1911, Lord Rosebery, in the chair, did not express a very high opinion of its intellectual or rhetorical qualifications. Lord Curzon, proposing the toast "*Floreat Etona*," said, "I cannot say in my day 'Pop' could fairly be described as a nursery of rhetoric, and yet I have known occasions upon which, amid loud applause, a member of 'Pop' has successfully addressed his audience for fifteen or twenty minutes."[7] Whatever its merits as a debating society, as Curzon observed, the example of Pop gave rise to a number of other debating societies at Eton and elsewhere "which, although they may not have inherited the social distinction of 'Pop,' certainly carried on its intellectual tradition."[8]

The young men who went up to university were able to continue honing their oratorical skills in a number of small, socially exclusive debating clubs that had formed at various colleges within the universities. These clubs were a part of a general increase of associational life and the organization of leisure time at the universities which began in the second half of the eighteenth century—most of which appears to have centered on gambling, drinking, and eating.[9] However, some clubs given over to more intellectual pursuits did emerge. In the late 1780s, for example, the future prime minister George Canning became the leading member of a select

Christ Church debating club known as the Speaking Society. Although Canning's own background was of a more dubious character, many of his fellow members issued from the highest social circles. Similar to Pop, collegiate debating clubs broadcast their exclusivity. The members of the Speaking Society, for example, wore special brown jackets with velvet cuffs and buttons bearing the initials D. C. P. and F., standing for Demosthenes, Cicero, Pitt, and Fox. Outward displays aside, legitimate political debate at this time was viewed as an aristocratic prerogative. Men like Canning who had to make careers (Canning's ambition as an undergraduate was the law) were advised to steer clear of such activities.[10]

Select collegiate debating clubs—often meeting as semi-private wine parties—continued to form well into the nineteenth century. For clubs like the Canning, the Chatham, the Palmerston, and the Russell, their names announced their political bent, and their social exclusivity endowed them with prestige. Sometimes they were debating clubs, sometimes they were "essay clubs" in which members prepared and read an essay, which was then discussed or argued over by the other members. The great difference between the two types was that in debating clubs the subject to be argued for or against was introduced extempore (although not infrequently from a memorized composition), while in essay clubs it was generated from a written text. Clubs formed after the inception of the Unions often provided a leadership cadre for the larger organizations. In one case—the only one it seems—an exclusive club was named for a current undergraduate, both a member of the club and the Oxford Union: the WEG, for William Ewart Gladstone.

The late 1810s and the early 1820s—the period in which the Cambridge and Oxford Unions were founded—favored the efflorescence of discussion. The end of nearly a quarter-century of armed conflict with France was followed by a relaxation of the various incentives—both coercive and voluntary—to speak with one (patriotic) voice. No longer, for instance, could the exigencies of war serve as an excuse to suppress calls for the reform of Parliament. Beyond the effects of peace breaking out, however, actions taken during wartime had also created or exacerbated other concerns. The formal joining of Ireland to the United Kingdom in 1800 had raised the question of granting full rights of citizenship to Catholics in England, Wales, and Scotland. Further, the issues surrounding Britain's imperial commitments were given added dimension by the fact that Britain had emerged from the Congress of Vienna with the largest empire in history.[11] Under these circumstances, once the war was over, it was natural that the young men from the "political classes" gone up to University would begin to debate some of these issues.

While the Union Societies owe some of their ancestry to the exclusive collegiate debating clubs, they were founded on very different principles. The Cambridge Union Society was formed in 1815 by the union of three small debating clubs, and held regular debates for two years.[12] In 1817, the attempted assassination of the Prince Regent prompted a host of repressive measures throughout Britain. In this atmosphere, any congregation of people—for whatever avowed purpose—fell under suspicion and severe restrictions were placed on public meetings of all kinds. The Cambridge Union was no exception. The Vice-Chancellor suspended the Union's activities claiming that they distracted the young men from their studies. (The Union sought to refute this charge by citing the large number of members who had taken high degrees and distinguished themselves in University examinations.) It appears, however, that University officials were most troubled by the Union's practice of debating current topics, such as the proposed suspension of Habeas Corpus in 1817. For four years, the Union continued as a reading society and in 1821 successfully appealed to the new Vice-Chancellor for permission to resume debates. The interdict was only lifted on the condition that debates on political questions would be limited to events occurring prior to 1800.[13]

In the 1820s, the Cambridge Union was marked by the strong presence of the early Cambridge "Apostles" (formally, the Cambridge Conversazione Society, an essay club). During that time, Apostles were not only among the most prominent speakers, but they also filled the Union's offices. Beginning in the 1830s, however, such active involvement in the Union came to be viewed as a very unapostolic way to spend one's time.[14] Apostolic fashion aside, however, the Union had succeeded very well in establishing itself as a fixture in undergraduate life. Shortly after arriving at Cambridge in 1828, the future Apostle Arthur Hallam wrote to his great friend and classmate from Eton, Gladstone, then at Oxford, that the influence of the Union at Cambridge "is very much felt here, extending even among reading men, who have actually no share in it, but are modified in one way or another by its spirit."[15]

Over the century, the growing importance of the Cambridge Union was reflected in its expanding physical life. At first, the debates occurred in an apartment at the back of the Red Lion Inn on Petty Cury. In 1832, the Union moved to the Hoop Hotel, into rooms that had been specially constructed for its use. Less than twenty years later, in 1850, the Union moved into what had once been a dissenting chapel, but soon began to contemplate building a new home for itself. Finally, in 1864, a plot of land behind the Round Church was obtained from St. John's College. Alfred Waterhouse, whose Manchester Assize Courts had just been completed to acclaim, was selected as the architect. The Union moved into its new Gothic premises in 1866. More land and buildings were added throughout the rest of the century.[16] Not least among the factors that prompted the Cambridge Union to begin planning for its new premises in the mid-1850s was the construction at that time of the new Oxford Union buildings. As one observer noted, "The comparison with the splendours of Oxford was specially humiliating to Cambridge."[17] In examining the Cambridge Union, perhaps no consideration is more important than the way it came to be overshadowed by the debating society it inspired at Oxford.

At Oxford, looking to the precedent of the Cantabrigians, a group of undergraduates got together in 1822 to form a debating society. Cautioned by the experience of the Cambridge Union, the Oxonians were careful to ensure the tolerance of the University authorities. As the revived Cambridge Union had done the year before, the United Debating Society formed at Oxford in 1823 limited its debates to "the Historical previous to the present century; and the Philosophical exclusive of Religion."[18] Of the 76 contributing members, 38 (50 percent) came from Christ Church, and 16 (21 percent) from Oriel.[19] In these early years, the Society's debates were often subject to disturbances from some of the less serious-minded members. By 1825, as a former United Debating Society president recalled, "One or two of the members had continually interrupted the debates by boyish folly, and (after all other modes of preventing it had been tried, and an opinion obtained that the rules gave no power of expulsion) the Society dissolved, and *immediately* re-formed as the [Oxford] Union [Society], leaving out the obnoxious members."[20]

From this point, the institutional strength of the Union grew steadily. As with its Cambridge counterpart, this can be seen in the history of the Oxford Union's physical life. At the beginning, debates were held in the rooms of individual members, a practice that quickly became impractical as membership increased. In 1829, following a dispute with the University authorities over obtaining permanent space, the Union moved its debates to rooms rented from Wyatt's Inn in the High Street, where they remained until 1853. Disputes with the owners who succeeded Wyatt led the Union in 1847 to begin planning the construction of new premises. The financing of the project was made possible through a loan from a Trustee of the

Union, and contributions from former members. The new premises constructed did not, however, provide sufficient space in which to hold debates. A debating hall was completed in 1857, decorated with original Pre-Raphaelite frescoes. (It was these buildings that inspired the Cambridge Union to build some of its own.) Eventually, however, even this hall proved too small for the ever-increasing membership, and a new debating hall was built in 1878. The old debating hall was adapted to hold the Union's library, which had begun with a set of *Hansard's Parliamentary Debates*, and by the turn of the century amounted to some 40,000 volumes.[21]

Although the Unions conducted their meetings in cramped and unappealing circumstances during the first decades of their existence, both aimed from early on to be more than just another debating society. By the middle of the nineteenth century, these institutional aspirations were realized. Both the Cambridge and Oxford Unions provided a distinctive lifestyle for their members. The expansion of the Societies' physical plants was as much cause as consequence of the popularity of the Unions. The physical and social amenities were comfortable for scions of the aristocracy and gentry, and attractive to socially ambitious young men from the middle classes. Indeed, the amenities for members became at least as important a part of the Unions' mission as debates. As set forth at the head of both Unions' rules, the societies existed for two purposes: to hold debates, and to maintain a library, reading rooms, and writing rooms. (Interestingly, holding debates comes first in Cambridge's rules, but maintenance of rooms comes first in Oxford's.) For the members' reading pleasure, the Oxford Union in the early 1850s was subscribing to 40 daily and weekly newspapers, eight theological newspapers, and 73 reviews and magazines—including the standard journals (*Blackwood's*, *Cornhill*, etc.), law journals, sporting journals, church magazines, and even a journal of phrenology.[22] The Unions also employed ample staffs of servants, supervised by a steward elected from the membership. (Union members caught giving a gratuity to a servant were fined.) By the turn of the century, according to the Oxford Union rule book of 1908, "The 'Union' now provides its members with all the luxuries of club life—writing, reading, smoking, and billiard rooms, and Library. Refreshments are supplied, and breakfast, luncheon, and dinner can be obtained."[23]

While the Union membership could only reflect the elite social character of Oxford and Cambridge undergraduates in the early and mid-nineteenth century, both Unions gradually eliminated some of their safeguards of social exclusivity such as nomination and blackballing. Indeed, as the Unions acquired definite institutional identities, the nature of distinction shifted from social prestige to oratorical strength. Votes in both Unions tended to reward the most powerful speaker, regardless of his politics and sometimes even which side of the issue he had championed. The Unions' offices—president, librarian, secretary, treasurer—were generally opened to those who had gained a reputation in the debating hall.

The general pattern for members who intended to "make their mark" in the Union was to rise for the first time only after careful planning and calculation, assessing the most propitious opportunity to gain the notice of the House. As later collectively described by four presidents of the Cambridge Union:

> Few of us who have broken the silence will ever forget how painfully we collated arguments and framed them in the grand rhetorical form; how anxiously we sought the president's eye; how fearfully we caught it; how nervously we arose to speak, forgot everything we had prepared, stuttered something visibly soporific and unquestionably irrelevant, and sat down with relief and confusion. Still, we had spoken, perhaps we might never speak again, but we had given to the debate, as it were, some of our personality, and had received in exchange some degree of confidence for future occasions.[24]

This broad characterization is borne out in numerous individual recollections. In the 1840s, the future President of the Cambridge Union and future Home Secretary, William Vernon Harcourt, wrote to his father following his first effort:

> My first speech was on the character of Mr. Canning, in which I am sensible enough that I broke down, though my friends were very good-natured and said "a successful first attempt" and all that. The truth was that intending only to make a declaration and not having the least idea I should lose my wits I went down without my notes, and found all at once as soon as I got on my legs that my heart was . . . in my stomach. However I was determined not to sit down and worked off as well as I could. This you may imagine was not a little disgusting, but I don't mean to "say die" and am going about this week calculating when I shall try the argumentative style.[25]

Any display of oratorical skill in such "back bench" interventions, favored one's selection to introduce a motion, or to deliver the main opposing speech. Success as a principal speaker typically led to selection for one of the Unions' various committees, followed in all likelihood by standing for election to an office. In some senses, enthused Lord Birkenhead around the time of the Oxford Union's centenary (as F. E. Smith, he had been President in 1894), it was a society open to talent.[26]

THE UNIONS AT WORK

In order to understand the kind of experience that Union members carried with them into public life, it is necessary to understand the workings of the Unions. By statute, debates at both Unions could be on any subject, other than theological questions. And indeed, the subjects debated were both many and varied. In 1826, the year of its second founding, the Oxford Union held debates on (in order): the benefit of mechanics' institutions to the "Labouring Classes," Charles I and Cromwell, George III, the Septennial Parliaments Act of 1716, the monopoly of the East India Company, cruelty to animals, usury, abolition of slavery, the system of unpaid magistracy, John Knox, primogeniture, unanimity of juries, Burke, the dissolution of the monasteries, Elizabeth I and Mary Queen of Scots, the decay of eloquence, the Austrian occupation of Italy, state control over Church property, the abolition of the Corn Laws, and Fox's attitude towards Revolutionary France. The agreements made by both Unions in their formative years not to debate contemporary issues was from the start observed in a nominal manner only (usually, by inserting into the motion "before 1800," or "up to" some earlier date in the century); and they soon fell entirely into abeyance. Thus, as just noted, the Oxford Union was debating the merits of the 1815 Corn Laws in 1826.

Along with the Corn Laws, many of the motions that the Oxford Union debated in 1826 reflected the concerns of the classes from which the Union's members issued: septennial parliaments, usury, and primogeniture. Divisions on these issues clearly upheld aristocratic interests—e. g. that unpaid magistracy is not desirable (Ayes 6, Noes 26), or that primogeniture is a good thing (Ayes 24, Noes 9). One might also add the Union's debate on the decay of eloquence to the list of aristocratic themes since, emerging from the Georgian era, eloquence was generally viewed as an aristocratic art (see chapter 2).

While Charles I, Cromwell, the French Revolution, and other topics reappeared often (in large measure because they provided convenient means to discuss contemporary issues by analogy), the overall tone of the Oxford Union's motions evolved rather rapidly. For example, in 1836, ten years after the motions discussed above, debates exhibited far more concern with current or very recent events—particularly parliamentary matters. That year, the Union debated the desirability of Peel's returning to office, legislation on the Irish Church, Palmerston's foreign policy, the character of Lord Brougham, the influence of the Radicals on the government, and confidence in the Melbourne's ministry. Even some subjects that were more historical in character were explicitly framed with reference to present conditions, for instance the motion "That an Administration, formed upon the principles of Earl Grey's Cabinet would be best calculated to meet the present exigencies of the Country."

In general, too, by 1836—to judge by the increased frequency of amendments and riders moved—the Union was exhibiting a greater degree of sophistication in legislative forms and parliamentary procedure. In these substantive and stylistic developments, one can observe the lasting effects of the tumultuous period between Catholic emancipation in 1829 and the Great Reform Act of 1832. In an atmosphere where basic constitutional assumptions were being questioned and overturned, a serious-minded debating society such as the Oxford Union could not but throw off its self-imposed constraints.

In addition to the kinds of motions that were actually debated, it is also important to look at the procedure of the Unions. The model for both the Cambridge and Oxford Unions was the House of Commons (in this sense, the Unions were among the earliest offspring of the "mother of parliaments"). Motions, amendments, and riders were all moved, debated, and divided upon according to the forms of Parliament or some close variant. Union Presidents performed functions similar to those of the Speaker of the House. In debates, Presidents could not speak on the motion from the Chair, but were vested with ultimate authority on rules, order, and discipline. It must have been rare, however, for young men who attained the presidency of their Union to imagine themselves future Speakers of the House—although one President of the Cambridge Union, William Gully, did eventually become Speaker. Rather, the presidency came to be seen as a first step to a see, the bench, or the cabinet.

Although there was no "government" in the parliamentary sense, Union presidents did perform duties that could be likened to those of a prime minister. As we have seen, the institutional mission of the Unions extended far beyond mere debates. Besides their Speaker-like functions, presidents wielded considerable power outside the debating hall—overseeing a sizable administrative apparatus that involved numerous departments (e. g. library, treasury, steward) and committees. It was as president or head of a department that many young Oxford and Cambridge men discovered their proclivity (or lack thereof) for executive management. In the last analysis, however, perhaps the most important aspect of Union presidency was that it was the highest position within these elite institutions (indeed, elite institutions within the elite institutions of Cambridge and Oxford). Like captains of the athletic teams, presidents of the Union automatically gained an elevated status in university society, and the distinction remained with them long after they went down.[27]

The Unions could not replicate the Commons' procedures in all respects. Since there was no government in the parliamentary sense, there was no legislative agenda to provide the matter to be debated. Nor were Union debates necessarily suggested by the vicissitudes, or demanded by the exigencies, of national life. In fact, from week to week, debates could be on any subject (other than matters theological). Most importantly, there were no established parties, or established party leaders. "The debate is not organized as a Parliament, so that the benches are occupied without distinction of party." [28] Of course, members spoke and voted in general accordance with their (or their families') Tory or Whig predispositions. However, even the Unions' great political rivalries appear to have been far more personal than political. One of the more famous Union antagonisms was that between Hilaire Belloc (a Liberal in those days) and F. E. Smith (a Conservative always) in the early 1890s. Yet, such rivalries were dictated largely by equality of debating or oratorical talents. Generally, the procedure of both Unions meant that "parties" and leadership formed with each debate, and disintegrated after. Members submitted motions to be debated (at Cambridge, by writing them in a book; at Oxford, by placing them in a box), which were then selected by the Unions' respective governing committees. The proposer of the selected motion (or an approved substitute) was obliged to open the debate on the day appointed for it. Similarly, after the motion was selected, those desiring to oppose it registered their names and were selected by the Unions' leadership. Votes depended on the persuasiveness of the speaker and the nature of the motion being debated.

Like Parliament, the Unions developed their own special conventions and expectations for speeches, as well as a particular style. To begin with, speeches could not be read. Exactly like speakers in Parliament, however, this convention did not prevent Union speakers from preparing their speeches to varying degrees. John Simon (President of the Oxford Union, 1896) recalled hearing F. E. Smith, with whom he shared a staircase in Wadham, "marching up and down his room in elaborate rehearsal" for Union performances.[29] The Unions' standards for the form and *appearance* of speeches were fully consistent with the requirements for successful public speaking in public life, most especially Parliament. As in Parliament, even when speakers had prepared and memorized their whole speech in advance, it was nevertheless critical for success that the speech be delivered in such a way as to seem an extemporaneous flow and not a recitation from memory.

Unfortunately, there are almost no records of actual Union speeches until the end of the nineteenth century. Neither Union took minutes of debates; their record books contain only motions, speakers, and votes. (Similarly, neither Union took minutes at their committee meetings.) Beyond the Unions' own records, their rules (like those of the House of Commons) for many years contained a statutory prohibition against reporting speeches. The Oxford Union's rules, for instance, included the following standing order: "No abstract or report of Speeches delivered at the Society's Meetings shall be published in any Newspaper or Periodical whatsoever. The President, with the concurrence of the Standing Committee, is empowered to take steps to prevent such publication."[30] By the last decade of the nineteenth century, such rules were no longer in effect and reports of Union activities were regularly reported in university magazines like *Isis* and *Cam*. Thus, in order to discuss the nature of Union speech-making during most of the century, it is necessary to rely upon the recollections and characterizations of contemporary witnesses.

With respect to the style of Union speeches, Birkenhead describes it as a "mixture of satire, humour, honesty, wit, and solemnity."[31] The "best authorities," he states, believe the origin of the Union style lies in Gibbon's ironic attack on the Christian Church. "It is," he says, "the style of youth—happy, irresponsible, mordant, treating serious subjects in a jesting, but omniscient, manner, and often fanatical about passing issues of little moment."[32] "F. E." himself provided some of the greatest examples of the Union style. In 1893, for instance, Belloc moved "That this House would approve of any measure which gave undergraduates a share in the Government of the University," and finished his eloquent speech with a peroration likening the University to a "lofty and well-proportioned cathedral, in which the representation of undergraduates would be a conduit and a drain for the buoyancy of youth." Smith opposed the motion and, after delivering a reasoned critique of Belloc's argument, parodied the mover's peroration with great, but savage wit: "When I contemplate the scheme of the honourable gentleman from Balliol [Belloc], I see it as a high, vast, lofty, well proportioned drain!"[33]

The kind of debating wit evidenced to a greater or lesser extent at the Oxford Union appears to have also obtained at Cambridge. Of the Union style of speaking, John Ellis McTaggart (President of the Cambridge Union, 1890) wrote: "I have made a speech at the Union crammed with epigrams, that being what the House expects from us. Nothing is easier than to create the Cambridge Union epigram. The recipe is, take any truism and convert it contrariwise. Thus, say that water kindles fire, or that refinement is the highest form of brutality, and the verdict of the Union is 'epigrammatic but cynical'."[34]

One author's satirical sketch of the Cambridge Union from 1849 describes Union members copying down verbatim speeches by Peel and Russell, and relates the story of how one undergraduate was about to deliver a speech copied from an 1809 number of the *Morning Advertizer* only to have another member deliver the same speech ahead of him.[35] It is hard to say to what extent this account is exaggerated, or even apocryphal. More important for the present purpose is the same author's description of how in debates the Unions tended to reward oratorical ability over substance:

> It always strikes me that the orators who are the most attended to are those who rave about the "glorious constitution," the "invulnerable church," and so forth, on the one side, and the fiery demagogues, who clamour for liberty of conscience, on the other. As for knowing anything more about the subject when you leave the room than when you came into it, that is out of the question. The sober, steady, seedy fellows from John's or Christ's, whom I am most anxious to hear, who appear to have read up the whole subject during the week, and to be really capable of giving information as to *facts*—these misguided men are, I say, invariably coughed down and growled back again to their seats.[36]

This characterization is borne out by William Everett, an American graduate of Harvard who sat out the Civil War in Cambridge. In a lecture delivered at the Lowell Institute, he said of Union debates:

> In general, they are death itself. There comes every now and then a season when a few active souls stir the Union into life. But even then the animation cannot create the habit of good speaking, to which the whole genius of the place [Cambridge University] is opposed; and the most intelligent audiences of Cambridge young men, always professing the most thorough contempt for rhetoric, are habitually carried off their feet by the most worn out claptrap.[37]

Everett's views are all the more interesting because he was not only a member of the Cambridge Union, but was elected President in 1862.

Occasionally, Union debates were enlivened by the presence of visitors. The Cambridge and Oxford Unions extended full privileges (to take part in debates and private business meetings, and to use the facilities) to each other's members, as well as to members of the Edinburgh Union Society (founded 1833), the Durham University Debating Society (founded 1835), and the College Historical Society at Dublin (re-founded 1843).[38] Thus, the Unions encouraged solidarity amongst themselves, expressing the shared interests as elite societies. Most important, however, was the relationship between Cambridge and Oxford. In 1829, a delegation of three from the Cambridge Union (Apostles all, and including Hallam) was invited to come to Oxford to debate the merits of Shelley versus those of Byron. Later, like the Boat Race, inter-Union debates would become annual events, thereby ritualizing the competition within a coherent framework of shared institutional values. The importance of the bond between the two Unions is clearly evident in a letter of February 1840 from the secretary of the Cambridge Union to his Oxford counterpart, anxiously inquiring whether there was any foundation to the report that a motion had been carried in the Oxford Union to exclude Cambridge Union members from its privileges. The Oxford secretary sent a prompt reply to assure his counterpart that no such resolution had even been contemplated, stating that such a measure "would be most subversive of that perfect spirit of amity between the sister societies so desirable to both parties."[39]

At both Unions, life membership admitted the occasional presence of old members in each Union's debates. It was Home Rule, however, that seems to have initiated the now-familiar practice of notables coming to address the Unions. When in 1887 the Cambridge Union debated the motion "That in the opinion of this House it is desirable to concede Home Rule for Ireland," the former Solicitor General, Sir John Gorst

(President, 1857) came up to oppose it. Of greater moment was the Oxford Union's Home Rule debate the following year, to which were invited Lord Randolph Churchill and John Morley—although they spoke on different nights and therefore did not debate each other. (Both had been members of the Union: Morley had taken part in debates but never held office; Churchill had been expelled for failing to pay his subscription.) Writing in the 1920s, Sir John Simon complained that the, by then, more common practice of inviting visitors was easily overdone by Presidents seeking to distinguish their terms by a great occasion.[40]

Such were the activities of the Unions that were commonly perceived to stamp a lifelong benefit on the participants. One indication is the recognition by 1850 that, alongside such familiar figures of university life as the Reading-Man, the Evangelical, and the Fast Man, a new type had emerged:

> I remark that there are some men who, betaking themselves to public life, on the first day of their entrance into this seat of learning, never, if I may so speak, retire into privacy till their assumption of the bachelor's gown. These are the men whose names are for ever figuring before us, on the lists, who discuss on all questions legal, political, poetical, historical, or metaphysical, who sit on debate nights at small tables, with glasses of water before them, and whisper mysteriously to the President every five minutes—these are the individuals whom I shall take the liberty of calling, for want of a better name the Unionic Undergraduates.[41]

The benefits of the Union experience for individuals could be taken for granted. It is not unusual for the vast biographies of Victorian notables to mention their subjects' activities in the Union in scarcely more than passing. (Indeed, the subject's entire university career is often given remarkably short shrift.) Yet, this taking for granted can also be read as a testament to the perceived importance of the Unions. Like a university education, membership in the Union came to be viewed as a matter of course for a great man—a thing that need neither be explained nor dwelt upon. Rather than the few lines devoted to Union careers in triple-decker biographies, perhaps a better indication of the importance attached to Union membership—and especially holding Union office—is that it appears regularly in the brief lives contained in that great national monument, the *Dictionary of National Biography*. When the biography of national greatness is pared down to its essentials, participation in the Union typically remains.[42]

If Union membership came to be considered *a priori* as a good thing, a number of memoir writers and biographers have attempted to articulate the real benefits. All these accounts strike essentially the same note. The advice of Raymond Asquith sums up the basic attitude: "Learn to speak at the Union, because if you can learn to speak there really well you can learn to speak anywhere."[43] Since (as will be seen in the subsequent chapters) public speech lay so much at the core of Victorian public life, the Union experience could prove highly advantageous—not only by honing oratorical abilities, but providing a venue in which to gain notice for those abilities. John Simon added the further point that the Union was an institution which provided new opportunities for displaying talents that might, in other circumstances, remain unnoticed or under-challenged. "One of the best things about the Union is that it gives the man from a small college, who may otherwise move in a limited circle, the opportunity of matching himself against the best of his contemporaries, and the thrust and parry of the debating hall are the finest preparations for more serious controversies afterwards."[44]

In addition to their size, organization, and influence, the Unions are significant as debating societies in the way they embodied and promoted a new conception of public speech: public speech for its own sake. The Unions manifested and institutionalized the belief that public speaking was a highly desirable skill to cultivate, but their debates were devoid of real consequences. Other than matters of private business (this includes highly acrimonious debates over books to be included in the library and newspapers to be subscribed to), no laws were enacted and the fate of nothing was decided. The Unions' debates on current issues such as the Corn Laws and Reform—as with those on Cromwell and regicide—affected nothing. The parties that opposed each other in the debating hall represented no constituencies, no "feeling of the country," no fixed political principles. They did not belong to a formal party, nor were they organized by whips. The reward of performance in the Union was the immediate gratification of acclaim from one's peers. (Birkenhead suggests that those immediate rewards, unlike the more delayed gratification of academic studies, go a long way toward accounting for the Unions' popularity as an undergraduate activity.) The only real effect of all these organizations was to hone the debating skills of the participants. In the words of Birkenhead, "Here was a contest which depended on nothing but the merit of the competitors."[45] It is also important to remember that the orators were young, and the Unions were, at their best, a maturing experience. Commenting on the Cambridge Union, the *Saturday Review* wrote in the 1860s: "It is not of course the value of the results, but the first energetic employment of youthful faculties, which makes such discussions pleasant to recollect and sometimes even to listen to. Great as is the nonsense sometimes contained in Union orations, they are not the less interesting as trials of the powers of the orator."[46]

FROM WYATT'S ROOMS TO WESTMINSTER: GLADSTONE AND THE OXFORD UNION

As the foregoing has shown, in a relatively short space of time the Unions became institutions of both note and influence. It is also true, however, that the Cambridge Union never equaled the prestige of the society it inspired at Oxford. To quote Birkenhead again, "what we yield to Cambridge in years we modestly reclaim in relative eminence. The rôle of British statesman [*sic*] owes on the whole, I think, more to the lists of the Presidents of the Oxford Union than it does to the heads of the sister Society at Cambridge."[47] Indeed, at the 1866 inaugural ceremonies for the new Cambridge Union building, Professor of Political Economy Henry Fawcett (Secretary, 1855), the "blind orator" who had been recently elected Liberal MP for Brighton, spoke of his hope that the new buildings would help the Cambridge Union gain on Oxford in terms of its influence in public life.

> Many of you have the power to speak, if you will only use the opportunity which the Cambridge Union Society places at your disposal, and you may thus give to Cambridge distinction in those things in which she has perhaps lost prestige. If we look to our right and left, we can probably call to mind many of those who were formerly members of this Union and who have helped make this University second to no seat of learning in the world in scholarship, in science, and in philosophy (loud cheers). But during the last twenty or thirty years she has not, in political distinction, attained the same prominence. In the late Ministry there were nine first-class Oxford men, and not one who had taken high honours at Cambridge. If the students of the present day will only give fair scope to their faculties,

> and avail themselves of the training which this Society will afford them, Cambridge may soon become as distinguished in politics as she is illustrious in learning and science.[48]

Any comparison of the contribution of the two Union Societies to British public life must take into account the tremendous boost the Oxford Union received from the career of one man. Gladstone's career both in the Union and afterward represents a kind of Union ideal—at least in structure, if not necessarily in substance. It was Gladstone above all others who seemed to embody the notion of the Union as a springboard for entry into the highest reaches of public life. As an Oxford undergraduate, with his characteristic energy, disputatious temperament, and previous debating experience in Pop, Gladstone quickly became a prominent figure in the Union. This, despite his claim that his interests as an undergraduate lay elsewhere: "during the larger part of my time as an undergraduate, my interests were not political but were either academical or theological. The records of the Oxford Union, to which I belonged, would show that I was neither a constant nor a frequent speaker there."[49] In the Union, Gladstone found ready acceptance from his fellow Etonians who, along with the Wykehamists, tended to dominate the Society. Further, in those years, Gladstone's college, Christ Church, provided one of the largest contingents of Union members and officers. Gladstone's ready powers as a speaker got him elected to the Union's committee, then to the post of Secretary in 1830, then to the presidency later that year.

The most famous speech in Union history was delivered in May 1831 when, on the proposition "That the present Ministry is incompetent to carry on the Government of the Country," Gladstone moved the rider "That the Ministry has unwisely introduced, and most unscrupulously forwarded, a measure which threatens not only to change the form of Government, but ultimately to break up the very foundations of the social order, as well as materially to forward the views of those who are pursuing this project throughout the civilized world" (on the rider: Ayes 94, Noes 38). One harbinger of things to come was that the speech lasted, by Gladstone's estimate, three-quarters of an hour—probably about as long as Union speeches got (later, they would be officially limited to 20 minutes). Although prodigious in the Gladstonian manner, the fame that this speech acquired did not derive from the merits of the speech itself. Rather, the speech grew in importance with the speaker. As Morley observes, Gladstone's "own future eminence made [the speech] in a sense historic."[50] Birkenhead is rather more hyperbolic when he states that Gladstone's Reform speech "is the only undergraduate effort which history has taken to its record."[51] However, although it would have been impossible to know in 1831 that this speech would launch one of the most brilliant political careers of the nineteenth century, it is a fact that the Union speech helped gain Gladstone a seat in Parliament. Gladstone's acquaintance at Christ Church and fellow Union member, Lord Lincoln, was so impressed by the speech that he persuaded his father, the Duke of Newcastle, to exert his influence and have Gladstone elected for his pocket borough of Newark. The future Prime Minister was duly elected to his first parliamentary seat in Britain's first reformed Parliament. Gladstone, so it seemed, had proceeded directly from Wyatt's rooms to Westminster.

As Gladstone's political fortunes and public profile rose—owing in no small part to his phenomenal oratorical powers—the Union, as a fixture in the emerging Gladstone legend, was afforded both a special place in the myth, and a share of the credit for Gladstone's success. But Gladstone's actual relationship with the Union went beyond its role in launching his career. Indeed, it continued throughout the rest of his days. As the young John Simon said in the eulogy he delivered in the Union: "He, throughout his whole life, with endless other interests to engage him, has remained constantly faithful in his attachment to the University which sent him into the world, and constant in his affection for, and interest in, the Society where he first revealed his marvelous gift of public speech."[52] One sign of Gladstone's enduring interest in the Union was how, during a busy visit to Oxford in October 1852, he took the time to look in on the Union's rooms.[53] Years later, in February 1890, on the occasion of what was to be his last visit to the University, Gladstone was invited to address the Union, and did so on the vestiges of Assyrian mythology in Homer.

This is not to say that the relationship between Gladstone and the Union was an uncomplicated one. For a start, Gladstone's political connection with the University itself proved to be problematic. From 1847 to 1865—that is, during the period of his political transformation from Peelite Tory to Liberal—Gladstone sat as one of the two MPs for the University of Oxford. Contested elections in university constituencies were considered a grave mark of disfavor, and Gladstone's seat was contested several times.[54] In addition to specific points of friction (such as his 1847 vote to remove Jewish disabilities), sections of the University constituency (Oxford MAs) reacted very unfavorably to the drift of Gladstone's politics, as when a vigorous, if unsuccessful challenge was mounted in July 1859 after Gladstone had accepted office in Palmerston's Liberal government. By the general election of 1865—the first which permitted votes sent by post from nonresident MAs—Gladstone's emergent Liberalism had sufficiently alienated his constituents to cost him his seat.

If the University electorate no longer wanted Gladstone as one of its representatives, Gladstone, for his part, appears to have tired of representing the University. During the 1859 contest, he had written to the University's other MP that while his constituents "have had much reason to complain, I have not had an over-good bargain. In the estimate of mere pleasure and pain, the representation of the university is not worth my having."[55] Although Gladstone had previously declined to be nominated for other constituencies, he permitted himself to be nominated for the new seat for South Lancashire in 1865.[56] Because of the tradition that university MPs may not address (and thereby, may not explain themselves to) their constituents directly, and because of the political constraints imposed by representing the University, Gladstone appeared before his new constituents of South Lancashire in 1865, as he famously described it, "unmuzzled" (see p. 242).

As the arch-Tory prig who had once presided over the Union evolved into the avatar of Liberalism, Gladstone's policies were often vigorously attacked in Union debates and rejected by its votes. It has even been suggested Gladstone did not attend the 1873 jubilee dinner because he felt at odds with the Conservative character of the Union, and even that the Union would not have received the Liberal Prime Minister with due courtesy.[57] Such speculations usually point to the *Times*' account of the banquet, which records that, during the Lord Chancellor's speech toasting "The Prosperity of the Oxford Union Society," his mention of Gladstone was met with "expressions of dissent."[58] Although Gladstone's diaries note his invitation to the jubilee banquet, they shed no light on why he declined the invitation.[59] It is impossible to know with certainty the real reasons—personal or political—why Gladstone declined to attend when so many other notables accepted, but the circumstances encourage conjecture.[60] It is certainly true that 1873 was a particularly difficult year in Gladstone's political career—one that included the falling popularity of his first government, his abortive resignation, cabinet embarrassments, and his assuming the duties of Chancellor of the Exchequer. Had Gladstone attended the jubilee, he would certainly have been obliged to make a speech. A speech of reminiscence at that point would naturally have opened up public discussion of his Tory past. Given his political fortunes that year, anything that might have underscored accusations of political inconsistency was clearly to be avoided. As it turned out, Gladstone spent the day of the jubilee at Hawarden, writing, reading, and felling trees.[61]

As to the expressions of hostility at the banquet when his name was mentioned, another interpretation seems possible. Two days after its account of the jubilee banquet, *The Times* printed a letter from a member of the Union that appears to absolve the jubilants from the charge that they behaved ignobly. According to this letter, the Lord Chancellor's mention of Gladstone was met with "a burst of cheering, which was so prolonged that the red-waistcoated official behind the chair held up his hand to try and stop the demonstration, and this it was that provoked the hisses and renewed cheering."[62] Political differences notwithstanding, Gladstone would have been without question the greatest ornament of that bejeweled banquet, as he was (and remains) the greatest ornament of the Union itself.

In fact, while partisanship may be a natural aspect of a large debating society, it did not create permanent cleavages among Oxford Union members. As John Simon wrote, at the Union "there are friendships to be made with the fiercest of your opponents which will last through life."[63] To believe that any ill will the predominantly Conservative Union expressed toward Gladstone was more than superficial is to misunderstand the nature of the Union itself. After Gladstone's speech against Reform in 1831, perhaps the most famous Oxford Union address—albeit for wholly different reasons—was F. E. Smith's speech on the occasion of Gladstone's death. This speech, coming from an ardent Conservative, was (deliberately) the finest expression of what Gladstone meant to the Oxford Union. Gladstone's death occurred during Eights Week—a time at which it had become traditional for the Union to offer debates of a more frivolous nature. In the light of Gladstone's death, Smith rose and moved that the Union adjourn. His speech on that occasion is justly considered a model of the memorial panegyric, and rewards reading in full. It said in part:

> Nearly seventy years, Sir, have passed since Mr. Gladstone sat in the chair you fill to-night. He enjoyed, in the discharge of your office, a wealth of contemporary reputation to which I conceive that none of his successors has even approximately attained, and during those seventy years all parties in this house have admitted him with ready assent the most illustrious ornament in the annals of the Society. Other great statesmen, Sir, have sat since Mr. Gladstone in your

> chair; there have debated within the walls of this Society poets like Swinburne, known wherever the English language is known, men of letters like Ruskin, and a long roll of prelates and judges, the mere recital of whose names would exhaust the patience of this house—yet I think it was said of none of these, as it was said of Gladstone the undergraduate, "A man is risen in Israel this day."
>
> In public some of us have exercised, from time to time, our wit and rhetoric against him, but in private, when we would give a high impression of this Society to those unfamiliar with its history, it was the name of Gladstone which rose first to our lips.[64]

At Gladstone's funeral in Westminster Abbey, the Union's President, Cyril Foster Garbett (later Archbishop of York), was officially invited to attend, and was assigned a stall—a final and public (albeit non-oratorical) sign of the strength in life of Gladstone's connection to the Union.

Gladstone's career in the Oxford Union became so compelling a tale because, atypically for Union performances, his Reform speech *did* have virtually immediate, real, and undeniably significant results. Because of his later fame, the Gladstone legend fails to appreciate that these consequences—at least, at first—were strictly *personal.* However early Gladstone came to be seen as a "coming man," it would take a number of years before the young parliamentarian plucked from the Union would begin to have a discernible impact on national life, and many more before it was clear that he was the dominant figure in British politics in the second half of the nineteenth century. Thus, as even the case of Gladstone demonstrates, if the Unions often had a profound influence on the lives of their members, the speeches those members delivered in the Unions influenced nothing at all. What Gladstone's career does reveal in this regard is that, as in so many other respects, he lived the transitions, and contradictions of his age. Elevated into the first reformed Parliament through the practices of old corruption, he came to notice through his speech against Reform in the new proving ground of public life, the Oxford Union.

THE INFLUENCE OF THE UNIONS ON PUBLIC LIFE

The Gladstone connection gave the Oxford Union, not only its reputation as a nursery of statesmen, but also a self-consciousness of its role as a starting point for great careers in public life. Certainly, not every member of the Unions achieved distinction. And as might be expected, it is even the case that young men who acquired a reputation at the Unions proved failures in their subsequent public careers. Birkenhead cites his old Oxford adversary, Hilaire Belloc, and the writer Herbert Paul as great Union orators who failed to catch the ear of the Commons: "What was regarded as a fount of amusement or an intellectual treat at Oxford was looked on by the House of Commons as a form of trifling or insincerity. The judgement was absolutely unjust, but it doomed two brilliant men to political impotence and sterility. They had achieved an immense success in one school, they could not adapt themselves to another, and found their consolation in the art of letters."[65] Birkenhead asserts, however, that these instances are exceptional. The overriding anecdotal impression is that the Union was the first proving ground for a successful public career. Those careers were not merely in politics and government, but also in the other oratorically-grounded sectors of public life, the clergy and the law.

To explore the realities behind both Unions' reputations, it is necessary to take account of the future career paths of their members. Since not all members were active speakers, however, it is most important to focus on those who participated in debates. To this end, the following analyses examine the young men who served as the Unions' presidents through 1873.[66] Besides being the fiftieth anniversary of the Oxford Union, 1873 seemed a good year to end the analysis since it affords each president at least a quarter century to establish a career before the end of the Victorian era. Further, even though the Cambridge Union came into existence eight years before its Oxford counterpart, the total number of presidents for each Union through 1873 is almost equal (173 for Cambridge, and 174 for Oxford), because during the three-year existence of Oxford's United Debating Society (1823–1825), there were 32 presidents (counting as one a president who held office twice).

The Union presidents came in large measure from the elite public schools. Of the 173 Cambridge Union presidents, I have found reference to the schooling of 142 (82 percent of the total). Of these 142 presidents, 64 (45 percent) attended the most prestigious endowed schools—Charterhouse, Eton, Harrow, Rugby, Shrewsbury, Westminster, Winchester (the old "Seven" public boarding schools), plus the elite day schools, St. Paul's and Merchant Taylors'—collectively known as the Clarendon Schools after the chairman of the 1864 Public Schools Commission that reviewed them (see pp. 66–67). Of the 174 Oxford Union presidents, I have found reference to the schooling of 114 (66 percent of the total). Of these 114 presidents, 78 (68 percent) attended the Clarendon schools. It therefore appears that the most elite public schools were somewhat better represented in the leadership of the Oxford Union than that of the Cambridge Union (in part, reflecting the undergraduate bodies as a whole). Compared to the rest of their respective universities, the Clarendon schools were disproportionately represented in the presidency of both Unions. In the period 1864–67, the segment of all undergraduates from the Clarendon schools was 22 percent at Cambridge and 35 percent at Oxford.[67] Therefore, even if *none* of the Union presidents for whom I could find no schooling information attended a Clarendon school, the proportion of those who did—37 percent at Cambridge and 45 percent at Oxford—was still much greater than the percentages for all undergraduates.

In terms of collegiate affiliation, the 173 Cambridge Union presidents were drawn from 17 colleges, although a significant majority—104 (60 percent)—came from Trinity. Since about one-third of Cambridge's undergraduates were at Trinity (roughly, 500 out of 1,500), the College was significantly overrepresented in the presidency of the Union. The college that provided the next largest number of presidents was St. John's with 16 (9 percent). The other 15 colleges had no more than seven presidents each, and eight of them had no more than three. The 174 Oxford Union presidents were drawn somewhat more evenly from 20 colleges. Of the total, 44 (25 percent) came from Christ Church, 28 (16 percent) from Balliol, and 22 (13 percent) from Oriel. The other 17 colleges contributed no more than 12 presidents each, and seven of them no more than three. Clearly, the large colleges dominated, but less so at Oxford than at Cambridge. The Unions were not quite the oratorical meritocracy that Birkenhead claimed. At Oxford, however, the broader distribution of presidents' collegiate affiliations lends some support to Simon's feeling that the Union provided opportunities for men from small colleges like his, Wadham (which contributed eight presidents, or 5 percent of the total in the period under review).

The academic achievements of the Union presidents were considerable. At Cambridge, from 1750 it was not necessary for candidates to offer any but mathematical subjects for examination. Of the 173 Cambridge Union presidents under review, 17 percent ranked in the first class of mathematical examinations as Wranglers. Cambridge established the Classical Tripos in 1824, but it was not a degree qualification until the 1850s. Further, students could not take the Classical Tripos unless they were at least a Junior Optime (third class honors) in the preceding Mathematical Tripos. However, while the University only required mathematical study, Trinity College—from whence the bulk of the Union presidents came—was famous for its emphasis on the classics. Of the 174 Oxford Union presidents, 141 (81 percent) appear on the University's list of honors and distinctions.[68] These achievements, like the Oxford curriculum, are overwhelmingly classical: 80 (46 percent) of the presidents took first class honors in classics, and an additional 33 (19 percent) took second class honors. Put another way, of those presidents who appear on the honors list, more than 80 percent achieved high distinction in the classics. Almost all of the remaining 20 percent received lesser classical honors. The presidents of both Unions were on the whole an academically prestigious group. For active members (as presidents surely were), the Unions were one of many academic and extracurricular activities in which, under enormous pressure to succeed, talented undergraduates competed. It is, therefore, not surprising that the officers of the Unions were accomplished in other areas of university life.

Our main concern, however, is what the presidents did after leaving Oxford and Cambridge. In order to provide some quantitative measure of the Unions' broad impact on public life, table 1.1 groups the presidents of each Union into general career categories. For these purposes, I have attempted to draw a rough distinction between careers that form a part of "public life" and those that do not. Thus, "Law," "Politics," and "Religion" appear under the rubric of public careers, while "academe," "letters," and "other" are classified as non-public careers. (For convenience, the five Oxonians whom I have identified as career civil servants—almost all of them rising to permanent under-secretaryships—have been added to the "Politics" category. No Cantabrigians are classified as civil servants.) While it is true that some of the scholars and authors were more influential on the public than some of the lawyers, MPs, and clergymen, I have made distinctions according to the nature of career areas, rather than the nature of individuals. Additionally, this separation is justified by the focus of this study on public speech. Career areas that I have classified as public are also those in which oratory of one kind or another was a central occupation. In the case of individuals who were active in more than one career area (e. g. someone who was both a barrister and an MP, or someone who was both a clergyman and headmaster of a school), I have attempted to classify them according to what appears to have been the *main* occupation of their lives.

As table 1. 1 shows, the presidents of both Unions went into the group of careers I have defined as public in virtually equal proportion—three-fourths of the total. Within the public group, Cambridge has a higher proportion of lawyers, and Oxford a higher proportion of politicians. The

TABLE 1.1 Cambridge and Oxford Union Presidents by Career Category

	Cambridge (1815–1873)			Oxford (1823–1873)			Totals		
	N	% of subtotal	% of Total	N	% of subtotal	% of Total	N	% of subtotal	% of Total
Law	50	38.8%	28.9%	28	21.7%	16.1%	78	30.2%	22.5%
Religion	55	42.6%	31.8%	58	45.0%	33.3%	113	43.8%	32.6%
*Politics**	24	18.6%	13.9%	43	33.3%	24.7%	67	26.0%	19.3%
SUBTOTAL	129	100.0%	74.6%	129	100.0%	74.1%	258	100.0%	74.4%
Academe	22	50.0%	12.7%	22	48.9%	12.6%	44	49.4%	12.7%
Letters	7	15.9%	4.0%	8	17.8%	4.6%	15	16.9%	4.3%
Other	15	34.1%	8.7%	15	33.3%	8.6%	30	33.7%	8.6%
SUBTOTAL	44	100.0%	25.4%	45	100.0%	25.9%	89	100.0%	25.6%
Totals	173		100.0%	174		100.0%	347		100.0%

*Includes civil servants.

proportion of each Union's presidents who went into religious careers is roughly equal—not surprising in light of the role both universities still played in clerical training. Similarly, the breakdown of careers I have defined as not public is about the same for both Cambridge and Oxford.

The breakdown of the career destinations of Union presidents can be compared to that for all Cambridge and Oxford matriculates.[69] Of the undergraduates who matriculated at Cambridge in 1848–49, 48 percent entered the clergy, 8.3 percent the law, and 0.4 percent government service. Of the Oxford matriculates in the same year, 50 percent entered the clergy, 5.0 percent the law, and 1.6 percent government service. For both universities, these percentages were virtually unchanged from the matriculates of 1818–19. By 1878–79, the pattern began to shift, with fewer matriculates going into clerical careers, and more into law and government service. Assuming these career categories are roughly comparable to those in table 1.1, Union presidents from 1815–1873 went into law and politics in significantly greater measure than all university matriculates, and went into the clergy to a significantly lesser extent. Among other things, these comparisons underscore the fundamental secularity of the Unions (no debates on theological subjects permitted) established at universities that were still essentially clerical training institutions.

The mere presence of ex-Union presidents across the major areas of public life, however, does not tell us how important they were in their respective fields. Because of the common perception that the Oxford Union has produced more important people than the Cambridge, a corollary issue is the relative eminence of the two sets of presidents. Table 1.2 shows one measure of public importance, the number of Union presidents who have entries in the *Dictionary of National Biography.*

By this measure, just over one-third of Cambridge Union presidents, and close to one-half of Oxford Union presidents led lives of the highest public note.[70] Table 1.3 groups the data in table 1.2 by the career categories in table 1.1.

The percentage of Oxford Union presidents through 1873 with entries in the *DNB* is over 1.4 times greater than that for Cambridge Union presidents. Particularly notable is Oxford's 1825–1834 cohort of which 62 percent have *DNB* entries. This especially talented group is the generation of Gladstone and included among its notable divines, statesmen, and lawyers Bishop Wilberforce, Cardinal Manning, Lord Elgin, Lord Chancellor Selborne, Archbishop of Canterbury Tait, and Chancellor of the Exchequer Lowe. (Cambridge has a higher percentage than Oxford only for

TABLE 1.2 Union Presidents in the *Dictionary of National Biography*

	Cambridge (1815–1873)				Oxford (1823–1873)			
	In *DNB*	Not in *DNB*	Total	% in *DNB*	In *DNB*	Not in *DNB*	Total	% in *DNB*
1815–24	10	19	29	34.5%	6	15	21	28.6%
1825–34	12	16	28	42.9%	26	16	42	61.9%
1835–44	4	28	32	12.5%	12	14	26	46.2%
1845–54	12	17	29	41.4%	17	13	30	56.7%
1855–64	13	16	29	44.8%	11	20	31	35.5%
1865–73	8	18	26	30.8%	11	13	24	45.8%
Totals	59	114	173	34.1%	83	91	174	47.7%

Note: Multiple-term presidents appear in year of first term only.

TABLE 1.3 Union Presidents in the *Dictionary of National Biography* by Career Category

	Cambridge (1815–1873)				Oxford (1823–1873)			
	In *DNB*	Not in *DNB*	Total	% in *DNB*	In *DNB*	Not in *DNB*	Total	% in *DNB*
Law	9	41	50	18.0%	8	20	28	28.6%
Religion	10	45	55	18.2%	29	29	58	50.0%
*Politics**	17	7	24	70.8%	28	15	43	65.1%
SUBTOTAL	36	93	129	27.9%	65	64	129	50.4%
Academe	15	7	22	68.2%	11	11	22	50.0%
Letters	5	2	7	71.4%	7	1	8	87.5%
Other	3	12	15	20.0%	0	15	15	0.0%
SUBTOTAL	23	21	44	52.3%	18	27	45	40.0%
Totals	59	114	173	34.1%	83	91	174	47.7%

*Includes civil servants.

1855–1864, but this is based on a small difference in the underlying numbers.) The percentage of Oxford Union presidents in public careers with entries in the *DNB* is over 1.8 times greater than that for Cambridge Union presidents. Particularly notable in these terms is Oxford's great preponderance in the "Religion" category—both numerically and percentagewise. Cambridge does have a higher percentage of politicians in the *DNB*, but it is based on a total number (24) that is a little more than half that of Oxford (44).

Another way to compare the public eminence attained by the presidents of the two Unions is to count the number of those who attained the highest positions in their fields. Table 1.4 shows the number of presidents of each Union who gained episcopal, cabinet, or judicial rank.

As this analysis shows, Oxford's greater total number of former presidents in those influential positions is attributable to the difference in the number of graduates who attained episcopal rank. Considering that nineteenth-century Oxford was a hotbed of religious controversy, perhaps this result should come as no surprise. What these figures, and those for judicial and cabinet ranks do not show are the qualitative distinctions to be made within each category. Of the jurists, Oxford's are the more eminent, with a Lord Chancellor (Selborne), a Lord Chief Justice (Coleridge) and a Chief Justice of Madras. Cambridge has only one jurist of this rank, Lord Chief Justice Cockburn. With respect to high cabinet officers, Cambridge, with four Home Secretaries (Cross, Harcourt, Normanby, and Walpole) one of whom (Harcourt) became Chancellor of the Exchequer, more or less equals Oxford, with four Chancellors of the Exchequer

TABLE 1.4 Union Presidents Who Attained Judicial, Cabinet, or Episcopal Rank

	Cambridge (1815–1873)		Oxford (1823–1873)		Totals	
	N	% of Total	N	% of Total	N	% of Total
Judicial	6	37.5%	5	21.7%	11	28.2%
Cabinet	7	43.8%	6	26.1%	13	33.3%
Episcopal	3	18.8%	12	52.2%	15	38.5%
Total	16	100.0%	23	100.0%	39	100.0%

(Gladstone, Goschen, Hunt, Lowe). That Gladstone also became Prime Minister tips the balance considerably in favor of Oxford. It is also significant that Gladstone was the only man to have been both President of a Union and Prime Minister in the nineteenth century. (In the twentieth century two other Oxford Union presidents, H. H. Asquith [1874] and Edward Heath [1939], would attain the premiership. No president of the Cambridge Union has become Prime Minister.) Although not included in this analysis, the Oxford Union's greater eminence in the political arena can also be seen in the presence of three colonial governors general (Bowen, Dufferin, and Elgin). The Cambridge Union presidents include a Speaker of the House of Commons (Gully). Looking to the episcopate, once again the Oxonians are the more eminent group with one Roman Catholic Cardinal (Manning) and one Archbishop of Canterbury (Tait), compared to Cambridge's Archbishops of Dublin (Trench) and Sidney (Smith).

Overall, these analyses show that, while the presidents of both Unions appear to have entered public life in roughly equal measure, those from the Oxford Union tended to be more successful. These analyses serve to confirm the contemporary and later impressions that the Oxford Union produced more eminent public men in this period. While these impressions should be qualified by noting that they were based on the careers of a relatively small number of influential individuals, the Oxford Union produced more of these individuals than the Cambridge Union.

There are two sides to undergraduate life, and both were particularly in evidence in early- and mid-nineteenth-century Oxbridge. The university men preparing themselves for careers in Parliament, the church, the law, or in other professions could take themselves and their work extremely seriously. By today's standards, and even perhaps by the standards of their own day, they were priggish and pompous. Yet, perhaps naturally for young men laboring under a great weight of expectations, these 19 and 20 year-olds could also be extremely silly and frivolous. Certainly, as many of the foregoing quotations have made clear, the Unions both took themselves very seriously, but also saw their fair share of frivolity.

The important part of the story of the Cambridge and Oxford Unions has nothing to do with the large number of members who—after the Unions moved out of rented rooms into their grand edifices—lounged in the smoking rooms, read the newspapers, but took no part in debates. Rather, the real importance of the Unions lies in the new connection between public life and oratory that they embodied. As Roundell Palmer described the value of the Union:

> A school for public speaking, where awkwardness might be brushed off, command of words and self-possession obtained, good and bad examples observed, and the lesson learnt that a too frequent speaker becomes a bore,—all without any serious penalty for mistakes or failures,—was not less useful than lectures and examinations to a young man intended for the bar, and hoping perhaps some day to obtain a place in Parliament.[71]

The emergence of the two Unions created a wholly new oratorical training ground for the young men that would gain positions in public life during the Victorian era. In their forms and aspirations, the Unions far exceeded the older collegiate debating clubs, but were also the most notable examples of a new wave of debating societies. With the Unions, the oratorical training of university students became, in effect, systematized. As never before, young men could gain the respect of their peers (and, in cases, the interest of their elders) through oratorical performance in these venues. In turn, the Unions created new styles and expectations for youthful orators. Even if at the beginning the Unions were not the miniature parliaments of their later fame, the connection between Unionic exertions and a future in public life was clearly in evidence from early on. The later careers of the Unions' presidents, along with those of other officers and active members, was the clearest display of how the Unionic influence had penetrated public life.

Women's Collegiate Debating Societies

Women—who only came to be admitted (for years as second-class citizens) to the ancient universities beginning in the 1870s—were, as one would expect, excluded from the Cambridge and Oxford Unions. Although the Unions debated admitting women at regular intervals over the ensuing decades (motions to do so inevitably defeated or neutered by amendment), they only extended full membership to women in 1963—close on a century after women first arrived at the universities. Nevertheless, for many of the ambitious women who studied at Cambridge's Girton College (founded 1869, incorporated 1872) and Newnham College (founded 1870, incorporated 1880), and for those who studied at Oxford's Somerville Hall and Lady Margaret Hall (both founded 1879) and St. Hugh's College (founded 1886), debating activities were a notable feature of their education. For men students, once the Unions became fully established, collegiate societies became the minor league of university debating. For women students, however, collegiate societies were the only venues of this kind available to them and therefore merit special mention.

Debating societies were established very early on in the life of the women's colleges: at Newnham in 1873, and at Girton in 1875. In 1882, a group of three Somerville students founded a debating society for women students, which in 1885 developed into the Somerville and Lady Margaret Halls' Debating Society. In this way, Oxford's women's colleges created the basis of a distaff Oxford Union. This Society was expanded into the United Halls' Debating Society in 1893 when the students of St. Hugh's were admitted to full membership. Although the forms of this Society followed the usual procedures of debating societies, there was also room for a certain plasticity in approach. At one point, the debates "bloomed out into a mock trial of a poacher in Wytham Wood, when the Principals and Tutors were jury, and the counsel for the prosecution was . . . Miss Ivy Williams, afterwards the first woman to be called to the English Bar."[72] But this was only one of numerous organizations at the women's colleges dedicated to the cultivation of oratorical skills. "Sharp Practice" clubs required members (in the words of one Somerville fresher in 1889) to participate in "a debate without preparation—anyone called upon must speak at this for three minutes or stand looking a fool."[73]

While this provides some sense of the range of speech and debate activities at the women's colleges, it is also very instructive to look more closely at the major debate activities at one college, Newnham. Recalling her undergraduate years, Blanche Athena Clough (Principal of the College, 1920–23) wrote, "we were very keen about our debates, which seemed to me then and for many years after I had ceased to be a student to be almost always stirring and stimulating occasions even if there was not a great deal of eloquence displayed."[74] The college's first Debating Society was formed while the college itself was still in a transient state. As one of the first Newnham students wrote, "it was perhaps characteristic that the debates were on social rather than political questions."[75] Even so, debates on total abstinence, teacher training, periodical literature, and the merits of George Eliot were accompanied by debates on such topics as land nationalization and the abolition of the House of Lords.[76] As a student wrote in 1883, among the college societies and clubs, "the Debating Society still holds a foremost place."[77]

Debates were held twice in each of the Winter terms and once in the May term. Like the men's Unions, fear and controversy were often the order of the day.

> Speaking in College was a terrifying affair: many who have since had experience apparently more formidable admit that no audience has ever given them such cold feet. Women's suffrage motions were at times defeated; at times carried by narrow majorities; it by no means followed that the student, *qua* student, had the opinions of the pioneer.[78]

One has the sense, however, that unlike the debates of the men—by the last quarter of the century so often a display of superficial cleverness and inherited politics—the women's debates were often a far more earnest exercise in honing an argument for *themselves* as intellectual leaders. One motion debated in 1883 was that "Women should not be encouraged to devote themselves to special intellectual pursuit, such devotion being injurious to their own happiness and the progress of the race."[79] The proposer of the motion and chief speaker in its favor was a student engaged in the very special intellectual pursuit of Natural Sciences. The debate, needless to say, was spirited. Intercollegiate debates with Girton began in 1885 and continued to be held on an annual basis (although with skips in some years).

After the Debating Society, Newnham's most important speech activity was the Political Society.[80] Organized in 1884, the Political, like the local parliament movement that arose around the same time (see below), was modeled on the House of Commons, complete with a Speaker, a government and opposition, and members sitting for "real" constituencies. Mock legislation was developed, debated, and divided upon. The work of the Society, including debates held weekly (every Monday except on Mondays following meetings of the Debating Society), was very demanding on its members—and most especially on the "government." As an account of 1884 describes, the members of the Political's ministry "have work enough to do in attending Cabinet Councils, and providing answers to the questions of a small but merciless Conservative opposition."[81]

Through the Political, students learned a great deal about parliamentary procedure and the intricacies of public issues. By the closing years of the century, the Political is reported to have become "the absorbing interest of all the competent."[82] In oratorical terms (particularly after the Debating Society decided to shift the emphasis of its debates on literary subjects), "the speaking is less ceremonious than at the meetings of the Debating Society, and fiery denunciation of honourable members opposite, and ridicule of their policy and arguments are rather encouraged than the contrary."[83] Also unlike the Debating Society, the membership of the Political was virtually co-extensive with that of the College. In the 1890s, minute books record a membership of around 150.[84] "On occasions," Clough recalled, when a close vote was expected everyone in the College was canvassed hotly and the Whips have been known to drag absentees out of their beds to vote."[85]

Given the social background of Newnham students at that time, it was also the case that "students whose fathers or friends were in Parliament occasionally 'coached them up' in arguments and prognostications."[86] Of certain inspiration to the students was Helen Gladstone, President of the Debating Society in 1881 and later Vice-Principal of the College. Although she never attended the debates of the Political, "in case her presence should be embarrassing," she was occasionally persuaded by the Liberal Whip to witness divisions.[87] In one amazing episode, a Liberal ministry under Clough took office in January 1886 "and threw themselves into the breach before Mr. Gladstone could get there, with a measure of Local Government for Ireland." Although this measure was rejected "in spite of the solemn warnings of its promoters," the Political's government introduced Gladstone's Home Rule bill in May and passed it with the assistance of the Radicals (a pyrrhic victory, it appears, since the Conservatives took over the following term).[88]

The Political enjoyed a heyday of twenty-odd years,[89] and it inspired the creation of similar organizations at other women's colleges, such as Somerville's Parliamentary Debating Society organized around the turn of the twentieth century.[90] In addition to the Debating Society and the Political, students at late-nineteenth-century Newnham participated in a number of impromptu debating activities. Like other women's colleges, there was a Sharp Practice Club in which each member was required "willy-nilly, to speak consecutively on the topic [drawn at random] . . . for five minutes, standing. The results are reported to be of a highly amusing character."[91] A similar sort of activity was practiced by a group known as "The Incapables" established in 1884 in Newnham's North Hall.

The significance of the debating societies that arose in the women's colleges goes well beyond being merely more examples of the popularity of such activities in this period. Nor are these societies simply a case of the women copying the men's colleges. The 1870s and 1880s, when the colleges and their debating societies were founded, was the period in which women began to gain entry into elected public life as members of school boards, poor law boards, and local government councils. By the late 1890s, about 1,500 women held local elected office.[92] Although the first generation of elected women drew on their public speaking experience as lecturers, campaigners, and fund-raisers,[93] the first generation of university women would benefit from the more formalized and structured preparation afforded by the various debating societies for their new and expanding role in British public life.[94]

Provincial Debating Societies and Local Parliaments

Debating societies were formed not only at elite educational institutions, but also throughout the country. When, later in the century, the new provincial universities were created, their students made sure to have their own Union societies on the Oxbridge model. But debating societies had also been formed in provincial towns from the early part of the century. Significantly, these societies were not organized for the benefit of students, but rather as an organ of adult (male) middle-class political culture. In the main, provincial debating societies helped to promote the creation of local elites. Such was the case with the Rochdale Literary and Philosophical Society co-founded in 1833 by the 22-year-old John Bright.[95]

In Bright's parliamentary constituency, Birmingham, an especially notable example of a provincial debating society was organized in 1846 by a group of young business and professional men. In 1855, this society merged with the flourishing debating society in nearby Edgbaston to form the Birmingham and Edgbaston Debating Society. Unlike the members of the Oxford and Cambridge Unions, the members of the Birmingham and Edgbaston Debating Society did not necessarily imagine careers for themselves in Parliament. Beginning with the Municipal Corporations Act of 1835 (providing for directly elected town councils), and continuing throughout the century with a variety of reforms and initiatives, local government developed into a major arena of British political life. In this context, debating societies in provincial towns provided young men with the first rung on the ladder to leadership in their town and region. As one of the Birmingham and Edgbaston Debating Society's presidents wrote: "This Society has proved a training school in which the intellectual athlete has prepared himself for the more vigorous, if not the more difficult, conflicts of public life; and it is a most gratifying fact that many of its members are baring an honourable and active part in the important public duties which are essential to the well-being of this town."[96]

While it is certainly true that the Society's members tended to become local notables,[97] some also gained national recognition. Of the 17 presidents of the merged Society between 1855 and 1873, five, or nearly one-third, have entries in the *Dictionary of National Biography.* The most significant person to hold the presidency of the Birmingham and Edgbaston Debating Society was Joseph Chamberlain. Chamberlain was not a natural public speaker, but over time his exertions in the Society helped him to cultivate the necessary attributes of aspirants to public life: the ability both to think on his feet and to speak well.[98] However difficult Chamberlain's path to public eloquence was, the Society proved one of the early vehicles by which he established himself as a leader among his peers. Yet, although Chamberlain attained national stature, it is also true that the base of his political power remained centered on Birmingham and the Midlands. The role of the Birmingham and Edgbaston Debating Society in forging a tight and powerful local elite can be seen, not only in how many of the Society's presidents became local notables, but also in the high proportion who became closely involved with Chamberlain's political career.

As debating societies at the public schools and the ancient universities could not help but reflect the largely aristocratic and gentry backgrounds of the students from which their membership was drawn, provincial organizations like the Birmingham and Edgbaston Debating Society reflect the political muscle acquired by the middle classes of Britain's new industrial urban centers. Later in the century, debating also became an activity promoted further down the social scale, sometimes even offered as entertainments in pubs. Another type of organization promoting debates was the political club, established by the expanding national party organizations as a means to integrate the newly enfranchised electors of the lower middle and working classes. As one historian has recently noted, these clubs "offered leisure and sporting facilities, newspaper rooms and libraries, lectures and debates, partly, at least, in an attempt to deepen the value of citizenship."[99]

The fullest realization of the debating club as an institution of popular political education came towards the end of the century with the creation in many towns and villages of debating societies modeled on the House of Commons.[100] Like Newnham College's Political society, the local parliaments, as they were called, replicated the representative structure, organization, forms, and procedure of the Commons. By 1883, there were over 100 such local parliaments with around 35,000 members.[101] In 1892, the National Association of Local Parliaments was formed to promote the movement and provide guidance to established and new organizations. Many local parliaments issued printed records of their proceedings, and some had their activities covered in the local press. The members of these societies were very earnest in the discharge of their "governmental" or "representative" duties. Indeed, sometimes local parliamentarians had to be reminded of reality, as illustrated by a retort from the Prime Minister (one Mr. Hedgeworth) of the Eastbourne House of Commons during an 1883 sitting: "I believe the object of this House is to enable members to join in subjects of debate. . . . [W]hatever Bill the local House might seek to introduce will not have the effect of repealing the existing Acts."[102]

The social composition of local parliament membership appears to have been fairly heterogenous. As one observer recorded:

> Side by side with [young men] . . . may be seen grey-headed men, magistrates, sober tradesmen, manufacturers. In a parliament of the West End of London, I have seen a (morganatic) cousin of the Queen . . . holding the office of First Lord of the Admiralty, while in a parliament in the north of the metropolis I have found a shoemaker discharging the analogous functions of Minister of War.[103]

Yet, although the membership was drawn from a broad social base (particularly in London), the greatest significance of the local parliaments lies in their function as, in effect, poor-man's Oxford Unions. From these societies, future working-class leaders and ambitious sons of the lower middle classes gained a practical education in politics and its oratorical medium. Despite the decidedly non-elite nature of local parliaments, it is a reflection on the changed nature of political society by the beginning of the twentieth century—as well as a reflection of the importance of debating societies in public life—that they, like the Oxford Union, can boast of former members who rose to the pinnacle of British public life: Ramsay

MacDonald of the St. Pancras parliament and Andrew Bonar Law of the Glasgow Parliamentary Debating Association.[104]

Conclusion

Debating societies could be seen as merely one manifestation of the nineteenth-century penchant for what could be called "serious recreation." But the political-oratorical education afforded by debating activities was, to judge by the statements of contemporaries, far more significant than their recreational functions. In all the forms discussed here—the public school club, the university Unions, the collegiate debating societies, the variety of local associations—and many others (including the legal debating organizations discussed in chapter 4), debating societies were both prevalent and prominent in the broader political culture of nineteenth-century Britain. The activities of debating societies were entirely academic in the sense that the motions and speeches and votes ultimately affected nothing. Yet, over the course of the nineteenth century, the various debating societies enabled a broad range of people to educate themselves in the techniques of public speaking—a crucial aspect of public life in Britain's gradually democratizing society.

The debating societies discussed here were formed by people who believed that the activity of debating was an important and valuable educational process, whether to prepare for future participation in national politics, to cultivate a local elite, or to facilitate upward status mobility. As schools for public speaking, these debating societies are all the more interesting because they were organized, not by school authorities or philanthropic groups, but rather by the members themselves. From the end of wartime repression, through the mid-Victorian boom, through the sharpening class tensions at the end of the century, debating societies came to provide the traditional "governing classes," the rising professionals, and the lower orders a distinctive vehicle of educational opportunity through public speech.

CHAPTER TWO

The House of Commons

IN THE COURSE of his late-Victorian youth, Winston Churchill determined that he would follow in the footsteps of his father, Lord Randolph Churchill, and become a professional politician in Parliament. Given young Winston's passion for reading the great British historians, it is unlikely that he failed to note Macaulay's declaration that "Parliamentary government is government by speaking. In such a government, the power of speaking is the most prized of all qualities which a politician can possess."[1] As a boy, Churchill avidly read the lengthy newspaper reports of parliamentary debates. On a number of occasions, he also witnessed government by speaking first-hand from the Visitors Gallery of the House of Commons, and remembered well hearing Gladstone deliver one of his last great speeches.[2]

To prepare himself for his future in the Commons, Churchill worked with therapists to overcome his speech impediments. Possibly connected with his efforts to shed his stammer and lisp, he also began to cultivate an oratorical style derived from what was regarded as the great tradition of parliamentary eloquence—a tradition that continued to be much discussed and analyzed during his early years.[3] To his own reflection in the mirror, he read aloud and often memorized the great speeches of the great parliamentary orators in this canon. As an MP, his speeches were carefully written compositions that sought to evoke the oratorical grandeur of Parliaments past. In the context of his political career before 1940, this style of speech had become out of place and could even be counted among his political liabilities.[4] Indeed, the parliamentary speech of Churchill's time owed far more to the pithy sarcasm and philippics for which his father was known than to the grand tradition of parliamentary eloquence that his romantic historicism led him to emulate.

It is perhaps inevitable that a discussion of parliamentary oratory written at the turn of the twenty-first century would begin with Winston Churchill, particularly since his international reputation was based largely on having "mobilized the English language and sent it into battle."[5] Yet it is not his twentieth-century oratorical feats that concern us here. Far more significant are the ways that Churchill's style of speech and his efforts to develop that style reflected the values associated with political eloquence during the age of Gladstone, in which Churchill spent the first quarter-century of his life. By 1913, a late-Victorian of an earlier vintage, Lord Curzon, could comment that Churchill was one of the few speakers in the House of Commons "who still cultivates, I will not say the classical, but the literary style, and at times practises it with great ability."[6]

Churchill's determination to learn how to speak like a statesman, and his understanding of what constituted first-rate political oratory, introduces a body of issues relating to the perception and realities of parliamentary speech in the nineteenth century. He was far from alone in his fascination with parliamentary oratory. As evidenced by the leading journals of opinion (*Blackwood's, Cornhill, Fraser's*, and the like) which regularly printed essays and series of essays devoted to analyzing the quality of speeches in Parliament, and the numerous diaries of memoirs of people in and around Parliament commenting on the traditions and current practices of speech-making, the nature of parliamentary oratory was one of the Victorian era's minor preoccupations. In particular, Curzon's description of Churchill's oratory points to two linked themes that were common to most nineteenth-century assessments of parliamentary eloquence: first, that parliamentary speech had experienced a qualitative decline; and second, that the quality of speeches was understood as a function of a kind of oratorical grandeur. Indeed, parliamentary oratory was viewed almost as a branch of literature in much the same way that the orations of Demosthenes and Cicero were integral parts of the classical canon, and oratorical grandeur was strongly linked to classical quotation.[7] This chapter will examine the nineteenth-century preoccupation with parliamentary speech, and explore the realities behind contemporary beliefs about the oratory of the House of Commons.[8]

The Golden Age of Parliamentary Oratory

In order to understand Victorian ideas about parliamentary oratory, it is first necessary to say something about the later eighteenth century—

the period that nineteenth-century commentators consistently described as Parliament's oratorical "golden age." Although the canon of parliamentary eloquence sometimes includes earlier figures—such as Oliver Cromwell and Lord Bolingbroke—the golden age is most often seen to have begun with the elder William Pitt. Yet, despite the towering reputation given to posterity by the much-read political memoirs of the age, the record of what the elder Pitt actually said is scanty at best. Almost all of the (incomplete) reports that exist are for speeches delivered in the Lords after the "Great Commoner" became the Earl of Chatham in 1770. Very little remains of the speeches he delivered in the House of Commons through which he gained his power and reputation. Thus Horace Walpole was prophetic when he wrote: "the memory of his eloquence . . . will remain, when the neglect of his contemporaries, and my criticisms, will be forgotten."[9] The oratorical legend handed down by Walpole and others aside, the elder Pitt's reputation as a speaker was certainly imbricated with his eventual standing as the hero of the Seven Years War and the architect of Britain's global greatness.

If there were not many of the elder Pitt's speeches for young Winston Churchill to study and recite, the same could hardly be said for the next great figure in the pantheon of parliamentary eloquence, Edmund Burke. Yet Burke's oratorical reputation was a mixed one. Although he was an eloquent and frequent contributor to debate, he found it difficult to command the attention of the House. As John Morley later wrote, "it is not wrong to say of Burke that as an orator he was transcendent, yet in that immediate influence upon his hearers which is commonly supposed to be the mark of oratorical success, all the evidence is that Burke generally failed."[10] In 1772, for instance, Horace Walpole opined: "His fault was copiousness above measure, and he dealt abundantly too much in establishing general positions. Two-thirds of this oration resembled the beginning of a book on speculative doctrines, and yet argument was not the forte of it."[11] Not only was Burke long-winded, but also the reception of his speeches at delivery was further impeded by his somewhat harsh voice and thick Irish accent. He acquired the reputation of a parliamentary "dinner bell"—when he got up to speak, members got up to leave. The fame of Burke's speeches rested on their *published* versions. In pamphlets based on his speeches, he sought (and often succeeded) to gain for his words the kind of reception that was denied at the time of their original, oral delivery. In terms of persuasion, the pamphlets succeeded where the orations did not. To quote Morley again, "the very qualities which are excellences in literature were drawbacks to the spoken discourses."[12] Thus, the legacy of Burke's speeches is literary and compositional rather than strictly oratorical.

Both the elder Pitt and Burke are routinely named in nineteenth- and early-twentieth-century histories of parliamentary oratory;[13] but in these accounts, discussion of the eighteenth century always focuses on the younger William Pitt and his principal political and oratorical rival in the House of Commons, Charles James Fox.

PITT AND FOX

The nineteenth-century view that the golden age of parliamentary oratory reached its zenith with the younger Pitt and Fox resulted, in part, from the fact that both men's achievements remained within living memory for some time. In different ways, both had emerged as heroes of the wars against Napoleon, and in an era that saw the emergence of party politics in the modern sense, both became icons for their respective political parties. With respect to their oratorical reputations, leaving aside the recollections of the older generation, the printed record of both the younger Pitt's and Fox's speeches was much greater than that of Chatham (as I will refer to the elder Pitt hereafter). Similar to those of Burke, the printed speeches of the younger Pitt and Fox, have a remarkably finished and literary quality, but they still read like speeches rather than compositions.

The younger Pitt was in a sense born, and certainly bred, to be a great parliamentary orator. Although (or because) Chatham had been schooled at Eton, he decided to have his sons educated by tutor at home. In addition to learning Latin, Greek, and mathematics before being sent off to Cambridge, Pitt's early education was augmented by special instruction in oratory from Chatham himself. To train the boy for public speaking, Chatham had his son extemporaneously translate Latin and Greek passages into English—an exercise designed to increase Pitt's facility for selecting the appropriate word.[14] This training was later borne out by the finished quality for which Pitt's parliamentary speeches were known. Further, in order to develop "sonorous elocution" Chatham had Pitt recite passages from Shakespeare and Milton.[15] Pitt is also recorded as having a thorough and accurate knowledge of the Bible.[16]

Chatham saw to it that Pitt developed into a confident, cultivated, and eloquent speaker. From his first performance in the Commons in 1781, Pitt gained a reputation as one of the foremost speakers in both substance and expression. This is particularly astonishing given the fact of Pitt's youth. He was not quite 22 when he entered Parliament, and first became Prime Minister at age 24. Thus, the commanding power of his oratory owed nothing to the gravitas of age. Contemporary approbation of Pitt's oratorical skill was perpetuated by succeeding generations of politicians, writers, and historians. To the present day, Pitt's qualities as a speaker are considered as tangible as, and inseparable from his other achievements as a statesman, and some of his speeches are the stuff of parliamentary legend.

Perhaps the most famous story about Pitt's parliamentary eloquence comes from his 1792 speech advocating the immediate abolition of slavery. The debate on the slave trade had been a long one, and the House had sat through the night. In the peroration of his lengthy speech, Pitt looked to the future prospects of civilizing Africa:

> Then may we hope that even Africa, though last of all the quarters of the globe, shall enjoy at length, in the evening of her days, those blessings which have descended so plentifully upon us in a much earlier period of the world. Then also will Europe, participating in her improvement and prosperity, receive an ample recompense for the tardy kindness, if kindness it can be called, of no longer hindering that continent from extricating herself out of the darkness which, in other more fortunate regions, has been so much more speedily dispelled.

He then crowned these eloquent words with what legend asserts was an impromptu quotation from Virgil:

> *Nosque ubi primus equis Oriens afflavit anhelis;*
> *Illic sera rubens accendit lumina Vesper.**[17]

According to Lord Stanhope, who heard the story from MPs who were present, "the first beams of the rising sun shot through the windows of the House in the midst of this final passage, and seemed, as Pitt looked

* Virgil, *Georgics* (Book I, 250–1): "when on us the rising Sun first breathes with panting steeds, there glowing vesper is kindling the evening rays." This and all subsequent translations from Latin authors are from the Loeb Classical Library editions of the works cited.

upwards, to suggest to him without premeditation the eloquent simile and the noble Latin lines with which he concluded."[18]

Like Pitt, Charles James Fox, was also well prepared to become a prominent parliamentary speaker, but as part of a much broader upbringing as a gentleman of fashion and cultivation. At Eton, Fox learned Latin and Greek according to the customary forms of composition, memorization, and translation. (He also learned French, and later Italian and some Spanish.) Fox too received an oratorical education, though perhaps not as deliberate and thorough as Pitt's. His father, Lord Holland, took him to see debates in Parliament on a number of occasions, and Eton's headmaster, Dr. Edward Barnard, regarded in his time as a great elocutionist, "attended carefully to the rhetorical training of the boys who had boroughs waiting for them as soon as they came of age."[19]

Fox was both a very cosmopolitan and a very cultivated man. At Oxford, although he moved in the fashionable society of gentleman-commoners, he was also an assiduous student. He was well read in the literature and poetry of the day (both English and French), and had a particular fondness for drama. His father's famous over-indulgence endowed him with great self-confidence, and he was also extremely well traveled. In short, Fox was nothing if not a man of the world, and a talented one at that. He was also a man of great personal charm (a quality that would later prove a substantial asset to Disraeli). In the House of Commons, which he entered in 1768, Fox became one of the best-regarded speakers of his day.[20]

The political rivalry between Pitt and Fox is inseparable from their oratorical rivalry. In private—like the worthy antagonists they were—each occasionally voiced sincere admiration for the other's speeches. During debates, however, it was a different story. Pitt might complain of Fox's "volubility that rendered comprehension difficult, and detection almost impossible."[21] Fox might critique Pitt's "verbose periods, and those big, bombastic sentiments which constitute, in general, the principal part of his orations."[22] When comparing the speeches of the two, it must be borne in mind that Fox was a far more cultivated man by late-eighteenth-century standards. However serious his application to his studies and his parliamentary duties, Fox had been brought up to be a man of fashion; Pitt had been brought up to be a man of government, and generally went about in society less. Further, in contrast to Pitt's ministerial career, almost the whole of Fox's political life was spent in opposition. Free from the constraints of office and cabinet solidarity, Fox could indulge his theatrical bent. His oratorical style was far more varied and extravagant than Pitt's, which was necessarily tied to articulating policy and leading the government party. Fox was free to attack; Pitt was constrained to defend. The roles of government and opposition also affected the manner in which they made their speeches. Pitt would deliver his speech and make no concessions to members entering the Commons chamber in the course of it. Fox, on the other hand, even at the end of a long speech, would return to his earlier arguments for the benefit of latecomers.[23]

Already in the first decades of the nineteenth century, the late-eighteenth-century House of Commons had acquired a legendary status. In an era of faction rather than party, politics was a far more personalized business than it later became. As one historian has written, there was a "distinctively *sturm-und-drang* quality" to British political life in the late eighteenth and early nineteenth centuries, characterized by a "special kind of emotionalism and violence" that produced "histrionics and highly charged rhetoric."[24] The emotionalism and rhetoric of Parliament in this era reflected the fact that Britain was at the center of a series of vast and violent global events: the Seven Years War, the loss of the American Colonies, the acquisition of an empire in the East, and a quarter-century of war against Revolutionary and Napoleonic France. Even the major "domestic" sources of impassioned parliamentary oratory were rooted in foreign concerns: the trial of Warren Hastings was about British rule in India, and the greatest constitutional debate of the period was over union with Ireland. The formidable nature of all these events—war, insurrection, empire—was the epic backdrop for debates over great principles and the accumulation of a great deal of parliamentary lore. Against this heroic lore, those in and around parliament in the nineteenth century compared their more lackluster realities.

QUOTATIONS IN SPEECHES

The era of Pitt and Fox was the standard by which Victorian analysts of parliamentary oratory measured contemporary speech-making in the House of Commons. In particular, they held that the excellence of this oratorical golden age was epitomized by the facility with which late-eighteenth-century MPs were able to draw from the well of classical literature in their parliamentary speeches. It was commonly asserted as fact that the MPs of this period routinely employed classical references and quotations, and that Latin served almost as a *lingua franca* among the parliamentary caste. Ultimately, the decline of oratorical classicism in Parliament was held to be the most significant index of a more general decline in the quality of parliamentary oratory.

When attempting to evoke the classical atmosphere of the eighteenth-century Commons, a number of nineteenth-century writers tended to repeat the same handful of stories, especially Pitt's 1792 speech on the slave trade. Another oft-repeated story was when Burke rebuked William Bagot for rising prematurely in the mistaken belief that Burke had concluded his speech. Bagot apologized for this breach of parliamentary etiquette with a quotation from Horace: *rusticus exspectat dum defluat amnis; at ille/ labitur et labetur in omne volubilis ævum.**[25] But an accurate qualitative assessment of eighteenth-century parliamentary discourse cannot be based simply on a few anecdotes.

A better way to gauge the classicism of the eighteenth-century Commons is to look at the frequency of classical quotation in the speeches of the younger Pitt and Fox. Both were among the best-educated MPs, and both had a facility for the classics. Both were also among the most frequent contributors to debates and were leaders in their respective political camps. Although it is a crude method given the incompleteness of the published record, one way to measure the extent to which they employed classical quotations and phrases is to count the number of Latin passages that appear in the standard collection of their speeches.[26]

Pitt's collected speeches contain reports of 147 parliamentary orations. Leaving aside routine Latin terms (*prima facie, ad infinitum, status quo*, and so on), these speeches contain a total of 15 significant Latin quotations—an average of one quotation for every ten speeches (although eight of the 15 quotations were made in the two-year period of 1792 and 1793). Fox also used Latin words and phrases frequently in his parliamentary speeches. Out of the 456 utterances in his collected parliamentary speeches, Fox employs full-length Latin quotations in fewer than 30—about six percent of the total. Even if these collections of Pitt's and Fox's speeches are incomplete, they are large enough to constitute a fair sample of each man's oratorical output in Parliament. It does not seem overly reductive, therefore, to conclude that both Pitt and Fox used Latin far more sparingly than their posthumous legends boasted.

In addition to Latin, Pitt and Fox also made a significant number of quotations from English literature, which they both knew well. Both nat-

* Horace, *Epistles* (Book I, ii, 42–43): " . . .the bumpkin waiting for the river to run out: yet on it glides, and on it will glide, rolling its flood forever."

urally drew on Shakespeare. Pitt appears to have stuck to better known authors like Pope.[27] Fox's selections were more wide-ranging: "it was often remarked that his quotations and allusions in his speeches from passages not commonly known in our dramatic authors, both serious and comic, were very frequent and very happy."[28]

Ultimately, while Pitt's and Fox's use of Latin quotations may have appeared impressive—both to those members who understood them and those who didn't—the extent to which they made a difference in political terms is questionable. The limitations of the parliamentary audience must always be considered. Certainly, as recorded by Nathaniel Wraxall, these limitations were borne in mind by the leading speakers:

> Mr. Pitt, who well knew how large a part of his Audience, especially among the Country Gentlemen, were little conversant in the Writings of the Augustan Age, or familiar with Horace, always displayed great Caution in borrowing from those Classic Sources. In the lapse of near fourteen years that I have heard him almost daily address the House of Commons, I question if he made in all, more than eight or ten citations. Fox and Sheridan, though not equally severe in that Respect, yet never abused, or injudiciously expended the Stores of ancient Literature that they possessed. Burke's enthusiasm, his exhaustless Memory, and luxuriant Imagination, more frequently carried him away into the Times of Virgil and Cicero: while [Isaac] Barré usually condescended, whenever he quoted Latin, to translate for the benefit of the Country Members.[29]

Most importantly, given the realities of later eighteenth-century parliamentary politics, Pitt's power and support in the Commons, and Fox's exclusion from both was determined to a significant degree by the crown. The enthusiasm of nineteenth-century commentators for late-eighteenth-century oratorical classicism notwithstanding, it is hard to imagine that quotations could have made a difference in the fate of a measure. Certainly, quotations added to the refinement and polish of speeches, but the eighteenth-century House of Commons was not so effete a place as to vote on practical measures according to the superior aptitude of a literary reference—even when it came from someone in such a commanding position as Pitt. When Pitt called for immediate abolition of the slave trade in 1792, impromptu Virgilian lines, however brilliantly applied, did not prevent the majority of members from voting for a motion to insert the word "gradually" into the bill. Indeed, what was a positive oratorical factor in whatever success Pitt and Fox enjoyed was their eloquence and debating power in English, which was, after all, the language they unquestionably employed—and employed so well—nearly all the time.

Structures of Parliamentary Speech

To the extent that Victorian parliament-watchers viewed Latin quotations as the ultimate expression of parliamentary eloquence, they also believed that in their own time the "genius of classical tradition has fled for ever from the House of Commons."[30] As one historian of parliamentary oratory lamented in 1913: "Until the nineteenth century Latin quotations were frequently given in the House of Commons. Now, Members of Parliament are an English-speaking brotherhood."[31] But the elegies for oratorical classicism in Parliament were not mere nostalgia. The perceived decline of Latin quotations in particular, and parliamentary eloquence in general, were explicitly rooted in a complex of assumptions about the past, present, and future of British political culture.[32] Most important were the ways that nineteenth-century observers of Parliament and parliamentary oratory proceeded from the firm belief that the 1832 Reform Act had significantly altered the social and educational composition of the House—and therefore its oratory—for the worse.

SOCIAL BACKGROUND OF MEMBERS

The connection between the waning "classical tradition" in Parliament and constitutional change was not confined only to those who wrote about parliamentary oratory in journals of opinion. It was commented upon in the same terms by major political figures as well. In the 1860s, for example, Disraeli described his efforts to recover what he believed to be the classical tradition of parliamentary oratory:

> There used to be well understood rules in the House of Commons in the old days (before the Reform), respecting quotations.
>
> No English poet to be quoted, who had not completed his Century.

> Greek & French never under any circumstances: Latin as you liked: Horace and Virgil by preference; then Juvenal.
>
> Now quotation (in the House of Commons) is what we are most deficient in. Very few will venture on Latin. But it is not that the House has relinquished quotation, but the new elements find their illustrations & exponents in illegitimate means. It is not merely, that they quote Byron & Tennyson before they have completed their quarantine. But Bright & Cobden, & all those sort of people, are always quoting Dickens & *Punch*, &c. Our quotations are either tawdry or trashy. The privilege of quotation should not be too easy. It should be fenced in.[33]

Fifty years later, Lord Curzon saw not only the decline of oratorical classicism in the nineteenth century, but also its fall. Where MPs had once been drawn from the aristocracy, they now came from the middle, and increasingly the laboring classes. Surveying the changes in parliamentary speakers and audiences from the Great Reform Act to the early twentieth century, he asked: "How many men are there in the House of Commons who have ever read an oration of Demosthenes, or could translate a speech of Cicero? Thus one class of model has altogether vanished."[34] Of the eighteenth-century parliamentarians he wrote that "Virgil, Horace, Cicero, Juvenal, even the later Roman poets, were more familiar to them then are Tennyson and Browning to us."[35] The practice of quotation from classical authors in Parliament, he declared, was "a moribund accomplishment," the vestigial remnants of which he labeled mere "popular tags."[36]

An excellent example of how nineteenth-century views of political eloquence were rooted in beliefs about the nature of constitutional change is an 1889 essay by Frederic George Kenyon, an Oxford classicist who later became Director of the British Museum. Among the classical civilizations, he wrote, all the necessary elements for the fullest development of political oratory were present only in Athens. Although Kenyon does not quite put it in these terms, these conditions all relate to the fact that Athenian political liberty extended only to a governing elite. In Athens, according to Kenyon, political orators and those they addressed shared the same education; the governing class had the leisure to talk and to listen; and political oratory had genuine power because the assembly was absolute and its debates moved the wheels of the state. He contrasts these conditions to Rome, which he finds not nearly as well suited to produce political eloquence of the highest order, not least because politicians who addressed public meetings descended to the level of the "uncultured mob."

Turning to modern political oratory, Kenyon asserts that only England has ever met his criteria for the production of genuine political eloquence. However, he finds the virtues of Athens in the oratory of the later eighteenth century, and the limitations of Rome in that of the nineteenth. In the second half of the eighteenth century, Parliament "had been long enough established to have learnt the resources of the language, and how to apply them to its art. It was not yet open to the debasing and chilling influences of reporting. The speaker addressed himself to an intelligent and educated audience, which, if not quick and emotional like the Athenian ecclesia, yet expected to hear good and careful speaking."[37] Thus, in this account, the highest political oratory was produced—and could only have been produced—under an aristocratic constitution. Of his own times, Kenyon writes that electoral reforms destroyed the conditions for true eloquence that had prevailed in the second half of the eighteenth century. The electorate was no longer composed of those with the culture or leisure to truly appreciate the arts of oratory. Writing only a few years after the Reform Acts of 1884–85, Kenyon laments the necessarily didactic function of addressing "a newly enfranchised, untaught, and hard-worked populace."[38] Under these debased and debasing circumstances, British political oratory could not but decline from its former heights.

As evidenced by Kenyon's essay, the traditions of eighteenth-century political oratory were seen by some as a great legacy bequeathed to the nation by the unreformed constitution. Accordingly, true eloquence of the kind practiced by Pitt and Fox was seen as a function of what was understood about the world of politics before 1832. In Curzon's words, real parliamentary eloquence—such as that of the late eighteenth century—was "the art of an aristocratic society, practiced under aristocratic conditions, in an aristocratic age."[39] Like many other writers on parliamentary oratory, Kenyon links changes in the quality of political eloquence directly to the belief that the 1832 Reform Act led to an immediate and dramatic shift in the composition of the House of Commons membership. "In less than a generation after the death of Charles James Fox [in 1806], the barriers which kept the public from a decisive share in politics were broken down, and the sovereignty transferred, in fact as well as in theory, from parliament to the people."[40]

Historians have conclusively refuted the nineteenth-century belief that the social composition of the Commons changed dramatically after 1832.[41]

In the words of one: "The Great Reform Act was both a landmark and a turning-point, but it would be wrong to assume that the political scene in the succeeding generation differed essentially from the preceding one."[42] Many studies have stressed the continuity of numerous facets of the pre-Reform Act political culture—the survival of pocket boroughs, active coercion, and electoral corruption, to name only the most obvious.[43] With respect to the social composition of the Commons, it is clear that the landed classes maintained their numerical majority, political influence, and parliamentary position throughout the nineteenth century. Despite the creation in law of a middle-class electorate in 1832, the Commons remained primarily aristocratic until after the reforms of 1884–85. Although the proportion of aristocratic MPs began to drop off after 1867, the landed presence predominated until the end of the nineteenth century, and continued to be strong well into the twentieth century.[44] Further, studies of the social composition of cabinets have shown that, irrespective of changes in parliamentary membership, the government of the nation in the nineteenth century ultimately remained in aristocratic hands.[45]

The argument for continuity across 1832 has also been made from the other direction—that the social composition of the Commons broadened significantly during the eighteenth century. In the parliaments of the first two Georges, "non-elite" MPs averaged around 16 percent of the Commons membership. By the turn of the nineteenth century, this proportion rose to as high as 23 percent, and had increased still further by the time of George III's death.[46] Thus, the election of significant and increasing numbers of non-aristocrats to the Commons had begun well before 1832. However, one must also bear in mind that, to the extent that "new men" did enter the Commons, their parliamentary career was typically but one aspect of their attempt to conform as closely as possible to the model of their social betters and advance their own and their descendants' social status.[47]

In light of this body of scholarship, the beliefs of those who attributed the decline of parliamentary oratory to a sudden change in the social composition of the Commons appear to be ill-founded. If the class representation of the Commons changed only slowly, and if "aristocratic" values continued to dominate the character of Parliament in the nineteenth century, then the explanations of contemporary observers for the decline of political eloquence that cited a dramatic alteration in the social origins of MPs cannot be correct. Broad generalizations about membership do not suffice to explain any changes in the style of parliamentary oratory.

EDUCATION OF MEMBERS

While the general decline of British political eloquence in the nineteenth century was conventionally seen as a function of extending the franchise, a number of commentators laid particular emphasis on what they believed to be the declining standards of MPs' education. In these accounts, the classical education common to the members of an aristocratic Commons produced a fuller development of, and shared appreciation for, political oratory. For instance, after writing at length about the classical erudition of eighteenth-century parliamentarians, the lawyer and essayist Abraham Hayward opined: "The altered constitution of the House since 1832 and still more, we fear, since 1867, has been in no respect more marked than the absence of that familiarity with the Latin classics, which renders it comparatively dead to quotations or illustrations drawn from them."[48] In another article from around the same time, the political writer T. H. S. Escott saw the decline in the quality of parliamentary speeches from the late eighteenth century as a function of what he claimed was a shift in educational values from classical (i.e. aristocratic) to scientific (i.e. middle-class) learning. He described the Commons as "the educational mirror of the nation" and wrote that, since the Reform Bill of 1832, "There has been a steady decrease . . . in the proportion of members of Parliament whose educational antecedents are those which were once deemed indispensable to every English gentleman, and matters have now reached such a pass that it is thought bad taste to make a Latin quotation, lest you should affront your next-door neighbour by the parading of an unknown tongue."[49]

A close look at those educational antecedents reveals a different picture. As already discussed, the landed interest was the dominant influence in Parliament throughout the nineteenth century. For the most part, aristocrats received the fullest education (poor scholars destined for the clergy being the major exception), and their education was overwhelmingly classical. The pattern of aristocratic schooling familiar to the nineteenth century took shape during the second half of the eighteenth century. Private instruction by tutors at home was increasingly replaced by education at public boarding schools. Between 1761 and 1790, more than three-fourths of peers' sons elected to Parliament were educated at Eton, Westminster, Winchester, and Harrow.[50] At the English universities, the eighteenth century saw both a general drop in admissions and a change in the social mix of students. Oxford and Cambridge became more socially exclusive as the poor scholars aiming for careers in the church came to be squeezed out by competition for admission and scholarships from sons of more affluent social groups.

Despite this shift in social composition, it has been argued that the *proportion* of elite sons entering Oxford and Cambridge actually declined during the eighteenth century (i.e. the overall size of the elite increased while the number of elite scions going to university remained constant). This decline has been attributed to a discrediting among the eighteenth century nobility and squirearchy of the value of a scholarly education for their sons. Admissions to Oxford and Cambridge experienced rapid growth only after the turn of the nineteenth century—growth due for the most part to increased matriculations among sons of the elite classes.[51] The growth in elite admissions was reflected in the proportion of MPs who had received a university education. Approximately 40 percent of the members returned to each Parliament during the period 1754–1790 attended an English, Scottish, Irish, or foreign university; by 1818, this proportion had increased to about 60 percent.[52]

Some portion of non-aristocratic MPs in the eighteenth century also attended the elite public schools and the traditional universities, but for different reasons—parliamentary life being the exception rather than the rule for people of their social backgrounds. Over the course of the eighteenth century, ambitious non-elite fathers did not see a compelling necessity to have their sons educated in the aristocratic fashion unless the boys were intended for careers at the bar, or were being groomed to preside as country gentlemen over landed estates purchased with the fathers' commercial wealth. At both the beginning and the end of the century, the proportion of non-elite MPs who had attended Oxford or Cambridge appears to have held at roughly one-quarter (some others attended Scottish universities). Data on the schooling of non-elite MPs is more problematic from a comparative standpoint, but of those returned in 1790, again roughly one quarter are recorded as having spent some time at either Eton, Harrow, Westminster, or Winchester.[53]

The shift to public education was an integral part of the formation of a new culture of public life in the eighteenth century.[54] According to one historian, the "most probable explanation [for this change in the pattern of aristocratic education] is the growing importance of Parliament in the national life after the Revolution of 1688 and the extent to which Westminster was replacing St James's as the centre of power and influence."[55] For the sons of the elite, the rough-and-tumble of public school came to be viewed as the appropriate training for Parliament. That aristocratic boys received their education together (hence "public") rather than individually at home, provided the basis for social cohesion as a governing class. This cohesion was aided by the fact that the classics and little else were taught at public school. (Private and home instruction, such as the younger Pitt's, also centered on classical languages and literature.) Beyond mere social cohesion, some scholars have seen the classical curriculum as an important ingredient in the creation among the aristocracy of a ruling-class ideology. Within Britain, "many members of the upper classes drew from it [the classical curriculum] not only vast personal pleasure, but also a pervasive code of values. Chief of these was the duty of service and a conviction of the rightness of patrician rule."[56] The classics also fed into the code of values that underpinned Britain's imperial enterprise.[57]

The Royal Commission appointed in 1861 to investigate the educational program at the nine most elite public schools (the boarding schools Charterhouse, Eton, Harrow, Rugby, Shrewsbury, Westminster, and Winchester, and the day schools Merchant Taylors' and St. Paul's) described a pedagogy that was little changed from that of one hundred years before:

> The means by which classical scholarship is acquired are, as is well known, the study of Latin and Greek grammar, the daily construing and the occasional translation into English of Latin and Greek writers, the repetition of passages, chiefly of Latin and Greek poetry, which have been learnt by heart, the practice of composition in verse and prose. Construing, repetition and composition are the chief employment of the upper forms.[58]

In summing up his six years at Eton during the first decade of the nineteenth century, the Judge John Taylor Coleridge recalled:

> I was full five years in the fifth form, and, during the whole of that time, week after week, the main teaching of the school was Homer, Virgil, and Horace. We never ceased doing Homer, Virgil, and Horace. No doubt the result of that is visible in Etonians, they are very familiar with quotations from Homer, Virgil, and Horace, and Horace they have almost by heart.[59]

At Winchester in the 1820s, Roundell Palmer, one of the most well-regarded parliamentary speakers of the nineteenth century (see pp. 212–15), also went through Homer, Virgil, and Horace (as well as Cicero, Livy, and Juvenal) several times. Along with the required weekly original verse and prose Latin compositions and public declamations in Latin, there was also the practice of "standing up," or reciting as many lines of a Latin or Greek poet as one could memorize between the Easter and Summer holidays (as well as construing such parts as required to demonstrate comprehension). Although it was hardly the norm, Palmer recalled more than one occasion on which a boy recited the entire *Aeneid*.[60]

The classical curriculum had its critics by the beginning of the nineteenth century, but any impulses toward broadening education at the endowed schools were largely frustrated by court decisions in 1803 and 1826 ruling that the schools' endowments could only be used to support the teaching of the ancient, or "learned" languages. While some innovation did take place (Samuel Butler at Shrewbury introduced English a regular part of the curriculum, and Thomas Arnold at Rugby did the same with modern history and modern languages), such changes were offset by the far slower pace of change at the more important institutions. For example, the largest and most prestigious of the public schools, Eton, did not even include mathematics as a regular subject until 1851. By the middle of the nineteenth century, most other public schools had introduced additional subjects such as mathematics, modern languages, or natural science. Nevertheless, as the Clarendon Commission report makes clear, the introduction of these subjects in no way displaced the classics as the main focus of instruction. Indeed, the report argued for maintaining the centrality of classics in public school education, discoursing on the "special fitness" of classical languages and literature for school instruction for disciplining the minds, morals, and world-view of students. "Beside this," the report observes, "it is at least a reasonable opinion that this literature has had a powerful effect in moulding and animating the statesmanship of political life in England."[61]

At Oxford and Cambridge, students who had passed through the public schools (and other grammar schools that primarily stressed classical learning) generally continued to study classical literature. Although Cambridge degree examinations consisted only of mathematical subjects, students continued to be instructed in classical literature in the colleges. At Oxford, the classics were the major subject of undergraduate study and examination. The reading lists of Oxford's largest college, Christ Church, show how Latin works dominated the reading lists for most of the eighteenth-century, although Greek literature (particularly the orators and tragedians) gained in prominence.[62]

In one form or another, the classics dominated English university education until the closing years of the nineteenth century, when modern history and English studies (originally viewed as a "poor man's classics") rose to prominence.[63] Gladstone, who went up to Christ Church, Oxford from Eton and took first class honors in both classics and mathematics, was one who found his university education wanting. In 1830, he wrote to his father: "I am wretchedly deficient in the knowledge of modern languages, literature, and history; and the classical knowledge acquired here, accurate, and useful, yet is not such as to *complete* an education."[64] Of course, Gladstone, as an excellent classicist, had somewhat more leisure to complain than his peers who were still struggling through their Virgil.

The education that Gladstone received at Oxford was considerably more structured than that of his eighteenth-century predecessors. The introduction of *Literae Humaniores* as an honors school in 1807 (following the 1801 statue requiring degree examinations) formalized and codified the classical curriculum.[65] At Cambridge, the Classical Tripos was established in 1824 (but not a degree qualification until the 1850s).[66] Classical education at the Scottish universities (at one time very strong in this area) had languished in the eighteenth century, but efforts were made to improve upon this situation following the critical report of a Royal Commission in 1830.[67] The University of London, founded in 1826, pioneered a broad curriculum that included scientific subjects and modern languages. Nevertheless, Greek and Latin were required for matriculation until 1873, and Latin until 1902. The provincial universities founded in the second half of the century stressed modern and scientific subjects, but neither the "governing classes" nor the ambitious sons of new wealth attended them.

It would appear, therefore, that classical education, rather than declining in the nineteenth century, was in fact strengthened in a number of respects throughout the educational "system" of the elite. Indeed, classical education yielded only very slowly and very reluctantly to modernization, and its position and value continued to be vigorously upheld well into the twentieth century.[68] This, combined with the enduring dominance of the landed interest in politics, and the extent to which the upwardly mobile "bought in" to the social habits of the elite (particularly in the area of education), argues for a nineteenth-century parliamentary world in which the repetitious study of classical literature remained a formative influence on the membership.

The true educational level of the late-eighteenth-century membership cannot be accurately determined short of a detailed biographical investigation of each MP. University education is an inadequate proxy measure. Of the 40 percent of MPs sitting between 1754 and 1790 who had attended a university, not all can be assumed to have emerged as proficient classicists. Although some certainly excelled in their studies, others doubtless muddled through their lessons and gratefully forgot all upon leaving university. And this is to consider only those who studied at all. There were also the gentleman-commoners—rich aristocratic sons who "had gone to the university merely because it was the thing to do."[69] Charles James Fox's apparent ability to move in his university's fashionable society while also acquiring a good education was the exception rather than the rule. It is estimated that only half of those attending Oxford during the eighteenth century earned BA degrees four years later. This proportion began to increase during 1790s and by the 1830s surpassed 70 percent, a level sustained for the rest of the nineteenth century.[70]

The absence of honors examinations in classics at Oxford and Cambridge until after the start of the nineteenth century makes it impossible to gauge MPs' classical learning in the age of Pitt and Fox with any degree of refinement. When classical honors were introduced at the English universities, 32 students received first or second class honors in *Literae Humaniores* at Oxford in the Easter term 1808 (compared to matriculations in that year of around 240), and 27 students received first, second, or third class honors in the Classical Tripos at Cambridge in 1825 (compared to matriculations in that year of 450).[71] Clearly, only a small proportion of university students managed to distinguish themselves in their classical studies (although in the eighteenth century, smaller student bodies may have made this proportion somewhat higher).

In comparison to the eighteenth century then, the nineteenth century had a larger number and proportion of young men from the governing classes entering university, a greater proportion of university-educated MPs, and an increased emphasis on classical learning at both the school and university level. The level of classical learning in Parliament was therefore probably higher in the first half of the nineteenth century than in the last half of the eighteenth century. Thus, just as nineteenth-century beliefs regarding a sudden change in the social composition of the membership were not justified, so too were claims that the overall educational level of MPs declined.

In their preoccupation with the contribution of classical learning to parliamentary oratory, nineteenth-century commentators tended to ignore the new and more significant ways in which the cultivation of public speaking was directly promoted within the educational system—in particular, the debating societies formed at the public schools and universities (see chapter 1). By the end of the century, the training of the debating society was understood to be a considerable asset to the politically ambitious. Winston Churchill, for example, writing of the many obstacles to his development as a public speaker, believed one of the most significant to be that he "never had the practice which comes to young men at the university of speaking in small debating societies impromptu on all sorts of subjects."[72]

THE COMMONS CHAMBER

In addition to the social class and education of MPs, no survey of the structures underlying the production of parliamentary speech can be complete without at least brief mention of the House of Commons itself. St. Stephen's Chapel, where the Commons met until the great fire that consumed the Houses of Parliament in 1834, could not physically accommodate anything near the full membership of 558 (after the 1707 union with Scotland), much less the 658 MPs after the union with Ireland in 1800. Estimates of capacity fall between 300 and 500 (although the latter figure is believed to be very optimistic).[73] The extremely crowded debates over the Reform bill in 1830–32 prompted the creation of a select committee to examine how to make St. Stephen's more commodious.

After the Chapel was destroyed in the fire, the specifications for the new Houses of Parliament drawn up in 1835 included, for the Commons, seating for 420 to 460 Members in the body of the House and accommodation for all the rest in the galleries, not exceeding 1,200 feet of sitting room in all (or 1.8 feet per member).[74] As it turned out, however, the realized design of Charles Barry, into which the Commons moved beginning in 1850, provided seating for only around 300 on the floor and 120 in the galleries (and gallery seats were disliked).[75] The specifications also stipulated that Gothic style was to be used for the New Palace of Westminster, as the re-built Houses of Parliament were officially styled. Nevertheless, in architectural terms, the idea that the palatial new structure "was no longer the classical 'British Senate House' of the eighteenth century, but a sublimer concept," must be held alongside the famous comment of Barry's collaborator, Augustus Welby Pugin, that the design amounted to "Tudor details on a classic body."[76]

Along with the Gothic style (considered by some to be the "Saxon" idiom), the new Commons chamber retained the oblong shape and opposing benches. In the words of a guidebook from the late 1850s, the rebuilt Commons chamber was kept "as small as possible . . . for the purposes of speaking and hearing without effort during the average attendance of members, which amounts to about three hundred."[77] Nevertheless, from the first tests of the new chamber in 1850, backbenchers complained about not being able to hear properly. Accordingly, the ceiling was lowered, but audibility remained difficult. In 1858, William White, the Doorkeeper of the House of Commons, noted that "when the chamber is full it is not a good place to speak in. Very few of the prominent speakers are successful in the modulation of their voices."[78] The fullness of the chamber also became a problem, particularly as the parliamentary parties developed greater organization and discipline. During major political controversies, such as the disestablishment of the Irish Church and later Home Rule, the new space proved as cramped as the old had ever been.

Although Parliament's surroundings, amenities, and support services were all grandly improved in the New Palace of Westminster, the Commons chamber itself retained the same basic size, structure, and architectural sensibility of its eighteenth-century predecessor. In doing so, it preserved what Winston Churchill (discussing a later rebuilding) described as "that intimacy . . . of debate and discussion, that freedom and that sense of urgency and excitement to which our Parliamentary proceedings have owed a great deal in the past."[79] Thus, the essential characteristics of the space in which the oratory of the golden age took place were unchanged. It was, fundamentally, not a space for grand oratory.

Patterns of Parliamentary Speaking

If the social composition of the Commons remained predominantly aristocratic, the education of MPs improved, and the new Commons chamber preserved the characteristics of the old, what other developments might have had an adverse effect on the quality of parliamentary oratory? One significant change in the production of parliamentary speech from the late eighteenth to the late nineteenth century, is the extent to which MPs actually got "on their legs" and delivered a speech.

THE LATER EIGHTEENTH CENTURY

The greatest portion of parliamentary speech-making in the later eighteenth century was produced by only a handful of members. Of the 692 MPs who at some time sat in the parliament of 1768 to 1774, only 303 (44 percent) have been identified as having spoken at all on public business. Of these 303 speakers, 62 (21 percent of those who spoke) spoke only once during the six years of the Parliament, and not more than 132 (44 percent of those who spoke) averaged roughly two speeches per session. In comparison, 40 members (13 percent of those who spoke, 6 percent of all members) each spoke on more than 100 occasions during the six-year period.[80] This general pattern also holds for the session of 1790, in which only 307 (55 percent) of the total 558 members spoke at all. Of those who contributed to debate in 1790, 19 members (6 percent of those who spoke) each spoke more than100 times, producing nearly 57 percent of the total contributions to debate.[81]

That few eighteenth-century members spoke, and that most of those who did spoke only rarely, should come as no great surprise. Most of those who did speak, did so only on matters of local or personal interest. The kinds of electoral pressures and partisan politics that would later provide more regular stimuli to back-bench speech-making had not yet developed. Further, other than career politicians and practicing barrister-MPs (see pp. 207–19), few members had any training, experience, or confidence as public speakers. Speaking in the small, intimate Commons chamber, surrounded by a highly critical audience could be a terrifying experience, and one that many vowed never to repeat.[82] Another factor that could have inhibited a member from getting on his legs was the intellectual disparities between the leading speakers and the rest of the membership. "Lord John Russell used to say that there were a dozen men in the days of Fox and Pitt who could make a better speech than anyone living in his time, but that there was not another man in the House who could even understand what they were talking about."[83]

It is also important to note the number of members who were present to hear orations. Attendance of more than 400 was considered by contemporaries to be a very full House in the eighteenth century.[84] Even a leading speaker like Charles James Fox could assume that "one-third of his audience was always either absent, or at Dinner, or asleep."[85] Further, it would appear that even the members who were both present and awake often paid little attention to debates—many of them preferring to engage in private conversation.[86]

In light of all this, the claims by nineteenth-century observers of parliamentary oratory that the later eighteenth century was an oratorical golden age due to the aristocratic constitution of the time do not hold up. The membership may have been predominantly (if broadly) aristocratic, but this social homogeneity does not appear to have been a stimulus to the oratorical output of members. Indeed, it appears that the conditions of political life in the later eighteenth century may have *inhibited* the production of oratory among the membership. Those that did speak did not make finer speeches because they were blissfully free from the obligation of politicians in a more democratic era to win the approval of the uneducated "mob."

THE NINETEENTH CENTURY

The conditions of parliamentary life in the first half of the nineteenth century were in many ways consistent with those of the later eighteenth century. The addition of 100 Irish members increased the number of seats at Westminster from 558 to 658 (until 1885), but the number of MPs who regularly attended debates remained about the same as in the later eighteenth century. An accounting of routine parliamentary attendance habits at mid-century is provided by Edward Henry, Lord Stanley (later the Fifteenth Earl of Derby), who analyzed the voting behavior of MPs during the session of 1856:

Of 653 applicable M.P.'s	Of total 198 divisions
1 (Duncan of Dundee)	voted 198 times
1 (Hayter)	190
14	absent 10–50 times
79	absent 50–100 times
243	100–150 absences
226	150–180 absences
82	from 180 to 197 absences
7	absent from all 198 divisions!

We have thus 315 members, or nearly half the entire House, absent from at least 150 out of 198 divisions, i.e. from three-quarters of the whole number. We have 558, or more than five-sixths, absent from

> above 100 divisions, or from more than half of the entire number. It is however to be noted that the session of 1856 was absolutely devoid of important business.[87]

The beginnings of modern party discipline in the 1860s would better ensure the presence of MPs during divisions.

Through the first half of the nineteenth century, it also remained the case that only a handful of individuals produced most of the speeches. In the 1847–48 session, six members spoke over 100 times for a total of 1,025 contributions to debate. In the 1852–53 session, nine members spoke over 100 times for a total of 1,869 contributions. Writing in 1854, Lord Stanley observed that, "In the present parliament, out of 646 members, 342 are not reported as having spoken at all: i.e. more than one half [53 percent] of the House still consists of silent members."[88] It was claimed that the addition of Irish members increased the proportion of members who spoke, based on the perception that Irishmen were little inclined toward silence.[89] However, if Lord Stanley's figures constitute a valid sample of parliamentary activity in the first half of the nineteenth century, Irish members do not appear to have made a significant difference to the aggregate loquacity of members. The proportion of speaking members is comparable to estimates for the later eighteenth century.

In the second half of the nineteenth century, more MPs contributed to debates, and those who did contribute did so more often. Table 2.1 lists the number of MPs recorded as speaking in the *Parliamentary Debates* at five-year intervals between 1835 and 1895.

As table 2.1 shows, the total number of MPs reported as contributing to debates increased steadily over the period (it is doubtful that growth after 1885 was attributable to the addition of 12 seats by the third Reform Act). Since the number of MPs who made three or fewer contributions remained roughly constant, the proportion of MPs who contributed to debate more often increased.

In the era of Pitt and Fox, a smaller number MPs spoke more often. The eighteenth century was the great era of patronage in Parliament, and the large number of placemen and MPs sitting for rotten boroughs only had to vote—not speak—to thank their patrons. The general explanation for the increasing number of MPs contributing to debates in the nineteenth century was that, compared to the 1830s, the Commons of the 1880s included "a larger number of men who treat its business seriously, who have come there with fixed opinions and definite aims, and who insist

TABLE 2.1 Contributions to House of Commons Debates

Session	Total MPs Reported*	MPs with 3 or Fewer Reports Number	% of Total
1835	365	130	36%
1840	315	123	39%
1845	311	104	33%
1850	344	100	29%
1855	384	115	30%
1860	407	103	25%
1865	364	115	32%
1870	444	122	27%
1875	429	117	27%
1880	441	117	27%
1885	479	109	23%
1890	504	123	24%
1895	513	141	27%

* Excludes the Speaker.

Source: Parliamentary Debates. Calculations by author.

on their claim to be heard on subjects in which they are interested."[90] Around the same time, another observer provided a similar explanation, albeit in a somewhat more negative vein:

> Members seem now [after the 1867 Reform Act] to feel more than formerly that in order to retain their seats it is necessary to keep themselves as much as possible in the minds of their constituents by their continual activity in the House of Commons, even though that activity may retard instead of advancing [*sic*] the progress of business. This may explain why it is that so many questions, useless or worse than useless, or of the most petty local interest, are continually addressed to the members of the Government in the House of Commons, and why so many wearisome speeches are persistently forced upon it by men who have nothing worth hearing to say.[91]

The increased loquacity of backbenchers by the last quarter of the century might be attributed to the shifting social composition of MPs after 1867 already discussed—membership increasingly becoming a means to elite status, rather than a consequence of it. Interestingly, although the five-year sampling of table 2.1 makes no allowance for the vicissitudes of legislative programs, it does suggest that the higher level of oratorical contribution after the Second Reform Act followed a trend of increasing participation that began around 1850. Greater participation in debates also reflected changes in the nature of the business of the House. As Lord Curzon wrote in 1913, "the House of Commons is much more concerned with legislation and much less with administration than a century ago."[92]

In the middle third of the nineteenth century, the shift to the legislative mode became pronounced. (It should also be noted that the administrative sector outside Parliament also greatly expanded during this period.) In particular, the rapid growth of the national railway network accounted for a substantial portion of the legislative volume. Beginning with repeal of the Corn Laws in the mid-1840s, continuing with Gladstone's great domestic reforms of the 1870s and 1880s, and finally with Home Rule, legislative issues increasingly went to the core of members' political and constitutional beliefs and produced several massive political realignments. In the last third of the century, the great political controversies debated in the House—the Eastern Question, Reform, Ireland—were even more likely to elicit participation from a membership that was increasingly composed of professional party politicians.

Another development that had significant consequences for the character of parliamentary speaking was the increasing use of the extra-parliamentary platform by politicians in the last third of the century (see chapter 5). In introducing the Third Reform bill in 1884, Gladstone described how the purpose of debates in Parliament had shifted from articulating great principles to working out the legislative details of measures:

> It commonly happens with regard to these large and Constitutional questions—and it is well that is should so happen—that, before they are proposed upon the responsibility of the Queen's government, they have attained to an advanced stage of progress in the public mind through discussion out-of-doors; and, in consequence, it is not necessary very long to detain the House with general arguments which, if they were entirely new, would undoubtedly be requisite in order to make a case for the introduction of a Bill.[93]

PRESS REPORTING

A further significant change that affected patterns of parliamentary speaking was the increased public access to MPs' speeches through the newspaper press.[94] If few could actually hear the great speeches delivered in the House of Commons, far more people read more accurate reports of them than was the case during the era of Pitt and Fox. In the eighteenth century, reporting of speeches was greatly inhibited by a variety of laws and practices that forbade publicizing the business of the House and blocked the access of strangers to proceedings. Indeed, the insularity of the Commons that resulted from the formal exclusion of the press and the absence of regular reports of debates contributed greatly to the legendary mystique of the period. Later generations' understanding of the culture of Parliament in this period depended to a great extent on the often gossipy memoirs of contemporary observers. The records that exist of speeches by the Pitts, Fox, and their contemporaries are most often based upon memory, surreptitious note-taking, and other indirect means. Sometimes these illegal reports were aided and abetted by MPs. (Members also frequently issued "revised" versions of their speeches as pamphlets.) In 1803, the House of Commons passed a resolution permitting members of the press to sit in the gallery, and William Cobbett began to publish parliamentary debates in regular installments based upon journalists' reports. Over the course of the nineteenth century, newspaper reports (corrected by the speaker) continued to be the main source for the "official" record of debates.[95]

In 1828, Macaulay wrote: "The gallery in which the reporters sit has become a fourth estate of the realm."[96] When the New Palace of Westminster opened for business in 1852, the permanent status of newspaper reporters was symbolized by the special gallery (and writing out room) expressly designed, built, and reserved for them in the new Commons chamber. Thus, while the space provided for MPs' debates in the new chamber did not change in its essentials from old St. Stephen's, the provision of space for reporters was perhaps the most significant alteration in the physical arrangements of the Commons.

Since even the best reports were not verbatim transcripts, there were periodic complaints by the membership. Disraeli, for instance, is reported to have quipped "I don't so much object to what they leave out, I am deeply annoyed at what they put in."[97] Even so, records of debates based upon newspaper reports continued into the twentieth century. (The House of Commons only assumed control over the reporting and printing of debates in 1909.[98]) With the rise of the newspaper press—greatly facilitated by Gladstone's fiscal reforms of the late-1850s and early 1860s (see p. 268)—a greater number of newspapers carried significantly more pages and cost significantly less money. Although seats in the Reporters' Gallery were made available only to members of the London press until 1881 (when the Gallery was extended), the provincial press contrived to gain entrance through various means and, beginning in the late 1860s, was able to purchase telegraphed reports from the new national news agencies. Thus, as the century progressed, metropolitan and provincial papers were able to provide fuller coverage of Commons debates to a readership that was both increasingly literate and increasingly enfranchised.

This readership, unlike its eighteenth-century forebears, could take in remarkably extensive reports of the previous evening's parliamentary proceedings, including the speeches of the leading members printed verbatim, or nearly so. The amount of coverage could be truly phenomenal. At the height of the Crimean War, for example, *The Times* of January 25, 1855 printed 25 columns of "Parliamentary Intelligence," as well as four columns of parliamentary comment—an estimated 58,000 words.[99] The increasing demand for, and demands of, parliamentary reporting were reflected in the growing size of the corps of newsmen in the Reporters' Gallery. In 1834, it is reported, the number of reporters did not exceed 60. By 1871, that number had increased to 105.[100]

The mid- and late nineteenth century was something of a heroic era for parliamentary reporting—an era which seemed to pass after the death of Gladstone. As a former director of a press agency wrote in 1905: "For years the reporters did their best work under the greatest of physical difficulties, supplying columns upon columns of speeches for which the country waited with an eagerness never since equaled and now regarded almost as an old time fable."[101] Thus, compared to the nineteenth century, the exclusion of reporters from debates and the limited extent of the press in the eighteenth century made MPs public figures on virtually an *ex-officio* basis. The new relationship between press and Parliament in the nineteenth century, and the massive growth in the number and size of newspapers, made MPs public figures in fact.

Parliamentary Oratory in the Nineteenth Century

The ways in which the character of parliamentary speech changed, or did not change from the "golden age" of Pitt and Fox can be illustrated through an examination of the oratorical careers of four of the nineteenth-century Commons' most prominent speakers: Peel, Gladstone, Bright, and Disraeli. (Chapter 4 looks further at parliamentary speech by focusing on leading barrister-MPs.) Although the House boasted other notable speakers in this period, such as Lord Palmerston and Lord John Russell, the four speakers dealt with here represented, and even embodied new models of parliamentary speech.

PEEL

Although Sir Robert Peel was the son of a wealthy provincial businessman (later a baronet and MP), he was characteristically raised and educated in the aristocratic manner: Harrow, then Christ Church, Oxford. As a youth, Peel had visited the Commons and heard Pitt, Fox, and other prominent speakers of the time. Immediately after graduating from Oxford in 1808 (achieving the first "double first" in classics and mathematics), Peel entered Parliament, and shortly thereafter the government. In the four decades of his political life, Peel held office for about 25 years.

With his strong background in the classics, Peel was well able to adorn his speeches with Latin quotations according to the established forms of parliamentary eloquence, and did so throughout his political career. In particular, because he changed his position on a number of important issues, he invoked classical authorities in self-defense. For example, during the debate on the third reading of the Roman Catholic Relief bill, Peel responded to accusations of political inconsistency by stating that it is the duty of a statesman to pursue the policies which he believes to be in the interest of the nation, not to blindly adhere to the same position heedless of new conditions.

> My defence is the same with that of all others under similar circumstances, and I shall conclude by expressing it in words more beauti-

> ful than any which I myself could use—I mean the words of Cicero—*Hæc didici, hæc vidi, hæc scripta legi, hæc de sapientissimis et clarissimis viris, et in hac republicâ et in aliis civitatibus monumenta nobis litteræ prodiderunt, non semper easdem sententias ab iisdem sed quascunque reipublicæ status, temporum inclinatio, ratio concordiæ postularent, esse defendendas.**[102]

Yet, if Peel was as ready as any of his golden age predecessors to invoke Latin in support of his cause, he was also perhaps even fonder of English quotations than orators past. Peel used English quotations only somewhat less frequently than Latin in his parliamentary speeches.[103] There is no discernible difference in the functions of Peel's English quotations. Like his Latin quotations they serve to augment his attacks, bolster his self-defense, and elevate his rhetoric. Indeed, Peel had a reputation for being a heavy user of quotations, and was even charged by some with poverty of thought for using so many. (In this light, Disraeli's 1846 description of Peel as an appropriation clause and a burglar of other people's intellect had oratorical, as well as political resonance.) In more than one thousand parliamentary utterances published in his collected speeches, Peel uses full-length quotations in around 60, or only 6 percent of the total. Possibly, this relatively sparing use of literary adornments contributed to the views of some contemporaries that Peel's speeches were plain and businesslike—an assessment that was for the most part transmitted to posterity. Given the value placed upon the traditions of parliamentary eloquence, it seems strange that, in 1845, at the height of his political power, Peel's speeches could be described as

> deficient in true eloquence. There is none of that lofty thought which follows a reliance on high principle. On the contrary, they eschew principles, and fight the battle on details. There is a want of "heart" in them. There are none of those sudden touches which stir

* Cicero, *Pro Plancio* (xxxix, 94)–the orator's speech on behalf of Gnaeus Plancius, who was accused of electoral fraud: "All my knowledge, all my experience, all my reading, all the testimony that the records of literature give us concerning men of wisdom and eminence in this and other states, goes to prove, not that men have held the same unvarying convictions till their death, but rather that they have adapted them to political circumstances, to the tendency of the times, and to considerations of public tranquility."

> the soul. They appeal to the thinking faculty, not to the moral nature or the passions. The language is correct, nay, faultless, without being powerful. The illustrations are apt and serviceable, but dry.[104]

Peel's reputation (even among his admirers) for being a dry public speaker was connected to several aspects of his life and career. One is the way in which Peel's oratorical style was seen to reflect his middle-class origins rather than his elite upbringing. Indeed, in several speeches, Peel drew attention to his middle-classness when claiming that his policies were more in touch with the spirit of the times than those of the opposition. It should also be noted that Peel spoke with a strong regional accent—more common among leading politicians than a hundred years later, but nevertheless a cause for some snobbery against him (and later Gladstone).[105] Additionally, by seeking to address his speeches to practical measures rather than great principles, Peel departed from the more sensational style and general emotionalism of parliamentary oratory that had been conventional at the time he entered the Commons. In 1845, he observed with satisfaction the increasing popularity of "speaking in simple unaffected language."[106] Although it would be wrong to claim that late-eighteenth-century parliamentarians did not traffic in practical measures at all, the challenges facing Britain after 1815 were of a very different nature and in Parliament, Peel was the first great oratorical exponent of that change.

Viewing Peel as a dry and businesslike speaker was made far easier by the fact that he entered political life at a time when the parliamentary spirits of the deceased giants, Pitt and Fox, were still very much alive. In stylistic terms, it is convenient to contrast Peel with his early political rival, George Canning. For example, Guizot, in his appreciative biography of Peel, writes that the young Home Secretary "had neither that splendour and fascination as an orator, nor, as a man, that charm, that seductiveness of character and success, which had gained for his rival [Canning] public admiration and enthusiastic friends."[107] Canning's parliamentary style was very much of a piece with the high eloquence associated with the late eighteenth century, and he was viewed in his lifetime as the greatest orator in succession to the younger Pitt. On Canning's death, it was said: "There died George Canning, the last of the rhetoricians."[108] A century later, Lord Curzon asserted that the golden age of British political eloquence that began with Chatham and reached its zenith with Pitt and Fox, died with Canning.[109]

It may be that Peel's middle-class background, combined with his emphasis on fiscal management and domestic reform, disposed people to describe his speeches as "businesslike." More perceptive observers, however, saw that there was far more to Peel's oratorical style than the prosaic qualities regularly ascribed to it. In 1833, Edward Bulwer Lytton saw Peel as redefining the nature of political eloquence: "It is a current mistake in the provinces to suppose that he [Peel] is rather sensible than eloquent. If to persuade, to bias, to soothe, to command the feelings, the taste, the opinions of an audience often diametrically opposed to his views, if this be eloquence, which I, a plain man, take it to be, than Sir Robert Peel is among the most eloquent of men."[110]

Peel's modern biographer has written that Sir Robert was "Temperamentally unfitted for oratory in the grand manner, he had no gift for the sublime passage or polished phrase." Yet, the last part of this verdict is belied by an appendix containing 33 highly-polished "maxims and reflections" uttered by Peel in the House of Commons.[111] Beyond this Peel could produce great flights of impassioned rhetoric. On one occasion, after speaking during the 1847 debate on commercial distress, an adjournment was moved on the same basis as that on which the younger Pitt moved an adjournment after a speech by Sheridan during the Warren Hastings trail—the speech was judged so effective that it was doubted whether the House was in a state to vote dispassionately.

Even if Peel's speeches were not as dry and businesslike as many claimed, they were also a significant departure from the more ornate styles of the later eighteenth century. The introduction to Peel's collected speeches describes them as "the sermons of the political mind."[112] Certainly, there is something about Peel's public character—as expressed through his speeches—that accorded well with the values of the early-nineteenth-century religious revival (see chapter 3). His speeches were a crucial component of the posthumous legend of Peel the virtuous statesman.[113] As one of the first modern statesmen, Peel's Latin quotations, like the toga on his Westminster Abbey statue, seem merely rooted in convention while expressing nothing of what made him remarkable in his time.[114] Particularly appealing to the early Victorians was the image of a man who acted on his convictions, and a politician who sought to work for the best interests of the nation, regardless of popularity. What was during Peel's lifetime often seen as his great defect—reversing his earlier opinions and policies—was reinterpreted in terms of his strength and integrity. In this light, his great speeches continued to be seen as acts of great political risk, but also came to be viewed as acts of great moral courage.

GLADSTONE

Gladstone, Peel's protégé and political heir, was without question the dominant orator in the House of Commons for most of the second half of the nineteenth century. By virtue of his natural abilities as a public speaker and the political conditions of the times (which he had a great hand in shaping), he, like no other, was able to govern by speaking.[115] In part, this can be seen in several oratorically based innovations in parliamentary politics that continue to the present day, such as turning the budget speech into a national event, and creating what became Prime Minister's question time. He was also, as will be discussed at length elsewhere (chapter 5), a pioneer in the use of platform speaking.

Yet, among the many paradoxes of Gladstone's life and career is that, while he was one of the greatest innovators in the history of British political oratory, he was also held out as the one brilliant exception by those who lamented the decline of the classical tradition in Parliament. Gladstone excelled in classical studies at Eton and at Oxford, and throughout his life he maintained a serious and active and passionate involvement with classical literature.[116] In addition to his political career and other literary output, he produced a number of long articles on classical subjects, the three-volume *Studies on Homer and the Homeric Age* (1859), *Juventus Mundi* (1869; a popularized version of the *Studies*), and translations of Homer and Horace. (The younger Pitt had also turned his hand to translating Horace.)

Gladstone's absorption with classical literature was not merely an intellectual diversion. The classics were an integral part of his social and political world. Certainly, excellence in the classical languages at public school and university were among the very few available means for overcoming one's provincial, mercantile origins, however wealthy. It has been suggested that Gladstone was something of a classical snob—particularly in the way that classical erudition often played a decisive role in his choice of personal political associations. Throughout Gladstone's life, "all the men to whom he was close . . . could confidently and happily exchange Latin and Greek quotations with him. John Morley's facility with the classics appears to have outweighed even his agnosticism."[117] In like manner, the classical attainments of Herbert Asquith played a crucial part in his winning Gladstone's affections. In this view, Gladstone's classical snobbery came at a heavy price. Key Liberal leaders like Joseph Chamberlain and Lord Hartington did not have the classical credentials to be admitted into the Grand Old Man's inner circle—thereby contributing to the schism over Home Rule and the failure of the great political project of Gladstone's later years.[118] This may be overstating the case; nevertheless, it is clear that Gladstone's fondness for the classics was an important element of his public persona.

As a public speaker, Gladstone used literary adornments from his earliest efforts. The surviving notes of his Pop speeches contain a Latin passage.[119] In this respect, it is safe to assume that Gladstone was not alone among his Pop colleagues—all seeking to emulate the renowned style of Pitt (and, in Gladstone's case at least, Canning), and armed with a store of memorized Latin passages. However, just as Pitt did not rely only on Latin authors to provide literary adornment for his speeches, neither did the Etonians. Gladstone's notes also record his quoting Milton.[120] In the Oxford Union, Gladstone—like the other old Etonians, Wykehamists, Harrovians, Salopians, and the rest of the public school boys that made up the membership—had at least the same fund of quotations at his oratorical fingertips.

In Parliament, Gladstone used Latin quotations frequently and his speeches provide numerous examples of his "depending on another untranslated Latin gobbet to lift him to the culmination of his argument."[121] Ironically, while the decline of Latin quotations was discussed as lying at the heart of the general decline of parliamentary eloquence, and while Gladstone was viewed as one of the few exceptions to this decline, he was also seen as being too classical. In 1846, for example, Gladstone's parliamentary style was criticized for his "unnecessary recourse to Latinised forms of speech."[122] By the 1870s, in discussing the way in which classical quotation had become bad form in the Commons, an author could write that "Mr. Gladstone is almost the only member of Parliament with whom the old spirit is strong enough to violate this rule of latter-day Parliamentary etiquette."[123]

Complaints about Gladstone's classicism doubtless arose from his style of delivery. He was not an eighteenth-century speaker, and could be mercilessly pedantic in his use of Latin quotations. This pedantic tendency is well-illustrated by his speech on the second reading of the 1851 Ecclesiastical Titles bill, in which he criticized Lord John Russell by recalling the latter's 1845 speech on the Maynooth grant. Where Russell in 1845 had merely given an English paraphrase of a passage from Virgil, Gladstone in 1851 could not resist reciting the original lines.

> I never heard a more impressive passage delivered by any speaker than one passage in the speech of the noble Lord upon the second reading of the Bill enlarging the endowment of the College of Maynooth. The noble Lord referred to some lines of Virgil which the House will not regret to hear:—
>
> *Scilicet et tempus veniet, cum finibus illis*
> *Agricola, incuruo terram molitus aratro,*
> *Exesa inveniet scabrâ rubigne pila:*
> *Aut gravibus rastris galeas pulsabit inanes,*
> *Grandinque effosis mirabitur ossa sepulchris.*[*124]

In the time-honored parliamentary tradition, Gladstone resorted to Latin when defending his character from his opponents' accusations. During the debate over the second reading of the 1866 Reform bill, Disraeli taunted Gladstone by recalling his famous Oxford Union speech of 1831 against the first Reform bill (see pp. 27–28). Gladstone replied by soberly describing the evolution of his views since his undergraduate days. Speaking of the Liberals, he said:

> You received me, as Dido received the shipwrecked Aeneas—
>
> *Ejectum littore egentem*
> *Excepti—*
>
> And I only trust that you may not hereafter at any time have to complete the sentence in regard to me—
>
> *Et regni demens in parte locavi.*[† 125]

Later in his long parliamentary career, Gladstone began to provide, if not translations, at least English paraphrases of his quotations. In 1883, for instance, in his speech on the second reading of the Affirmation bill, Gladstone asserted that the parliamentary oath made no sense now that Parlia-

* Virgil, *Georgics* (Book I, 493–7): "Yea, and a time shall come when in those lands, as the farmer toils at the soil with crooked plough, he shall find javelins eaten up with rusty mould, or with his heavy hoes shall strike on empty helms, and marvel at the giant bones in the upturned graves."

† Virgil, *Aeneid* (Book IV, 373–4): "A castaway on the shore, a beggar, I welcomed him and madly gave him a share in my throne."

ment had shed most of its other religious safeguards. On this point, he quoted a six-line passage from Lucretius, but then assisted his audience—still in a very pedantic manner—to a better understanding of its meaning: "'Divinity exists'–as these, I must say, magnificent words set forth—'in remote, inaccessible recesses of which we know noting; but with us it has no dealing, with us it has no relation.'"[126] Whether Gladstone included this and similar paraphrases in his later speeches out of consideration for those who heard his speech in the Commons chamber, or for those who read it in the newspapers is uncertain.

Gladstone's career as a parliamentary orator provides ample evidence that, contrary to the assertions of various nineteenth-century analysts, the greatness of parliamentary speech did not derive from the facility with which the speaker adorned his speeches with classical quotations. That he was certainly the greatest classicist/politician of his age has little to do with his status as the greatest orator-statesman of the nineteenth century. Despite his excellent knowledge (and regular use) of the ancient languages, Gladstone was an oratorical modernist in politics. The most outstanding and commanding characteristic of his parliamentary speeches was his absolute mastery of legislative detail. Gladstone "was hardly ever caught out and, when he was caught, was at his most formidable."[127] This mastery of detail became clearly evident in the two long speeches that made his national reputation: his demolition of Disraeli's budget in 1852, and the introduction of his own first budget in 1853.

Gladstone was almost unique in his ability to discuss a budget with verve. (Lloyd George exhibited plenty of verve when discussing the "People's Budget" of 1909, but his enthusiasm was clearly for its political, rather than its fiscal substance.) It is instructive to compare Gladstone's 1853 budget speech with what was up to then considered to have been the greatest budget speech—that of the younger Pitt in 1798. On this occasion, Pitt described to the House his proposal to levy an income tax to support the extraordinary costs of the war on a current basis, as opposed to further reliance on debt. While it is a thorough and well-turned speech, it is essentially a methodical outline of the new taxation plan without, in Pitt's words, "that accuracy of detail which can only be derived from practice."[128]

Gladstone's speech, on the other hand, was a far more substantial and far more detailed disquisition on the nation's major revenue sources and expenditures—their past, present, and future.[129] At four and three-quarter hours in the delivery, the speech entered into the upper reaches of Parliament's oratorical endurance records. National finances were far more complex by 1853 than in Pitt's time, and Gladstone embraced the complexity—particularly in the considerable attention he paid to explaining the bases on which various revenue and expense items were projected. Yet, if the matter was inherently dry, Gladstone's almost lyrical exposition was far from it. In his diary, Lord Stanley wrote that Gladstone's budget speech was "an extra-ordinary effort of rhetorical skill: no fault could be found except too great length and a hackneyed quotation from Virgil spoiling a fine peroration."[130]

As recalled by his long-serving Parliamentary Private Secretary, Arthur Godley, Gladstone's recipe for financial speeches was to get up the figures "'thoroughly and exhaustively, so as to have them absolutely at your fingers' ends, and then give them out as if the *whole* WORLD was interested in them'–with tremendous emphasis upon 'the *whole* WORLD'."[131] Through his ability to effectively convey his own enthusiasm for, and command of the budget as a dynamic fiscal and political instrument, Gladstone not only established himself as a national figure, but also placed Lord Aberdeen's Whig-Peelite coalition government on a secure footing which it had not before enjoyed.[132] In a longer perspective, given the realities of political management and parliamentary insularity in the eighteenth century, Pitt had no need to generate any kind of demagogic enthusiasm for his financial measures—nor does it seem likely that he could have even thought of delivering financial speeches as if to the "*whole* WORLD."

Comparisons between the speeches of Gladstone and Pitt are also useful in showing how parliamentary oratory reflected the change in the work of the Commons from (in Curzon's formulation) an administrative to a legislative mode. Pitt was known as a great administrator who guided his nation through the most serious threat to its existence that had yet been experienced. Gladstone was known as a great legislator—albeit, ultimately, a quixotic one—who significantly reformed and modernized the British state. In addition to their budget speeches, the contrast between Pitt and Gladstone stands out in their speeches on Ireland. On January 31, 1799, Pitt addressed the House on incorporating Ireland into the union of Great Britain.[133] As Pitt himself said, his purpose was to explain the intentions of the government, the principles of the measure, and the advantages of union for both the Empire and for Ireland. His lengthy speech describing these points concluded with eight brief resolutions that outline, in general terms, the general plan of the government. Specifics are few and far between.

Eighty-seven years later, on April 8, 1886, Gladstone sought to undo the consequences of Pitt's success.[134] After describing the inadequacy, and indeed the immorality, of the current system of governing a restive Ireland through an endless succession of coercion acts, Gladstone laid out specific legislative proposals in considerable detail. He described the functions, composition, and competence of the new Irish legislature, as well as the powers reserved to Westminster. Then, he turned to provisions for the executive, the courts, the constabulary, the civil service, and the Post Office. Finally, he addressed (in even more detail) questions of taxation and finance. On most points, he not only gave full explanations for the necessity of his proposal, but also discussed why his recommendations were better than alternative formulations. Thus, where Pitt had offered arguments and rationales to support general resolutions, Gladstone described a substantive and detailed program.

Gladstone was a great creative legislator, and his greatest speeches in the Commons tend to be those introducing complex bills: in addition to his budgets, the 1866 Reform bill, the 1869 Irish Church disestablishment bill, the 1870 Irish land bill, and the 1886 and 1893 Home Rule bills. Yet, command of details alone does not explain Gladstone's ability to hold oratorical sway over the Commons. His best parliamentary speeches were animated by his powerful sense of the moral correctness of his position and, usually, the immorality of the position he opposed. Thus, a more equitable scheme of taxation was described as "a sacred aim."[135] The Treaty of Berlin was criticized because "I am not quite sure, however, that the world has the same clear and strong conviction with respect to the standard of our moral action as it has with respect to the standard of our material strength."[136] Home Rule must be taken up because attempting to govern Ireland through "ineffectual and spurious" measures of coercion "is morally worn out."[137]

It is probably true that Gladstone's greatest oratorical legacy was outside the House of Commons. Nevertheless, he was also the dominant force in parliamentary debate during the last third of the century. In an era of increasingly complex legislation—amplified by his own penchant for "big bills"—Gladstone's greatest strength as a parliamentary speaker was to argue his case as effectively on arcane details as on great moral principles. He did this at great length, and kept people listening. As in so many other aspects of his life, Gladstone's style of parliamentary speech not only suited, but also helped to shape the age through which he passed.

BRIGHT

John Bright is somewhat anomalous in the present examination, as he was in Parliament itself. Unlike Pitt, Peel, Gladstone, and Disraeli, Bright was never Prime Minister or even, like Fox, the head of his party. Even in his pre-parliamentary career opposing the Corn Laws, Bright was always subordinate to Richard Cobden. In Parliament, Bright was self-consciously an outsider. Nevertheless, no discussion of nineteenth-century parliamentary oratory can exclude him. Perhaps this fact alone is sufficient evidence of the changes in parliamentary life from the late eighteenth century to the mid-nineteenth. In the eighteenth century, an outsider like Sheridan could win renown as among the first rank of parliamentary speakers, but his theatrical background occasioned much disrespect throughout his parliamentary career. Bright, on the other hand, became one of the most well-respected figures in Parliament—even for those who were diametrically opposed to his views. As discussed earlier, it took almost the whole of the nineteenth century before the social composition of the Commons began to reflect the broadening franchise in both membership and spirit. It is also true that new men from more humble backgrounds were entering Parliament all along. In the case of Bright, these new influences had a disproportionate effect on the history of parliamentary oratory.

As a Quaker, Bright did not attend public school or university. In fact, his formal schooling was relatively meager. After attending a succession of Friends' schools to age fifteen, he records that he "had learned some Latin and a little French, with the common branches then taught in such schools as I had been placed in. Reading, writing, arithmetic, grammar and geography—no mathematics and no science."[138] While working for his father, he also worked to improve himself through extensive reading. At this time Bright also began to develop as a public speaker in the local debating society (which he helped to found), in lectures on temperance, and in speeches for repeal of the Corn Laws. By the time he entered Parliament in 1843, Bright was already a noted platform orator (see chapter 5). Thus, like his ally Cobden, Bright entered Parliament with an educational background and an oratorical training that was fundamentally different from most of the membership. A quarter of a century later, this was still remarked upon. As the future Lord Chief Justice, John Duke Coleridge wrote of Parliament in 1866: "Dear old Latin and Greek still lead us, you see, and I cannot think of any very eminent men, except Bright and Cobden, who are not men of some education."[139]

As Coleridge's comment makes clear, however, despite both his lack of classical education, and his oratorical apprenticeship on the popular platform, Bright came to be regarded as one of the great parliamentary speakers of his time—consistently placed alongside, and sometimes even above Gladstone. It had not always been that way. The prejudice against people of his background (particularly so unassimilated a character as Bright) holding a seat in Parliament was strong. In the 1840s, a few years after Bright had first entered Parliament, it was snobbishly observed that

> there is a rough, coarse vigour in his style of speaking, which is attractive at a public meeting, while it rather puzzles the House of Commons. It does not exactly square with their idea of what a member of parliament ought to be, and yet they cannot quarrel with the bold and uncompromising expression of opinion, restrained and regulated by that respect which even *parvenues* have for custom, from one who, by the suffrage of a legally constituted body of his fellow-countrymen, has acquired the right to speak.[140]

It was, however, Bright's qualities as a speaker that eventually won him the highest respect. By the 1870s, the parliamentary observer Henry Lucy did not hesitate to describe Bright as "the orator *par excellence* of the House of Commons."[141]

As a public figure, Bright's appeal was rooted in his perceived honesty and simplicity.[142] In particular, Bright's style of parliamentary speech came to win praise for its "Saxon" plain-spokenness. Even in some of his more overwrought passages, like "The angel of death has been abroad throughout the land; you may almost hear the beating of his wings,"[143] are simple in their meaning, direct in their imagery, and vigorous in their cadence. Bright's gestures were modest, and his manner of speaking subdued (although it is recorded that his voice carried extremely well in the Commons chamber). Despite his elaborate preparation of certain passages and his perorations, those who heard Bright never accused his speeches of artifice.

To a far greater degree than those contemporaries in his oratorical class, Bright's parliamentary speeches were filled with quotations from a host of sources: newspapers, letters, dispatches, old parliamentary debates, and poetry. Not surprisingly, he hardly ever used Latin. One of the few examples occurred in 1851 during the debate on the Ecclesiastical Titles bill. Bright drew attention to the fact that none of the "holy men" of the House—by which he meant pious Anglicans like Gladstone—were exerting themselves in favor of the bill. "It has been said '*Multæ terricolis linguæ, cœlestibus una*' [Mortals have many languages, divinities one]. But it does not appear that the celestials in this House are more agreed about the matter than any of those who feel little regard for Protestantism or Catholicism."[144] This was hardly an attempt to conform to traditions of parliamentary eloquence. Rather, Bright used the Latin to mock the Anglicans in the language of their own class and education.

On another notable occasion, however, Bright's attempt to use Latin ended badly. On July 16, 1869, during a debate on the Irish Church bill, Bright replied to Disraeli's warnings against the bill: "I have seen the right hon. Gentleman just as angry about many other great questions. I have seen him come down—as I might say if I were not afraid of being thought classical—*crinis disjectis*, with disheveled hair." To Gladstone's horror, Bright had used the wrong declension. While some of the more classically erudite members chuckled, the Prime Minister was observed hastily writing a note to inform his colleague of the error.[145]

If Bright was unable to produce long quotations from Latin authors, his parliamentary speeches were studded with English quotations, which he used to either solemn or wryly humorous effect. "His style had no specific model," according to one biographer, "but his command of language grew out of his sustained reading in Milton and Byron, Shakespeare and Spenser."[146] Naturally, Bright's Quaker upbringing left the Bible as the strongest of his literary influences. His speeches regularly contained Biblical references—from the Old Testament in particular—such as the "Angel of Death" and, most enduringly, chiding Robert Lowe and his followers for retiring into "what may be called [their] political cave of Adullam" over the 1866 Reform bill.[147] In addition to the Bible, Bright's quotations covered a broad literary range, from children's verse ("Satan still some mischief finds / For idle hands to do"[148]), to popular poets like Thomas Chatterton, to Ben Jonson. Many of the quotations serve to emphasize his position as an outsider and his parliamentary independence. In one particularly amusing aside, Bright takes time away from criticizing Lowe for backing off his party's Reform bill (the cave of Adullam speech), and pokes fun at Gladstone and government men for their love of office.

I do not object for a moment to a Member of this House for being fond of office. The Chancellor of the Exchequer probably lives much more happily in office than he would live if he were out of it, though I do not think he will live quite so long. I do not complain of men who are fond of office, though I could never comprehend the reason they like it so much. If I may parody, or if I may make an alteration in a line or two of one of the most beautiful poems in our language, I might ask—

For who, to dumb forgetfulness a prey,
That pleasing, anxious office e'er resigned,
Left the warm precincts of the Treasury,
Nor cast one last, long, lingering look behind.[149]

Bright's oratory was distinctly outside the golden age tradition of parliamentary eloquence. In particular, in his *crinis disjectis* speech, Bright indicates his rejection of classical oratory in his desire not to be "thought classical." The plain-spoken honesty of Bright's oratorical style, and his perceived determination (to borrow a later phrase) to speak truth to power, were integral parts of his popular appeal and enduring legend: "A Foxite adduced Pitt's preference of Latin Compounds as an all-sufficient proof of habitual ambiguity. Apply a similar test to Mr. Bright and no further proof will be needed of his straightforwardness."[150] Since Bright's fellow MPs did not think him "classical" as a parliamentary orator, it is especially ironic that Bright was popularly presented and appreciated in explicitly classical terms. In one of many examples, his careful preparation of speeches was likened to "the great orators of Greece and Rome."[151] Even more significant, he was hailed in classical terms as the "Tribune of the English People."[152]

DISRAELI

Like Bright, Benjamin Disraeli was a natural parliamentary outsider who achieved a commanding position in the Commons. The oratorical styles of both men were original contributions to parliamentary speech. Unlike Bright, however, Disraeli played with the surface, if not the substance of the classical tradition. Disraeli was substantially less adept at the classics than he affected to be. His schooling was respectable, but certainly not comparable to those forcing-houses of classical learning, the public schools. Nor did he attend university. Yet, it is certainly one indication of the enduring importance of classical education for a gentleman's status and respectability in the nineteenth century that Disraeli apparently felt his deficit in this area so keenly. Both in life, and through some of his fictional alter egos, he constructed a myth of overcoming the defects of his education through heroic self-study of the classics. "The truth would seem to be that he contrived . . . to make himself a fair Latin scholar and retained in after life a moderate familiarity with the great Roman authors; but that his Greek was scanty in the beginning, and, in spite of his efforts after leaving school, remained scanty to the end."[153] In another account: "Disraeli probably was quite genuine in his love of the classics, but, like Stanley Baldwin, he rested that love upon somewhat shaky foundations. However, he knew enough to bandy Latin quotations in the House of Commons, and, luckily, it was not the form to do so in Greek."[154] As part of his personal myth-making, Disraeli made far greater claims for his use of Latin quotations.

> When I took the lead of the Opposition, I, temperately & discreetly, somewhat revived the habit of classic quotation. (I had done it before to some degree, when I had got the ear of the House.) Applied with discretion, it was not unsuccessful; & I was rather amused in the course of time to find Lord John Russell, who was then Prime Minister & Leader of the House, brushing up his classical reminiscences & coming down frequently with Virgilian passages, so that he might keep up the credit of his party.[155]

Although it is certainly not the case that Disraeli single-handedly breathed new life into the traditions of oratorical classicism (far abler classicists such as Gladstone did not have this effect), he did far more than merely "bandy" Latin quotations. In fact, to look at Disraeli's use of Latin quotations is to gain insight into the qualities—rhetorical, oratorical, and personal—that set him apart from what were understood as the traditions of parliamentary oratory. Take, for instance, Disraeli's use of a quotation from Horace in his attack on Peel during the debate on the third reading of the Corn Importation bill on May 15, 1846:

> But was it not strange that, after so much agitation, after all these Machiavellian manœuvres, when the minister at last met the House and his party, he acted as if we had deserted him instead of his having left us? Who can forget those tones? Who can forget that indignant glance?

> *Vectabor humeris tunc ego inimicus eques:*
> *Meæque terra cedet insolentiæ*:*
>
> which means to say, "I, a protectionist minister, mean to govern England by the aid of the Anti-Corn-Law League; and as for the country gentlemen, why, I snap my fingers in their faces."[156]

On one level, the Horatian lines cleverly cloak Disraeli's attack in the "time-honored" traditions of parliamentary debate. Horace lent an institutional legitimacy to the condemnation of a figure so established as Peel by one so marginal as Disraeli. The passage and its Latin quotation evoke the heightened emotional pitch associated with some eighteenth-century speeches. Disraeli did not lead up to the quotation, but rather seemed as if he would use it, in the eighteenth-century manner, for a dramatic, rhetorical flourish. However, instead of finishing with the quotation, Disraeli continued with his pointed, sarcastic paraphrase. The sheer insolence of his paraphrase (his real purpose) gained additional shock value from its contrast with the stately Latin lines that preceded it.

Another significant example occurs in a speech from 1849 on the motion for a select committee to inquire into the state of the nation. On this occasion, Disraeli brought in a classical quotation with a far more showy effect.

> I was reminded the other day when reading a passage in the works of the greatest Roman statesman, of the truth that the present is only a reproduction of the past. It would, perhaps, be pedantic in me to quote the passage to the House, who are well acquainted with it; but it is where Cicero tells Atticus, in the last years of the great epoch when he flourished, that a new disease had fallen upon the State; that the State is dying of a new disease; that men in all conditions joined in denouncing everything that was done; that they complained, grieved, openly lamented; that complaint was universal, but that no remedy was proposed by anyone; and he says that there is a general idea that resistance without some fatal struggle was impossible, although it were resistance against that which all disapproved; and that the only limit of concession appeared to be the death of the

* Horace, *Epodes* (XVIII, 74–75): "Then as a horseman I'll ride upon thy hated shoulders and the earth shall give way before my unexampled might."

republic. I think the passage runs somewhat thus:– *"Nunc quidem novo quodam morbo civitas moritur, et cum omnes ea quæ sunt acta improbent, querantur, doleant, aperteque loquantur et tam clare gemant, tamen medicina nulla affertur, neque resisti sine internecione posse arbitramur, nec finem cedendi videmus, præter exitium."* * [157]

Unlike the impromptu nature ascribed to some of Pitt's quotations, this one was clearly well-prepared in advance (as, doubtless, was the quotation used against Peel). Indeed, in his extended introduction, Disraeli was deliberately drawing attention to the fact that he was about to deliver a Latin quotation. His claim to have been casually reading Cicero "the other day" rings false. The quotation was not a display of classical erudition, but rather a deliberate affectation—including Disraeli's coy admission that it would be pedantic to recite the passage, and his facetious statement that the House would be well acquainted with it.

Disraeli also drew on English literature in his speeches—quotations and allusions that (as an English literary man himself) probably came to him with much greater facility than the Latin ones. In an 1843 speech against a motion for remission of import duties, he quoted Milton when discussing Whig views linking civil and commercial freedom: "License they mean, when they cry liberty!"[158] In his 1846 speech on the Address, attacking the Peel ministry for choosing posterity over party, Disraeli called upon the House to look at the government: "Throw your eyes over the Treasury Bench. See stamped on each ingenuous front, 'The last infirmity of noble minds.' They are all of them, as Spenser says, 'Imps of Fame!'"[159] Significantly, as Disraeli grew into a party leader and national statesman, quotations from or allusion to English literature in his parliamentary speeches became less frequent.

What sets Disraeli apart from some of the other orators discussed here is the way that his "classicism," ironically, was an outgrowth of his Romanticism. His cultivation of respectability through a Parliamentary career and the veneer of classical banter co-existed with his cultivation of difference in his youthful dandyism (velvet and chains) and in his early politics

* Cicero, *Letters to Atticus* (Book II, 20): "Now the state is dying of a new disease. The measures that have been passed cause universal discontent and grumbling and indignation . . . and people are now venting their disapproval openly and loudly, yet no remedy is applied. Resistance seems impossible without bloodshed: nor can we see any other end to concession except destruction."

(Radicalism, followed by Radical Toryism). These striking stylistic contrasts of Disraeli's early career expresses his desire for a kind of acceptance that he knew would never be given by an aristocratic and fundamentally anti-Semitic establishment. In the words of Lord Blake, Disraeli "was determined to conquer the great world partly because he knew that he could never belong to it."[160]

The working of Disraeli's contradictory impulses is revealed in the famous near-disaster of his maiden speech, in which he attempted to gain respectability through the accepted channel of parliamentary speaking, while at the same time asserting his difference (and superiority) by delivering a speech which defied the conventions of the House. According to the accepted forms, a new member should spend some time observing practiced parliamentary speakers. When he is ready to make a speech of his own, he should be modest in his aims, and not try the patience of the House with grand language or high-flown rhetoric. By tradition, a maiden speech respecting these conventions will be listened to with respect, and applauded by both sides of the House when it is done. As that keen observer of parliamentary manners Anthony Trollope wrote: "There are many rocks which a young speaker in Parliament should avoid, but no rock requires such careful avoiding as the rock of eloquence."[161] The great exception in parliamentary lore—as one might expect—is the younger Pitt's maiden speech which, according to the legend, was entirely spontaneous and moved him instantly into the oratorical front rank of Parliament.

Disraeli, in his maiden speech, sought to deliver an oratorical knockout blow. He began the speech sensibly enough, but then launched into a peroration heavy-laden with rhetorical embellishments, including a pastiche of classical allusions and Latin tags.

> He wished, before he sat down, to show the House clearly their position. When they remembered, that in spite of the support of the honourable and learned member for Dublin [Daniel O'Connell] and his well-disciplined band of patriots, there was a little shyness exhibited by former supporters of Her Majesty's Government; when they recollected the "new loves" and the "old loves," in which so much of the passion and recrimination was mixed up between the noble Tityrus of the Treasury bench [Russell] and the learned Daphne of Liskeard [Charles Buller]–notwithstanding the *amantium ira* [lovers' quarrels] had resulted, as he had always expected, in the *amoris integratio* [renewal of love]. . . .[162]

After a few more impossibly convoluted clauses, Disraeli gave up amid the shouts and laughter, uttering the famous vow with which he sat down: "the time would come when they would hear him."

There is a consensus among Disraeli's biographers that his being prevented from finishing his speech was a blessing in disguise. Had he been allowed to conclude his baroque oration, Disraeli's maiden speech would have turned from a fiasco into a failure. "If Disraeli's peroration had been listened to in silence it might have blasted his Parliamentary reputation for ever."[163] Instead, Disraeli was granted a reprieve—a chance to gain "the ear of the House," as Richard Lalor Sheil advised him after his debut, by getting rid of his genius for a session and making the House long for his wit and eloquence.[164]

When discussing Disraeli, it is important always to have the question of style in mind, for in many ways, Disraeli is all about style. Few other politicians have used personal style so effectively. Therefore, like much in his political career, Disraeli's pretensions to keep oratorical classicism alive can be seen as striving for an aesthetic statement in politics. In this aesthetic, Latin quotations were a symbol, a stylistic evocation of parliamentary greatness based on aristocratic preeminence. For Disraeli, Latin quotations symbolized the political order before 1832, and more especially before the constitutional betrayals of Peel.

Yet, by far the most important aspect of Disraeli's parliamentary oratory had nothing to do with his attempts to uphold the classical tradition of parliamentary debate. Rather, what distinguished his speeches then, and has given them lasting renown, was Disraeli's mastery of and expansion upon another tradition. Like Fox, Disraeli's political identity was formed in opposition, and he excelled in the opposition MP's role as a mocker and a scorner of the government. Curzon records the opinion of those who remembered Disraeli that, even in his prime, "he was not an orator by nature or art." He was, however, a master of "the jeweled phrase, the exquisite epigram, the stinging sneer. He was like a conjuror on a platform, whose audience with open mouths awaited the next trick." Moving from simile to metaphor: "He was an actor in the guise of a politician."[165] In rather more prosaic terms, Lucy wrote: "Just as the merits of the pudding at a school dinner are gauged by the frequency of the plums which occur in a slice, so is the success of Mr. Disraeli's speeches measured by the number of sparkling sentences distributed throughout an oration."[166] There is, as Lord Blake has shown, a clear affinity between Disraeli's ironic and epigrammatic humor, and that of the great wit of the late nineteenth century, Oscar Wilde.[167]

As a phrase-maker, Disraeli was prolific. Monypenny and Buckle—who claim that the pre-eminent quality in Disraeli's speeches "was the power of phrase-making and phrase-adapting"[168]–list 148 individual "phrases and catchwords" in their index. Most of these phrases occurred in the course of parliamentary speeches. Without entering into an extended discussion of Disraeli's phrase-making, the enduring quality of many of his phrases is evident in the recitation of a few: "that fatal drollery called a representative government"; "the Prayer Book may be divine, but it is also human"; "we have legalised confiscation, consecrated sacrilege, condoned high treason"; "plundering and blundering"; "the mass in masquerade"; "the palace is not safe when the cottage is not happy"; "an armistice is certainly not a peace any more than a courtship is wedlock." A few of Disraeli's most famous coinages were Latin—for example, *Imperium et Libertas*—but they have far more to do with phrase-making than with any classical tradition of Parliament.[169]

The Disraelian style of parliamentary speaking came to be viewed as enormously appealing. It was also highly influential, and its influence was hardly confined to members of Disraeli's own party. One great student of the Disraelian style was the Liberal William Vernon Harcourt, who emulated the Conservative leader by using atypical word-choices in alliterative combinations, for example (where Harcourt perhaps overdid it) "the ill advised railing of a rash and rancorous tongue."[170] The advanced Liberal Edward Jenkins, in his maiden speech actually employed a phrase of Disraeli's when he attacked "political somnambulism," and attempted to achieve a similar effect by discussing "hysteric statesmanship." The Radical Charles Dilke, it was observed, "contents himself with copying the most bizarre of Mr. Disraeli's alliterations, as when he told the House . . . that publicans were perplexed, the parsons persecuted, and the Dissenters disgusted."[171] Ultimately, it was as an epigrammatic, sarcastic phrase-maker that Disraeli bequeathed his greatest legacy to parliamentary speech.

The Decline of Oratorical Classicism?

As the great-nephew of Macaulay, biographer of Bright, and son of the Liberal MP and statesman (and biographer of Fox) Sir George Otto Trevelyan, the historian G. M. Trevelyan had vast personal and professional knowledge of Parliament. With respect to parliamentary speeches, he observed that, "In the seventeenth century, Members of Parliament quoted from the Bible; in the eighteenth and nineteenth centuries from the classics; in the twentieth century from nothing at all."[172] We have already seen that the great speakers of the golden age of parliamentary eloquence appear to have used Latin quotations considerably less than later claimed for them. In this light, can oratorical classicism in Parliament still be said to have declined, and even fallen in the nineteenth century?

THE NINETEENTH CENTURY

How did the oratory of the four great figures of the Victorian Commons discussed here—Peel, Gladstone, Bright, and Disraeli—measure up to contemporary views of the traditions of parliamentary eloquence? With respect to their knowledge of the classics and their use of Latin quotations in Parliament, the four represent a spectrum of ability and application. At one extreme is Gladstone, who was supremely well-versed in the classics and who used Latin quotations with relative frequency. Gladstone's oratorical classicism highlights some of the contradictions that defined him: his classical stylings looked back to earlier traditions of parliamentary discourse, while productions such as his great budget speeches set an entirely new tone. Gladstone's new tone derived in large measure from Peel. Peel had received essentially the same classical education as Gladstone and had derived nearly equal benefit. Although he used Latin quotations, the emphasis Peel gave to English quotations can be seen as representative of the new, more practical parliamentary style he embodied.

Even though Gladstone and Peel had both come from non-landed wealth, their fathers had provided them with all the opportunities necessary to enter into a political world still dominated by the classically educated aristocracy. Disraeli and Bright entered political life as true outsiders. Disraeli had an incomplete education, but as a stylist in politics recognized the importance—both practical and symbolic—of Latin quotations. Disraeli was very much a new-style politician, but draped himself to the extent possible in traditionalism. Finally, at the opposite end of the spectrum from Gladstone was Bright, who had almost no classical education. Among the many ways that Bright represented a new spirit in parliamentary politics was the way he made a virtue of being unclassical. Thus, reflected in their oratorical classicism (or lack thereof), we see the way in which Disraeli more or less "faked it" as part of his efforts to gain a degree of acceptance from the political establishment, and Bright rejected it as part of standing virtuously outside that establishment.

Given nineteenth-century views on the decline of oratorical classicism in Parliament, it is both ironic and revealing that what is arguably the greatest single instance of dueling with Latin quotations in the House of Commons occurred in 1866 during the debates over the Liberal Reform bill of that year. In this protracted contest, Gladstone and Robert Lowe sought to out-do each other over the lesson to be drawn from the second book of the *Aeneid* and its account of the Trojan horse. On the first night of debate, Gladstone said that no one should view the bill as Trojan horse filled with armed men ready to burn and plunder the sacred city.

> We cannot join in comparing it to that *monstrum infelix* [ill-omened monster]—we cannot say —
>
> "— *Scandit fatalis machina muros,*
> *Fœta armis: mediæque minans illabitur urbi.*"*[173]

Lowe, who opposed the bill even though he sat in the Liberal interest, responded the following night. Like Gladstone, Lowe had an excellent knowledge of classical literature, having been a prefect in the top form at Winchester and gained first class honors in classics at Oxford. He also followed in Gladstone's footsteps as a leading speaker in, and then President of, the Oxford Union. At the end of his speech against the bill, Lowe disputed the validity of Gladstone's use of Virgil. He said that, since Gladstone could not find in his large classical repertoire a quotation to describe "the state of perfect bliss to which this Bill would introduce us," he used a quotation to describe what the bill was not. Referring to the many previous attempts to bring in a second Reform bill, Lowe then asked the House to "attend to the sequel" of Gladstone's passage:

> I am no believer in *sortes Virgilianæ* [Virgilian lots] and the House will see why in a moment—
>
> "*O Divum domis Ilium, et inclyta bello*
> *Mœnia Dardanidûm! Quater ipso in limina portæ*
> *Substitit, atque utero sonitum quater arma dedêre.*"

* Virgil, *Aeneid* (Book II, 237–40): "The fateful engine climbs our walls big with arms . . . and glides threateningly into the city's midst." Gladstone elided the first half of the second sentence.

But that is not all—

> "*Instamus tamen immemores, cæcique furore,*
> *Et monstrum infelix sacratâ sistimus arce.*"*

Well, I abominate the presage contained in the last two lines; but I mix my confidence with fear.[174]

A month later, on the first night of debate on the second reading of the bill, Gladstone returned to the Trojan horse. By describing the measure as no *monstrum infelix,* Gladstone had, he said, endeavored to warn critics away from this line of attack. In his impatience, however, Lowe, "as though this instead of being a warning had been a hook that had been baited to allure him, rushed straight at his mark, and with portentous emphasis delivered the two lines from which my words were taken—." After quoting the two lines again, Gladstone asked the House: "What is the 'monstrum infelix?' Who are the persons contained within its hollow side? They are the voters at £7."[175]

The final volley in this tournament occurred towards the end of the month, on the seventh night of debate on the second reading. At the end of a long speech, Lowe stated that he and the Chancellor of the Exchequer had but one area of common ground left to them: the second book of the *Aeneid.* He compared Gladstone's returning to the "poor old Trojan horse" to a moth returning to the flame that singed its wings. He then asked the House's permission to give "one more excerpt from the history of that noble beast," promising thereafter to "turn him out to grass."

> The passage which I am about to quote is one which is, I think worthy of the attention of the House because it contains a description not only of the invading army of which we have heard so much, but also a slight sketch of its general —
>
> "*Ardus armatos mediis in mœnibus adstans*
> *Fundit equus, victorque Sinon incendia miscet*
> *Insultans: portis alii bipatentibus adsunt,*

* Virgil, *Aeneid* (Book II, 241–5): "O Ilium, home of the gods, and ye Dardan battlements, famed in war! Four times at the gates' very threshold it halted, and four times from its paunch the armour clashed; yet we press on, heedless and blind with frenzy, and set the ill-omened monster on our hallowed citadel."

Millia quot magnis numquam venêre Mycenis."

In other words–

"The fatal horse pours forth the human tide,
Insulting Sinon flings his firebrands wide,
The gates are burst; the ancient rampart falls,
And swarming millions climb its crumbling walls."[176]

As one writer later commented, this protracted debate between Gladstone and Lowe "left the Trojan horse without a leg to stand on."[177] The anti-classical Bright must surely have had the Trojan horse in mind when, after the first night of debate, he spoke of the "cataracts of declamation" that had been poured out over whether the borough franchise should remain at £10 or be reduced to £7.[178] Certainly, the contest between Lowe and Gladstone took classical pedantry in parliamentary debate to a very high level. Yet, to make the point of their dueling quotations more generally understood, Gladstone had employed close paraphrase, and Lowe had finally provided a complete translation. Like eighteenth-century oratorical classicism, the volley of quotation was something shared between the speakers and a few others who appreciated it. The job of convincing the membership in general was left to the English language. For all the pedantry, the Trojan Horse appeared rather briefly in speeches lasting several hours and containing numerous quotations from Shakespeare and other English poets.

Perhaps the best way of concluding an assessment of oratorical classicism in the Victorian House of Commons is to note that, of all the columns of Latin uttered in debate, the most famous and genuinely effective instance consisted of a single three-word phrase. The phrase was uttered in 1850 by Lord Palmerston—regarded by many as a singularly un-eloquent parliamentary speaker—at the end of a five-hour speech defending himself from a majority of members opposed to his gunboat diplomacy in the Don Pacifico affair. In his peroration, Palmerston reduced the entire matter down to the question of whether Britain would guarantee the safety of its subjects abroad, so that a Briton could say like a Roman "*Civis Romanus sum*" (I am a Roman citizen).[179] The analogy was clear, the message simple, the Latin comprehensible. According to Lord Stanley, it was "an expression equally eloquent, popular, and indiscreet."[180] Although more debate ensued (including some classical pedantry from Gladstone), Palmerston had reversed the tide of opposition—aided in no small measure by this supreme example of a Latin tag.

THE MEANING AND LEGACY OF ORATORICAL CLASSICISM

G.M. Trevelyan's claim notwithstanding, the story of oratorical classicism in Parliament—and its decline—could be carried well into the twentieth century along with those leading politicians who, like Churchill, spent their formative years in the age of Gladstone. Arthur Balfour and Asquith were both excellent classicists. Stanley Baldwin was far more modest in his classical attainments. Yet, like Disraeli, Baldwin's classical pretensions underscore the continued, if ever-waning force of the tradition of oratorical classicism. Churchill, hated and barely learned classics. He recalled how as a boy he had been told that "Mr. Gladstone read Homer for fun, which I thought served him right."[181] Later on, Asquith used to get a physically pained expression on his face when Churchill "sometimes adorned a Cabinet discussion by bringing out one of my few but fanciful Latin quotations. It was more than annoyance; it was a pang."[182] In the postwar era, the single outstanding example of a classicist-politician was the late Enoch Powell.[183] Significantly, he was one of the period's strongest (if, ultimately, most infamous) political orators.

That oratorical classicism was a powerful symbol of parliamentary tradition and greatness in the nineteenth century is abundantly clear from contemporary discussions. In their focus on the perceived decline of oratorical classicism from the age of Pitt and Fox, however, Victorian critics failed to understand its evolution. Latin quotations in the nineteenth century served a different, broader set of oratorical means and rhetorical ends than in the eighteenth-century "golden age." On the whole, both Pitt and Fox—man of government and man of opposition, respectively—used Latin quotations in similar ways and for similar effects: to attack, to defend, and to adorn. Disraeli and Gladstone—Pitt and Fox's heirs as political and oratorical rivals—responded to, rather than continued these conventions. Disraeli (man of opposition) used Latin quotations to acquire greater political legitimacy for himself. Gladstone (man of government) used Latin quotations in part from his own classical inclinations, but more importantly as one of many ways of displaying his mastery of the forms and business of the House.

In contrast with the moralism of nineteenth-century politics and the relatively circumspect behavior of nineteenth-century politicians, those who bemoaned the decline of oratorical classicism in Parliament did so in reference to a romanticized view of the political world of the eighteenth century. Underlying the complaints about nineteenth-century oratory, was a picture of an eighteenth century that was as noble in achievement as it was corrupt in practice, its protagonists as brilliant as they were dissolute. As George Otto Trevelyan wrote about the age of Fox:

> those who have not clearly before their minds the nature of that vital change which has come over the circumstances of English public life during the last hundred years will never understand the events of the eighteenth century, or do justice to its men—men who were spurred forward by far sharper incentives, and solicited by far fiercer temptations, than ours, and who, when they held a straight course, were entitled to very different credit from any that we can possibly deserve.[184]

Curzon is another who betrays his sneaking admiration for the political world of the eighteenth century, where politicians "spoke as they dressed, and moved, and I may add, drank, with a fine profusion, and in the grand style."[185]

For nineteenth-century critics, oratorical classicism was the symbolic essence of this "grand style" as expressed in parliamentary speech. The manner in which eighteenth-century MPs were later believed to have been able to infuse their speeches with references to and quotations from classical literature was seen not only as testimony to their brilliance—both individual and collective—but also as indicative of the timeless greatness of the "British Senate" itself. Thus, claims that the "classical spirit" was on the wane in the Commons can be understood on one level as coded complaints against a perceived lack of grandeur in nineteenth-century political style.

Yet, oratorical classicism was more than a stylistic concern—even for Disraeli. In general, as one scholar has written, "to study Victorian classicism is to attempt to deal with Victorian culture on its own terms."[186] Given the importance of classicism in Victorian culture, it is indeed significant that (leaving aside the recitation of classical texts in the schools and universities), Latin quotation in Parliament was its major spoken manifestation. Thus, concerns over oratorical classicism underscore the centrality of public speech at this time. Ultimately, oratorical classicism in

Parliament was a half-invented tradition in the nineteenth century that was both misunderstood and misinterpreted by contemporaries, while new influences affecting nineteenth-century politics re-shaped the nature and utility of speech in the House of Commons.

Conclusion

A recent historian of the preoccupations of nineteenth-century politicians has observed that the ways in which the changing political world was understood by contemporaries by no means followed a coherent line of thinking. Instead, notions of political change became attached to what he describes as "symbols unimportant in themselves"—among them, the perception of a new "coarseness" in parliamentary debate.[187] Yet, as this chapter has attempted to show, the perceptions and the realities of parliamentary speech were more than mere symbols and far from unimportant in themselves.

As the introduction to the 1853 collection of Peel's speeches states: "The interest of Parliamentary Oratory has of late years greatly increased."[188] Among leading statesmen, the preoccupation can be observed—to take but one notable example—in Lord Stanley's diaries, in which he routinely comments on the oratorical efforts of his parliamentary colleagues. The quality of parliamentary speech was also of no small interest to backbenchers, as evidenced by the diaries of Sir John Trelawny.[189] Public interest can be seen in the regularity with which articles on parliamentary oratory appeared in journals of opinion, and the extended descriptions and discussions of speech-making in that great Victorian literary genre, the parliamentary novel.

The nineteenth century was not uniquely self-conscious about its parliamentary oratory. Nevertheless, it is striking that no other period in modern British history seems to have been so self-critical in this respect while at the same time producing so considerable a collection of first-class speakers. By contrast, later-eighteenth-century Britain appears to have been satisfied with the quality of its oratorical talent. Twentieth-century Britain has complained much about the failure of its political oratory to measure up, but the complaints appear to be far better justified than they were in the nineteenth century.[190] Churchill, whose oratorical style incorporated a studied antiquity, has proved to be pretty much the only exception.

Contemporary concerns over the relative state of parliamentary eloquence notwithstanding, the fact remains that, beginning in the middle of the nineteenth century, more people were speaking in the House of Commons, and they were speaking more frequently. Further, parliamentary speeches were being carried to a greater number of people through the expanding national and provincial press. In this context, the changing styles of parliamentary speech—from the rhetorical to the explanatory (for measures), from the denunciatory to the deflationary (for people)—reflected the increasingly public role of the House of Commons and its debates. In an era of democratic expansion in which the political agenda was dominated by questions of domestic reform and the words of MPs were more available to the public, the kind of hothouse parliamentary oratory characteristic of the late eighteenth century was insufficient for the political requirements of the time.

CHAPTER THREE

Religion

IN TERMS OF quantity, quality, and popularity, the second half of the nineteenth century could claim to be the greatest era for religious oratory in British history.[1] The famous "religious census" of March 30, 1851 shocked contemporaries by calculating that, of the estimated number of persons in England and Wales able to attend religious services of some kind, *only* 58 percent (40.5 percent of the total population) had actually attended (fewer, it was reckoned, given the fact that some people attended more than one service).[2] A similar (albeit less accurate) census in Scotland recorded 61 percent of the population attending services.[3] In terms of oratorical consumption, the censuses indicate that nearly 7.3 million people in England and Wales and 1.75 million people in Scotland heard a sermon that particular day. Such a nationwide survey of religious observance was never repeated; however, the 1851 censuses provide a rough measure of the listening audience for sermons on the cusp of a period that saw a significant quantitative and qualitative improvement in religious oratory. By the 1880s, an estimated 2 million sermons were preached in Britain every year.[4] This averages out at over 38,000 sermons per week, or one weekly sermon for around every 800 people.[5]

By the middle of the nineteenth century, the experience of churchgoing for members of Established and Nonconformist churches had been largely transformed by the success of the evangelical movement, and its emphasis on preaching "The Word." Indeed, the wide diffusion of evangelical values in the first half of the nineteenth century succeeded to the extent that much of what is popularly considered "nineteenth-century" is, at its root, a general manifestation of the evangelical temperament.[6] Unquestionably, the evangelical movement produced new expectations for the experience of worship; nevertheless, ascribing the mass popularity of preaching in the second half of the nineteenth century simply to the success of evangelicalism neither explains, nor does justice to the dazzling variety of oratory and orators that contemporaries heard from the pulpits of that time.

Structures of Preaching

The number of professional speech-makers in religion was far greater than in any other area of public life. Parliament had only 658 members in the Commons and around 400 in the Lords, and in each house active speakers were a small minority (see pp. 71–76).[7] In the law, there were between 500 and 1,000 practicing barristers (see pp. 170–71). Among major denominations, the 1851 censuses counted 17,621 Anglican clergymen in England and Wales, 1,225 Wesleyan Methodist ministers, and perhaps another 1,000 ministers in other Methodist sects. There were also 1,124 Church of Scotland ministers, 763 Free Church of Scotland ministers (split from the Church of Scotland in 1843), and 950 Catholic clergymen.[8] Additionally, there were the ministries of Baptist, Unitarian, and a host of other smaller denominations. Further, a number of Nonconformist denominations, particularly the Methodists, relied heavily upon lay preachers. One can assume that all of the Nonconformist clergy were preaching to a greater or lesser extent. The same cannot be said for the Anglican clergy, although the proportion not performing parish duties had fallen from around 50 percent at the beginning of the century to 15 percent by 1850.[9]

While the number of parliamentary seats remained essentially the same and the number of practicing barristers increased very little, the number of clergymen and ministers increased significantly. In the forty years between 1851 and 1891, the Anglican clergy of England and Wales grew by nearly 40 percent. Although the numerical increase of the Anglican clergy was probably as large as, if not larger than that for all the other denominations combined, the non-Anglican ministries increased at greater rates during this period: the Church of Scotland by around 50 percent, the Free Church by around 60 percent, and Methodist denominations by 60 percent to 70 percent. Additionally, there are other important denominations for which data is insufficient to calculate growth but which surely grew in this period, such as the Congregationalists (with more than 3,000 ministers in 1901) and the Baptists (with 2,000 pastors in 1901). Special mention should also be made of the Salvation Army, whose flying corps of preachers grew from 36 in 1876 (the first year for which data is available) to 4,170 in 1897. Catholic clergy experienced by far the greatest percentage growth between 1851 and 1891—more than 200 percent—largely in response to the growing concentrations of Irish immigrants.[10]

While it is clear that the personnel of preaching was large and that it grew significantly over the course of the nineteenth century, these facts alone do not convey the extent to which religious speech came to be so deeply enmeshed in the public culture of the times. This can begin to be shown by examining two aspects of how preaching came to be more widely and more prominently embodied: in the built environment, and in print.

CHURCH-BUILDING

Space is integral to all considerations of oratory, and nineteenth-century Britain saw a massive expansion of the space in which preaching took place. For the Church of England, the church-building movement that began around 1810 was the project not of Evangelical clergy, but of High Church laymen led by the prosperous London wine merchant, Joshua Watson. Responding to demographic shifts that left the existing churches of industrializing North able to accommodate only a small portion of the people, Watson and his associates formed the Church Building Society in 1818 (incorporated in 1828) to raise a private fund and make grants to assist the construction of new churches. They also helped persuade Lord Liverpool's government to put through the 1818 Church Building Act, providing £1 million of public funds for building Anglican churches to be disbursed by a Church Building Commission that included Watson and other members of the Church Building Society.

This £1 million was granted on an *ad hoc* basis to fund, if not the full costs of constructing new churches, then the greater part of them. Parish contributions in the form of subscriptions and loans were considerably smaller. By 1821, the Commission had supported 85 church-building projects (out of 158 applications) that together provided seating for an additional 144,190 people.[11] More than £900,000 of the grant had been committed while less than £150,000 had been raised from private sources.[12] In 1824, successful lobbying resulted in a supplemental grant of £500,000, which the Commission disbursed according to the practice of the Church Building Society by providing smaller sums to parishes willing to cover the bulk of the expense. By the time the Church Building Commission was dissolved in 1856, the £1.5 million of public funds allocated for church-building (plus around £200,000 of interest earnings) had been matched by private sources amounting to nearly £1.4 million. These funds built 615 new churches accommodating around 600,000 worshipers.[13]

The number of new Anglican churches increased at an accelerating rate during the first half of the century: by 111 in the 1810s (some funded by the 1818 grant), by 328 in the 1820s, by 785 in the 1830s, and by a staggering 1,409 in the 1840s.[14] After the peak of the 1840s, the number of new churches built per decade dropped back down to the level of the 1830s and remained roughly constant from the 1850s through the 1880s (an average of around 720 new churches per decade).[15] By the 1880s, the church-building boom began to taper off with only 656 new churches, followed by 512 in the 1890s. In addition to the new construction, existing churches were rebuilt, renovated, and extended throughout the nineteenth century. The rebuilding of churches rose sharply beginning in the 1840s with 7,144 rebuilt between 1840 and 1875 (compared to 1,727 new churches built in the same period).[16] By these means, many thousands of additional sittings were provided to parishioners.

What is most extraordinary about the church-building "boom" of the 1840s is that, unlike the efforts of the 1820s, it was accomplished without the benefit of new parliamentary grants. Peel was unwilling to antagonize Nonconformists by providing public funds to build Anglican churches. In 1843, however, new legislation made it easier for the Church to partition old parishes even when there was as yet no church. By further facilitating the Church's ability to grow and respond to demographic realities, the motivation for the 1843 act was akin to that underlying the 1818 act. In the wake of Waterloo, building more churches in populous areas and requiring a proportion of the new sittings to be free had been seen as a way to combat the appeal to the poorer classes of godless Jacobinism as well as Methodism and other forms of New Dissent.[17] Similarly, the 1843 act was a response to fears raised by the Chartist agitations of the previous year.

One effect of the 1843 legislation was to add a new dimension to the expansion of the Church of England. In addition to growth determined by bishops' diocesan planning, the Church also began to expand according to the strategies that had long fueled the growth of Nonconformist denominations. A clergyman "went into a suburb or a slum some way from any church, and opened a room for Sunday worship, in a shack, a living room, a conservatory."[18] In this way, church building and extension were supplemented by the holding of Sunday services in licensed rooms and a variety of other places. In the industrial region of Oldham and Saddleworth, for example, "Most of the new churches of the 1840s and 1850s began in some such building, or in converted cottages, hired rooms, and, in one case, . . . in a purpose-built wooden church with seating for 150."[19]

In the absence of parliamentary grants, the construction and refurbishment of churches were funded from private sources. In the diocese of London, for example, of the £2.7 million expended on building, repairing, and extending churches between 1840 and 1875, more than £2.5 million came from private benefaction.[20] Generally, the reluctance of churchwardens and ratepayers to bear the cost meant that the clergyman had to look to his family, friends, landowners, and the Church Building Society to finance his project. One Lincolnshire incumbent who managed to get his church restored stated that if he had not had "the greatest landowner in the place coming forward to give money and countenance to it I should have had very great difficulty indeed in getting the thing done. The people said, 'Oh it lasted our father's time, it will last ours, and we think you had better let things alone.'"[21] In industrial towns, absent the patronage of the local landowner, Anglican clergymen had little recourse but to deal with the seemingly inscrutable bureaucracies and incomprehensible priorities of the Church Building Commission and the Church Building Society.[22]

Nonconformist denominations also expanded their physical presence at an aggressive pace in the first half of the nineteenth century, although obviously without the benefit of state grants. In general, Nonconformists built chapels only after a potent preacher had already built a congregation. Where, according to the 1851 census, Anglicans had added 2,698 new places of worship with a total of 1,028,032 sittings between 1801 and 1851, over the same period Nonconformists added 16,689 new places of worship with a total of 4,013,408 sittings. (The Anglicans, however, began the century with 11,379 places of worship.)

The Methodist presence expanded rapidly before 1850, particularly in new urban and industrial communities. Wesleyan Methodists—the main body from which other Methodist denominations (e.g. New Connexion, Primitive Methodists, etc.) split off—increased from 825 chapels with 165,000 sittings in 1801 to 11,007 chapels and 2,194,298 sittings in 1851.[23] In 1818 (the year the Anglicans launched the Church Building Society, the

£1 million grant, and the Church Building Commission), the Wesleyans created a Great Chapel Fund to support chapel-building. By 1851, however, all Methodist denominations taken together had already gained more than 60 percent of their total nineteenth-century increase in membership.[24] In the second half of the century, the rate of increase for new Methodist chapels established would fall with the slowing in membership increases.

Growth in churches and chapels for other Nonconformist denominations also slowed after mid-century. The Baptists, for example, increased the number of their churches in England and Wales from 1,426 in 1838 to 1,992 in 1861 (an average annual increase of 1.5 percent), compared to an increase in all of Great Britain from 2,082 in 1861 to 2,777 in 1891 (an average annual increase of 1.0 percent).[25] In the second half of the century, other kinds of Nonconformist facilities providing religious oratory emerged and enjoyed rapid growth, such as the "preaching stations" of the Salvation Army.

In general, therefore, the formal structures in which religious oratory was listened to experienced their most remarkable period of growth in the first half of the nineteenth century, with further steady growth continuing for several decades more. There was, of course, considerable local variation and in some areas church-building peaked in the 1860s. Events in Scotland produced a somewhat different chronology. An extended wave of church building followed for several decades after the Disruption of 1843 as Free Church adherents raised funds to provide new churches for the evangelical ministers who had "walked out" of the established Church of Scotland. But this followed earlier evangelical efforts to build additional churches within the Establishment.[26] Between 1801 and 1841, 816 new places of worship were erected in Scotland, most (562) between 1821 and 1841. In the decade following 1841, no fewer than 1,032 places of worship were erected—710 (69 percent) by the Free Church.[27] In these ways and others, the building of churches and chapels throughout Britain in the first half of the century was a concerted commitment of resources resulting in a vast (if uneven) expansion of space for religious worship, and also for preaching.

PREACHING AND PRINTING

In addition to the growth in the number of professional preachers and the expanding space for religious oratory, the nineteenth century also witnessed a boom in religious publishing—a great deal of which was connected to preaching. The greatest growth in religious publishing occurred in the second half of the century, with more books on religious subjects published in the 1870s (7,653) than during the thirty-two years from 1814 to 1846 (7,268). The peak decade for religious publishing was the 1880s, during which the number of religious titles reached 8,640.[28]

In the eighteenth and early nineteenth centuries, volumes of sermons were published for the use of the clergymen who did not write their own (some of these books were even printed in a copperplate script to appear hand-written). But developments in the nineteenth century changed the nature and functions of printed sermons.[29] The increasing number and popularity of professional preachers helped generate a market for their own printed sermons, while at the same time (thanks to Gladstone's fiscal reforms of the 1850s and 60s) it became far easier to have sermons published. Thus, printed sermons changed from a resource for clergymen in the pulpit, to a new kind of pulpit—a new means for preachers to broadcast their message. Beginning in the 1860s, the expansion of periodical publication following the lifting of the paper duty led to a fundamental shift in the principal mode of sermon publishing.[30] Where printed sermons had hitherto primarily consisted of the publication of composed works in volume form, extempore preachers now produced a durable *oeuvre* in pamphlets, magazines, and newspapers with the aid of shorthand reporting. Like the publication of platform and courtroom speeches (see pp. 180 and 268–72), sermons printed in media designed for broad distribution played an important role in spreading preachers' reputations beyond their locality.

The religious periodical press also expanded significantly in this period.[31] By 1864, there were 196 magazines considered to be of a "decidedly religious character." During the last four decades of the century this number nearly trebled to 543 titles by 1900.[32] Most religious periodicals printed sermons in one form or another. Some publications were specifically denominational. The general trend in the second half of the century, however, was to publish sermons from a wide range of denominations—the criteria for publication being the excellent qualities of the sermon rather than its theological position. *The Homilist* (1851-77) was a particularly successful example of this ecumenical trend (although it published written rather than preached sermons). The periodical explicitly announced that there would be no "denominationalism" and no "polemical Theology." It further declared its aim "is not to supply sermons for indolent or incompetent preachers, but stimulus and tonic for the true-hearted, hard-working, and genuine teacher. It does not deal in the 'ready made,' but in the raw material." By the end of its quarter-century run, *The Homilist* had achieved total sales of more than 130,000.[33]

The religious "penny press" was also extremely popular during this period. These weekly periodicals—many of which enjoyed a large circulation and were popular with advertisers—printed a range of religious matter including sermons. *The Christian Herald*, for example, boasted a circulation of more than 195,000 a week and featured sermons in every issue, as well as in its penny monthly supplements. One contemporary estimated that eight leading titles of the religious penny press enjoyed a combined circulation of from 1.25 to 1.5 million every week.[34] Perhaps the most sermon-oriented and ecumenically minded penny weekly was the highly successful *Penny Pulpit*. Each number was entirely devoted to printing sermons preached by ministers of various denominations. Numerous similar periodicals brought together the sermons of Anglicans and Nonconformists of all stripes, and (as discussed later) these served as a model for some of the leading preachers to issue series of their own sermons.

The quantitative increases in the personnel of preaching, the places in which they preached, and the reach of their sermons in print are eloquent testimony to the various ways in which religious oratory became increasingly prevalent in the cultural life of nineteenth-century Britain. What these data do not speak to are the qualitative questions about how preaching was experienced by its producers and its consumers. Some sense of this can be conveyed through looking at efforts to improve the competitive position of the Church of England through oratory.

Enhancing Anglican Preaching

If, as Lytton Strachey quipped, "the Church of England had slept the sleep of the . . . comfortable" for many generations,[35] this was nowhere more evident than in the general view of Anglican preaching at mid-century. Building more churches was no guarantee that more people would fill them. As the newly consecrated Bishop of London observed in 1856, it would "be wrong if we mistake the erection of churches for the spread of the Gospel throughout the land."[36] This bishop, Archibald Campbell Tait, was one of a number of influential Anglican clergymen who identified, and acted upon the need to improve the quality of preaching in the Church of England.

TAIT'S LEADERSHIP

Evangelical sympathies had been a barrier to advancement within the Church. In 1856 and 1857, however, Palmerston filled vacant sees with clergymen of a pastoral, rather than the typical "high and dry" theological bent. The "Palmerston bishops" worked to expand church-building and pastoral outreach efforts, and they took a particular interest in improving the quality of Anglican preaching. For example, during his lengthy tenure as Bishop of Ripon from 1857 to 1884, Robert Bickersteth consecrated 157 new or rebuilt churches plus numerous mission rooms. He also brought religion to the masses in person by preaching to colliers at the pit mouth, to navvies at the waterworks, and to factory workers during their lunch. In his first charge to the clergy of his diocese, Bickersteth "spelt out clearly the value he placed on fervent preaching and he may have been unique among Anglican bishops in preaching more and more frequently during his episcopate."[37]

In general, the Palmerston bishops advanced the influence of the Evangelical party. Nevertheless, it was the Latitudinarian Tait who became one of the most active and visible promoters of preaching within the Church of England. His 1856 appointment as Bishop of London was controversial: he was no theologian, he was Scottish, and he had not occupied a lesser see beforehand.[38] From a primarily educational career at Balliol and Rugby, Tait stepped into one of the most—and perhaps *the* most—prominent public roles in British religious life. Encompassing more than two million people, London was by far the Church of England's largest diocese and, in the mid-1850s, the largest diocese in the world. Despite its vast size, however, the diocese of London still had far fewer places of Anglican worship than many other sees—a problem that Tait's much-admired and long-serving predecessor, C. J. Blomfield, had worked hard to address through vigorous church-building campaigns. Because London was the nineteenth century's world city, the Bishop of London was *ex officio* far more significant than his mitered colleagues, and certainly eclipsed his nominal superior, the Archbishop of York, if not that of Canterbury.

Tait was rarely considered an especially eloquent orator, although few would claim he was not an effective speaker either in the pulpit or in the Lords. In addition to argumentative powers that were first observed in the Oxford Union (of which he had been President in 1833),[39] contemporary accounts record that his oratory exhibited that most important nineteenth-century characteristic, *earnestness.* Whatever the limitations or strengths of his public speaking, Tait's oratorical output was considerable—particularly during his years as Bishop of London. In addition to preaching and speaking in churches—such as at special Sunday evening services he organized for working people in the North and East of London—Tait gained considerable notice in the Spring and Summer of 1857 by giving open-air addresses throughout his diocese.

> His diary shows him going off from the House of Lords to speak to a shipload of emigrants in the Docks, from the Convocation discussions on Church Discipline to address the Ragged School children in Golden Land, or the omnibus-drivers in their great yard at Islington. He preached to the costermongers in Covent Garden Market; to railway porters from the platform of a locomotive; to a colony of gypsies upon the Common at Shepherd's Bush, and this without in any way relaxing the accustomed round of confirmations and sermons and committees which must always occupy a bishop's time in addition to his huge correspondence.[40]

However, Tait's leadership in expanding the reach of preaching was not confined to his personal example. During his tenure as Bishop, and after 1869 as Archbishop of Canterbury, he used the influence of his office to raise the standard of preaching for Anglican clergy. Shortly after his ordination, he beseeched his clergy to "go forth into the highways and hedges, and proclaim in the simplest words at their command the Gospel of a living Saviour."[41] In his five-hour primary charge of November 1858 delivered under the dome of St. Paul's, Tait addressed a wide range of issues, but laid special emphasis on improving the quality of preaching—the most important external aid to worship.[42] While conceding that no systematic professional training could be guaranteed to produce consistently first-rate ministers, he stressed the need to correct the shortcomings of the clergy at an early stage in their careers: "young men may be taught to compose and speak with force and fluency; a thorough acquaintance with Scripture may be communicated; and useful hints may be given for the difficult duty of reaching, both in public and private address, distressed and ignorant human souls."[43] He also attempted to impress upon his clergy the need to consider the nature of their audience: "When a man sets himself to prepare a sermon or to preach, I beg him ever to remember that the measure of his being a good or a bad preacher, must be by conveying his distinct ideas to the understanding, and calling up religious feelings in the hearts of the people (of whatever class they are) to whom he is speaking."[44]

This stress on improving the quality of preaching as an institutional responsibility can certainly be understood in the context of the 1851 religious census. Not only was less than half the population attending religious services, but also Anglican worshipers only barely outnumbered Nonconformists. By the example of his own preaching efforts, and in his first charge, Tait attempted to shake up Anglican complacency and make the case forcefully that the Church of England needed to compete more effectively. In 1862, Tait's second charge continued to urge better preaching by stressing the unique oratorical demands of life in the ministry and the consequent responsibility to improve the quality of religious public speech.

> We have heard of late a great deal of criticism on our preaching. . . . I need scarcely touch on what is alleged as to the indistinctness of utterance, or a dull monotony of manner. All persons who are called to speak in public may find at first that they are liable to these faults. The misfortune is, that while other speakers who labour under them are soon obliged to correct their faults, or else find their opportunities of speaking gone, by the fact that no one requests them to speak, or if they do speak no one stays to listen, we clergymen, on the contrary, whether we can or no, are obliged to speak in public every week; it is an essential part of our office; and a considerable number of persons is obliged to sit patiently, and at least appear to listen to us. We have not the benefit of that practical criticism of our defects which soon teaches men in other professions either to amend or be silent.[45]

Although Tait stated that "the matter of our sermons is of course far more important than the manner,"[46] he continued to urge his clergy to take into account the class and educational background of their congregations, to speak to them in a manner they can understand, and to draw examples from the scriptures with which they can most readily identify. In fact, while Tait's first charge had implied much of this, his 1862 charge explicitly laid out practical advice and general guidelines for preaching. He ruled it "out of the question" to preach other people's sermons or even to use a digest of another's thoughts, thus effectively demanding the end of what had been a common practice among Anglican clergymen. While he did not advocate speaking extempore over reading composed sermons, he stated that "whether written or directly spoken, the sermon is a speech"[47]—and to be a really good preacher, one must be comfortable with both styles. He urged his clergy to prepare carefully for their sermons, observing that without appropriate preparation, the speech cannot succeed. He spoke of the need to be able to expand upon, or curtail prepared material as circumstances require, as well as the need to be aware of the impression being made on those listening. Finally, he urged his clergy to make a study of the sermons of the best divines of the past, and for more experienced clergymen to take a hand in mentoring new clerics in their early oratorical efforts.

Tait's charges both acknowledge the Church of England's oratorical shortcomings and offer frankly worldly solutions to the problem. That the general state of Anglican oratory was seen as a matter for remediation at this time was due in part to the criticism of the established Church by Nonconformists, and the 1851 revelation that the Church of England held only a slender majority of those who worshiped. That oratory was a particularly important factor was convincingly demonstrated by the new kind of popularity that an increasing number of preachers—both Nonconformist and Anglican—began to generate beginning in the 1840s. Tait's recommendations to his clergy read like a basic primer for any public speaker—originality, preparation, adjusting material in delivery, awareness of the audience. With sermons, he observed, "it will be here as in other oratory."[48]

It is impossible to measure the extent to which Tait's advice contributed to the improvement of preaching in the diocese of London. Nevertheless, there is evidence that his message did not fall on deaf ears. For example, the Church Homiletical Society formed around 1874 embodied all that Tait had recommended in his charges with respect to preaching. Indeed, Tait, by then Archbishop of Canterbury, headed the list of the Society's distinguished Church patrons. The Society was dedicated to "the training and improvement in Preaching of the younger Clergy and Candidates for Holy Orders."[49] To this end it held monthly general meetings in which lectures and discussion addressed the subject of preaching and its improvement. Local branches of the Society pursued similar activities on a more intimate scale. The Society made arrangements for experienced clergymen to provide private homiletic tutoring to novice preachers or those seeking improvement. Members could also send in the texts or outlines of proposed sermons for blind criticism—criticism that the Society assured members would be directed toward manner rather than matter. Through its monthly organ, *The Clergyman's Magazine* (1875-98), the Society circulated to its members a variety of articles and other material useful for preaching. It is also notable that the advertisements carried by the magazine include works relevant to preaching from Nonconformist as well as Anglican sources. The reach and influence of the Society can be judged by the fact that in its first five years, *The Clergyman's Magazine*, issued more than 200,000 copies.[50] This works out to an average circulation of 40,000 per year during a period in which the target audience—the episcopal clergy of England and Wales—numbered around 21,000.

CATHEDRAL SERVICES

Allied to his drive to improve the quality of Anglican preaching itself, Tait was also instrumental in popularizing preaching through innovative use of space. In particular, he promoted the use for oratorical purposes of the Church's most spectacular, but least used, physical resource: the cathedrals. Amid the ecclesiastical reforms of the first half of the nineteenth century, the cathedrals had remained something of a problem. Although the 1840 Dean and Chapter Act empowered the Ecclesiastical Commission to redistribute cathedral endowments for other needs within the Church, the question of how best to use cathedral establishments remained. Even when cathedrals were in locations that had not been emptied by the demographic shifts of industrialization and urbanization, they were still virtually moribund. In his 1851 novel *Yeast*, the clergyman Charles Kingsley described an afternoon service at St. Paul's:

> The organ droned sadly in its iron cage to a few musical amateurs. Some nursery-maids and foreign sailors stared about within the spiked felon's dock which shut off the body of the cathedral, and tried in vain to hear what was going on inside the choir. As a wise author—

> a Protestant too—has lately said, "the scanty service rattled in the vast building, like a dried kernel too small for its shell." The place breathed imbecility and unreality and sleepy life-in-death, while the whole nineteenth century went roaring on its way outside.[51]

Despite the work of a Commission in the mid-1850s to "inquire into the state and condition of the cathedral and collegiate churches in England and Wales," little notice was paid to its recommendations.[52] In 1855, the abolition of the twenty-person limit on Anglican worship outside a church finally permitted Evangelical clergymen to experiment with the methods of successful Nonconformist preachers by holding large services "out-of-doors" or in public halls. In 1857, under Tait's auspices, a course of services held at Exeter Hall—a venue previously used for large Nonconformist services—drew a capacity crowd (*The Times* observing a "decided preponderance" of men).[53] High Churchmen opposed to such non-Anglican forms of worship objected to using unconsecrated sites like Exeter Hall when London's cathedrals stood empty.[54] Tait could rent public halls, but use of the cathedrals required the approval of the dean and chapter. In 1858, however, he convinced both Westminster Abbey and St. Paul's to hold services in their naves.

Westminster Abbey agreed to a six-month trial period in order to see if people would actually come and, if they did, to determine if the fear of some clergymen that cathedral services would decrease their parochial congregations was justified. At the first service, on January 3, 1858, attendance well exceeded expectations. The *Times* reporter, judging by externals, thought that there were few there who were not of the "better classes." When the huge "concourse of persons" that had gathered outside the Abbey surged through the door in "a most unseemly and violent manner," it presented "a scene of such confusion as rather resembled the gallery door of a theatre on boxing-night than the entrance to a place of worship."[55] In addition to being unprepared for the crowd, no provision had been made to heat the January-cold Abbey. The audience shivered through the sermon by Dean Trench, even though it was difficult to hear him from the special pulpit that had been erected in the nave. These and other shortcomings (later remedied) did not prevent an even larger crowd from lining up the following Sunday.

Judging the Westminster Abbey experiment a success, Tait finally overcame the reservations of St. Paul's venerable Dean Milman. At the first service on November 28, 1858, around 4,000 people were admitted after waiting outside for hours and a great number were turned away. The crowd was observed to consist predominantly of men; in social terms, "it was a middle-class assembly, and not the upper section of it."[56] From a pulpit in the eastern corner of the South Transept, Tait himself delivered the sermon. Although St. Paul's was heated before the service, the Bishop fought a losing battle with the Cathedral's acoustics. "From a great tub-pulpit decked in green velvet Bishop Tait boomed upwards into the echoing dome for nearly an hour, and even the front rows could scarcely distinguish a word."[57] The following Sunday, a sounding-board was placed over the pulpit to help convey Milman's sermon to the once-again capacity audience.[58]

These experiments demonstrated that great numbers of people were willing to attend cathedral services, even when climate and audibility were less than ideal. The size of the audiences at these early efforts was certainly due in part to the novelty of the events. Cathedrals are spectacular, otherworldly settings, and the idea of attending a service in the nave must have been exciting in its own right. It was, in short, an "experience." In the ensuing decades, nave services continued to draw in and captivate large audiences. In 1876, after beholding a service at Westminster Abbey, Disraeli is reported to have exclaimed: "I would not have missed the sight for anything; the darkness, the lights, the marvelous windows, the vast crowd, the courtesy, the respect, the devotion—and fifty years ago there would not have been fifty persons present."[59]

After a period of resistance, cathedrals outside the metropolis followed the example of Westminster and St. Paul's, and also drew in great crowds. At York in 1867, no less than 2,000, and sometimes as many as 3,000, people showed up for the 7:30 p.m. service. At Ely in 1872, out of a population of more than 5,000, an estimated 1,200 to 1,300 worshiped at the cathedral every Sunday.[60] At Bristol, nave services began in 1882 and also drew large crowds.[61] As Archbishop, Tait repeatedly urged cathedral chapters to improve their old preaching arrangements and encouraged rural cathedrals to open their pulpits to preachers with the proven ability to attract audiences:

> The custom of introducing extraneous preachers, at special evening services on Sunday, began in the Metropolis at Westminster Abbey, under Dean Trench, and Dean Milman speedily followed the example at St. Paul's. The best Anglican preachers in England one after another are now to be heard in these two cathedrals, whether they belong to the cathedral body or whether they do not.[62]

Thus, the enhancements to worship involved in cathedral services came to be joined with the drive to improve the quality of Anglican preaching.

Preaching Stars

In the second half of the nineteenth century, a number of divines achieved unprecedented fame by virtue of their abilities in the pulpit. What was unprecedented was not that their renown rested on their preaching—for certainly preaching formed the basis of much of John Wesley's and George Whitefield's positive appeal—but rather their concentration in number and the scale and range of the audiences they were able to attract. The climate for preaching was very different one hundred years after Wesley's time—the example of Wesley himself having contributed greatly to the change in that climate. By no means, however, were the preaching stars of the later nineteenth century all from the evangelical camp. They represented a broad range of denominations and intra-denominational parties. Despite the doctrinal and stylistic differences among these preaching stars, they were discussed and analyzed together, and even ranked. Further, their listening (and reading) audience extended well beyond the members of their respective denominations.

EARLY EXAMPLES

Two of the earliest nineteenth-century preaching stars who had a national impact were from Scotland, and the pulpit careers of Thomas Chalmers and Edward Irving helped point the way for the more established period of preaching celebrity after 1850. Chalmers gained some notice from his pulpit exertions as minister of Kilmeny (Fife) from 1803. It was, however, following his evangelical conversion in 1810 that Chalmers's preaching career began to ascend to its legendary heights. Where previously he had spent little time readying his sermons, these preparations now "engrossed the leisure of the whole preceding week."[63] Chalmers's regional fame spread and in 1815, he was nominated by the Town Council of Glasgow to be minister of the Tron parish. As one witness to Chalmers's first sermon in Glasgow (an Oxford student and son of a Scottish minister) recorded, "most unquestionably, I have never heard, either in England or Scotland, or in any other country, any preacher whose eloquence is capable of producing an effect so strong and irresistible as his."[64]

Between 1815 and 1817, Chalmers "reached the height of his power and influence as a preacher, attaining an eminence perhaps unsurpassed in the history of the Scottish pulpit."[65] Even on a Thursday forenoon, the Tron church, built to hold 1,400, would be filled with 1,500 to 1,600 people.[66] In an attempt to accommodate his hearers, Chalmers experimented with delivering the same sermon twice daily, but even this seemed to have no effect on the crowding.[67] Chalmers's reputation in Scotland was consolidated by a series of six hugely popular discourses delivered in 1815 and 1816 on astronomy (an early passion of his) in relationship to Christian theology. These discourses reached a wider British public through their publication in 1817. Although up to this time volumes of sermons did not typically sell well, *The Discourses on the Christian Revelation, Viewed in Connection with Modern Astronomy* sold 6,000 copies in ten weeks and eight further editions were issued that year, bringing total circulation of the *Discourses* to 20,000—one of the best selling volumes of sermons ever to appear in Britain.[68]

In May 1817, Chalmers traveled to London, where he preached to great crowds. The chapels at which he was scheduled to appear were invariably filled beyond capacity hours before the service was scheduled to begin. In an effort to control this, tickets were issued and a newspaper announcement instructed that, although the service would begin at eleven o'clock, "it is requested that those holding tickets may be at the chapel at the opening of the doors, at half-past nine o'clock, to prevent disappointment."[69] A broad section of London society came to hear the Scottish preaching sensation, from Lords and literati to soldiers and shopkeepers, as well as clergymen of other denominations. Chalmers's great success in the capital further enhanced his standing in Glasgow and Scotland.

Ultimately, however, Chalmers came to take a rather jaundiced view of his own preaching celebrity.[70] Although he certainly continued to preach and attract great audiences, his disillusionment with pulpit success led Chalmers to take his ministry in other directions. Preaching became secondary, a vehicle to promote the social improvement causes—the achievement of "the godly commonwealth"—that increasingly became the focus of his work. His preaching formed "a boiling, foaming current, a mingled stream of exposition, illustration, and application, directed to the one great object of moving his audience to action."[71] Ultimately, his greatest fame was achieved as leader of the Disruption of 1843 and the creation of the Free Church of Scotland.

Irving, one of Chalmers's assistants, also brought a new style of preaching celebrity before a national audience.[72] In 1822, dissatisfied with life in Chalmers's shadow, he accepted an invitation to minister to the small congregation of Scottish Presbyterians at the Caledonian Chapel in Hatton Gardens, London. The great celebrity that Irving acquired shortly after coming to London has sometimes been attributed to a remark by Canning who, during a Commons debate on the relationship between talent and good pay in the Church, stated that in a marginal and unendowed church he had lately heard the most eloquent sermon in his experience. Canning's public compliment led people from fashionable society to descend upon the little Caledonian Chapel. In short order, the small, poor, Scottish, Presbyterian congregation to which Irving had been called became a large, wealthy, London, heterodox one. "The crowds that rushed to his church had scarcely ever been equalled in London."[73] Irving's loquacity—delivering sermons lasting two and three hours—does not appear to have dampened the excitement. In 1827 Irving moved to a new larger church built for him in Regent's Square. In these, the last few years of his career and life, however, Irving became increasingly grandiose, extravagant, and apocalyptic while some members of his following began to speak in tongues. Shortly before he died a broken man, Irving was formally charged with heresy and stripped of his orders.

Important preachers continued to appear throughout the first half of the century. However, even though some of their names came to be known nationally, these preachers did not attain the level of national renown that Chalmers and Irving had shown to be possible. At Brighton, for example, Frederick William Robertson achieved considerable local celebrity before his untimely death from a brain tumor.[74] Although his success was based upon his qualities as a preacher, he found the burden of preaching overwhelming. In 1848, he wrote to a cousin of

> the wear and tear of heart and mind in having so constantly, and in so unassisted a way, to speak on solemn subjects. A man who is by profession bound to speak for present effect—for, except in the present, what can speaking do?—necessarily injures himself and his character. I do not mean in the way of popularity; for I find nothing seducing in that, and would gladly, joyously give it all up tomorrow for a calmer life; but I mean in the destruction of repose, and the inability to see any truth in its quest for beauty.[75]

This reluctance to play the role of the great preacher may be one reason why Robertson's wider reputation and wider influence as a preacher was entirely posthumous—based primarily on the five volumes of his published sermons. The great success of the published sermons is even more remarkable since they are derived from imperfect shorthand notes, or summaries that he wrote for friends.

Another regional, but more widely recognized, preaching phenomenon was Birmingham's George Dawson.[76] In 1844 Dawson was invited to minister to the dwindling congregation at Birmingham's Mount Zion Baptist Chapel. Although few felt they knew what Dawson actually believed in, they were captivated by his preaching, which displayed, according to one witness, "an affluence and intensity of thought, a vehemence of movement, a brilliance, a tenderness, an energy."[77] Dawson revived the Baptist congregation, and his eclectic approach drew in members from other denominations in Birmingham's large Nonconformist population. "Congregationalists found his sermons startlingly original: Unitarians . . . were sufficiently impressed for one of them to say that this was the preaching for which they had longed all their lives."[78]

After he resigned from Mount Zion in 1845, Dawson and the large number of supporters he had acquired in so short a time set about building him his own chapel. The "Church of the Saviour" opened in 1847 and became a fixture in the religious and civic life of Birmingham. From his "preacher's platform," Dawson delivered sermons emphasizing the obligations of everyday life, particularly the importance of one's duties as a member of the Birmingham community. Not only did Dawson preach the "civic gospel," he also made his church as much a social as a religious institution, providing education for children, night classes for adults, public lectures, and relief for the poor. Further, in public lectures, ostensibly on literary or historical subjects, Dawson "chaffed popular prejudices, denounced popular vices, tore down popular idols, and made his lecturing a crusade against whatever he supposed to be hostile to the intellectual freedom and the moral health of the country."[79]

Strong preachers continued to fill the Scottish pulpit, although few attracted the kind of attention throughout Great Britain that Chalmers did. Among the most notable Scottish preachers of the generation after Chalmers was Thomas Guthrie. As a divinity student, he had paid considerable attention to the art of elocution believing that, as he wrote, "the manner is to the matter as the powder is to the ball."[80] He always wrote out and memorized his sermons but, according to one observer, the difference between the composed and the extempore "was by his vivid imagination and quick sympathies reduced to a minimum, if not wholly obliterated."[81]

Beginning his preaching career in the rural seaboard parish of Abirlot, he moved to Edinburgh in 1837 and quickly established himself as one of the city's most popular preachers. The Free St. John's church he built in the poor district of West Bow and presided over until his retirement in 1864 was attended by a large congregation, which encompassed a social range that astonished contemporaries. Even Chalmers's son-in-law and biographer found Guthrie's appeal remarkable:

> I believe there is not on record another instance of a popularity continued without sign or token of diminution for the length of an entire generation. Nor is there upon record the account of any such *kinds* of crowds as those which constituted continuously, for years and years, Dr. Guthrie's audiences in Free St. John's. Look around, while all are seating themselves; you have before you as mixed and motley a collection of human beings as ever assembled within a church. Peers and peasants, citizens and strangers, millionaires and mechanics, the judge from the bench, the carter from the roadside, the high-born dame, the serving maid of low degree—all for once close together.[82]

"Wales," as one (Welsh) religious historian wrote in 1918, "has not produced any preachers who could be classed with" the leading preachers of England and Scotland. "It need hardly be said that the range of the influence of the English and Scottish pulpits has been infinitely greater than that of the Welsh pulpit.[83] The first statement is most certainly unfair to the extremely vigorous, revival-soaked preaching culture in Wales's Established and Nonconformist churches. Many Welsh preachers enjoyed large followings and celebrity throughout the Principality.[84] The writer's point about the wider influence of Welsh preachers is, however, well taken. The national renown of the best Welsh preachers was certainly inhibited by the general isolation of the Principality during the nineteenth century, and the fact that the ministry in Wales (both Anglican and Nonconformist) was conducted for the most part in the Welsh language.[85] At the end of the century, David Lloyd George would carry elements of the Welsh preaching style to the wider British public in a different, but no less crusading oratorical context (see Conclusion).

The success of even the most notable English provincial and Scottish preachers notwithstanding, what made the second half of the nineteenth century a great age of preaching was the accumulation of a critical mass of popular preachers in London. The population of the metropolis was large enough to sustain the diversity, proximity, and popularity of a great many regular preachers, plus those that regularly came in from the provinces to hold meetings. The combination of the relatively large concentration of middle-class Londoners and the scarcity of respectable entertainments for the serious-minded filled the churches, chapels, cathedrals, tabernacles, and temples. The large concentration of working-class people and the poor brought in the revivalists. Besides the regular London population, there was the constant stream of tourists—their presence facilitated by macadamized roads and the railway—for whom hearing a certain preacher, or a number of preachers was one of the major attractions. International tourists from France, Germany, and the United States also came to the capital with preachers on their itineraries.

Without discussing every star preacher, something of the wide theological and homiletical range of religious oratory one could experience in London in the latter half of the century can be represented by two of the most successful preachers of the Victorian era who so neatly bracket that range: the Calvinist Baptist Charles Haddon Spurgeon, and the Tractarian Anglican Henry Parry Liddon.[86] While their theologies and the character of their sermons were poles apart, both Spurgeon and Liddon gained enormous renown and preached to hundreds of thousands of people from all walks of life. Their location in London made unprecedentedly large congregations and national celebrity possible. Like Dawson at his Church of the Saviour, both preachers were identified with the large structures that housed their audiences: Spurgeon at his Metropolitan Tabernacle in Southwark, and Liddon at St. Paul's Cathedral. They were the most prominent examples of the great age of preaching, the beginning of which can be dated from shortly after Spurgeon's arrival in London in 1853.

SPURGEON

Spurgeon was arguably the most popular and the most prolific preacher in nineteenth-century Britain. In his day, he was a figure of national and international standing—the subject of a profusion of newspaper and journal articles, popular biographies, collections of anecdotes, and various other sorts of "Spurgeonalia."[87] Spurgeon was raised amid preaching. His grandfather (with whom young Charles lived for a number of years) was a Congregational minister and his father a lay pastor.[88] As a small boy, Spurgeon is reported to have played preacher to a congregation of his siblings. The Calvinist orthodoxy of his upbringing caused Spurgeon's early teens to be marked by intense spiritual self-examination, resolved at age fifteen by his conversion on hearing a Primitive Methodist sermon (on Isaiah 45: 22—"Look unto Me, and be saved, all the ends of the earth").[89] Despite his Congregationalist upbringing, Spurgeon joined the other form of Calvinist Nonconformity prominent in the South and East of England and became a Baptist.

In 1850, the sixteen-year-old Spurgeon preached his first sermon during a cottage prayer meeting. The oratorical abilities he displayed on this occasion, particularly when combined with the novelty of his youth, quickly led to invitations to preach at other cottage meetings and chapels. Two years after preaching his first sermon, he was asked to become pastor of the Baptist congregation at Waterbeach (Cambridgeshire), where his preaching led to a doubling in the size of the congregation within a year. In 1853, Spurgeon was invited to deliver some sermons at the Baptist church in New Park Street, London, which was seeking to revive its declining fortunes. The following year, he agreed to become the church's pastor. During the four years of his apprenticeship in Cambridgeshire, Spurgeon had shown himself to be not merely an able preacher, but an energetic one. From his first sermon in August 1850 to his move to London in April 1854 (176 weeks), Spurgeon preached around 670 times.[90]

At New Park Street, Spurgeon rapidly fulfilled, then exceeded, expectations. As *Vanity Fair* recalled in 1870 without too much hyperbole, the chapel "soon overflowed with his audiences, so that the narrow streets were blocked, and the public-houses were crowded with those who could not find room in the chapel."[91] Less than a year after Spurgeon became pastor of the moribund congregation the church required enlargement. While New Park Street was closed for renovations, Spurgeon moved his services to Exeter Hall. The notion of holding religious services in a secular public hall was controversial at the time, but highly successful. The spectacle of the twenty-year old preacher filling Exeter Hall to capacity (around 5,000 people) and the overflow clogging a major London thoroughfare further advanced the Spurgeon phenomenon. His startling success and the publicity it generated assisted the passage that summer of Lord Shaftesbury's bill to remove the ban on holding Anglican services for more than twenty persons outside a church, and inspired Bishop Tait to hire Exeter Hall for Anglican services. Opponents of both the bill and the use of public halls for Anglican worship spoke derisively of "Spurgeonism."

When Spurgeon returned to New Park Street in 1855 it was clear that the enlargement just completed could not accommodate the size of audience he now regularly drew. After preaching in an open field he wrote, "I climbed to the summit of a minister's glory. My congregation was enormous, I think ten thousand, but certainly twice as many as at Exeter Hall."[92] Spurgeon re-engaged Exeter Hall the following year, but it too was no longer adequate. While plans were made and funds raised for the construction of a building sufficient for his needs, Spurgeon moved his services to another secular venue—the Surrey Gardens Music Hall, which held up to 12,000 people. Tragedy joined celebrity and controversy when, on October 19, 1856, someone raised an alarm of fire in the middle of a crowded service. The ensuing stampede resulted in seven deaths and numerous injuries. The incident gave some temporary ammunition to Spurgeon's critics, but the overall effect was simply to further spread the news of the young preacher who could command such crowds. In 1857, Spurgeon preached at the Crystal Palace to an audience that, according to the turnstiles, numbered 23,654. Two months later, an Anglican clergyman was not far off the mark when, in a carping letter, he wrote that the chief characteristic of Spurgeon's preaching "seems to be that its effectiveness is in proportion to the multitude addressed."[93]

In 1861, Spurgeon commenced services at the Metropolitan Tabernacle. Located near the Elephant and Castle in Southwark, the Tabernacle was built with 3,600 seats, additional seating (side flaps, seats in the aisles, etc.) for 1,000, and room for more than another thousand to squeeze in. At capacity, therefore, the Tabernacle held around 6,000 people. Thus, with three services, Spurgeon preached to around 18,000 weekly. In design, it was not a church, but rather a great preaching hall. On the outside, rejecting the Gothic Revival style that was becoming standard even for Nonconformist chapels, the front of the Tabernacle featured a neoclassical portico and columns. Inside, there was no altar, or pulpit, or any other elements of church architecture. Spurgeon delivered his sermons from behind the railing of a gallery that projected out over the Tabernacle's floor. Soon "Spurgeon's Tabernacle" was one of the sights to be seen when visiting London as well as (if one could get tickets) a Spurgeon sermon. Although he did manage to deliver a few sermons elsewhere, a significant portion of his correspondence is devoted to declining invitations due to work, ill health, or both. As he later wrote to another popular minister, Henry Allon:

> I cannot leave my pulpit for any cause but illness, for, alas, that cause takes me away so much. Moreover if I c[oul]d do so I w[oul]d be in an evil case—since the moment I went for one I sh[oul]d have to do it for another or give grievous offence. I am happy in having the love of my brethren but it rather embarrasses me at times.[94]

The Tabernacle's official congregation count passed 5,000 in 1877, and reached its highest level in 1882 with 5,427 members. Although there was some fall-off after 1882, the congregation never fell below 5,300 during the last nine years of Spurgeon's ministry and life.[95] According to contemporary observations, the crowds that gathered to hear the Pastor of the Tabernacle were predominantly lower middle class and upper artisanal in character, with a higher than usual proportion of men in attendance (notable because women were believed to be generally more susceptible to preaching, particularly of the evangelical variety). "The congregation seems very equally divided among males and females, and consists almost exclusively of the middle class. There is no symptom of the very poor, or, to judge by outward appearance, of the very rich."[96] A few years later, another reporter noted: "We do not observe any of the very poor." Instead, the congregation appeared "to be in the social zone between the mechanic and the successful but not fashionable tradesman. We find no one as low as a working man, no one who follows any liberal or learned profession."[97] George Eliot readily apprehended the lower-middle class profile of Spurgeon's audience. After accompanying a friend to a Tabernacle service in 1870, she wrote snobbishly of Spurgeon's "superficial, Grocer's-back-parlour view of Calvinistic Christianity."[98]

Although the Tabernacle was large, the Pastor's ability to draw listeners was much larger. Spurgeon managed this demand in a number of ways. He preached twice on Sundays and once during the week. Those wishing to attend one of the Tabernacle services were required to obtain tickets beforehand. Perhaps most important in accommodating demand, however, was the Tabernacle staff, which according to numerous accounts was expert at packing in the crowds. These measures notwithstanding, Spurgeon still could not meet the demand to hear him preach. In the late 1870s, therefore, he began to ask his regulars to forego attendance once per quarter in order to leave the Tabernacle free for all comers. These "open houses" proved quite successful and routinely filled the Tabernacle to capacity. The press regularly commented, not only on the size of these special audiences, but also their social breadth. One newspaper account of an open service in 1878 describes the Tabernacle

> thronged by members of different religious sects and of different nationalities, many of the French, German, American, and other tourists at present sojourning in London being observable amongst the congregation . . . . The gentler sex were decidedly in the minority, which is seldom the case with religious assemblies, but which may be accounted for by the fact that numbers present had come long distances, and towards evening the aspect of the weather had grown threatening. Every quarter of London had, in all probability, contributed to the throng, and perhaps well-nigh every shire in England. Judging by outward appearances, the great bulk of those present belonged to the middle-class, though the poor and well-to-do were fairly represented. There was a tolerable sprinkling of ministers scattered throughout the building, a popular Congregational divine occupying a prominent seat in the lower gallery. The sombre dress of the gathering, as a whole, was relieved by the scarlet uniforms of some half a dozen soldiers—not that the presence of the military is anything new in the Tabernacle.[99]

In addition to preaching to crowds at the Tabernacle and elsewhere, Spurgeon built up around himself a large, multifarious empire. Other than the orphanage he founded, most of Spurgeon's enterprises capitalized in one way or another on his oratory. Pastor's College (now Spurgeon's College), founded in 1856, provided instruction in theology, but its real significance lay in the way it functioned as a kind of oratorical master class. It did not accept novices, but rather men who had already served for at least two years in the pulpit and had demonstrated some aptitude for preaching. Spurgeon himself conducted the preaching class. Ten years after its founding, Pastor's College alone accounted for one-third of the students at Britain's nine Baptist colleges, and at least one-third of the revenues. By the time of Spurgeon's death in 1892, nearly 900 men had received their training at Pastor's College.[100]

Perhaps the greatest outgrowth of Spurgeon's oratorical powers was the printing of his sermons.[101] Spurgeon's sermons had begun to appear in the *Penny Pulpit* soon after his arrival at New Park Street. As Spurgeon recalled in his autobiography, "I conceived in my heart the idea that, some time or other, I should have a 'Penny Pulpit' of my own."[102] In 1855, inspired by the good sales of his sermons in the *Penny Pulpit* and confident of his abilities and "market," Spurgeon, with his friend the publisher Joseph Passmore, launched his own weekly series of printed sermons, the *New Park Street Pulpit*, later continued as the *Metropolitan Tabernacle Pulpit*.

The production of Spurgeon's printed sermons was a highly organized process over which the preacher exercised absolute control. The Metropolitan Tabernacle had a *de facto* "press gallery" where a shorthand scribe took down the sermon as delivered.[103] Spurgeon would then personally edit successive longhand drafts and proofs before the sermon was finally published.[104] That Spurgeon's sermons were virtually uniform in length made the publication process easier. "Constant habit," he described, "enables me generally to give the same amount of matter on each occasion, the slight variation almost surprises myself; from forty to forty-five minutes' speaking exactly fills the available space and saves the labour of additions and the still more difficult task of cutting down."[105]

Spurgeon's sermons sold extremely well in Britain and elsewhere (especially in the United States), and they were eventually translated into a great number of languages. By the time Spurgeon's *Pulpit* produced its five-hundredth weekly number in March 1863, more than eight million copies of his sermons had been sold world-wide.[106] The revenues supplemented Spurgeon's vigorous fund-raising efforts for his various institutions and causes. After Spurgeon's death in 1892, enough sermons remained to continue the weekly series until 1917—and beyond but for wartime paper shortages. The 3,561 collected sermons run to 63 large volumes. The posthumous output of his sermons, and the extent to which they continue to be read, fully justified Spurgeon's epitaph from Hebrews 11:4, which became the motto for Spurgeon's empire after his passing: "He being dead yet speaketh."

Spurgeon's preaching ability was his capital—the source of his fame and fortune, the basis of his power and influence. During his life and afterwards, many have sought to understand his phenomenal and enduring success. According to one contemporary:

> His mind teems with large, practical thoughts of common interest; he is a master of the language daily employed by the middle classes of London; he has a voice which enables him to easily convey his words to the most distant member of his audiences. These are indis-

> pensable conditions to success in moving masses of English people. And they must be conjoined; neither of them can safely be absent or appear by substitute.[107]

A somewhat more critical contemporary assessment does not vary greatly in its identification of the important elements of Spurgeon's preaching style: "Energy, and violence, and homely similes, and a powerful voice are the elements upon which his popularity seem to rest."[108] More critical still—but also agreeing with these other accounts—was George Eliot, who credited Spurgeon with "a fine voice, very flexible and various; he is admirably clear in his language," but "was shocked to find how low the mental pitch of our society must be, judged by the standard of this man's celebrity."[109]

Later analysts have viewed Spurgeon's sermons as models of evangelistic preaching: his voice was clear and expressive; his speech was straightforward and colloquial; he discussed the day's Biblical text with analogies that recommended themselves to his audiences' common observations and experiences; he delivered his message, not to the mind, but to the emotions of his hearers. In addition to his oratorical skills, Spurgeon projected moral authority in his strong vocation, in his undoubting, if crude, understanding of Calvinistic doctrines, and in his unscholarly, but thorough knowledge of the Bible.[110] As the manner of his speech was plain, the matter of his sermons was simple. He found his sermon in the text, rather than using the text to introduce a sermon on a given topic, theological or otherwise. As one contemporary commentator in the religious press put it, part of the power of Spurgeon's preaching lay in the way he used the text as a "seed truth" from which grew his sermon.[111] The same writer (in rather overwrought prose) also identified the simple message that underlay the "inexhaustible variety" of Spurgeon's prolific output:

> The preacher is discussing essentially the same familiar truths over and over again; he is presenting the same great Saviour to lost sinners, with what might seem lavish fidelity to the spirit and even to the letter of the written Word; and yet his setting forth of truth, his shades of thought, and his modes of illustration, always arrange themselves in new forms and colours, with well nigh the variety of the combination and tints of the clouds at setting sun.[112]

Spurgeon adhered rigidly to his own simple theological views and proved quite willing to separate himself from those who did not agree with them—notably the Evangelical Alliance in 1864, and the Baptist Union in 1887. His willingness to sever useful alliances underscores the power and self-sufficiency attained by the Spurgeon empire. On the other hand, this evident self-sufficiency also reflects some natural, or self-imposed limits on the Spurgeon phenomenon. With a following that was highly personal, Spurgeon does not appear to have contemplated transforming his empire into his own sect or denomination—even when he thought the general state of the Baptist faith was in decline. Additionally, although his reputation and influence were national, Spurgeon's power base always remained local to South London. His printed sermons may have enjoyed astounding world-wide sales, but the success of the printed sermons was predicated on the success of their initial "live" delivery in securing and holding a mass audience.

But all of this hardly explains why Spurgeon was acknowledged in his time and afterwards as "the most famous preacher in an age of great preachers."[113] It is always difficult to identify the factors that lie at the root of a popular phenomenon. It is far easier to see how interest was sustained than how it was first sparked. For Spurgeon, as in so many cases, success was generated by success—lots of people came to hear him, because lots of people were already coming to hear him. All accounts of his life depict Spurgeon as a fully developed preacher of the highest caliber from his first sermon in a Cambridgeshire cottage at age sixteen, and perhaps this was the case. Certainly, he must have absorbed a great deal of practical knowledge about preaching from his grandfather and father, but this does not account for the phenomenon he so quickly became. After all, although Spurgeon began his career in a region where Baptists and Congregationalists were the dominant form of Nonconformity, according to the 1851 religious census, only 4.5 percent of the population were Baptists. Relative to the population of England, Baptist membership leveled off beginning in the 1840s, and began to decline from the middle of the 1880s.[114]

Spurgeon's youth certainly played an important part in his attracting notice. As a "boy preacher" he was a novelty act in an era and an area where public entertainment was scarce. Indeed, after his move to London, it took some time for those outside preacher's sway to treat him seriously. This did not prevent Spurgeon from gaining a large following. The interest of a boy preacher lies not simply in his youth, but also in his ability to preach in a manner that seems beyond his years. That Spurgeon was made pastor at the tender age of eighteen is testimony to the seriousness with which his abilities in the pulpit were viewed, but one cannot divorce his early appeal at this point from the fact of his youth. It was not long, however, before the moon-faced, long-haired, buck-toothed lad who revived the New Park Street Chapel grew into the obese, bearded, gouty man who continued to hold large audiences rapt at the Metropolitan Tabernacle. Spurgeon carried into his mature career the great lesson of his days as a boy preacher: the motivations which lead people to come through the chapel doors are of no importance; once they are seated under his pulpit, the preacher's job is to convince them. The same principle was later applied to the quarterly open houses at the Metropolitan Tabernacle, as Spurgeon's closing remarks on one such occasion demonstrate: "Our preaching is so much like a fiddler's play, people come to see how we do it. Now I don't care what you think of me so long as you can see something in what I say."[115]

A significant aspect of Spurgeon's more lasting public appeal is indicated by the way he was regularly likened to that other great contemporary Nonconformist orator, John Bright. These comparisons reflect an aspect of Spurgeon that the biographical literature typically plays down or passes over altogether: his involvement in secular politics. In fact, as one scholar has convincingly shown, the Pastor of the Tabernacle was politically active to a significant degree, particularly during the period from the late 1860s to the mid-1880s.[116] In his writings, speeches, correspondence, and conversation, Spurgeon openly avowed his support for the Liberals and he was seen by some as "the greatest single influence in South London in favour of Liberalism."[117]

Those who compared Spurgeon and Bright sometimes mention physical characteristics—a strong face, a "homely" figure.[118] Most important, however, the connection between the two men rested in the main on the qualities that were ascribed to both men's oratory. After being taken to one of Spurgeon's lectures, Matthew Arnold wrote that it was "a most striking performance, and reminded one very much of Bright's."[119] According to one newspaper's description of a crowded service at the Tabernacle, the prayer was "delivered with as musical an intonation, as clear an enunciation, and a diction as purely Saxon as Mr. Bright's."[120] In an obituary, another newspaper wrote that the "web of his speech was as simple as that of John Bright's, and the effect he produced on his hearers was strikingly similar."[121]

However, it was not only the quality of Spurgeon's body, voice, and diction that led people to compare him to Bright. Spurgeon was viewed as the religious counterpart to Bright's "tribune of the people." An 1879 article on Spurgeon in the pulpit could have as easily been written about Bright in Parliament: "It is pleasant to hear once more half an hour of wholesome Saxon all aglow with earnestness and sparkling with homely wit. You yield yourself irresistibly to its fascination, and cannot help feeling that after all this is better stuff than most of the fine talking and Latin quotations and elaborate periods heard elsewhere."[122] As might also have been said about Bright, "The British public had arrived at the conviction that he [Spurgeon] was absolutely sincere, simple, unpretending and straightforward."[123] Thus, both Spurgeon and Bright enjoyed a lasting public appeal based on their perceived earnestness and plain-spoken Englishness (the "Saxon" qualities). In addition, Spurgeon and Bright were cheered for their ability, not only to outshine the forces of tradition in their respective areas of public life (the Church of England and aristocratic Parliament), but also, in a sense, to elevate religion and politics morally through their oratory. As one journalist wrote of Spurgeon: "His influence is not confined to his own neighborhood nor his own denomination. In the Church of England and in other Churches, his example has provoked more earnest and efficacious preaching."[124]

LIDDON

Spurgeon can be seen as having extended the evangelical pulpit in unprecedented ways and on an unprecedented scale. However, to attribute captivating religious oratory, mass congregations, and general influence on social mores wholly to evangelicals—Nonconformist or Anglican—is to overlook one of the most important examples of a preaching star to emerge in the second half of the nineteenth century. Henry Parry Liddon stands out as the single greatest demonstration that one did not need to be evangelical in the slightest to achieve great popularity in the Victorian pulpit. Liddon was a leading Tractarian—indeed, he was, among other things, the official biographer of Edward B. Pusey, whose name became synonymous with the ultra-High Church party that emerged from the Oxford Movement of the 1830s and 1840s. Taken along with those of the other great preachers of his time, Liddon's career exemplifies, not only the deep appeal of preaching in the second half of the nineteenth century, but also its breadth.

Liddon's first religious influences, his mother and his aunt Louisa, were strongly evangelical, and his penchant for religious life was manifested quite early. Like Spurgeon (and, doubtless, many other nineteenth-century children), young Liddon liked to play clergyman. Different from the young Spurgeon, however, (and a foretaste of his later ritualism), it is said that he preached to congregations of his playmates wearing a sheet of newspaper for clerical vestments.[125] Beyond make-believe, Liddon began to compose sermons when still a boy. Unlike his newsprint surplice, these early sermons reflected his evangelical surroundings, with titles like "The Danger of Procrastination" and "Preparation for Judgement." As he got older, Liddon's evangelical inclinations began to fade, as can be seen in a notebook of sermons composed in 1844 while he was at King's College School. Sermons with titles like "On Love" and "On Death" are more meditative in character and display less of the evangelical preoccupation with personal salvation.[126] According to the reminiscences of some schoolmates, Liddon was "a Priest among boys,"[127] and he appears to have already decided on taking holy orders before he went up to Oxford in 1846.

Liddon did not cut a great figure in undergraduate society. He joined the Union, but was not an active member.[128] His energies were focused on spiritual development. He affiliated himself with John Keble, whom he later described as "the best and wisest man whom he had known intimately in life,"[129] and found in Pusey a lifelong mentor. At Oxford, Liddon shed whatever vestiges of his evangelical upbringing that remained. The sermons he composed as an undergraduate, such as "The Communion of Saints" and "The Terms of Penitence," bear the unmistakable imprint of the Oxford Movement. In general, Liddon's life at Oxford and immediately afterward conformed to the pattern for beginning Anglican clerical life. He took his degree (a second in Classics) in 1850, and obtained the Johnson Theological Scholarship in the following year. In 1852 he began work as a curate in Wantage (Berkshire) where he preached his first sermon, and a year later was ordained a priest.

Before his ordination, Liddon traveled to Rome. Following the Anglican defections to Catholicism that had so damaged the Oxford Movement a few years earlier, this was perhaps the way for a serious young Puseyite to test his Anglican convictions. Certainly Liddon was tested. No less a person than Pius IX's Chamberlain, Monsignor Talbot (who had "gone over to Rome" in 1847), actively pursued Liddon's conversion. Whether Liddon was ever genuinely tempted or not, nothing strengthens convictions like rejecting advances. Having stared Catholicism in the eye and not blinked, Liddon returned to England confirmed in his high Anglican Puseyism.

Following his ordination, Liddon spent roughly the next decade in various educational institutions: Vice Principal of Cuddesdon College (a High Church theological school), and Vice Principal of St. Edmund's Hall, Oxford. After illness made it necessary for him to leave St. Edmund's in 1862, he was appointed Select Preacher to Oxford. Two years later, he began working under the High Church Bishop of Salisbury, Walter Ker Hamilton. In 1870, Liddon was installed into the position where he gained the greatest renown, Canon of St. Paul's Cathedral in London.

The influence of Pusey, Keble, and Hamilton was strong and enduring (Liddon was even successful at turning his staunchly evangelical Aunt Louisa to a fuller appreciation of the sacraments by the time of her final illness[130]). In addition to writing Pusey's biography, Liddon was also instrumental in establishing the even more durable memorials at Oxford, Keble College and Pusey House. Notwithstanding setbacks (such as being forced to resign from Cuddesdon during a public scandal over the College's "Catholic" teachings), Liddon upheld the Puseyite cause with uncompromising vigor. He inveighed against the Broad Church *Essays and Reviews* (1861) and later against the treachery of the High Church *Lux Mundi* (1889). He also strongly opposed the secularization of the universities. In Church matters, he was actively concerned with points of ritual worship, such as insisting on the correctness of a priest facing East when celebrating the Eucharist, or arguing against dropping the Athanasian creed from Anglican worship—stands which brought him into direct conflict with Archbishop Tait.

Where Liddon differed from his mentors was in the manner in which he applied his Tractarian beliefs. The Oxford Movement did not lay great stress on preaching. John Henry Newman's sermons to Oxford students were famous and influential, but they were far from the greater part of his work. Their accomplishments in the pulpit aside, Pusey and Keble were primarily concerned with justifying their positions through theological scholarship. Liddon, on the other hand, found his true calling in preaching rather than scholarship. (Perhaps one reason for this was Liddon's belief in his unfitness as a scholar because he attained only second-class honors at Oxford—a fact he later felt disqualified him from accepting the offer to become the first head of Keble College.) In 1864, Pusey criticized Liddon for concentrating so much of his energies on his sermons at the expense of scholarship: "Called on Dr. P., who was very sharp. . . . 'You preach sermons an hour long at St. Paul's, and nobody hears you, and you are knocked up for a fortnight afterwards. You have done nothing.'"[131] If his youthful efforts at writing sermons are any indication, Liddon had early developed an inclination toward preaching. And although emphasizing preaching was considered by many to be a Low Church sort of thing, Liddon managed to wed his affinity for the pulpit with his ultra-High Church views. In particular, rather than the popular preaching of Protestantism, he made a study of the great ecclesiastical preachers of Catholic France.

Although Pusey's contention that nobody heard Liddon at St. Paul's was surely wrong, he was correct in identifying the self-sacrificing element of Liddon's preaching. Liddon regularly exhausted himself in the pulpit, and was sometimes incapacitated for several days after the effort. Preaching on the Victorian scale could take a considerable physical toll. For Liddon, this was so from the outset of his career. Writing to his Aunt Louisa in 1853, the young curate described his heavy preaching burdens and their physical effects:

> Yesterday evening [Wednesday] I preached an extempore sermon in the parish Church on Isaiah 53.4 three quarters of an hour long, and have quite lost my voice in consequence, besides having a swollen throat. But I need to be better tomorrow: I had preached a rather shorter one on Tuesday and suppose that the two coming together were too much for me. Any how I shall have to preach again tomorrow [Friday] evening, Saturday, and Sunday so that you see we really have plenty to do.[132]

Leaving his cure did not relieve Liddon's oratorical burdens. There was plenty of preaching to be done in and around Cuddesdon. Liddon's abilities in the pulpit gained wider renown when he was asked by Bishop Wilberforce in 1858 to deliver a course of Lenten sermons at Oxford—a course he continued for many years. The recognition he gained from these sermons led to many offers to preach all over the country. Although his duties at St. Edmund's Hall (including well-attended theological lectures) obliged him to decline many offers during this period, he also accepted a good number. In 1860 alone, in addition to his other work, Liddon preached 42 sermons in various places around the country.[133] Liddon occasionally registered some regret at the length of his sermons: "The sermon about an hour in length—This is a wretched mistake."[134] Similarly, of an Easter Sunday in Sarum he wrote: "Preacht in evening on *Ps: 118:24*: at St.

Thomas'. *1* hr. *20* minutes. Not so tired as on Good Friday evening. Feel again that I have preacht too long a time."[135]

Throughout the 1860s, Liddon added to his oratorical and pulpit successes, including delivering the Bampton Lectures (at short notice!) in 1866, and preaching to the Queen in 1868. In 1870, the Bishop of London asked Liddon to give a course of Lenten sermons at St. James's in Piccadilly (one of London's most affluent areas) and to deal particularly with the religious difficulties that faced educated society. Despite the length of the lectures (upward of three hours each), St. James's was thronged throughout Liddon's course.

> For several Sundays the space in front of the church has, more than half-an-hour before the beginning of the service, been thronged by a fashionable concourse, which has eagerly waited for the opening of the door, and has pushed in to the lobby with the unceremonious vigour of a plebeian mob a the pit-entrance of a theatre on a 'first night.' Elegantly-dressed ladies have endangered shawls, bonnets, and tempers in the crush; fashionably-dressed men have not scrupled to use their physical strength to get a good place; and, five minutes after the opening of the doors, every free seat has been filled. By three o'clock not a single seat has been unoccupied, and throughout the service the passages have been crammed.[136]

These oratorical triumphs notwithstanding, what Liddon was best known for in his time, and best remembered for afterward, was his preaching at St. Paul's. In the early 1860s, when cathedral services were still a recent innovation, he was invited to preach at both Westminster Abbey and St. Paul's. Liddon's diary records his great excitement at preaching his first cathedral sermon at the Abbey in June 1861. Accustomed to large congregations by the standards of local churches, at the Abbey he experienced his first audience of thousands: "Between *2000* & *3000* in Nave of Abbey; wh[ich] was perfectly full."[137] Although Liddon would ultimately be identified with the cathedral pulpit, his early experiences of cathedral preaching were not all so positive. In 1863, he preached his first sermon at what would eventually become *his* pulpit, St. Paul's, and was far from satisfied with himself: "Did as well as I could: but feel that the sermon was a miss. The Dean told me I was 1 hr. 10 min. & that I exerted myself too much to be heard."[138]

On Easter Sunday 1870, ten days before his installation as Canon of St.

Paul's, Liddon preached at the Cathedral to a congregation of 8,000 people.[139] Each of St. Paul's four canons spent three months of the year "in residence," during which time they would deliver sermons. In his first year, Liddon's months of residence were set as May, September, and January. This schedule conflicted with his duties as Ireland Professor of Exegesis at Oxford, so beginning in 1871 his residence was shifted to months when the University was in recess—April, August, and December. As a result of this change, Liddon was in residence during the most popular holidays: Easter, Advent, and Christmas.[140]

Liddon delivered his first sermon as Canon after the accepted fashion, from the choir. The following week, however, he decided to move closer to the congregation seated in the nave and "went into [the] Dome Pulpit."[141] To that point, preaching from under the dome had only been done for special Sunday services during the Winter. Liddon made it his regular practice. Thereafter, Liddon always entered in his diary "Preached under Dome," as though the novelty never quite wore off. In addition to making him more immediate and audible to the congregation, Liddon's move beneath the dome enhanced the drama of his performances in several ways: the area under the dome provided a more spectacular and monumental backdrop to his oratory; he filled the vast space with his voice; and the acoustics of the dome area gave his voice greater effect. Despite successes in bringing in large numbers of people, cathedral services had failed to duplicate the kind of oratorical excitement of to be found at places like the Metropolitan Tabernacle. Liddon's great success as a cathedral preacher was precisely that he did not aim for an evangelical effect, but rather produced an oratory that was suited to the venue.

Although his wider oratorical reputation had already been established by his earlier cathedral preaching and the Piccadilly sermons, Liddon's regular presence at St. Paul's during the most popular holidays gave him a celebrity unprecedented for an Anglican clergyman. As a younger colleague later recalled: "His sermons at St. Paul's for twenty years formed a central fact of London life."[142] Published collections of his sermons enjoyed brisk sales and went into several editions during his lifetime. His sermons also appeared in pages of the religious press and in the *Penny Pulpit.* Liddon invariably preached to a full nave, although his sermons had not grown any shorter. In his case, as one observer described, "you will not, however, be fatigued, but will merely fancy that your watch has played you a trick when you consult it at the end of the discourse."[143] Visitors to London, whether from other parts of Britain or from other countries, made certain to see Liddon at St. Paul's. After discussing an American tourist who had "booked" Liddon for the previous Sunday, one writer observed in 1884, "Most of the people who go to hear the eloquent Canon . . . would pay—and very liberally—to get seats near the pulpit."[144] In 1880, Archbishop Tait held out Liddon's St. Paul's as an ideal to be emulated by other cathedrals:

> It must be granted that St. Paul's Cathedral has no easy task, in the very centre of modern civilization, surrounded by four millions of people, a vast number of whom have no connexion with the Church which St. Paul's typifies. Yet I am bound to say that, during late years, a great work has been done in that cathedral. No one can enter it on a weekday or on Sunday without seeing that it has laid hold of the hearts of the people of that great metropolis.[145]

In his preaching career, Liddon delivered both extempore and composed sermons. At the outset of his curacy he wrote out his sermons, but soon the demand for his preaching made extempore preaching a necessity. Later, at both Cuddesdon and St. Edmund's Hall, the responsibility of providing theological instruction to university students naturally led Liddon to compose his sermons and lectures. Outside these collegiate institutions, however, he continued to deliver extempore sermons for his heavy schedule of preaching engagements. After Liddon became Canon of St. Paul's, he wrote out his sermons with particular care and seldom deviated from the text. His composition was facilitated by the fact that, after going to St. Paul's, Liddon seldom preached elsewhere, but there were also practical considerations. The effort to master the acoustical dynamics of St. Paul's and to be heard by the audiences that filled its large nave was a tremendous strain. Liddon "used to say that he found the constant effort to control his voice so as to suit the acoustic conditions of the Cathedral distracted his attention and made clearness of thought more difficult."[146]

Liddon's sermons were long—typically over an hour, and sometimes over an hour and a half. Even Liddon himself thought his sermons too long, but the nature of his sermons conduced to length. This is because, instead of emotional appeals, Liddon's sermons presented arguments. "When he preached," one hearer recalled, "it was a substantial, a large meal for the mind and spirit that was eaten at the table he spread."[147]

Compared to a sermon of spiritual exhortation, which is rhetorical in character, an argumentative or didactic sermon follows its logical course to its reasoned conclusion. A preacher has far more flexibility when building to a rhetorical climax: it is easier to jettison ideas and save time when the purpose is to evoke certain feelings among the congregation. One cannot so easily elide points of an argument without that argument losing its overall force and effect.

In addition to the great number of Liddon's sermons that were published, he also left behind many of the pages of notes from his extempore sermons.[148] These outlines clearly reveal the general pattern of Liddon's argumentative structure—a structure that has been epitomized as follows:

Introduction.
Part I.
  Objection I.
    Answer.
  Objection II.
    Answer.
Part II.
  Division 1.
  Division 2.
  Division 3.
  Division 4.
Part III.
  [Digression.]
Appeals.
  Consolation.
  Exhortation.[149]

While this is a composite structure not fully observed in any single sermon, it does represent the general form of Liddon's outlines. What the outlines reveal is that Liddon's sermons were not only highly organized, but also elaborate in their argumentative structure. This can be contrasted to the extremely simple structure of Spurgeon's sermons-for example, in 1859 sermon on Hebrews 12:2 ("Looking unto Jesus the author and finisher of our faith; who for the joy that was set before him endured the cross, despising the shame, and is set down at the right hand of the throne of God."):

I. <u>There was even in the dying Saviour's heart a deep joy.</u>
It sounds from the cries.
"Father forgive them"
"Today shall thou &[c.]"
"Into thy hands &c."
"It is finished."
The joy that was set before him shone over all.

II. <u>The cross is bright with joy to us.</u>

what we see.
1. There we see God's love to sinners
2. There we see Christ's love to death
3. There sin is ended and evil overcome
4. There Satan is defeated
5. There death is slain.

There are also views available.
To sufferers Jesus their companion
To sinners Jesus their friend
To the weary Jesus their rest
To the warring Jesus conquering
To the preacher Jesus the attraction
To the love of unity Jesus the centre
To the doubting Jesus the guarantee
To the dying Jesus the pioneer.[150]

Spurgeon's sermons neither made an argument, nor proved a case. The Truth—the rightness of what he was saying—he took to be self-evident. It was not disputation, but exhortation. Liddon's sermons, however, were not necessarily less clear as a result of their analytical character. The structure may have been complex, but the language was not. This is clear in an example selected almost at random:

> Let us try to take it to pieces. Let us ask ourselves why he [St. Paul], a man who knew what words meant, a man of reason rather than of impulse, a man whose life expressed the sincerity with which he uttered this very expression—let us ask ourselves why he called his master's religion "the glorious Gospel of the Blessed God."[151]

As one observer put it, Liddon was "master of a style lucid, explanatory."[152] While his discourses were long and involved, Liddon's pulpit manner was characterized by "a total freedom from pomposity."[153] Examining the secret of Liddon's success, another contemporary account stated: "In the first place, he has something to say. Instead of clap-trap sentiment, or vague declamation, he gives the results of long study and careful thought."[154] He led his audiences through the progress of his argument, and his practice of raising, then answering objections to his own premise made his sermons a far more engaging discourse than simply informing the congregation on the correctness of a particular belief or doctrine.

All these aspects of his sermons—the sense of analytical precision, clarity of language, explicit structure, and thorough exposition—were viewed in terms of the quality by which Liddon was most generally known in the pulpit: his *earnestness*. In his sermons, Liddon conveyed his own firm beliefs, and presented positive arguments to support those beliefs. One of the best descriptions of the impression Liddon made upon hearers is contained in an 1876 letter from the future Archbishop of Canterbury, E. W. Benson:

> His beautiful look and penetrating voice are powerful over one, and then his reasoning is very persuasive. He does not make leaps, and dismiss one with allusions, or assume that one knows anything. He tells it all from beginning to end, and seems to assume nothing. But all his physical and intellectual structure is quite swallowed up in spiritual earnestness, and he is different to other preachers, in that one feels that his preaching is in itself a self-sacrifice to him—not a vanity or a gain.[155]

IV. OTHER PREACHING STARS

While Spurgeon and Liddon were arguably the most prominent London preachers, there were many others from across the theological and homiletical spectrum that helped make the second half of the nineteenth century a great age of preaching. To sample this range briefly, among the most successful and well-regarded were the Broad-Church Anglican Frederic William Farrar,[156] the very Broad-Church Anglican turned independent Stopford Augustus Brooke,[157] the Congregationalist Joseph Parker,[158] and the Methodist William Morley Punshon.[159]

Like Spurgeon and Liddon, three of these preachers were identified with the places in which they delivered their sermons. Farrar, after many years as a master at Harrow and head master at Marlborough, was made a Canon at

Westminster Abbey and Rector of St. Margaret's, Westminster (thus, unlike Liddon, Farrar had regular parochial duties in addition to those of a Canon). Brooke gained his great fame as a preacher at two proprietary chapels in London: St. James's Chapel on York Street from 1866 to 1875, and the Bedford Chapel on New Oxford Street from 1875 to 1894. Both these chapels were on the small side—seating around 400 and around 600, respectively—but Brooke filled them to overflowing. Before he seceded from the Church of England in 1880, Brooke had also been able to hold the attention of large audiences as a guest preacher at Westminster Abbey.[160] Parker, after a successful ministry of eleven years in Manchester, accepted an invitation in 1869 to minister at London's languishing Poultry Chapel with the understanding that a new and larger space would be constructed for him. In 1874, after some interim moves, Parker preached his first sermon at the "City Temple," a great classical edifice erected on the Holborn Viaduct, which could hold up to 3,000 people. Punshon did not become identified with a particular pulpit because, according to the Methodist practice, he was posted to circuits for only a few years at a time. Nevertheless, much of his preaching career was spent in various parts of London. Punshon was particularly successful at increasing the size of already thriving circuits and reviving moribund ones to the point that they divided to form several new circuits.

In the pulpit, all of these preachers had an appeal that was both large and broad, and each exemplified a different style of preaching. At Westminster Abbey and St. Margaret's, Farrar became one of London's major preaching attractions, and people came to see him in both his jobs. His style of preaching depended upon his venue. In the intimate St. Margaret's, he delivered extempore sermons that were known for their simple, informal, and good-natured tone. In Westminster Abbey, like Liddon at St. Paul's, he preached from written texts in a more elaborate, but also a more crowd-pleasing oratorical style. As one contemporary wrote of Farrar at the Abbey, "his ornate periods, metaphors, tropes and far-fetched comparisons diffuse ecstasy among those worshipers who derive their wisdom from penny newspapers."[161]

Brooke's affinity for preaching was great and manifested itself from the beginning of his clerical career. Less than a year after delivering his first sermon (and only a few days into his honeymoon), Brooke wrote to his brother, "I do so long to be in that little box (the pulpit) again. It is the only place and time in which I feel truly alive."[162] His highly composed sermons were famous for their polished literary qualities, and he combined elements of Broad Church theology like the humanity and historicity of

Jesus with Romantic literary themes like Love and Nature. Brooke's sermons appealed to educated sensibilities and his well-to-do audiences (often including prominent Tories) listened happily to his sermons criticizing materialism and social injustices. As Brooke wrote, "all my radicalism goes down their thrapple without a wry face."[163]

Parker was known for an epigrammatic style that gave his sermons on tried-and-true themes an air of novelty, as well as for (like Spurgeon) stressing the application of the Scriptures' key lessons to everyday life. The impression left by Parker, as one witness enthusiastically recalled, was one of "originality, individuality, freshness, richness, suggestiveness."[164] Punshon preached in the great Methodist tradition—pyrotechnic and hard-driving. Parker described Punshon's preaching as "rhetorical, theatrical, external, and thunder-like. It would, however, be a great mistake if any man regarded Punshon's discourses as mere conjuring in words."[165] Palmerston called Punshon the "Prince of Preachers"[166]—an epithet that would later, and more enduringly, be applied to Spurgeon.

The broad appeal of these four preachers can be seen in their audiences. As a leading attraction in one of London's two cathedrals, Farrar enjoyed the kind of diverse audience that comes to witness a spectacle. Brooke's audience is a little more complicated to assess. One member of the congregation attempted to describe the range and variety of his congregation:

> Opposite me in the gallery, I used to see Mr. Justice Mellish—one of the subtlest lawyers of his time. . . . After the sermon, I have seen Matthew Arnold walking thoughtfully down the staircase, detached and analytical. Neurotic women of Fashion and great place have I beheld, enraptured and enthusiastic, in the front seats. The young man about Town was present occasionally. . . . Then there were active members of Parliament, busy professional men, and quiet men of Letters, pretty ladies, and here and there the anxious young man, still troubled, because of his youth, to solve, or not to solve, the riddle of the world.[167]

Parker's capacity audiences at the City Temple tended to be largely male, and are reported to have covered a social range from workers to Members of Parliament. Further, at his Thursday afternoon services, ministers of denominations ranging from the Salvation Army to the Roman Catholic Church were regularly observed.[168] Punshon's broad appeal is evident in his great success at building and rebuilding Methodist circuits wherever he went. At the beginning of his career, one can see the demand across denominational lines for the kind of preaching that men like Punshon had to offer. In 1845, a group of Anglican parishioners at Marden, Kent, rejected their incumbent over the unacceptable level of his ritualism. Punshon, who was sent to answer the request, joked that he was now the incumbent of Marden. "There are, of course, no Methodists in the place and I shall have to try, under God, to *make* some."[169]

Extending their pulpit activities, all of these four preachers published their sermons in book and pamphlet form. Parker even had his own Spurgeon-like media outlet, the *Fountain*, which published his extempore sermons and prayers as reported from a shorthand writer's notes.[170] Additionally, all of these preachers engaged in a host of other lecturing and writing activities. Before becoming Canon at Westminster Abbey, Farrar had spent most of his career as a master or headmaster at public schools. During this period he wrote several novels centered on public school and university life. Later on, he also authored several historical novels and a host of other works. His greatest literary achievement, however, was his best-selling popular biography, *The Life of Christ* (1874). Brooke had a full-fledged second career as a man of letters.[171] He wrote a biography of F. W. Robertson, which became an important document for the Broad Church movement, and later on produced several volumes of literary, poetic, and dramatic criticism. In addition to his writing, Brooke mounted Sunday afternoon lecture series at his chapels that aimed both to break down what he felt to be the artificial boundaries between the sacred and the profane, and to broaden his appeal to the well-educated who did not normally go to church. At Bedford Chapel, he also started a debating society that counted George Bernard Shaw, William Morris, and Sidney Webb among its regular participants. Similarly, Parker used the City Temple for a host of quasi-religious lectures and similar activities. Punshon too had a significant career as a popular lecturer through which, over the years, he raised a significant amount of money for Methodist church-building and other causes.

There were also a number of notable women preachers in this period, even though no major denomination allowed women a place in the ministry. A tradition of preaching by women in Methodism was officially terminated by the Wesleyan Conference of 1803, although women in some Methodist sects (e.g. the Primitives) continued various kinds of preaching activities until the middle of the century.[172] By the middle of the century, however, women had become far more prominent in religious life generally. In terms of ministry, the profusion and experimentalism of religious activity encouraged a number of inspired women to discover their gift for preaching and apply it in a variety of circumstances.[173]

One of the most successful, if short-lived women preachers was Geraldine Hooper. Born to a genteel provincial family in Bath, Hooper was not remarkably pious until her conversion around age eighteen. Her ministry began with "family worship" prayer meetings for the poor. Soon, however, she began to preach in ever larger spaces, as increasing numbers of people who came to see the novelty of a "lady preacher" began to attend on a regular basis. Hooper was quickly launched upon a career as a public evangelist and was soon preaching in barns, halls, and the out-of-doors to audiences of thousands throughout southern England and beyond. Her largest audience may have been at Dunstable (Bedfordshire), where on several occasions, in a covered and heated space between two large factories, she preached to 7,000. Such irregular venues went hand-in-hand with the poor and working-class character of those to whom she most often preached. At one of her Dunstable services, it was observed, "Men with brawny arms and horny hands, wiped away the tears coursing down their cheeks."[174] When preaching in chapels and town halls, her audiences were liable to include more representatives of "respectable" society.

As a lady preacher, Hooper was the object of much criticism in religious circles (based on passages in the Bible that were interpreted as prohibiting women from preaching), as well as heckling at her services. Some clergymen are reported to have changed their views after hearing Hooper preach, and she also appears to have been adept at handling the unruly members of her audiences. On numerous occasions she was described as a female Spurgeon: "She is to her sex what Spurgeon is to her father's—a powerful, earnest, and most successful preacher of the Gospel."[175] Marriage did not affect her seemingly tireless preaching schedule, but the physical strain of her peripatetic evangelistic life was enormous. As one historian has written about in-demand Methodist preachers: "Over-worked, some of them all but preached themselves to death, but the popular thirst for eloquence could never be completely satisfied."[176] Hooper was 31 when she died. According to her friend and biographer, in the ten years from the time she first started preaching in 1862 until her death, Hooper "preached Christ not less than between four or five thousand times, and rarely without winning souls."[177]

Along with preaching colossi like Spurgeon and Liddon, these examples give some indication of the kind of mass popularity that preachers were able to attain during the second half of the nineteenth century. This popularity was achieved across the religious spectrum, throughout the country, and among all social classes. Both the production and consumption of religious oratory attained new heights in this period. That this was so need not be attributed wholly to the spiritual hunger of the Victorians at one extreme (since many were quite unconcerned with religion), or the relative paucity of mass entertainment at the other (since many were genuinely pious). Indeed, this was also a great period of atheist and agnostic public oratory, such as the famous debate at the British Association meeting in 1860 that pitted the evolutionist Thomas Henry Huxley against Bishop Samuel Wilberforce, or the meetings of the National Secular Society at which Charles Bradlaugh and Annie Besant drew audiences in the thousands.

One way that the profusion of preaching can be understood is within the wider context of public speech and public life in later nineteenth-century Britain. Before turning to more general conclusions about the production and consumption of religious oratory, however, the connection between preaching and public life is perhaps nowhere more evident than in the interactions between some of the era's most popular preachers and its leading statesman-orator.

The Word in Man: Gladstone and the Great Preachers

The connection between Gladstone's profound personal religiosity and his prodigious public career is one of the most important and most difficult questions with which Gladstone scholars have wrestled.[178] Gladstone was one of the most prominent High Churchmen of his time; yet his temperament owed more to the strict Presbyterianism and Low Church evangelicalism of his forebears.[179] Indeed, in both his public and private lives, Gladstone has been seen as one of the great avatars of the evangelical spirit with which the age is so often identified. His diaries reveal the great extent to which his private life was taken up with religious matters. In public life, it has been convincingly argued that the principal intersection of Gladstone's political and religious views was his desire to foster "religious nationality," but "from the mid-1870s Gladstone came to recognize that his personal religious opinions had to remain personal if he hoped to achieve political results."[180] Yet Gladstone's turn to the secular in politics by no means meant that his public life as Prime Minister and head of the Liberal party was devoid of religious interest or satisfaction. The ongoing linkages between Gladstone's public political and private religious worlds is clearly evident in his often overlooked, but extremely suggestive connections with a number of the most noted preachers of his time.

Gladstone's connections with great preachers underscore the broader connections between oratory, religion, politics, and personality in later nineteenth-century public life. Without offering a systematic study of Gladstone's relationships with his contemporaries of the cloth, these connections can be illustrated through his personal and political dealings with four of the era's most notable and successful pulpit figures: Liddon, Spurgeon, Parker, and Brooke. As a student and practitioner of oratory, Gladstone admired these preachers' powers in the pulpit. As a vigorously religious man, he sympathized with the essence of their Christian message. As a politician who helped create a new kind of mass politics, he observed their ability to bring together vast and diverse congregations. For their part, these preachers saw Gladstone as a man doing God's work in the secular world, and their approval and support helped to validate his sense of his own role in public affairs.

PERSONAL AND POLITICAL CONNECTIONS

As already described, Liddon, Spurgeon, Parker, and Brooke were very different people holding very different religious views and approaches. Accordingly, Gladstone related to and dealt with each in different ways. Of the four preachers, Liddon was most similar to Gladstone in background and religious outlook. Both had matriculated at Christ Church, and they shared a lifelong devotion to Oxford. Both had emerged from evangelical backgrounds to become High Churchmen. It is not surprising, therefore, that these two men should have great respect and sympathy for one another. Gladstone's diaries record many meetings and conversations with Liddon over a span of some thirty-odd years, and his papers include a great deal of correspondence between the two, written during the same period. In 1870, during his first ministry, Gladstone presided over Liddon's appointment as Canon of St. Paul's. Gladstone clearly valued Liddon's ability to convey High Church views so well to so many. In 1885—when seeking (unsuccessfully) to persuade Liddon to accept a bishopric—he wrote that "in this age of unparalleled conflict between belief and negation, Dr. Liddon is the greatest personal power in the country on the side of belief."[181]

Although there was much common ground between Gladstone and Liddon, Gladstone's connections with great preachers reached well beyond people of similar education and religious views. There is no better proof for this than his dealings with Spurgeon.[182] Spurgeon's correspondence with Gladstone began in 1869, when the Pastor of the Tabernacle was well established and the "People's William" had just begun his first ministry. On a number of occasions, Gladstone invited the Pastor to dinner or breakfast, but Spurgeon consistently declined the invitations—stating (typically for him) that he was either too busy, too ill, or both.[183] Despite his consistent refusals to dine, Spurgeon's letters to Gladstone were always warm and admiring. Gladstone himself came to regard the Pastor of the Tabernacle as a genuine man of God, even though Spurgeon was a Baptist with notably unsophisticated theological views (certainly compared to Gladstone's own). In 1884, in a letter congratulating Spurgeon on his upcoming fiftieth birthday, Gladstone wrote that, leaving aside their differences on particular points,

> There happily abides a vast inheritance of truth which we enjoy in common, and which in its central essence [is] found, as I rejoice to think, the basis of the faith of Christendom. I therefore ask to unite my voice with the voice of thousands in acknowledging that singular power with which you have so long testified on the world "of sin[,] of righteousness, and of judgement" and the splendid uprightness of public character and conduct which have I believe contributed perhaps equally with your eloquence and natural gifts to win for you so wide an admiration.[184]

Spurgeon was hardly the only leading Nonconformist preacher with whom Gladstone became familiar. Parker, to judge from his autobiography, took considerable pride in his connection with Gladstone.[185] It appears that Gladstone first took an interest in Parker after reading his book *Job's Comforters: A Religious Satire* (1874), which depicts the unsuccessful efforts of agnostics like Mill and Huxley to relieve Job's sufferings. Gladstone is reported to have described the work as worthy of Swift.[186] After reading it, he invited Parker to have breakfast at Downing Street. Parker (unlike Spurgeon) accepted, and was shortly astonished to find that he had breakfasted with the Prime Minister on the morning of the government's resignation.

Beyond their religious and personal affinities, these great preachers also tended to support Gladstone's politics. The strength of Gladstone's religiosity led the majority of Nonconformists to place their political faith in him.[187] The Nonconformists were a bulwark of the Liberal party and many ministers were active in secular politics. A description of "Preachers of the Day" from 1884, for example, asked readers to forgive Parker's "incessant introduction of Gladstonian politics in connection with holy things."[188] Spurgeon, as already discussed, threw his considerable weight behind Liberal policies and candidates. (A persistent legend had the Pastor declaring that he would vote for the Devil if the Devil were a Liberal—a story Spurgeon took pains to deny.) In his letters to Gladstone, as in public utterances, Spurgeon regularly expressed his support for policies like the disestablishment of the Irish Church (endorsed by political Nonconformity as the prelude to disestablishing the Church of England).[189] Gladstone could only have appreciated the political support of a Pastor who held sway over so large a congregation.

The political connections between Gladstone and Liddon were fundamentally different than those between Gladstone and the Nonconformists. Gladstone and Liddon were primarily religious, rather than political allies. Most of their correspondence is taken up with ecclesiastical matters and Church politics. So, for instance, Liddon welcomed Gladstone's entry into the Palmerston cabinet in 1859, but as a means of putting a brake on the Prime Minister's "mischief" in Church appointments. In the mid-1870s, however, religion and secular politics combined with great consequence for Liddon, and for Gladstone. It was Liddon who began to give some coherence to the diffuse feelings of outrage provoked by reports of massacres of Christians by Turks in Bulgaria. On August 13, 1876 he delivered a stirring sermon at St. Paul's, telling his audience that they would be complicit in the atrocities in the sight of God if they failed to act against the Disraeli government's pro-Turkish policy. As he recorded in his diary that day, "an effect was produced."[190] As both an orator and organizer, Liddon played a decisive role in creating a crisis of national conscience over Britain's policy in the East.[191] Ultimately, this moral/political climate created the great opportunity for Gladstone to begin staging his political comeback.

The sermons and pronouncements of Liddon and a few other like-minded High Churchmen were soon reinforced by large meetings of Nonconformists organized to protest the atrocities. In this matter, Nonconformists were more than willing to pay homage to the Puseyite preacher. *The Methodist*, for example, described him as the "preacher of the Gospel, the subtle theologian, who is now our political oracle."[192] Liddon, however, recognized that for the agitation to have real effect a politician of the first order was needed. He attempted through various means to prod Gladstone into becoming part of the crusade. Although there were many factors and calculations that ultimately prompted Gladstone first to join, and then to lead the campaign, there is no doubt that the personal influence of Liddon was highly significant.

Among other things, the Bulgarian atrocities agitation gave Gladstone the opportunity to become acquainted with another leading London preacher, Stopford Brooke. Brooke was an organizer of, and Gladstone a speaker at, the National Conference on the Eastern Question on December 8, 1876. Although Gladstone was wary of Brooke's religious views, Brooke's admiration for Gladstone is clear in a flattering letter of 1878. Brooke quoted at length Milton's letter to the Duke of Parma's ambassador to France, Philaras of Athens, waxing lyrical about the valor and supreme eloquence of the ancient Athenians, his wish for their descendants to be free of the Ottoman yoke, and his desire for the recovery of the ancient values. To Gladstone, Brooke wrote how he found the passage "very interesting in its testimony to the influence of Greek on English Literature" (certainly a subject to warm Gladstone's heart), "very interesting politically now, and it pleased me to think that in Milton's words I heard your voice."[193]

If Gladstone and some of these great preachers found a common interest in the protests over the Bulgarian atrocities, Home Rule proved more divisive. From some of them, Gladstone's assertion that Britain's governance of Ireland was "morally worn out"[194] received considerable support. Brooke, who had been born and raised in Ireland, was an active and outspoken advocate for Home Rule. Parker, who had been an active participant in the Bulgarian atrocities campaign, was one who sought to help Gladstone's Home Rule policy through both word and deed. He even arranged for Gladstone to come to his house and deliver an address on Home Rule to a group of Nonconformist ministers.[195] Following this event, Gladstone wrote in his diary that, "I owe these people a good deal which I cannot pay."[196]

Spurgeon viewed Home Rule very differently. Despite his strong Liberalism, the Pastor had declined to take part in the organized protests over the Eastern Question—but he did deliver a public prayer to "change our rulers, oh God, as soon as possible."[197] When it came to Home Rule, however, Spurgeon joined the active opposition. Although he continued to profess personal loyalty to Gladstone, Spurgeon could not abandon his fellow Protestants in Ireland to a Catholic majority, and so he spoke out against the bill. After Spurgeon's death in 1892, both supporters and opponents of Gladstone's 1893 Home Rule bill distributed flyers quoting Spurgeon in support of their respective positions. Those for the bill quoted comments by Spurgeon on Gladstone's superior vision as a statesman; those against quoted the Pastor's statements against Home Rule.[198]

Liddon, in contrast with his early leadership role on the Eastern Question, appears to have been far more indifferent with respect to Home Rule. Evidently, the prospect of Protestants being left in the hands of a Catholic majority bothered the Tractarian Canon of St. Paul's far less than the Baptist Pastor of the Tabernacle. "As to Home Rule," Liddon wrote in 1887, "I have what the Liberals call 'an open mind'."[199] Consistent with the way that their relationship centered on questions of religious doctrine and ecclesiastical politics, it seems that Home Rule was not a matter Liddon and Gladstone found necessary to discuss very much, if at all. Describing Gladstone's visit to Oxford in 1890, Liddon wrote: "I had long conversations with him about the Old Testament, [the liberal Catholic theologian] Dr Döllinger, and the old Tractarians. Not a word about Ireland."[200]

ORATORICAL AFFINITIES

Gladstone's interest in Liddon, Spurgeon, Parker, and Brooke was hardly confined to personal and political connections. The fame that these four men gained in the pulpit also provided a crucial link. Gladstone was a great student of rhetoric and oratory. In particular, he had a deep appreciation for preaching, and he consumed a lot of it. During his youth, Gladstone's diaries show him taking in two or three sermons every Sunday. As a schoolboy, his father took him to hear Edward Irving. Gladstone later recollected:

> About the year of 1823, the eloquence of Mr. Edward Irving drew crowds to his church in London which was Presbyterian and in or near Hatton Garden. These crowds were largely supplied from beyond his own persuasion. It required careful previous arrangements to secure comfortable accommodation. The preacher was

> solemn, majestic (notwithstanding the squint) and impressive; carrying all the appearance of devoted earnestness.
>
> My father had on a certain occasion, when I was still a small Eton boy, taken time by the forelock, and secured the use of a convenient pew in the first rank of the gallery. From this elevated situation we surveyed at ease and leisure the struggling crowds below. The crush was everywhere great, but greatest of all in the centre aisle. Here the mass of human beings mercilessly compressed swayed continually backwards and forwards, I suppose as the sense of the situation became intolerable in one quarter or another.[201]

In 1830, the young Gladstone also heard Thomas Chalmers preach at Oxford (in a Baptist chapel), and reported to his father: "I need hardly say that his sermon was admirable and quite as remarkable for the judicious and sober manner in which he enforced his views as for their lofty principles and piety. He preached, I think, for an hour and forty minutes."[202]

Throughout his adult life, as the diaries make clear, Gladstone continued to take in a vast number of sermons both from the pew and through print. In addition to evidencing his connoisseurship, the diaries also show the extent of Gladstone's own preaching. Gladstone delivered sermons on a number of occasions beginning in 1833 with the last reference occurring in 1868. On at least one occasion, he even appears to have done what he described as "a little street preaching."[203] Between 1834 and 1866, he composed at least 195 short sermons. After he married, the sermons were delivered to his family and servants with Sunday's household prayers.[204] In 1877, Gladstone also delivered a speech on preaching at a conference on "Pew and Pulpit" held by Parker at the City Temple. Most of the attendees were clergymen and ministers representing a wide denominational range. Recalling the event, Parker wrote: "His knowledge of the subjects connected with preaching simply astonished all experts in that art. Mr. Gladstone spoke about preaching as if he had never spoken on any other subject."[205]

On that occasion, although he was purposefully ecumenical in his address, Gladstone sought in particular to defend Anglican preaching from the oft-repeated charges of being "commonplace." To the loud cheers of his audience, he said that criticism of Anglican preaching reflected not a problem with the preachers, but rather, "some deficiency in that healthy appetite by which they ought to be received by the pew."[206] Gladstone certainly appreciated the fact that the appetite of those in Liddon's pews never seemed to fail. He considered Liddon "nearly the first to associate a great thinking force with the masteries of a first rate preacher,"[207] and when asked (by Parker) for his opinion on the greatest Anglican preacher, replied: "In mental power through his sermons, Canon Liddon, perhaps."[208] Yet, few Anglican preachers could match Liddon's achievements in the pulpit, and there were occasions when even Gladstone found Anglican preaching wanting. One evening in 1879, Gladstone sat in a church in Marylebone, filled to less than one-tenth of its 2,000 sittings, "while the Rector, perfectly complacent, delivered a sermon which I can only call pious chatter, perfectly effete, on a grand text (Nathan & David) which he did nothing to open. In the evening I read Spurgeon's vivid & noble sermon of last Sunday on the crisis & the wars: what a contrast!"[209]

Two years later, Gladstone let it be known that he was interested in attending a service at the Tabernacle. On hearing this, Spurgeon wrote: "If it ever be so, allow me the pleasure of seeing you accommodated & placed where you need not be observed."[210] On January 3, 1882, Gladstone wrote to make arrangements to come to the Tabernacle on the following Sunday evening.[211] Spurgeon, with great consideration for what he imagined would be the need for discretion, sent Gladstone instructions to come to the Tabernacle's back gate, where he would be met by members of his staff. With a peculiar combination of deference and boastfulness he added: "I feel like a boy who is to preach with his father to listen to him. I shall try not to know that you are there at all, but just preach to my poor people the simple word wh[ich] has held them by their thousands these 28 years."[212] (From a former *wunderkind* preacher who far surpassed his father's lay preaching efforts at an early age, Spurgeon's first sentence is particularly revealing.)

In his diary for January 8, Gladstone noted: "In the Ev[enin]g went with Willy to Mr. Spurgeon's Tabernacle. Saw him before and after."[213] As the newspapers reported:

> THE PREMIER AT THE METROPOLITAN TABERNACLE—The Right Hon. W. E. Gladstone and Mr. W. H. Gladstone, M. P., occupied seats in Mr. Spurgeon's pew at the rear of the preacher's platform, on Sunday evening. The Tabernacle was crowded. Mr. Spurgeon, who preached, took for his text Mark v. 30 and 31. On leaving, the Premier expressed himself greatly pleased with the visit.[214]

Distressed over the intrusion of the press, Spurgeon wrote to assure Gladstone that he had had no hand in it. Gladstone's cordial reply thanked

Spurgeon for allowing him to attend and dismissed his concern over the publicity with the observation that his "life is passed in a glass bee hive."[215]

For some months after, Gladstone's attendance at the Tabernacle generated a stream of correspondence and commentary in the newspapers.[216] As might be expected, a number of Gladstone's fellow High Churchmen were deeply disturbed, and even felt betrayed by his going to the services of so prominent and popular a Nonconformist. Many other journalists and letter-writers, however, looked on the incident with favor as a demonstration of the premier's broad-mindedness and his evolution from his early "stern and unbending" days. Although the controversy over Gladstone's visit to the Tabernacle died down soon enough, the connection between the two orators was never quite forgotten. In 1885, for example, as Gladstone's majority in Parliament dwindled, a small piece in the satirical magazine *Moonshine* humorously suggested that, after his ministry failed, "Mr. Gladstone would become co-pastor of the Metropolitan Tabernacle, and fill up his time translating 'Paradise Lost' into Gladstonese."[217]

Certainly, both Spurgeon and Gladstone must have been pleased with how the affair came off. The Pastor clearly gained public prestige from the Premier's attendance, as well as the personal gratification of being recognized by a man he admired. Gladstone, head of a party that drew great strength from its appeal to Nonconformist moral sensibilities, gained in political terms from associating with the most popular Nonconformist preacher of the day. Beyond political benefits of this sort, Gladstone, who was inventing a mass politics based on extra-parliamentary speeches, must also have been curious to observe the techniques of another great oratorical institution. As one newspaper column commented: "A man of Mr. Gladstone's culture, conscientiousness, and oratorical powers would naturally wish to hear for himself how Mr. Spurgeon keeps together six or seven thousand people for years; all of different minds, and of varied though not very broad education."[218]

Whether or not Gladstone drew lessons from the success of the great preachers, he placed great value on their abilities in the pulpit. In the case of Brooke, good preaching even appears to have gone a long way to overcoming Gladstone's theological disapprobation. Gladstone was, to say the least, very ambivalent regarding Brooke's ultra-Broad Church religious views. According to his diaries, Gladstone first heard Brooke preach in 1867. On that occasion, he described Brooke as "striking but unbalanced & wild?"[219] A second hearing nearly a decade later, in 1876, produced a somewhat mellower response: "very noteworthy, a little perilous."[220]

In later years, Gladstone's appreciation for Brooke appears to have increased further, perhaps because once Brooke separated from the Church of England in 1880, the "peril" that Gladstone perceived in his sermons was no longer an Anglican concern. Gladstone may also have been one of the many who admired Brooke for his integrity in voluntarily leaving the Church when he no longer believed in its doctrines. Certainly, Gladstone must have appreciated their alliance in protesting the Eastern Question, and later, Brooke's outspoken support for Home Rule. Ultimately, however, preaching was the key. In 1897, at the very end of Gladstone's life, Brooke sent him copies of some of his works of literary criticism. In his cordial letter of thanks, Gladstone wrote: "I am afraid there are important questions on which we might not agree; but I remember with pleasure an intense sympathy with which I once heard you preach at Westminster Abbey (what I called) a sermon against respectability."[221] Brooke returned the compliment, and then some. Remarkably, he not only distilled many of the main themes of his sermons into a few lines, he also placed Gladstone at the center of them:

> No, I suppose we do not agree in many things, though I only know of theology. However theology includes all. And I should be sorry for *myself*—honouring you as I do—did not all controversies seem to me now useless sorrows. I only know of one thing needful, to love if possible in some degree as Jesus loves. You have done that, if I may say so without impertinence, & with some hope of pardon. You have so lived & thought that you have kept the soul alive in England, at a time when men from all sides attacked it. That some ideal life, life founded, that is, on those invisible & primal ideas of the nature of God & man by which the human race exists & moves—is still in England, is in great part your work. That is to love the human race.[222]

QUESTIONS OF INFLUENCE

What kind of influence did these various connections with great preachers have on Gladstone's public life? Influence is a particularly difficult thing to assess, but several varieties of potential influence suggest themselves. There is no way to determine the extent to which the new kind of preaching celebrity served as a model for Gladstone's innovative use of the political platform; but certainly these preachers had been successfully reaching large and diverse audiences from the pulpit and through printed sermons well before Midlothian. Gladstone was something of a frustrated divine in any case, and if the success of the preachers lay in a kind of quasi-secular appeal, Gladstone's platform crusades succeeded in part through their near-religious quality (see p. 244).

There is some evidence that Spurgeon's preaching influenced Gladstone's platform speaking at least indirectly. The public outrage over the Bulgarian atrocities in 1876, and Gladstone's ability to make political capital of it through stirring oratory and moral exhortation, occurred in an atmosphere strongly colored by the hugely successful revival tour of Britain and Ireland mounted by the American evangelists Dwight L. Moody and Ira D. Sankey in 1873-75. Gladstone saw Moody and Sankey in 1875, and he recorded the sight as "wonderful & touching in a high degree."[223] A number of scholars have viewed Moody and Sankey as an important example and precondition for the new political style adopted by Gladstone beginning in 1876.[224]

For his part, however, Moody had been strongly influenced by Spurgeon. In 1867, during his first trip overseas, Moody was one of the tens of thousands who attended the Pastor's mass services in the Islington Agricultural Hall (London's largest building) while the Tabernacle was being renovated.[225] When he returned to England with Sankey, Moody's preaching was described by some as "pseudo-Spurgeonesque."[226] And despite Spurgeon's wariness of revivalism in general (and of Moody in particular), the Pastor's unprecedented popularity throughout England and beyond clearly paved the way for the success of the Moody and Sankey tour. As Moody's biographer has written, Spurgeon "created attitudes among Englishmen which made them sympathetic toward the American when the latter arrived in 1873."[227] In this way, Spurgeon set the stage for Moody and Sankey, who then set the stage for Gladstone.

If the great preachers' ability to acquire and sustain large, mixed audiences through both oratory and print helped prepare the way for Gladstone's great political/moral crusades, at least equally important to his public career were the ways in which his relationships with the great preachers provided him with both political and personal validation. The correspondence and recollections of Liddon, Spurgeon, Parker, and Brooke all reveal a deep mutual appreciation between the preachers and Gladstone based on the firm belief that, notwithstanding differences over the details, they were all doing God's work by promoting a core of Christian values to the public at large through word and deed. The specifically religious reassurance he received from men who held sway over large congregations must have greatly aided Gladstone's process of sublimation when, in the mid-1870s, he came to recognize that it was politically expedient to keep his personal religious views to himself.

The validation provided by the great preachers may have had even deeper meanings for Gladstone as a person, and for his conduct in public affairs. It is abundantly clear that Gladstone had a sense of his own special, divinely ordained mission in life. To take one of numerous expressions of this in his diary, here is Gladstone in 1879 discussing his innovations in the technique of politics over the three years from the Bulgarian atrocities agitation to the Midlothian campaign:

> The word spoken was a word for millions, and for millions who themselves cannot speak. If I really believe this then I should regard my having been morally forced into this work as a great and high election of God. And certainly I cannot but believe that He has given me special gifts of strength, on the late occasion especially in Scotland.[228]

Although Gladstone did not publicize his sense of his own calling, it was sufficiently in evidence to give rise to comments such as Henry Labouchère's often-quoted (though likely apocryphal) remark that, while he had no objection to Gladstone's habit of concealing the ace of trumps up his sleeve, he did object strongly to his reiterated claim that it had been put there by Almighty God.[229]

The success of Liddon, Spurgeon, Parker, and Brooke in doing God's work was taken to be evident in their great oratorical powers, their large followings, and their wide renown among all classes of people. From their correspondence it is clear that, if these great ministers felt they had a divine calling, they also felt they shared it in some way with the great Prime Minister. This could only have helped to justify Gladstone's belief in his own special destiny in public affairs. In his later years, Liddon is reported to have said, "When Gladstone is gone, then we shall feel that we had a prophet among us."[230] Spurgeon is perhaps the most effusive. Borrowing his language from the Psalmist, the Pastor of the Tabernacle wrote on one occasion: "The sense of right will be to you as a sword and buckler, and if again deserted by the recreants as you may be, you will stay yourself upon the Eternal God in whose custody the jewels of right and justice are ever safe." [231] Even after he broke with Gladstone over Home Rule, Spurgeon agreed with, or at least endorsed, Gladstone's view of himself as a providential actor. In 1891, during the Pastor's final illness, Gladstone sent the preacher a letter of sympathy. On his wife's letter of acknowledgment, Spurgeon penned a postscript: "Yours is a word of love such as those only write who have been into the King's country, and have seen much of his face."[232]

Conclusion

For both Anglicans and Nonconformists, the nineteenth century was a period in which the *experience* of religious observance received increasing emphasis. Although ritualism was a contested issue, a number of enhancements across the denominational spectrum transformed the conditions of worship. By the 1860s, organs, choirs, and the singing of hymns were all increasingly prevalent in services. In the architectural realm, even Nonconformist chapels came to be built in the ecclesiastical Gothic style. Inside Anglican and some Nonconformist churches, decoration and furnishing became more ornate. Finally, Anglican, and occasionally Nonconformist clergy began to adopt more elaborate costume.[233] If Victorian religion was truly characterized by an "evangelical consensus,"[234] the result is a Victorian paradox: for in order to instill religious beliefs in a greater number of individuals, the experience of worship became far more spectacular and far less intimate, more public and less personal.

The popularity of preaching in the second half of the nineteenth century must be understood within the context of this broader trend toward experience in worship. Certainly, it cannot be explained simply in sectarian or doctrinal terms. This is not to deny the positive religious appeal of the great preachers, but good preaching seems to have been more of a priority to a large number of their hearers. The size and diversity of the audiences that preaching stars attracted is indicative of how preaching could transcend particular religious views. Tait, as Bishop of London, seems to have recognized this by charging his clergy with improving the quality of their oratory, not in terms of their sermons' religious content, but in the style of their delivery. Treating the production of religious oratory in essentially secular terms was balanced by a paradoxical secularity about the consumption of preaching in the second half of the nineteenth century. People from a broad range of social and educational backgrounds attended the services of various notable preachers. Certainly, some did so out of curiosity or because it was the thing to do; but the fact that these preachers were famous enough to make attendance broadly fashionable indicates the extent to which hearing leading religious orators provided entertainment value.[235]

At its height, the Victorian consumption of religious oratory was epitomized by the practice of "sermon-tasting."[236] The available variety and quality of preaching—particularly that concentrated in London—made sermon-tasting both possible and enjoyable. A Norfolk Baptist like Edward Clodd, while working as a bank clerk in London, made a point of taking in the sermons of all the noted divines, Nonconformist and Anglican.[237] Sermon-tasting was also a great occupation among clergymen of all denominations. The Rev. Alexander White of St. George's United Free Church in Edinburgh recalled how "The first Lord's day I ever spent in London I was happy enough to hear the three preachers in all London I was anxious to hear. In the forenoon I heard Mr. [F. D.] Maurice preach; in the afternoon I heard Dean Stanley; and in the evening Mr. Spurgeon."[238]

Those unable to taste sermons directly could read an ecumenical variety of the sermons of great preachers printed for mass consumption. The ecumenical spirit with which preaching was consumed was also reflected in the major journals of opinion, which printed numerous articles on preaching and preachers of all kinds. In an 1884 article in *Temple Bar*, for example, the author surveys the London preaching scene running the spectrum from Liddon to Parker:

> The sectarian doctrines of these various clergymen must be left out of account in such a review, it is only intended to describe the preachers as they appear to the chance occupant of a pew, who has entered their respective churches—not undevoutly indeed, nor in hypocritical spirit, but with the purpose of weighing what he hears and of observing the manner in which it was delivered.[239]

Other signs of how the quality of preaching was treated ecumenically include newspaper surveys asking readers to vote for their favorite preachers. In March 1887, the Christian newspaper, *The British Weekly*, asked its readers to fill in and send a coupon with the names of the three greatest preachers in each of five denominational categories. The vote in the "Preacher Coupon" competition was reported to be very heavy. The results were as follows:

Anglican	F. W. Farrar (Broad Churchman)
	H. P. Liddon (High Churchman)
	W. C. Magee (Evangelical)
Baptist	C. H. Spurgeon
	Alexander Maclaren (of Manchester)
	John Clifford (of London)
Congregationalist	Joseph Parker
	R. W. Dale (of Birmingham)
	Henry Allon (of Islington)
Presbyterian	Oswald Dykes (of Regent Square)
	Donald Frasier (of Marylebone)
	Thain Davidson (of Islington)
Methodist	Hugh Price Hughes (of the West End)
	Mark Guy Pearse (of London)
	Charles Garrett (of Liverpool)[240]

In September of the same year, the magazine *Great Thoughts* ran two similar competitions, but without denominational categories. In these contests, readers were asked to rank the "20 Greatest Preachers During the Victorian Era."[241] In both competitions (the first with 222 entrants, the second with 762), first place went to Spurgeon. Farrar and Parker ranked below Spurgeon (their places reversed in the second competition), followed by Liddon. Both lists mixed together a broad range of denominations and church parties, including Anglicans William Boyd Carpenter (the Broad Church Bishop of Ripon) and Samuel Wilberforce (the High Church Bishop of Oxford), the Methodist Punshon, the Catholics Newman and Manning, and the Congregationalist R. W. Dale.

In addition to the ways in which preaching was produced and consumed, the physical context is particularly important to understanding nineteenth-century religious oratory. A vast number of new permanent churches and chapels were constructed, existing churches and chapels were extended and re-furbished, and Anglican cathedrals acquired a new identity as oratorical venues. Based on the accumulating evidence that the poor did not in general attend formal worship at a church or chapel, outreach efforts led to the creation of new kinds of spaces for worship, most notably the mission room. Successful Nonconformist preachers built grand edifices to contain their large congregations—the Metropolitan Tabernacle, the City Temple, the Church of the Saviour. Additionally, preachers of all denominations began to use spaces that had been built for secular purposes—the Surrey Gardens Music Hall, public halls such as Exeter Hall and the Islington Agricultural Hall, town halls, theaters, and (in the country) barns. The era also witnessed the creation of a great deal of temporary and semi-permanent spaces for preaching, such as the covered space between two Dunstable factories where Geraldine Hooper preached to 7,000 at a time. Finally, open-air preaching ceased to be confined to itinerant Methodists emulating Wesley, with even several Anglican Bishops numbering among its practitioners in the second half of the nineteenth century.

Examining the manner in which preaching of various kinds was delivered in the second half of the nineteenth century and the conditions under which it was received yields another paradoxical result. The extraordinary popularity of preachers—the extent to which unprecedented numbers came to hear them, read them, and build or procure buildings for them—may make it appear as if religion was the paramount concern of people at this time. Yet it was also a period in which religion was beset by controversy from within, and doubt and disaffection from without. Part of the way religion sustained itself in this increasingly hostile, increasingly secular environment was by becoming unwittingly, in effect, *less* religious through oratorical popularity and the widespread use of religiously informal or grandly spectacular venues for preaching. The pulpit also became less religious through the overt political identification of preachers. As John Morley noted in 1891: "The pulpit is now social, as the platform is, too often just as party and political in the worst sense."[242]

The Victorian age, a historian of religion in Britain has written, "was the last to appreciate and practise great oratory, whether in Parliament on the platform, or in the pulpit. The leading preachers were the counterparts of the politicians, public lecturers, and actors of the day."[243] The vast crowds that gathered to hear celebrity preachers did not, for the most part, do so because of the preachers' denomination or religious views, but rather on the strength of his or her preaching. London, in particular, afforded a wide variety of first-rate religious oratory that was liberally partaken of by both residents and visitors. That the great preachers, and even many of the lesser ones, were well-attuned to their audiences' taste for oratory helps explain the (for today) remarkable reports of people, not more pious than most, who routinely sat through two, or even three Sunday sermons—in all likelihood averaging an hour apiece. In addition to the quantity and quality of preaching they produced, a significant number of preachers catered to the public taste for oratorical events through lecture series and similar offerings that they either performed themselves, or organized through their churches. None of this is to say that preaching and related activities had degenerated into mere entertainment. Nevertheless, the complex of developments that underlay the phenomenal success of the preaching stars clearly reveals the extent to which mainstream religion ceased to be primarily a matter of individual worship and increasingly came to center on public oratorical display.

FIGURE 1 The Nursery of Statesmen: The Oxford Union in 1873.

FIGURE 2 The Golden Age of Parliamentary Eloquence: The Younger Pitt addressing the House of Commons in 1793 (after Hickel)

FIGURE 3 Old Man Eloquent: Gladstone delivers his peroration in the 1886 Home Rule debate

FIGURE 4 The Fourth Estate of the Realm: The reporters' gallery in the House of Commons in 1867

FIGURE 5 Oratorical Reformer: Archibald Campbell Tait

FIGURE 6 Preaching Star: Charles Haddon Spurgeon at the Metropolitan Tabernacle

FIGURE 7 Preaching Star: Henry Parry Liddon at St. Paul's Cathedral

FIGURE 8 Oratorical Theater: The Tichborne Trial, 1871. John Duke Coleridge cross-examines the Claimant

FIGURE 9 Platform as Happening: Gladstone on Blackheath in 1871. Note the range of activities and diversions taking place during the speech

FIGURE 10 Platform and Press: Gladstone and a contingent of reporters on Blackheath in 1874

CHAPTER FOUR

Law

IN MAY 1856, two months after the formal conclusion of the Crimean War, the attention of large segments of the British public focused on the trial of William Palmer, the Rugeley poisoner. Later, the legal scholar Sir James Fitzjames Stephen, who was present during the greater part of the proceedings, would claim that it was one of the most significant trials in the history of English criminal law.[1] Even before the trial commenced, interest was high. Local feeling was so manifestly against Palmer that, in order to assure a fair trial, the government called upon the Attorney General to prosecute the case and rapidly carried through an act of Parliament (19 Vict., c. 16) permitting the Court of Queen's Bench (the chief court of criminal jurisdiction) to order that certain offenders be tried at the Central Criminal Court instead of the appropriate local assize.

Certainly, the crime—the alleged repeated poisoning by Palmer of John Parsons Cook for financial gain—was sensational enough, as was the widely held belief that Palmer had also poisoned his wife and his brother. Adding to the interest of the case itself was the legal talent assembled to try it. The Lord Chief Justice, John Campbell, presided. The prosecution was led by Attorney General Alexander Cockburn and included one of the bar's rising courtroom stars, Edwin James. Originally, Palmer was to have been represented by the renowned Charles Wilkins, but the barrister had fled to Boulogne to avoid his creditors. In Wilkins's stead, the defense was led by Serjeant William Shee—like Cockburn, James, and Wilkins, among the most highly regarded lawyers and courtroom orators of his time. The courtroom was crowded throughout the trial, and the Old Bailey (as the Central Criminal Court was known) was surrounded by many more wishing to get in. In the interests of order, the sheriffs issued a limited number of tickets and denied access to anyone without one.[2] Although neither the defendant nor the victim was high-born, a number of notable aristocrats—including Earls Derby and Grey—attended throughout the trial, and the Duke of Cambridge (the Queen's cousin) was present on at least one day.

At the heart of the trial were the speeches. Cockburn's speech for the prosecution was generally measured in tone, seeking to give logical force to a complicated circumstantial case and impress it upon the minds of the jury. His painstaking narrative exposition attempted to show that the murder was only the culmination of Palmer's many lesser, but equally calculated evils. In his four hour opening speech, Cockburn first sought to establish motive by leading the jury through the complex web of Palmer's sordid business dealings and financial relationship with Cook. The Attorney General then had to convince the jury that, even though no strychnine was found in Cook's body, Palmer had nevertheless poisoned the victim with strychnine as evidenced by the manner in which he had died.[3]

"The defence," according to Fitzjames Stephen, "was by far the least impressive part of the trial, but that was mainly because there was really nothing to say."[4] Yet, even if there was nothing to say, Shee said it with style and at considerable length. The defense counsel's address to the jury occupied no less than eight hours in length. With no evidence to establish his client's innocence, Shee attempted simultaneously to raise doubts in the jury's mind about the soundness of the prosecution's case and its witnesses, and to generate unease among the members about the possibility of condemning an innocent man. In a bold and striking move, Shee exceeded the usual boundaries of the defense counsel's role and declared: "I commence his [Palmer's] defence, I say it in all sincerity, with an entire conviction of his innocence."[5] Rather than merely seeking to chip away at the facts as presented by the Attorney General, Shee's declaration (reiterated later in his speech) increased the dramatic tension of the trial by pitting the rhetoric of absolute conviction against the prosecution's thorough, but circumstantial case. The defense was followed by a final speech by Cockburn of around four hours. The trial concluded with a two-day summation by Lord Chief Justice Campbell. On May 27, after retiring for an hour and eighteen minutes, the jury returned with a verdict of guilty.

After the jury delivered their verdict on Palmer, *The Times* delivered its verdict on the whole trial: "For twelve days the public has watched with eager anxiety every phase of this memorable trial. Never in late times has a case of murder aroused such universal interest, never have such pains been taken to insure perfect fairness in the inquiry, never have the proceedings extended to such a length."[6] For the historian, the Palmer trial represents more than a mid-century *cause célèbre.* The fascination, the spectacle, the drama, and the length of the trial were all very much bound up in recent transformations in the structure of courtroom procedure. As far as the practice and experience of the courtroom went, most of these transformations were related in one way or another to the changing nature and function of speech in the law.

Structures of Barristerial Oratory

Legal histories of England[7] tend to overlook or obscure the fact that it was only during the first half of the nineteenth century that barristers became the principal courtroom speakers, and that the structure of courtroom procedure became focused on barristers' speeches. Indeed, many aspects of today's courtroom procedure—such as the opening and closing speeches of opposing counsel—are products of the nineteenth century. Despite this, accounts of nineteenth-century law are typically dominated by the great reforms of legal institutions and the shift to a more humane administration of justice through vast reductions in the number of capital offences and the elimination of public execution. Too little attention has been paid to how this period of reform affected the law as practiced—in particular, the increasing orality of courtroom procedure. On the whole, according to a recent study, legal historians have failed to pursue "the socio-historical study of law as advocacy, rather than law as the interpretation of texts. This is important because the oral, dialectic nature of law has seemingly been forgotten—historians of law emphasize the court structure and the written texts, never the way that law has been a necessary and consistent strand of oral or spoken tradition."[8] Although a fuller discussion of legal orality in nineteenth-century England would include judges and solicitors, this chapter deals almost entirely with the men of the bar.[9] Barristers were the professional orators of the legal world and (for the most part) only barristers had the right of address in court. It was their job to speak, and their professional reputation and livelihood depended on their speeches.

The expansion of legal oratory took place, and was responded to on a number of levels. The combined effect of a number of reforms beginning in the late 1830s and continuing throughout the rest of the century was to give counsel and their speeches a far larger role in an increasing and more widely distributed number of courtrooms. The rising oratorical demands on the profession can be seen in the production of handbooks to advise the aspiring advocate, and in the efforts of law students to supplement their education with training in public speech. At the same time that oratory was becoming more of a professional reality and more of a professional concern, the nature of barristerial speech was subjected to new levels of public criticism while the oratorical performance of barristers in the courtroom became the object of greater public fascination. Further, at the same time that barristerial speech figured more prominently in the courts and in public, barristers also expanded upon their traditional numerical and oratorical presence in Parliament.

Like MPs and preachers, barristers were—at least in theory—professional public speakers. The greatest limit on a barrister's public speaking, however, was not inclination but opportunity. One could get elected to Parliament and never show up. One could become a clergyman and never preach. The practicing barrister, on the other hand, was in business in order to speak in court. The only question was the extent to which he was able to do so. Four sets of structural developments are critical to understanding the production and consumption of legal oratory in nineteenth-century England. First, are the changes in the professional structures within which the men of the nineteenth-century bar lived and worked. Second, are changes in the institutional and procedural structures that shaped the exercise of barristers' professional calling. Third, are the increased presence and distribution of physical structures that embodied the law and the courtrooms in which barristers made speeches. Finally, there is the character of barristers' audiences both inside and outside the courtroom.

THE PRACTICING BAR

A large body of research on the nineteenth-century bar has described the evolution of its formal structures and institutional culture, changes in its size and composition, and the emergence of various other professional outlets for its members.[10] The size of the Victorian bar has proved to be perhaps the most vexing question. Part of the problem is that far more people were called to the bar than actually practiced, and even greater numbers had been students at an Inn of Court without ever being called. Contemporary reports and census data show a large increase in total bar membership over the course of the nineteenth century—from close to 600 at the beginning of the century to more than 4,000 toward its end. Nevertheless, regardless of how many men were called to the bar, the most important statistic—from both a sociological and an oratorical perspective—is the growth of the *practicing* bar. In this respect, contemporary accounts seem poorly founded—such as the 1846 observation that the practicing bar could count 3,000 members compared to 456 in 1809.[11] The most thorough scholarship on the size of the practicing bar estimates that there were really only between 450 and 1,010 practicing barristers in 1835, and between 660 and 1,450 in 1885.[12] Thus, the practicing bar—of which active courtroom speakers were a part—remained small, and such growth as it did experience did not keep pace with population.

The main reason for the relatively small number of practicing barristers is that there were so few opportunities to practice, and very little room for expansion. The structure of the judicial calendar, with its alternation of superior court sessions and assizes, permitted a few leading barristers to acquire a disproportionate share of the briefs. According to one contemporary account:

> It would surprise any one who is not well acquainted with the English profession to learn what a very small number of barristers suffice to carry on the business of a court, though the simple reflection that in the nature of things one case only can be heard at one time by one court, and that four barristers are as a rule sufficient for each case, may tend to explain the fact that the same names keep continually recurring in nearly every newspaper report of the proceedings of a given court. The institution of circuits of course carries this still further. When justice is administered in six or seven large towns successively, it happens not unfrequently that the same man is engaged in every important case that occurs in six or seven populous counties.[13]

The limited opportunities at the bar can also be seen in the way that a small elite among practicing barristers reaped enormous financial rewards at the expense of the bar's rank and file.[14] Briefless young barristers became a cliché in nineteenth-century Britain. In his first two years of practice after being called in 1863, the legal earnings of W. S. Gilbert amounted to only £75.[15] The Judge in Gilbert and Sullivan's operetta *Trial by Jury* (1875), recalls a start at the bar much like Gilbert's own: "When I, good friends, was called to the bar, / I'd an appetite fresh and hearty, / But I was, as many young barristers are, / An impecunious party."[16] To succeed, young barristers needed to get the attention of solicitors, paradoxically, by proving themselves in the courtroom first. If they were fortunate enough to have solicitors for relatives, friends, or in-laws, barristers could receive briefs immediately after their call. (Gilbert's Judge, for example, turned his career around by marrying the ugly daughter of a rich attorney.)

Over the course of the nineteenth century, the bar transformed from something like a medieval guild to an essentially modern profession. As the role of barristers expanded, a variety of factors, both external and internal, broke up the patterns and assumptions of the bar's old corporate life.[17] One of the most important developments was the improved rapidity and convenience of travel. At the beginning of the century, the pattern of life at the bar revolved around the provincial assize circuits. Twice a year, amid much pageantry and ritual, the same group of barristers and judges went on their chosen circuit, during which they traveled, worked, dined, and sought amusement together.[18] In the second half of the century, however, the railways brought about the end of the carnival and camaraderie of the circuits. Now, instead of several barristers sharing a carriage for the duration of the circuit, individual barristers could travel to the various assize towns directly from London. Personal associations between leading barristers and judges (themselves former barristers) remained, but they were increasingly based on mutual *professional* recognition rather than membership in the cozy closed society of the circuit. As orators, therefore, barristers ceased to perform as part of an ensemble, and increasingly became soloists.

The development of the nineteenth-century bar was shaped, not only by new material circumstances such as railways, but also by the tension between external pressures for reform and internal resolve for self-determination. In most respects, the nineteenth-century bar did not readily embrace the amendment of its professional life—particularly when the impetus came from outside. In spite of all the reforms it adopted, the bar clung tenaciously to as many of its old privileges as possible. Most notably, the bar and its friends succeeded in thwarting the durable idea of reorganizing the four Inns of Court into a legal university. The bar insisted on, and maintained, self-government and self-regulation, but also adapted in response to external challenges. These changes altered the conditions surrounding the exercise of the barrister's defining function: speech.

As will be dealt with at length below, the bar was subjected to new kinds of general public criticism. By the 1860s, a number of public scandals involving members of the bar prompted the four Inns of Court to cooperate in new ways to better regulate the profession and more effectively discipline its members.[19] One consequence of this new level of public scrutiny and professional organization was to restrict the real and perceived abuses of speech by barristers in the earlier more *laissez-faire* professional environment. By the middle of the century, the status of legal education also became a subject of public concern and prompted the formation of parliamentary select committees. Eventually, this led to a revived law curriculum at Oxford and Cambridge, as well as the introduction of examinations at the Inns of Court (compulsory after 1872). Although improved knowledge of the law among barristers was not inherently at odds with the production of quality courtroom oratory, the new emphasis upon legal knowledge along with greater professional discipline situated barristerial oratory within structures (and strictures) that were considerably different from those in which the barristers of the first half of the century had practiced.

LAW REFORMS AND THE ROLE OF BARRISTERS

In addition to changes in professional practices and institutions, the legal context for barristerial oratory was also transformed over the course of the nineteenth century. Like the bar, the English legal system at the beginning of the century had changed little from its medieval origins. Professional representation of parties by barristers had become increasingly prevalent during the eighteenth century, but the older pattern of the Judge examining the witnesses was still common.[20] But even if the barristerial presence was increasing at the beginning of the nineteenth century, the structure of the administration of justice provided limited opportunities for legal speech. Minor criminal offences were dealt with four times a year in summary trials at local quarter sessions presided over by Justices of the Peace. Major criminal cases and civil suits were tried by Judges at either the provincial assizes or the national superior courts in London. Assizes were held twice a year (and only once in some northern counties), while the superior courts were held in limited sessions—in the common law courts, four terms of three weeks each. Evidentiary and procedural rules in place at the beginning of the century also effectively limited the opportunities for courtroom oratory. In criminal cases especially, counsel for accused felons were only permitted to address points of law and cross-examine, but could not make speeches to the jury.[21] In theory, the judge saw to it that the accused was tried fairly. In equity courts, evidence consisted of written depositions, and *viva voce* testimony was prohibited until the 1870s. Finally, there was virtually no system of appeal.

Nineteenth-century legal reforms greatly increased the scope of barristerial oratory. The first significant innovation was the creation in 1834 of a Central Criminal Court at London's Old Bailey Sessions House to serve as a permanent assize with jurisdiction over London and the surrounding counties. Unlike the national superior courts, the Old Bailey held sessions at least twelve times a year. Although for a time their colleagues regarded Old Bailey barristers with some degree of disdain, the Central Criminal Court soon became the great cockpit of courtroom talent. In 1836, the Counsel for Prisoners Act (6 & 7 Will. IV, c. 114) provided perhaps the most powerful impetus to forensic display. The Act gave prisoners on trial for felony the right to "make full answer and defence thereto by counsel learned in the law."[22] Previously, although as many as three-quarters of persons apprehended were accused of felonies,[23] counsel could only make speeches in treason or misdemeanor cases.

Permitting accused felons defense by counsel was for a long time opposed by the majority of lawmakers. By the early 1830s, however, the general climate for reform proved more favorable. Both supporters and opponents understood that the bill would significantly extend the role of barristers in the legal system by making criminal trials increasingly dependent on advocacy. (It was generally felt, however, that addresses by counsel in civil cases were desirable due to what was believed to be the greater complexity of the matters in dispute.) *The Law Magazine*, for instance, wrote that the bill would only help barristers who were "young, rash, inexperienced, and anxious to attract attention by a flashing oration, or a burst of indignation against the prosecuting leader or the judge, and we really tremble to think of the intemperate scenes that will be presented, and the shocking consequences that may ensue."[24] Introducing the second reading of the Lords' bill in 1836, Lord Chancellor Lyndhurst conceded that "in some degree something like warmth and zeal would make its appearance in the courts of criminal justice," but observed that speeches by counsel in misdemeanor trials did not seem to affect the order, decorum, or tranquility of those proceedings.[25]

If the Counsel for Prisoners Act "afforded the Bar a greatly extended sphere of professional practice, together with enormous opportunities for forensic display,"[26] subsequent statutes governing the oratorical structure of trials further extended the potential for increased barristerial oratory. In civil trials, prior to the 1854 Common Law Procedure Act (17 & 18 Vict., c. 125), the first speech was made and the first evidence called by the party on whom the burden of proof lay. Then opposing counsel opened his case and called evidence. If the opposing counsel called evidence, counsel for the party with the burden of proof could reply; but if opposing counsel called no evidence, counsel for the party with the burden of proof had no right to reply. In the latter case, counsel for the party with the burden of proof could not sum up or explain the examination and cross-examination of his witnesses. After the Act, counsel for the party with the burden of proof was allowed to address the jury a second time to sum up the results of his evidence even if the defense called no witnesses. If opposing counsel called witnesses, then he too had the right to sum it up in a speech.[27]

Eleven years after the Common Law Procedure Act, barristers in criminal trials also gained additional opportunities for speech-making. Under the 1836 Counsel for Prisoners Act, if the defense called witnesses, it was not permitted to make a final reply to the prosecution's summation. Since calling witnesses meant giving the prosecution the last word, it was not uncommon for defense counsel to take the risk of dispensing with evidence from witnesses.[28] Under the 1865 Criminal Procedure Amendment Act (28 & 29 Vict., c. 18), if the defense called no witnesses, the prosecution could address the jury a second time for the purpose of summing up his evidence. If the defence did call evidence, it was permitted to open the case, call witnesses, and sum up the evidence; then the prosecution had the right to reply.[29]

For both civil and criminal trials, then, the new laws encouraged additional speech-making by barristers. It should be noted, however, that other factors limited opportunities for oratorical display. The 1854 Common Law Procedure Act permitted consenting parties in civil trials to have their case decided upon by a judge alone. As a result, the use of juries in civil trials declined, and by the end of the century only half the civil trials in High Court were by jury.[30] By the time the 1865 Criminal Procedure Amendment Act entered the statute book, the number of criminal trials in the superior courts had declined from the heights of the 1840s and early 1850s, when between 25,000 and 30,000 people were committed for trial each year.[31] (A sign, possibly, of the "age of equipoise," or the introduction of police in the 1840s.) Nevertheless, as a result of the legislation affecting courtroom procedure, barristerial oratory was more prominent in trials generally. Since the most important and contentious civil cases continued to be tried by jury, these proceedings continued to demand the full powers of barristerial oratory. Likewise, the oratorical efforts of counsel did not diminish with the declining number of criminal trials.

The reach of legal oratory was also significantly expanded by structural innovations in the administration of the law. Perhaps the most important of these was the creation of the County Court system in 1846. The old quarter sessions were replaced by approximately 500 new provincial courts grouped in 60 circuits established to hear civil cases involving matters of small monetary value. In their early days, County Courts' cases were generally not large or serious enough to require counsel. Later, with enlarged jurisdiction and more complex cases, the County Courts provided greater scope for advocacy and advocates. Although a significant amount of minor litigation was transferred to them, County Courts generated far more in the way of new legal business. In the first five years of their existence, they heard on average 433,000 cases annually, compared to an annual average of about 100,000 proceedings begun in the superior courts in the years before 1846.[32] Indeed, the County Courts provided a new outlet for the underemployed junior bar, and came to be viewed generally as advantageous to the profession (even if it behooved a junior barrister in the late 1840s to keep quiet about his practice in the County Courts).[33]

Ultimately, the introduction of County Courts enlarged legal oratory in several ways. As they were more numerous and sat for much longer periods than the quarter sessions, County Courts expanded both the space and time allotted to advocacy. Further, despite the best efforts of the bar and its friends to establish a monopoly over advocacy in the County Courts, solicitors as well as barristers were allowed to serve as advocates. In fact, this opening appears to have given rise at an early date to solicitors who acted exclusively as advocates. To take the experience of one court: "In 1857, 150 attorneys had appeared in the Birmingham County Court but practically all business was conducted by three men [solicitor-advocates] who did nothing else."[34]

A number of other structural reforms had the effect of strengthening the position of advocacy within the law. Beginning in the 1830s, a variety of special courts and jurisdictions outside the common law paradigm—courts without the need for professional common law advocates—were either curtailed or eliminated.[35] In the superior courts, procedural and structural reforms also emphasized the increasing dominance of the common law over the largely parallel systems of law in the Admiralty, ecclesiastical, and equity courts. Some Admiralty jurisdiction passed to the

County Courts, while jurisdiction over probate and matrimonial causes formerly held by the ecclesiastical courts was transferred in 1857 to the secular courts. Beginning in the 1850s, a series of acts brought the equity, or Chancery courts into ever closer integration with the common law courts. The Judicature Acts of 1873 and 1875, the culmination of Victorian legal reform, rationalized the superior courts into a single hierarchy and created a court of appeal. As part of this, the Acts provided that the Chancery division should try actions with oral evidence instead of the written affidavits on which it had formerly relied.

NEW COURTHOUSES

The production and consumption of legal oratory was also conditioned by the construction of new court buildings throughout England. Although the subject can be dealt with here only briefly, the physical space devoted to the administration of the law—and therefore, in part, to legal oratory—expanded considerably in the nineteenth century. The spread of court buildings in the nineteenth century was very much a product of the new legal recognition given to urban centers beginning with the 1835 Municipal Corporations Act, and the subsequent creation of assizes at major towns like Bristol, Manchester, Liverpool, and Birmingham. The 1846 County Courts Act also created additional need for courtrooms throughout the country.

Thus, despite the enduring centralization of the law, a number of developments encouraged the spread of court buildings in the provinces. Provincial courthouses were erected in towns with populations ranging from several thousand to several hundred thousand. Table 4.1 lists a number of the new courthouse buildings constructed outside London between 1830 and 1900.

The Manchester Assize Court was by far the most important provincial courthouse and made Alfred Waterhouse an architect of national standing. Gladstone, stopping by the nearly completed building between speaking engagements (he became MP for South Lancashire less than a year later), thought the new courts "beautiful."[36] A few years later, *The Times* called the Manchester Assizes "the best courts of law in the world."[37] Twenty years later, Birmingham's Victoria Law Courts also provided a grand, architecturally significant edifice for its recently conferred assize. In addition to the new courthouses, many more provincial courtrooms were

TABLE 4.1 Some Provincial Courthouses Constructed Between 1830 and 1900

Date(s)	Town	Building	Cost	Pop. (000s)
1834	Bradford	Court House		23
1834	Leeds	Court House		123
1837–38	Bodmin	Court House		7
1841–43	Boston	Sessions House	£10,000	13
1842	Spalding	Sessions House		8
1847	Dudley	Court House		3
1850	Mansfield	Court House		9
1857–8	Preston	Court House	£2,889(est.)	6
1859–64	Manchester	Assize Court	£118,050	303
1860–65	Salford	Court House		64
1861	Barnsley	Court House		13
1865–70	Bristol	Assize Courts	£12,000(est.)	154
1865–66	Elgin	Court House	£4,110	6
1865	Horncastle	Courthouse		5
1868–71	Manchester	Police Courts	£68,982	339
1871	Barnsley	Court House		23
1882	Birmingham	County Court		437
1883	Birkenhead	Sessions Court	£30,000(est.)	84
1887–91	Birmingham	Victoria Law Courts		478
1890–92	York	Law Courts		50

Data from Colin Cunningham, *Victorian and Edwardian Town Halls* (London: Routledge & Kegan Paul, 1981), Appendix III: "A Chronological List of Town Halls, 1820–1914," pp. 252–299; and Colin Cunningham and Prudence Waterhouse, *Alfred Waterhouse, 1830–1905: Biography of a Practice* (Oxford: Clarendon, 1992), p. 212.

constructed within new public buildings designed to house a range of local administrative functions. This was the case in buildings for larger towns like the Leeds Town Hall (1853–58), as well as for smaller towns, like the Welshpool Courthouse and Town Hall (1869). In one notable instance, St. George's Hall in Liverpool (1841–56), two separate projects for a new assize court and a new town hall ended up being fused into one building.

In London, the construction of the new Royal Courts of Justice (1872–82) on the Strand was incontestably the most significant court-building project in nineteenth-century Britain.[38] The Westminster fire of 1834 had spared the courts that Sir John Soane had built amongst the buttresses of Westminster Hall in the 1820s, but these courts were already inadequate by the time of their completion. As the number of judges was increased in response to the new legal demands posed by England's rapidly growing, urbanizing, industrializing population, courts and other legal facilities became scattered throughout London. The vast new court building designed by George Edmund Street and constructed for about £2 million was intended to consolidate all these dispersed courts. (It also made the courts convenient neighbors to the Inns of Court.) Further, the new Law Courts embodied the recent fusion of Common Law and equity from the Judicature Acts. It was the last great public building in London to adhere to the Gothic Revival, and boasted a huge, cathedral-like vaulted central hall around which were arranged the courtrooms.

Before the construction of the new Law Courts, London's courtrooms were often cramped, makeshift quarters described in the memoirs of one barrister as "those holes situated at Westminster."[39] Some acquired expressive nicknames such as the "cock loft" and the "dog hole." The Central Criminal Court was no better: one historian of the Old Bailey recalled seeing "very many famous trials held in these horrible, ill-ventilated and insanitary old courtrooms."[40] The shape of English courtrooms was generally rectangular, with the judge's bench lining one of the long sides facing the prisoner's dock. Jurors and witnesses occupied sets of sharply graded seating along the side walls between the dock and the bench. Spectators occupied galleries overlooking the floor.[41] Even in the grand new Law Courts on the Strand, with its monumental central hall, the courtrooms remained relatively small. They continued to be rectangular and oriented along the length of the room. The public galleries stretched across the rear of the courtroom provided limited seating. Street's design sought to ensure good visibility and audibility (as well as economy of space) for the spectators.[42] According to one judge, however, the new courtrooms were constructed so that counsel could not hear the judge, the judge could not hear the witnesses, and the jury could hear neither.[43] Thus, like the House of Commons in the New Palace of Westminster (see pp. 70–71), the new courtrooms within the new Law Courts were not created on a grander scale, but merely housed within a vast, imposing, and more amenable edifice.

AUDIENCES

In the courtroom, barristerial speech was listened to by three separate audiences, each with its own particular significance: the judge, the jury, and the spectators. This was different from other areas of public life.

Although spectators were often present in the Commons, an MPs' real audience was the membership. Similarly, preachers and platform speakers also effectively addressed themselves to one audience.

As an audience, the formal concern of judges with the laws relevant to the case places them beyond the present consideration of barristers' oratory. Juries are of course very relevant. Compared to parliamentary, church, and public audiences, barristerial oratory was formally aimed at the smallest number of people—twelve. The composition of juries could be a study in itself. Briefly, however, the 1825 Juries Act (6 Geo. IV, c. 50) established a uniform set of minimum property qualifications to be met by juries in all legal venues (assizes, quarter sessions, etc.). But jurymen were not gentlemen, and vice versa. Peers were exempted from jury service, as were legal and medical professionals. In the main, therefore, juries were drawn from various strata of the middle classes.

As for spectators, the overall composition of this audience is difficult to ascertain. Press reports often note the presence of aristocrats in the courtroom and describe their special seating arrangements, often on the judge's bench itself. Comments about "regular" spectators are few, although it is sometimes observed that they are from the "respectable" classes. At assizes, the spectators were naturally townspeople. Attendance at the trial was both a matter of local interest and part of the general festivities that surrounded the assizes. The practice of charging admission to trials, abolished in 1860, probably discouraged most poor people from attending (and until 1868, public hangings provided free entertainment). Press reports and legal memoirs also regularly comment on large numbers of ladies having been present in various trials—ascribed in some instances to the charms of the defendant. Particularly when persons from the upper classes were involved, trials took on the character of social outings.

Through press reports of speeches, barristers (like politicians and preachers) also had a vast indirect audience. In the middle of the century, at the same time that procedural reforms provided barristers with more opportunities for oratory in the courtroom, the various taxes and duties which had fettered the newspaper press were being removed (see p. 268). Newspapers increased in size and number, as did circulation and readership. For the trials in which the public took the greatest interest, verbatim reports of courtroom speeches by leading counsel ran to many columns in papers like *The Times*, and were carried in whole or in part in the local press. In this way, counsel who might previously have only been known in the metropolis and in the area of their assize circuit gained national recognition.

The Nature of Barristerial Oratory and the Training of Courtroom Orators

Barristerial oratory is shaped by a paradoxical relationship between efficacy and eloquence. This paradox is, in part, a function of the special nature and purpose of barristerial oratory as compared to other kinds of public speech. First, it is the most adversarial form of oratory. In trials, opposing counsel engage in a head-to-head contest and seek the opposite outcome from each other—guilty or not guilty, liable or not liable, and so on. In Parliamentary debates MPs usually speak as part of a party or faction and do not necessarily seek outcomes opposite from those sought the other party, but often speak to *modify* measures. Sermons, while sometimes condemnatory, are non-adversarial because the preacher is the sole speaker. Like preachers, platform orators, although partisan in their message, speak without formal opposition (hecklers are not on an equal footing with the speaker). Other kinds of public speaking occasions, such as civic celebrations, are usually consensual affairs in which any adversarial tendencies among the speakers are deliberately smoothed over.

Barristerial oratory also differs from other kinds of public speech because of its quantity. In the major trials of the period, barristers' speeches could last over the course of several days. This compares to the parliamentary record of five hours or so (e.g. Palmerston's Don Pacifico speech and Gladstone's 1853 budget speech), and sermons only rarely over one and a half hours. The incredible length of some trial speeches resulted from the need for barristers to re-present the evidence and testimony in a way to help the jurors make sense of it all and lead them to the desired verdict. Barristerial oratory is also the most directly consequential—the other end of the spectrum from debating society speeches that affect nothing. At the end of a civil trial, with some material form of recompense or redress typically at stake, one party wins and the other loses. At the end of a criminal trial, the stakes are even higher for the defendant: freedom versus imprisonment or death. Unlike parliamentary debates over things like taxes (where some people will gain financially and some lose) or foreign policy (where lives may be lost in military action), the consequences of barristerial oratory are direct and individual.

As a result of these characteristics, the virtues of barristerial speech were not necessarily tied to notions of eloquence. In his 1849 treatise on advocacy, the barrister William Forsyth wrote: "It must be admitted that eloquence has always been rare amongst the advocates of England."[44] Fifteen years later, Fitzjames Stephen had an only slightly more favorable view: "The bar are a robust, hardheaded, and rather hard-handed set of men, with an imperious, audacious, combative turn of mind, which is sometimes, though not very often, capable of bursting out in the form of eloquence."[45] One late-nineteenth-century barrister, Montagu Williams—himself regarded by contemporaries as among the bar's leading speakers—considered a number of great nineteenth-century barristers to have been exponents of what he calls the "solid style" of courtroom oratory: "I do not refer to heaviness of manner, but to solidity of appearance, robustness of speech, and a general air of good English honesty. This style is very taking with juries of the country."[46]

The notion that eloquence is somehow at odds with good barristerial speech should not be taken as a sign of indifference to the quality of barristers' speeches. Even though the outcomes of trials were acknowledged to depend principally upon the facts of the case, a barrister's ability to obtain briefs and thus earn a living was still directly correlated to his powers of speech in the courtroom—whether on the winning or losing side. In professional terms, the impression made by a barrister on his third audience—the courtroom spectators—could be more significant than his success with his first two audiences, the judge and jury.

To the extent that definitions of eloquence incorporated classical models, oratorical classicism was cautioned against in the strongest terms. As the major nineteenth-century handbook for advocates warned: "Let him [the barrister] be ever so eloquent, fluent, pleasing in tone or graceful in manner—let him boast the possession of every other qualification of the orator, and he will assuredly fail of success as an Advocate if he should address his audience in expressions borrowed from the classical tongues." The author instead recommended using simple, honest "Saxon"—"the language of the people of England."[47] The question of over-eloquent speech was sometimes framed in terms of the different social and educational backgrounds of barristers. An article in *The Law Times* from 1886 set out this issue in explicit terms:

> Technical knowledge is at the bottom of success at the Bar. University men will not acquire it—they prefer lofty eloquence—and hence non-university men do better. And such men are not necessarily less cultivated—they do not reduce the tone of the Bar . . . unless Uni-

> versity men condescend to drudge in practical legal labour for the three years of their studentship they will always be beaten by the men who do.[48]

The bar was divided between those who had received an upper-class education at Oxford or Cambridge before joining an Inn of Court, and those who went directly to the Inns—typically with the benefit of a small inheritance or a coveted scholarship. Although young men from aristocratic and gentry families frequently entered one of the Inns (considered useful for eldest sons who would go on to inherit estates and become local Justices of the Peace), the membership of the practicing bar was typically made up of younger sons and men from the middle classes. As the profession with the greatest social prestige, the law provided men of inferior social status a route of upward mobility particularly (as will be discussed later) when combined with a career in Parliament.[49] If the Inns were the natural places to which ambitious young men from the middle classes gravitated, many of their students also came to see their destiny outside the bar. For example, both Disraeli (articled to a firm of solicitors) and Gladstone (a university graduate) were students at Lincoln's Inn, but neither stayed long enough to qualify for the bar.

It is not surprising that university-educated barristers were sometimes accused of talking over the heads of their juries and addressing "the tradesman and the farmer in a language for whose every fourth word the perplexed twelve need an interpreter."[50] Since legal education did not include any formal training for speaking in court, one might expect Oxbridge barristers to fall back on the hothouse oratorical styles of the Unions. William Frederick Pollock (the son of Peel's Attorney General) remarked that "as a law student, and afterwards for eight years at the bar, I do not remember ever having received any hint or instruction upon the management of the voice when using it in public, either from my father or any one else."[51] When the Inns of Court set about considering the ways to improve legal education, this crucial aspect of barristerial practice was entirely neglected.[52] Traditionally, aspiring and newly minted barristers learned their lessons in courtroom oratory by hanging about the courts and observing the leading advocates of the day in action.

Outside university debating societies, some barristers acquired public speaking experience before entering an Inn of Court from performing on the stage. Law students and young barristers also appear to have exercised their nascent powers of oratory—while at the same time entertaining themselves and others—in mock trials. One particularly interesting training ground was the Judge and Jury Society, a theatrical group devoted to putting on mock trials in which audience members were encouraged to participate. The Judge and Jury (discussed further below) was very popular with law students and lawyers, and its founder boasted that law students "cannot have a better school than it affords, not certainly in intricate points of law, but in eloquence, aptitude of response, and ingenuity of reply."[53] Barristers and others also organized mock-trials on an impromptu basis, as when a group of barristers on the Northern circuit in the early 1860s (including young W. S. Gilbert) regularly got together with a group of actors on tour in Liverpool and amused themselves with various kinds of improvised theater, including mock-trials. As the actress Marie Wilton recalled: "We had several mock trials. . . . It was interesting to hear the clever speeches, all about nothing, delivered by the rising young barristers. I was sometimes the judge and gave imitations of the various gentlemen I had seen on the bench. My robe was a pink wrapper, and my wig made of cotton wool." [54]

Most significant for the direct cultivation of oratorical skills by aspiring barristers, however, was the establishment of debating societies for law students.[55] A few years before the founding of the Eton Society or the Cambridge Union (see chapter 1), students at the Inns of Court established the Forensic Society in order to improve their oratorical skills through debate.[56] The Forensic held weekly debates on both legal and general topics (although, like the Oxbridge Unions, religious topics were excluded). In his influential series of essays on the training and practice of advocates written in the 1840s, Edward Cox strongly urged law students to join the Forensic.[57] A little later in the century, the Forensic Society appears to have given way to what eventually proved to be a far more important legal debating club: the Hardwicke Society, named after the eighteenth-century Lord Chancellor.[58] The Hardwicke held weekly debates on "legal, political, and Social subjects."[59] Members of the four Inns and the corresponding institutions of the Scottish and Irish bars were eligible to join the Society, although in the early years attendance was small. For the first quarter-century after its founding in 1848, the Hardwicke held its debates in a succession of coffee houses. Beginning in 1874, it was perhaps a sign of the Society's rising profile within the legal world that it was permitted to use a lecture room in the Inner Temple.[60]

Writing in 1920, the *Morning Post* hardly exaggerated when it stated that the Hardwicke Society was where "most of the eminent counsel and judges of the Victorian and present eras have voiced their youthful rhetoric"[61]—a claim that the Society itself later routinely reiterated at its annual dinners.[62] Hardwicke members included the future Lord Chancellors Halsbury, Herschell, and Russell of Killowen, and Attorney General Henry James (who could have been Gladstone's Lord Chancellor but for his opposition to Home Rule). Many more members became judges and eminent counsel. Some members, like the positivist philosopher Frederic Harrison, distinguished themselves in other areas of public life. Of all the Hardwicke's notable alumni, however, it was Edward Clarke whose great success at the bar and in Parliament was most strongly identified with the Society. With formidable drive and natural talent, Clarke rose from extremely humble circumstances to become one of the great courtroom orators of his time, a QC, an influential Conservative MP, and one-time Solicitor General (he refused further office and legal promotion rather than impair his large professional income). Clarke called the Hardwicke "the best debating society I have ever known,"[63] and regularly urged aspiring barristers to join. At the Society's annual dinners, he routinely spoke about his personal debt to the Hardwicke and its great contribution to law and public life generally.[64]

In addition to debating societies, other developments assisted the oratorical education of barristers, such as the revival of "Moots" at Gray's Inn.[65] In the Tudor and Stuart eras, *Motes* in which legal questions were argued by students before an Inn's benchers had been an integral part of legal education, but the practice declined and fell into disuse by the end of the seventeenth century.[66] In the nineteenth century, lobbying by students led Gray's Inn to revive the Moots in 1875 as a practical exercise in oral legal argumentation. The restored Moots were held twice per term before a court consisting of a president (typically, a legal dignitary invited for the occasion) and the benchers of Gray's Inn. Students from all four Inns could participate. Significantly, the training provided by the Moots was in legal argumentation rather than general debate. In the wake of the creation by the Judicature Acts of a supreme court of appeal, the revived Moots sought to conform as closely as possible to appellate proceedings. Thus, combined with the various debating societies that flourished during the century, the revival of Moots shows both a diversification of opportunities for oratorical training, and the perceived need of law students to be kept current with the oratorical consequences of broader structural changes in the law.

Orality and Morality: The Case of Barristerial Speech

Amid the all the changes in the nature, function, scope, and context of legal oratory over the course of the nineteenth century, how did people perceive and react to barristerial speech? The most important development in this respect was the preoccupation of both the profession and the wider public with what was seen to be the inherent immorality of lawyers' speech.[67] Such concerns are as old as advocacy itself,[68] but a number of factors combined to give them particular emphasis in Victorian Britain.

On the surface, it seems paradoxical that the morality of legal oratory became a source of public anxiety in mid- and late-nineteenth-century Britain. This period could be seen as one in which the law was placed on a far more humane basis—for example, in the wholesale elimination of capital offenses, and in the creation of an appellate system. Indeed, it has been argued that the later nineteenth century witnessed "the development of a far more respectful and even admiring regard for the law."[69] However, this phenomenon was essentially a shift in the *intellectual* climate based on parallel advances in jurisprudential thought and legal education. "Public moralists" like Fitzjames Stephen may have believed in, and promoted the law's "high, quasi-religious, function,"[70] but this was not—nor was it perceived to be—the world of the practicing barrister.

The nature of legal argumentation ran athwart the Victorian obsession with speaking the truth. Mendacity was particularly abhorrent to nineteenth-century bourgeois culture.[71] In the words of Thomas Henry Huxley, "veracity is the heart of morality."[72] Viewed in this light, counsel representing a guilty party too effectively became guilty themselves of abetting a criminal. As Jeremy Bentham wrote in 1827: "What the non-advocate is hanged for, the advocate is paid for and admired."[73] But in Bentham's time, the oratorical tools of the barrister as courtroom accomplice were (in criminal cases) essentially limited to attempting to discredit prosecution witnesses during cross-examination. With the successive reforms of courtroom procedure over the course of the century, barristers gained far greater scope to ply their oratorical and rhetorical skills in aid of their client. More generally, intensified suspicion of lawyers' motives and practices in the Victorian period also coincided with what some historians have viewed as a fundamental transformation of Britain's social structure wrought by the "rise" of the professions.[74] In a society becoming increasingly aware of and dependent upon the organization and self-regulation of specialized knowledge and services, it is easy to imagine that lawyers—the most established, visible, and elite profession—could become a natural lightning rod for the unease that inevitably accompanies broad social transformations.

The deep anxiety with which legal oratory came to be viewed in the Victorian period also had more proximate causes. Only four years after the 1836 Counsel for Prisoner Act, one particular speech by one particular barrister seemed to realize all that was potentially morally corrupt in the nature of barristers' work and barristers' speeches. This speech—the infamous address to the jury by Charles Phillips in the Courvoisier trial of 1840—catalyzed professional and public debates over the immorality of advocacy that flared up periodically and never fully subsided throughout the rest of the nineteenth century.

Phillips was one of a number of successful Irish barristers who made names for themselves in English courts during the nineteenth century. Called to the Irish bar in 1812, he was known in the Irish courts for his fervid forensic eloquence—particularly in cases where emotions more than points of law were salient.[75] After establishing a reputation in a string of "criminal conversation" and breach of promise cases, Phillips moved to London to expand his professional horizons. On joining the English bar in 1821, he appeared to realize all the English stereotypes of over-florid Irish loquacity. Phillips's friend and sometime courtroom antagonist, Henry Brougham, is reported to have said, "I should call it horticultural not floricultural eloquence," and some referred to him derisively as "Counselor O'Garnish."[76] Although professional opinion as to the merits of Phillips's style was divided, his oratorical powers soon gained him a leading practice in the criminal courts (in spite of his modest command of the law). His courtroom renown was such that he was the only barrister holding no official position interviewed by the 1835 Lords' select committee preceding the Counsel for Prisoners Act. [77]

Phillips might well have been remembered as a leading example of a type of legal oratory in the first half of the nineteenth century, but he achieved a more lasting fame for his defense of the Swiss valet François Courvoisier against the charge of murdering his employer, Lord William Russell.[78] Briefly, in May 1840, Lord William (Lord John Russell's uncle) was found slain in his London house. The assailant had attempted to make it appear as if Lord William had been murdered by an intruder, but investigators concluded that the house had not been entered from the outside and charged Courvoisier with the crime. Because of the victim's social rank, the trial generated a great deal of public interest, resulting in a crowded courtroom: "the anxiety to witness the proceedings, particularly by those who compose the higher classes of society, was beyond all precedent."[79] Additional seating was set up and special provisions were made for the "higher classes," including chairs placed on the judge's bench and a special box of seats. According to one legal observer, the judge "was so hemmed in by the extensive draperies of the surrounding ladies that he had scarcely room to move and looked disgusted at the indecency of the spectacle."[80] Ultimately, however, the notoriety and importance of the Courvoisier trial were due to Phillips alone.

Courvoisier maintained his innocence well into the trial, but when Lord William's stolen plate was located and Courvoisier identified as the man who had left it for safekeeping the valet became frightened and confessed his guilt to Phillips. His client's confession notwithstanding, Phillips not only continued to defend Courvoisier, but also used rhetorical tactics in his speech to the jury to cast suspicion upon some of the female servants, impugn the Police's motives, and (as Shee would do in the Palmer trial 16 years later) frighten the jury with the chance that they might condemn an innocent man. If they returned an erroneous guilty verdict, he warned: "It will haunt you in your sleep and hover round your bed. It will take the shape of an accusing spirit, and confront and condemn what you do before the judgement seat of your God. So beware what you do."[81]

Although Phillips's address "was listened to with breathless interest by the most crowded Court we ever witnessed, and at the conclusion of it many present were affected even to tears,"[82] the jury deliberated for less than ninety minutes before returning a guilty verdict. A few weeks later, 30,000 people turned out to see Courvoisier hanged. The controversy over the Courvoisier trial began when *The Times* reported "Courvoisier's Confession of Guilt."[83] *The Times* praised Phillips for making "the best of a very bad case," but others writing in the press argued that the barrister had gone too far by deliberately employing falsehoods to acquit a man whose guilt was known. In the legal press, some writers were highly critical of Phillips, while others maintained that the barrister's tactics were fully consistent with the standards and practices of advocacy.[84] In fact, when Courvoisier confessed his crime to Phillips, the barrister consulted with an assisting judge at the trial, who told him it was his duty to persevere.[85] Nevertheless, the apparent mendacity of Phillips's defense of Courvoisier had provided the public and the legal profession with a concrete realization of all that was in theory morally questionable about advocacy.

The immediate excitement generated in the wake of the Courvoisier trial soon abated, but the questions given new life by the controversy surrounding Phillips's actions never fully disappeared.[86] The customary low view of barristers was also reinforced by other professional scandals. In the 1845 Tawell poisoning case, for example, the defending counsel, Fitzroy Kelly (later Solicitor General and Attorney General) was heavily criticized for being too willing to heed testimony suggesting that the odor from the victim's stomach could have resulted from her eating apple pips. In 1861, the prominent barrister and MP Edwin James was actually disbarred for professional misconduct. In the early 1870s, another successful barrister, Edward Kenealey, conducted a defense in so scandalously violent and inflammatory a manner that he was censured in public and vigorously sanctioned within the legal community. These and other instances of barristerial corruption and bad behavior helped keep the legal profession on the defensive for most of the nineteenth century. They also led, in course, to the bar taking a firmer hand it its own self-discipline. However, the greatest public moral anxiety continued to stem not from the actions a few rotten apples (or, in Kelly's case, apple pips), but rather from the questions surrounding the misuse of rhetoric and oratory to defend a bad cause. Thus, twenty years after the Courvoisier trial, one can find Fitzjames Stephen defending the practices of advocacy against what he stated was the commonly-held view that barristers "'do twist evidence; they do, as far as they can, pervert and obscure the truth, and their standing and success in their profession is determined by the ability with which they contrive to do so.'"[87]

The underlying concerns of the general public were to a large extent shared by the profession as a whole. An early reaction to the problems of the bar in the 1840s was a series of prescriptive essays by the barrister Edward Cox that appeared in *The Law Times* between 1847 and 1852 (with additional installments published in the late 1850s). These essays, collected under the title *The Advocate*, are infused with the necessity of an advocate to adhere to a high standard of Christian morality in his personal and professional life. In all things, Cox wrote, honesty (usually rendered in capital letters) is paramount:

> It is plain that many persons flatter themselves they are honest, if they keep their hands from picking and stealing. But HONESTY means a great deal more than abstinence from *Theft*. It means fair dealing in *every* transaction, public or private; truthfulness of speech;

> frankness of deportment; readiness to HEAR ALL SIDES of every question, and to judge all men . . . by the same standard, meting out to them the same measure of charity in the construction of their motives, words and acts.[88]

Although Cox's work was the most comprehensive nineteenth-century handbook for barristers, its moral exhortations do not appear to have lowered the temperature of public and professional concern over barristerial speech. In 1864, *The Law Times* commented that the debate over the morality of advocacy "has languished occasionally; but it has never died out among the public, and in the Profession it has been, and is, eagerly canvassed, because to us it daily presents itself in a practical form."[89]

This remark was prompted by what had been the latest flare-up of the debate over the advocate's duty—an exchange during a great dinner in the Middle Temple Hall between no lesser, and no less eloquent personages than Lord Brougham, the former Lord Chancellor, and Lord Chief Justice Alexander Cockburn. Brougham stated that "the first great quality of an advocate" was "to reckon everything subordinate to the interests of his client," and that "no greater misfortune could befall the administration of justice than an infringement of the independence of the bar, or the failure of courage in our advocates." This statement was in full accord with Brougham's declaration during his defense of Queen Caroline in 1820:

> To save the client by all expedient means—to protect that client at all hazards and costs to all others, and amongst others to himself—is the highest and most unquestioned of his duties; and he must not regard the alarm, the suffering, the torment, the destruction, which he might bring on any other.[90]

In reply, Cockburn asserted that the advocate must retain his honor: "The arms which an advocate wields he ought to use as a warrior, not as an assassin. . . . He ought to know how to reconcile the interests of his client with the eternal interests of truth and justice." The problem, as observed by *The Law Times*, is that:

> The judge, the Bar, the audience and the newspapers may applaud the counsel who has adhered to the principle enunciated by the LORD CHIEF JUSTICE, and exclaim against him who has followed the doc-

> trine of CHARLES PHILLIPS; but the clients will certainly prefer the latter to the former; and briefs come from clients and conduct to fame and fortune.[91]

It is certainly a sign of the extent to which the name of Phillips came to symbolize those aspects of legal speech that were perceived to be the worst that *The Law Times* associated Cockburn's name with the virtuous position, but substituted Phillips's name for Brougham's as representing the "client's interest" position. Indeed, *The Law Times* took pains to assert in subsequent numbers that Brougham's upholding of the client's interest position on this occasion did not necessarily mean that he believed that barristers should emulate the kind of behavior associated with the name of Phillips.[92]

The heightened level of public opprobrium to which the legal profession—and the nature of advocacy in particular—was subjected in the mid-nineteenth century was mirrored, extended, and sustained by the popular literature of the period.[93] Eloquent testimony to the "rise" of the lawyer, solicitors and barristers appear throughout nineteenth-century fiction. The works of Charles Dickens—most famously *Bleak House* (1853)—present a legal world that is generally (aside from some kindly solicitors) inhumane and concerned far more with its own perpetuation than with serving the interests of justice. Dickens drew not only upon his first-hand experience of the law, but also "a long tradition of popular and literary hostility toward lawyers, who generally appear—in, say, Jacobean and Restoration drama, and in eighteenth-century fiction—either as musty crabbed half-wits or, more often, as unscrupulous rogues."[94] Although barristers do not play a great part in his works, when they do appear they and their practices are always presented as essentially immoral. In *The Old Curiosity Shop* (1840–41), for example, we find the barrister who is "in dreadfully good spirits" after a trial in which he "very nearly procured the acquittal of a young gentleman who had had the misfortune to murder his father."[95]

Dickens's most famous depiction of a barrister is Mr. Serjeant Buzzfuzz from *The Pickwick Papers* (1836–37). Although *Pickwick* was published a few years before Charles Phillips's fall from grace, the episode—a trial for breach of promise, the climax of which is Buzzfuzz's absurdly misleading speech—enjoyed a separate, and extremely popular existence when Dickens added it to his repertoire of public readings in the late 1850s.[96] In the 1880s, the legal memoirist William Ballantine wrote that the trial depicted by Dickens "is a burlesque, and yet there is nothing impossible in a deaf judge or an inflated address by counsel, and a speculative firm of attorneys may be found even during the present days of purity."[97]

Later in the century, even W. S. Gilbert was not above trafficking in popular prejudices against barristers. Gilbert's few unsuccessful years as a barrister made a deep impression upon him and he may not have been entirely ironic when having the Lord Chancellor in *Iolanthe* (1882) declare: "The Law is the true embodiment / Of everything that's excellent."[98] Nevertheless, the popular theater was not the place to buck convention. In *Trial by Jury*, the judge recounts his youth at the bar and his great success at getting the guilty acquitted.

> The rich attorney [his father-in-law] was good as his word;
> The briefs came trooping gaily,
> And every day my voice was heard
> At the Sessions or Ancient Bailey.
> All the thieves who could my fees afford
> Relied on my orations,
> And many a burglar I've restored
> To his friends and his relations.[99]

While Dickens and later Gilbert certainly helped to sustain the general prejudice against lawyers, nowhere are the post-Courvoisier attitudes toward barristers more evident, and nowhere did they enjoy a greater audience, than in the works of Anthony Trollope. According to one late Victorian assessment, "Trollope was in his lifetime more popular than any of his contemporaries. Twenty years ago [in the 1870s] it would hardly have been an exaggeration to say that half the novels on the railway bookstalls were his."[100] The *National Review* may have overstated the case when it claimed in 1863 that Trollope had around one million readers; nevertheless, by his own account, the author's works brought him, on average, £4,500 a year in the 1860s and 1870s—a considerable income indicative of a very large readership.[101]

During the period of his greatest popularity, Trollope's widely read novels both represented and reinforced prevalent negative views of the advocate's practice. (Trollope's father had failed at the bar.) Sometimes his critical view of barristers comes in the form of throwaway comments—such as the remark about a pathologically untruthful woman who, "if the sex could have its rights, would make an excellent lawyer."[102] In other works, such as his *Life of Cicero* (1880), the criticism of advocates is more sustained. Trollope generally aims to rehabilitate the Roman orator's reputation by showing him to have approximated Christian values. This is marred only by Cicero's legendary advocacy, for he spoke "without reference to the truth or honesty of the cause, and when he did so, used all his energy for the bad, as he did for the good cause." He "preferred lies in perfect language to truth in halting syllables." But, Trollope admonishes the modern barrister, "we seem to forget that more should be expected from us, than from those who lived two thousand years ago."[103]

While these comments certainly broadcast the author's views, Trollope gives fullest consideration to barristerial immorality through his creation Chaffanbrass—perhaps the most active barrister in Victorian fiction. Trollope describes Chaffanbrass as the "great guardian of the innocence—or rather not-guiltiness of the public."[104] Although he appears in three separate works,[105] Chaffanbrass's character and powers are shown to greatest effect in the novel *Orley Farm* (1861–62). In this work, Lady Mason is brought to trial on a charge of perjury related to her illegal holding of an estate based on a forged will. Although (unlike Courvoisier) she does not confess her guilt to them, Lady Mason's lawyers have no doubt that she is guilty of both perjury and forgery. True to his calling, Chaffanbrass gets his client off, while caring nothing for her innocence or guilt. Indeed, embodying the lowest possible estimate of a barrister's morality, Chaffanbrass finds the greater professional challenge in the probability of Lady Mason's guilt.

Although practically the whole of *Orley Farm* is a sustained attack on the barrister's misuse of oratory in the courtroom, two passages serve to illustrate the dominant anxieties over the practice of advocacy—anxieties widely read novels like this helped exacerbate. The first condemns the barrister's profession for thriving on the thwarting of truth:

> There were five lawyers concerned [with the Orley Farm case], not one of whom gave to the course of justice credit that it would ascertain the truth, and not one of whom wished that the truth should be ascertained. Surely had they been honest-minded in their profession they would all have so wished—have so wished, or else have abstained from all professional intercourse in the matter. I cannot understand how any gentleman can be willing to use his intellect for the propagation of untruth, and to be paid so for using it. As to Mr Chaffanbrass and Mr Solomon Aram [the Jewish solicitor]—to them the escape of a crimi-

> nal under their auspices would of course be a matter of triumph. To such work for many years they had applied their sharp intellects and legal knowledge.[106]

The second passage amplifies Bentham's idea that the barrister using his oratorical powers to get a guilty person acquitted shares the defendant's guilt:

> Considering the lights with which he had been lightened, there was a species of honesty about Mr Chaffanbrass which certainly deserved praise. He was always true to the man whose money he had taken, and gave to his customer, with all the power at his command, that assistance which he had professed to sell. But we may give the same praise to the hired bravo who goes through with truth and courage the task which he has undertaken. I knew an assassin in Ireland who professed that during twelve years of practice in Tipperary he had never failed when he had once engaged himself. For truth and honesty to their customers—which are great virtues—I would bracket that man and Mr Chaffanbrass together.[107]

Twelve years later, Trollope had not greatly moderated his views on Chaffanbrass or his line of work, even though the barrister reappears to defend a wrongly accused hero: "The duty of an advocate defending a prisoner [says Chaffanbrass] is to get a verdict of acquittal if he can, and to use his own discretion in making the attempt."[108] The significance of Chaffanbrass is that, although he may not have fairly represented the bar overall, there were in reality enough public scandals involving barristers' actions to lend the fictional stereotype the appearance of an archetype. In the hands of a great popularizer like Trollope, the appeal of the negative stereotype was far stronger than the positive case for advocacy and advocates that people like Fitzjames Stephen sought to make in legal and literary journals.

Victorian concerns over the morality of advocacy clearly reflected the intersection of two broad socio-cultural trends: the moralizing and the professionalizing of British society. That traditional suspicions of courtroom oratory and courtroom orators became inflamed in the second half of the nineteenth century is another instance of how Victorian Britain was suffused with oratory. In a sense, however, barristerial oratory can be seen as a special case of public speech gone wrong. Parliamentary speaking, bound by constitutional traditions and codes of civility, was regarded as generally high-minded. Preaching, of course, existed for the purpose of moral elevation. Platform speaking (even when charged with demagoguery) typically claimed to champion lofty goals. In contrast, courtroom oratory was regarded as, when necessary, a form of lying to achieve an unworthy end (i.e. acquittal of the guilty).

Beyond the nature and aims of different kinds of public speech, there is also the nature of the orators. Feelings about the immorality of advocacy could only have been enhanced by the ambiguities of barristers' social position. Overall, nineteenth-century barristers were regarded as gentlemen, but only just barely. Barristers' gentlemanly status certainly derived in part from the fact that spending some time at an Inn of Court (albeit, with no intention of studying for, or being called to the bar) was an accepted practice among the landed classes. Further, there was always a contingent of active barristers rubbing shoulders with aristocrats and gentry in Parliament. Nevertheless, barristers as a whole were not exactly "respectable." Ultimately, practicing barristers engaged in that most ungentlemanly of economic activities: providing services for a fee. As the bar became a more prominent institution in English public life, the efforts of practicing barristers to overcome the tradesman's stigma can be seen in the invented tradition (dating from the late eighteenth century) that the small hood attached to the back of barristers' robes was actually a wallet into which fees could be deposited by client without embarrassment to the barrister.[109]

In general, the heightened anxieties over barristers' speech is the contrasting case to the positive connections—through public speech—between moral concerns and public life discussed in other chapters. In the culture of public life in the second half of the nineteenth century, honest speech was virtuous speech. Whether the speech was plain or elaborate, its perceived honesty was one of the most important factors underlying the success of Bright and Gladstone, Spurgeon and Liddon. The heightened concerns in both fact and fiction over the inherent dishonesty of barristers' speech demonstrate the vitality of the connection between moral values, oratory, and public life.

The Law as Oratorical Theater

Like the criticism of the advocate's profession, the analogy between law and theater has a long pedigree. "From time immemorial," wrote one barrister in the 1920s, "advocates have trained themselves to give histrionic displays in the legal dramas in which they were engaged. The bar and the stage have always been kindred professions."[110] As early as the first century B.C., Cicero both likened the law court to a stage and urged young courtroom orators to study the great star of the late republican stage, Roscius.[111] At the very core of the kinship between stage and bar—beyond technical considerations of voice, diction, pace, stress, and so on—is that both actors and advocates must *persuade* their respective audiences, if only temporarily, in accordance with the particular role they are performing.[112] As a barrister who was the son of actors wrote:

> It has often been said, and truly, that in the actor's art and the advocate's there is much in common. I am often made to think of that in court. To begin with, each is playing a part, and to play it well his most urgent element is sincerity. Without it the actor will leave you cold. So will the advocate. He may fear or even be sure that he has a bad case. But he must so act his part as to give the impression that he believes in it entirely. It is his only chance of touching a jury.[113]

Indeed, it is the artifice of persuasion that links the traditional prejudices against barristers and actors.[114]

Scholars in several disciplines have explored the notion of law as theater.[115] Among historians of Britain, E. P. Thompson, discusses "the pomp of the assizes (and all the theatrical style of the law courts)," and "the terrible theater of the law" as part of the apparatus of public theater employed by the Hanoverian gentry to exhibit its authority and exact deference.[116] Looking to France, Katherine Fischer Taylor's architectural history of the *Palais de Justice* in Paris takes a most literal view of the theater of the law by considering the courtroom as a performance space. Convincingly, Taylor connects the orality of the courtroom to its physical surroundings: "The architectural effect of oral procedure is to convert the courtroom to a stage, in which space, sight lines and acoustics are critical."[117]

Although this point is particularly important for nineteenth-century Britain in light of the enhancements to oral procedure and the great growth in the number of court buildings discussed earlier, the analogy with cross-Channel developments is not straightforward. The late-nineteenth-century French magistrate and legal reformer Jean Cruppi admired what he saw as the *un*theatrical nature of British courtroom procedure and the *un*dramatic character of British trials.[118] Perhaps it is true that British trials did not, on the whole, measure up to France's protracted *drames judiciaires.* "Of late years," wrote Fitzjames Stephen in 1864, "we have had monster trials in England, but they have been short in comparison with the monster trials of France."[119] (Stephen attributed this mostly to differences in the nature of French proceedings and the desire on the part of France's decentralized courts to make the most of any *cause célèbre* that came their way.) Nevertheless, it would have surprised a great number of Victorian lawyers to be told that their trials were undramatic affairs in which the public took little interest.

The key to the drama of the Victorian courtroom is the way in which it was an *oratorical* drama. As procedural reforms increasingly shaped the structure of trials around the oratorical contest of opposing counsel, speeches to the jury came to have at least equal, if not greater importance than cross-examination in both civil and criminal trials. In criminal trials the dramatic focus might have been diverted away from the barristers and their speeches if the prisoner in the dock had enjoyed the right to give evidence on oath, but the right of the accused to speak as a sworn witness was not granted until the 1898 Criminal Evidence Act (61 & 62 Vict., c. 36).[120] Thus, in criminal trials, barristerial oratory assumed its greatest significance—in both legal and dramatic terms—between 1836 and 1898.

The oratorical drama was further enhanced by the fact that the leading courtroom speakers belonged to the same small group of barristers who more or less monopolized the major trials. The reasons people flocked to trials of this kind were not confined to the theatrical appeal of seeing justice meted out in response to a crime. Indeed, the old final act of this kind of the courtroom drama—public execution—had become increasingly rare.[121] Peel's reforms of the late 1820s and additional measures in 1837 drastically curtailed the number of capital offences. The last public execution took place in 1868. The rarity of public executions after 1838 caused them to become far larger and more spectacular events.[122] Consequently, the carnival theatricality of hangings diverged even further from the stage theatricality of the courtroom, in which the characteristic axis of dramatic tension had shifted from judge and prisoner to opposing counsel.

By the second half of the nineteenth century, the dramatic satisfactions of the law were no longer to be found in witnessing punishment, but rather in seeing a great oratorical contest between the known gladiators of the courtroom stage. Although the subject matter of trials—heinous murder, upper-class scandal, and the like—may have generated the initial excitement, the action was played out primarily through barristerial oratory. Ultimately, what the people crowded into small, ill-ventilated courtrooms came to see (and the crowds seeking admission wished to see) were speeches—sometimes very lengthy—by opposing counsel.

BARRISTERS AND ACTORS

Before looking at how the drama actually played, a significant but unexplored aspect of the connection between law and theater in nineteenth-century Britain merits at least brief consideration: the density of personal, social, and professional relationships between lawyers and actors. To begin with, it appears that many actors viewed the bar as the best available route for their sons' upward social mobility. Determined that his son, William Charles Macready, should become a barrister and a gentleman, the actor-manager William Macready took the first step and sent him to Rugby.[123] On the basis of young Macready's declamatory abilities, his Rugby tutor remarked that the boy could succeed in either of the two main avenues of social advancement open to the non-landed: "I know this rare talent may be turned to good account in the Church or at the Bar; it is valuable everywhere."[124]

When asked by the headmaster about following his father onto the stage, Macready declared both his intention to become a barrister and his extreme dislike of the actor's profession.[125] He was being educated as a gentleman and in the early nineteenth century, as in Cicero's time, acting was not a gentlemen's occupation. Until Rugby and legal aspirations were set aside for good when Macready *pére* ran into serious financial troubles, Macready sought the kind of respectability that his father could never attain. Although he became one of the greatest actors of his day, Macready remained bitter that he would never be considered a true gentleman—a social status that would have been automatically (even if tenuously) conferred on him as a barrister.[126]

Like the senior Macready, numerous other theatrical parents throughout the century aspired to the bar on their sons' behalf. For example, the leading actor of the latter part of the century, Henry Irving, sent his son up to Oxford to read law. Soon, however, young Harry Irving disappointed his father by giving up barristerial pursuits and reverting to the stage.[127] Irving's contemporary at Oxford, George Pleydell Bancroft, the son of the famous actor-managers Sir Squire and Marie Wilton Bancroft provides another, but more (legally) successful example. Although his connection with the theater remained strong, Bancroft became a successful barrister and eventually advanced to become Clerk of Assize for the Midland Circuit.

It was not uncommon in the nineteenth century for barristers to have had some experience on the stage. Two of the more notable examples were Charles Wilkins and Edwin James. The details of Wilkins's early life are sketchy, but what is known suggests he had a natural penchant for oratory that took many forms before he became a barrister.[128] At one point, he joined a group of strolling players touring the Midlands and is reported to have performed imitations of the elder Kean and other actors at the Shakespeare Jubilee.[129] His legal career began during the election campaign at Newark in 1832, when Wilkins mounted the hustings to speak in favor of the Liberal candidate, Serjeant Thomas Wilde (later Lord Chancellor Truro). The impromptu speech caused a sensation, and shortly thereafter Wilde sponsored Wilkins's entry into the Inner Temple.

James was the son of a leading London attorney, and grandson of an MP who had moved among the likes of Fox and Sheridan.[130] Possibly it was Sheridan's influence that made James determined to join the theater. Overcoming his father's resistance, James apprenticed at small private theaters specializing in popular melodramas. Lessons from a leading teacher of stage acting taught him the standard approaches to melodramatic and tragic performance: exaggerated voice, expression, gesture, and movement. Although James was performing regularly during this period, he failed to garner either the recognition as an actor or the financial rewards he required. So, when his father offered to pay the necessary fees and enroll him as a student in the Inner Temple, James accepted and began his legal career.

At the bar, both Wilkins and James proved to be great successes. At the height of their careers, they were earning as much as £7,000 per year. Both advanced to higher professional status: Wilkins became a Serjeant-at-Law, and James a QC. Further, James entered Parliament and very nearly became Solicitor General. In the courtroom, both were known for the melodramatic quality of their speeches.[131] One observer recalled how, defending a poor girl charged with robbing her master, Wilkins successfully moved first the jury, then the whole courtroom to tears. "The consequence, I need not say, was the acquittal of the prisoner (guilty or not), who never imagined before that she had been so wronged."[132] Later on, after the 1849 trial of George and Maria Manning for murder, one report opined that it might be more convenient to transfer court proceedings to theaters, "the judge, counsel and other performers would welcome the better ventilation; the orchestra would be at hand to accompany Mr. Charles Wilkins [who represented George Manning] and other eloquent gentlemen in the chanting parts of their oratory."[133]

James's training in melodrama also stood him in good stead. Among the high points of his courtroom performances was his speech as counsel for Dr. Simon Bernard, a Belgian doctor living in England who had conspired in the unsuccessful 1858 plot to assassinate Napoleon III in Paris. Although James had spent much time during the prosecution's evidence questioning the legality of trying a foreign citizen for a crime committed on foreign soil, his speech for the defense dwelt little on the law. Instead, he sought to inflame the jury's chauvinism by characterizing the entire proceeding as France dictating to the British government. At the conclusion of an already overwrought performance, James pulled out all the stops:

> Tell the prosecutor in this case that the jurybox is the sanctuary of English liberty. Tell him that on this spot your predecessors have resisted the arbitrary power of the Crown, backed by the influence of the Crown-serving, time-serving judges. Tell him that under every difficulty and danger your predecessors have secured the political liberties of the people. Tell him that the verdicts of English juries are founded upon eternal and immutable principles of justice. Tell him that, panoplied in that armour, no threat of armament or invasion can awe you! Tell him that, though 600,000 French bayonets glittered before you, though the roar of French cannon thundered in your ears, you will return a verdict that your own breasts and consciences will sanctify and approve, careless whether that verdict pleases or displeases a foreign despot, or secures or shakes and destroys for ever the throne which a tyrant has built upon the ruins of the liberty of a once free and mighty people![134]

The jury returned a verdict of not guilty.

Despite their great success at the bar, both Wilkins and James came to bad ends. They lived well beyond even their large professional incomes and incurred enormous debts. After abandoning the Palmer trial to avoid his creditors, Wilkins ended his days financially ruined and broken in health. James was ultimately disbarred for professional malpractice (most seriously, for borrowing money from the defendant in a case in which he was acting for the plaintiff with the promise of an easy cross examination) and died penniless.

The examples of Wilkins and James notwithstanding, theatrical experience did not necessarily lead to melodramatic careers at the bar. Before attaining considerable legal distinction in his short life, Frank Lockwood had acted in a number of amateur performances, and even one professional one, while still a law student.[135] Another leading barrister of the last third of the nineteenth century, Montagu Williams, had been a member of the provincial touring company of the well-known amateur actor Captain Disney Roebuck before taking up the law.[136] While part of Roebuck's company, Williams formed a more lasting link to the theatrical world when he met his future wife, the daughter of the noted actors Robert and Mary Anne Keeley. According to Williams, a long conversation with his father-in-law convinced him to abandon the theater and to study for the bar. Thus, like other theatrical parents, Keeley identified a better life for his daughter (via her husband) with a career at the bar.

Beyond his own theatrical experiences, Williams's life also evidences the strong personal connections between the legal and theatrical worlds. Through his in-laws, Williams came to be acquainted with many theatrical and literary people. Further, the Keeleys were able to advance their son-in-law's prospects by throwing dinner parties for their notable legal friends.[137] Personal friendships between lawyers and actors abounded. The Bancrofts, like the Keeleys, had a wealth of lawyers as close friends from the early days of their careers.[138] While still reading for the bar, Frank Lockwood met and formed an enduring friendship with William and Madge Kendal.[139] William Frederick Pollock was a close friend of Macready and even edited the actor's memoirs. Thomas Noon Talfourd, a lawyer who also penned a number of tragedies, was known for hosting parties at his large house in Russell Square attended by a miscellaneous company of eminent counsel, struggling young barristers, painters, poets, and actors.[140] Talfourd's son, Francis, was called to the bar in 1852 and even practiced occasionally on circuit, but gained his greatest renown as a writer of burlesque extravaganzas.

Some of the friendships between barristers and actors were a product of the peripatetic nature of both professions. Theatrical tours of the provinces were sometimes scheduled to coincide with the general festivities surrounding assizes. Both lawyers and actors were strangers in the town, and remained somewhat separate from town society—the lawyers isolated by professional etiquette, the actors by prejudices against theaterfolk. For example, Squire Bancroft began a life-long friendship with the future Lord Chief Justice Russell of Killowen when, in 1864, the former was playing in Liverpool and the latter was a struggling young barrister on the Northern circuit.[141]

Lawyers and actors also regularly mixed in London's tavern and club life. Even if lawyers were not "brought up in the theater" like George Bancroft, or had not married into it like Montagu Williams, they nevertheless routinely enjoyed the company of actors at taverns like Evans's and clubs like the Garrick, both located in Covent Garden. At Evans's, according to Ballantine, "Artists, lawyers, writers, actors, and men of fashion congregated in the hall of a night."[142] Ballantine also devotes a whole chapter of his memoirs to evoking the scene at the Garrick: "it was naturally sought by actors, poets, artists, and novelists, and members of the graver professions were only too glad to relieve the labours of the day by the society of all that was distinguished in literature and art."[143] The Garrick was founded in 1831 as an actors' club, but by the 1850s was losing its exclusively theatrical identity as the number of literary, military, and professional members increased. By mid-century, the Garrick was common ground for lawyers and actors to talk, drink, and gamble.[144]

A particularly interesting variant on the circuit, tavern, and club connections between the legal and theatrical worlds was the Judge and Jury Society established in 1841 at the Garrick's Head Hotel in Bow Street. For the amusement of the customers, the Society featured semi-participatory entertainment in the form of mock trials. As described by the Society's founder, "Lord Chief Baron" Renton Nicholson: "The trials are humorous, yet containing matter sufficiently grave for the exercise of serious eloquence, as well as the lighter *badinage* of flowing repartee and fluent satire."[145] Nicholson's own legal training consisted of several trials for insolvency and a few turns in jail. When taking over the proprietorship of the Garrick's Head, he conceived of the Judge and Jury as a way to stimulate the Hotel's business. Advertisements for the Society consisted of sham reports of the "courtroom" proceedings in which the plentitude and cheapness of food and drink at the Hotel were prominently mentioned. In a short time, the Society became quite popular, and remained so even when it relocated to other venues. According to Nicholson, "Members of both Houses of Parliament, statesmen, poets, actors of high repute, *cum multis aliis*, have visited the Judge and Jury Society. It has been no uncommon occurrence to see the jury composed of noble lords and M.P.'s."[146]

In the twenty years of its existence (it appears to have died with Nicholson in 1861), the Judge and Jury Society assumed a full range of legal forms. While the Society operated out of the Garrick's Head, for example, the Hotel was styled in advertisements as Garrick's Inn, where students could "have what they like for dinner, or choose from the *culinæ* supply of the day—an arrangement which makes the eating terms more agreeable than at any other Inn of Court."[147] At various times, Nicholson and his stock players took their act on tours of the provinces—effectively, going on circuit. Most amazing, however—and a sign of the popularity of the Society and its leader within the legal community—Nicholson, when appearing in real courtrooms, continued to have his mock-legal standing recognized by lawyers, Sheriff's officers, and even judges.[148] In a dense multiplexing of law and theater, the last scene of the barrister-playwright Frank Talfourd's popular burlesque extravaganza, *Shylock, or the Merchant of Venice Preserved* (1853), depicts the trial of Shylock as a meeting of the Judge and Jury Society presided over by an actor playing Nicholson![149]

The multiplicity of familial, social, professional, and associational connections between the law and the theater, had several implications for the nature of barristerial oratory. Barristers were not strangers to theatricality. Many barristers identified with actors and the acting profession, and felt sufficiently kindred in personal and professional terms to cross the barrier of social respectability separating the two groups. Leading barristers with experience of the stage made full use of their theatrical training. Thus, for aspiring barristers, theatrical models of oratory were available not only on the stage, but also in the courtroom. Young barristers also had access to and participated in a variety of performance activities—such as amateur theatricals and mock trials of either the impromptu or organized variety—which reinforced the connections between the law and the theater and helped to shape the way that barristers spoke in court.

Toward the end of the century, although the connections between the legal and theatrical worlds remained, changes in both professions altered the character of the relationship. Both the legal and acting professions were attaining new levels of respectability. In the law, new levels of professional discipline sought to remove the stigma of the various legal scandals of the early part of the century and end the *laissez-faire* practices of a number of barristers.[150] In the theater, actors increasingly came from good social and educational backgrounds, while leaders in the profession increasingly pressed their claim for greater status and legitimacy. A new level was reached in 1895 when Queen Victoria (on Gladstone's recommendation) knighted the effective head of the actor's profession, Henry

Irving.[151] In both law and theater, the freewheeling days of the early and middle nineteenth century were over.

ORATORICAL DRAMA

The existence and popularity of the Judge and Jury Society underscores some of the ways in which trials in mid-nineteenth-century Britain were appreciated as oratorical theater, of which the Palmer trial that opened this chapter can be seen as something of an archetype. The facts of the case meant that both sides were completely dependent on the speeches of their counsel to produce the necessary levels of persuasion. Further, the nature of the facts required that the speeches of opposing counsel be in markedly contrasting styles. In the absence of direct evidence of strychnine poisoning (i.e. an eyewitness to Palmer putting the poison in Cook's food), the prosecution's case could be made only through explanation and making sense of often confusing and conflicting testimony. In complete contrast, the speech for the defense relied very heavily on high emotional rhetoric. In these ways, the drama of Palmer's guilt or innocence was conveyed to the audience through Cockburn's and Shee's lengthy speeches.

The theater of later nineteenth-century trials can be seen in greater depth through examining the oratorical dimension of one of the most dramatic trials of the era: the first trial of the Tichborne Claimant. If the Palmer trial was one of a number of *causes célèbres* in British legal history, the trials of the Tichborne Claimant could claim to be the legal cause of the century. The first (civil) trial was a piece of oratorical theater on an epic scale. It makes the Palmer trial seem brief and straightforward. To strip an extremely convoluted story to its barest essence, in 1866, a butcher living in Australia claimed to be Roger Tichborne, the heir to a baronetcy and estate who had been lost at sea in 1854. Although the Claimant (as he came universally to be known) was accepted by Tichborne's surviving mother and a few others, most family members and many acquaintances declared him to be a fraud. The Claimant could not positively establish his identity as Roger Tichborne. Both sides engaged in an extensive public relations battle (the Claimant more successfully) and much legal maneuvering (the Tichborne family more successfully). Thus, before the Claimant finally entered the courtroom in 1871, public interest in the case had been sustained for several years.[152]

The first trial, in which the Claimant as plaintiff sought legal recognition as Roger Tichborne, was a protracted affair carried out over ten months from May 1871 to March 1872. In accordance with the great public interest generated by the case before the commencement of the proceedings, the courtroom was consistently filled to capacity and graced by the presence of various curious notables including on one day the Prince and Princess of Wales. With expectations for the trial very high, the success of the drama *as* a drama depended upon the speakers. The courtroom was not a grand stage but a cramped space at Westminster. Additionally, as a civil trial, "whatever may have been the wishes of some of the visitors, no chance existed of the principal performer [the Claimant] ending his days in company with the Ordinary and executioner."[153]

The cross-examination of the Claimant by John Duke Coleridge, Solicitor General and leading counsel for the family, was one of two climactic pieces of oratorical theater during the trial. It lasted for twenty-two days between June 2 and July 6, 1871. In this dialogue (with occasional interjections from Lord Chief Justice Cockburn, the jury foreman, and the Claimant's counsel), Coleridge sought to show the Claimant's ignorance of essential facts of Roger Tichborne's known life and experience, while the Claimant sought, in the areas for which he had no answer, to leave things as murky as possible. As drama, the contest between Coleridge and the Claimant was surpassed in the nineteenth century only by the cross-examination of Oscar Wilde by Edward Carson during Wilde's 1895 libel action against the Marquis of Queensbury—a cross-examination so damaging that Wilde was forced to drop the suit.[154] Coleridge was not as successful against the Claimant as Carson was against Wilde; nevertheless, his tenacious pursuit of the extremely slippery Claimant was very well regarded, and his refrain during the cross-examination, "Would it surprise you to know. . . ?" became a popular London catch-phrase for some time.[155]

Later, after the witnesses for the Claimant had been called and examined, Coleridge produced what must certainly be regarded as the high-water mark of nineteenth-century legal oratory. Between January 15 and February 21, 1872, Coleridge delivered a twenty-six-day address to the jury in which he vigorously sought to show the Claimant was a fraud. Although his mandate did not require it, Coleridge not only asserted that the Claimant was not Roger Tichborne, but also made the dramatic claim that the Claimant's real identity was Arthur Orton, son of a Wapping butcher. During the speech, Cockburn (no supporter of the Claimant) wrote to Coleridge: "I congratulate you on having turned the tide of general opinion. I find people in the world are everywhere giving up the Claimant."[156]

In this, however, the Lord Chief Justice was too optimistic. The Claimant was non-suited, then successfully prosecuted for perjury and sentenced to fourteen years penal servitude. Nevertheless, the battle over the Claimant waged by his huge following endured for a number of years, and even continued to some extent after his death in 1898.[157]

There is no question that the Tichborne affair was a grand drama, and that the first trial—including Coleridge's twin peaks of oratorical heroism—was its climax. During the course of Coleridge's great speech, the *Saturday Review* derisively compared the trial to the theater: "It has been the fashion of late to run pieces on the London boards in a way that twenty years ago would have made managers and the public stare. By a singular coincidence the legal drama has suddenly followed the prevailing fashion."[158]

The dominant feature and dramatic focus of the first Tichborne trial was not its spectacle, but its speeches. The *Daily News* described the great anticipation which attended the opening of Coleridge's address to the jury: "There were more people waiting patiently outside, and more people in court [than on all previous days of the trial]; there was greater excitement and stronger exhibition of feeling than on any of the days on which the claimant was under examination."[159] The same paper further observed that, for this courtroom audience, space previously unoccupied for "affording a view of nothing but the clock and the ceiling, were now as much sought after as the most eligible situations were on any previous day."[160] The account also gives a sense of the dramatic qualities of Coleridge's speech itself which do not necessarily come out in the usual printed text.

> With great deliberation of manner, and with all the appearance of having weighed his words well, the Attorney-General remarked that he would show, or at least try and show that the claimant was "a cunning and audacious conspirator" (a pause), a perjurer (another longer pause), a forger (a look, as it seemed of quiet triumph at the jury), an imposter (in a slighting tone this, as if that part of the question were already proven), and a villain (a slightly melodramatic accent on the last word, and a full stop).[161]

The final comment to be made about Coleridge's performance as *oratorical,* rather than theatrical drama relates to gesture. Certainly, cramped and crowded courtrooms did not generally allow for much gesticulation by barristers.[162] Coleridge was particularly anti-gestural. His characteristic pose when speaking, as evidenced by many illustrations, was to stand leaning forward with his hands placed firmly on the table before him. In the words of a humorous rhyme about the trial: "This is the Attorney General who stands, / And speaks for weeks without raising his hands."[163]

As illustrated by the Palmer and Tichborne trials, barristers' speeches, particularly those of star counsel, held the fascination of the Victorian public. Although these trials—one criminal, one civil—were among the most sensational of their time, other courtroom causes could have been used to make the same point. In trials, the initial interest will always be generated by some combination of the nature of the cause (murder, divorce, bankruptcy), and the nature of the persons involved (particularly if they are wealthy and powerful). Yet, from the perspective of the drama of the courtroom, these elements only establish the plot. The way that the drama is played out is based on the structures of courtroom procedure. As we have seen, the legal reforms of the last two thirds of the nineteenth century produced a courtroom procedure that gave unprecedented emphasis to barristerial oratory. Thus, if the playing out of the trial was indeed dramatic, the drama was realized in greatest measure through the speeches of counsel. But procedural structures alone do not produce drama. The procedure must be appreciated *as* drama. It is clear, however, that barristers' speeches were indeed a focus of dramatic interest—most clearly evident in the crowds that sat through them, as well as the newspaper accounts, which sought to convey or describe the speeches in dramatic terms for the many unable to gain admission.

"The 'D____d Lawyer' Spirit of the House": Barristers in Parliament

The extent to which questions of morality and theatricality were central to the understanding of barristers' speech in the nineteenth century can be seen very clearly in that notable repository of legal talent: the House of Commons. Beyond the courtroom stage, many barristers stood for, and were elected to Parliament. That a significant portion of MPs was associated with the legal profession was nothing new in the nineteenth century. As one historian has observed, however, "given the special interest attaching in the nineteenth century to questions of patronage, reform, and social change, the enormous representation of the Bar takes on a special colour."[164] Thus, as a group, nineteenth-century barrister-MPs experienced a variety of new pressures both as politicians and as professionals. As parliamentary speakers, barrister-MPs constituted a distinct category by virtue of their specialized oratorical training and experience. No account of legal (or parliamentary) oratory can be complete without examining this group.

BARRISTER-MPS

Like the bar itself, lawyers in Parliament have resisted precise quantification. One of the main difficulties has been determining the precise nature of a given MP's status in the legal profession: whether he merely attended an Inn of Court, or was called to the bar; whether he practiced law but dropped it upon entering Parliament, or continued an active legal career. But even if methods of counting have differed, all those who have studied the subject agree that the number of barristers in Parliament increased significantly during the nineteenth century. Although a large number of MPs had some kind of legal training or experience, the most important question for an examination of public speech in public life is how many MPs were practicing barristers. It is this group that is the most likely to have been successful in the law's oratorical arena.

Between 1754 and 1790, the Commons included no fewer than 120 practicing English barristers and 20 practicing Scottish advocates (an average of 30 barristers and 6 advocates per election).[165] From 1790 to 1820, 165 MPs are believed to have made a career of the law.[166] During these two periods then, the proportion of MPs who were practicing barristers was 7.1 and 7.7 percent, respectively.[167] Over the course of the nineteenth century, the number of lawyers in Parliament increased by a significant margin. The proportion of *all* lawyers in the House of Commons may well have doubled from around 11 percent in the 1830s to around 20 percent in the 1880s.[168] To gain some sense of the growing presence of *practicing* lawyers in Parliament during the second half of the nineteenth century, table 4.2 draws upon a count of lawyer-MPs that excludes "lawyers" more strongly associated with other occupational categories (e.g. landowner, industrialist). According to this analysis, the proportion of practicing lawyer-MPs (almost all of them barristers) increased by 50 percent in the fifteen years between 1865 and 1880.[169]

Facilitating the upwardly mobile barristers' entry into national politics were their earnings at the bar, and their connections with members of the landed classes, which had been made either at university or at the Inns of

TABLE 4.2 MPs Chiefly Associated with the Legal Profession

General Election	Lawyer-MPs England	Wales	Scotland	Ireland	Total	Seats	% of Total Seats
1865	38	1	3	14	56	658	9%
1868	39	3	4	11	57	658	9%
1874	39	4	5	21	69	658	11%
1880	52	7	2	22	83	658	13%

Data from William Henry Whiteley, "The Social Composition of the House of Commons, 1868–1885" (PhD diss., Cornell University, 1960), Appendix I, p. 578.

Court. In terms of social background, from the late seventeenth through the middle of the early nineteenth century, the majority of lawyer-MPs appear to have come from the lower strata of the landed classes and from the professional and commercial classes. Relatively few were sons of peers. A number had been born into very humble circumstances.[170] In the second half of the nineteenth century, most lawyer-MPs continued to come from middle-class backgrounds. As a whole, the social profile of barrister-MPs in 1880 may have improved over that of a century before. According to one analysis, 40 percent of barrister-MPs in 1880 came from the aristocracy or gentry.[171] However, the practicing barrister-MPs—those without independent means and dependent on their legal earnings—most likely continued to come from lower gentry, professional, and commercial backgrounds.

Most barristers with parliamentary ambitions recognized the need to establish themselves in the legal arena first and attain a level of financial security.[172] "It is not supposed to be a good thing for a briefless barrister to try to enter politics," wrote the struggling young barrister James Bryce in 1868. "When a professional reputation has been gained, 'tis another thing."[173] Parliament may have been the best way to advance one's legal career, but these ambitions typically came at a financial cost. The demands of parliamentary membership could, if taken seriously, interfere with a barrister's practice. Accepting government office generally meant a drastic reduction in a successful barrister's income. Young barristers who got elected to Parliament without first establishing themselves in the legal arena would need, like Trollope's Phineas Finn, to get themselves noticed by the leaders of their party and appointed to junior governmental office as soon as possible. Succeeding thus, young barrister-MPs could only pray that the government to which they were attached—perhaps the sole source of their livelihood—would be long lived. More consistent with the general pattern is the career of Finn's legal mentor, Mr. Low:

> At a certain point in his career, supposing his career to have been sufficiently prosperous, it becomes natural to a barrister to stand for some constituency, and natural for him also to form his politics at that period of his life with a view to his further advancement, looking, as he does so, carefully at the age and standing of the various candidates for high legal office.[174]

Trollope's views on the political pragmatism of barristers, and the role of Commons membership in professional advancement were not mere cynicism. From 1830 to the Home Rule schism of 1886, the political affiliation of barrister-MPs was predominantly Liberal. But since the Whig and Liberal parties were ascendant in the national politics of these years, it should not be surprising that more barrister-MPs were elected in the Liberal interest, even if equal numbers of Liberal and Conservative barristers sought election. In terms of advancement, the Whig and Liberal parties were in government for around 41 years, compared to fewer than 15 years for the Tory and Conservative parties; thus, they were most often in the position to fill vacant judicial offices, and junior and senior ministerial positions.[175]

LAW OFFICERS

The general reputation of lawyer-MPs was that "they are usually birds of passage" in the House of Commons "on their way to some more permanent resting place."[176] The most important positions for barristers in the House of Commons, as well as the best stepping-stones for further advancement in the law, were the senior law offices: the Attorney General and his deputy, the Solicitor General. The offices of Attorney and Solicitor General embodied a wide range of responsibilities—some wholly legal, such as serving as leading counsel for Crown prosecutions; some wholly political, such as upholding in Parliament the legality of positions taken by other government ministers; and some a combination of the two, such as providing legal advice to the government and its ministries.[177] (The

Attorney General was also, after 1814, titular head of the English bar.) Additionally, until the end of the nineteenth century, the Attorney and Solicitor General continued their private practices—their standing with solicitors and juries further enhanced by their official position. The men who filled either or both of these offices typically proceeded to the judicial bench, or attained the highest (and most lucrative) legal-political office, the Lord Chancellorship. The Lord Chancellor was effectively Speaker of the House of Lords, which was also theoretically the highest court of appeal for most of the nineteenth century. Thus, just as the established church, in the form of senior bishops, contributed a number of prominent orators to the upper house, so too did the legal profession.

In considering the legal contribution to the Commons, it is important to note that the offices of Attorney and Solicitor General, in addition to a number of more minor ones, were important and lucrative positions open exclusively to members of the legal profession. Indeed, as the parliamentary essayist Henry Lucy observed, the expectations for barrister-MPs were far different from those of an "ordinary" MP:

> A man may hang about an under-Secretaryship of State for years and look no higher than finally to be Secretary, a promotion to which he has no prescriptive right, and may only hope to earn. With the barrister who, being in the House of Commons, steadily fixes his eyes on the Solicitor-Generalship, the case is different. Once made Solicitor-General, whilst the immediate professional advantages are soothingly solid, the Lord Chancellorship is a plum which no one can say hangs above his reach.[178]

Between 1830 and 1895, 42 men filled the offices of Solicitor General and Attorney General. Of these, 80 percent went on to higher positions within the law: 11 became Lord Chancellor, and another 23 were appointed to some form of judicial office. Only three appear to have made politics their final career: J. E. Gorst, who became a Financial Secretary to the Treasury and an organizer of the Conservative party; William Vernon Harcourt, who served as Home Secretary and Chancellor of the Exchequer; and Henry James, who might have been Gladstone's Lord Chancellor or Home Secretary in 1886 but opposed Home Rule and later served as Chancellor of the Duchy of Lancaster in Salisbury's Unionist government. Edward Clarke, Solicitor General in Salisbury's first administration, declined further offers of promotion, but remained active as both an MP and a barrister.[179]

For a barrister-MP with a successful practice, agreeing to serve as one of the law officers almost certainly meant a significant reduction in income because the job interfered with one's ability to take cases. Edward Clarke declined further office for just this reason. While the law officers received remuneration for their official duties and continued to be briefed by private clients, the demands of their official duties and parliamentary attendance inevitably decreased their ability to sustain the more profitable private side of their business at its previous levels. John Duke Coleridge, in an 1872 speech against debarring government law officers from maintaining a private practice, claimed that he had already "lost between a third and a half of my private practice by taking office."[180]

Law officers received no salary until 1871; instead, their remuneration consisted of various official fees for advising on cases forwarded from other departments and government officials. The uniform official fee of three guineas for such work was viewed as very small. Other income accrued to the law officers from adjudicating on petitions for patents, and a host of other matters. In 1850, Attorney General Sir John Jervis estimated that his total official income for the three previous years had averaged around £10,000 per year.[181] In 1871, the old system was replaced with annual salaries of £7,000 and £6,000 for the Attorney and Solicitor General, respectively, with some supplementary fees allowed, but many abolished.

While the political and professional gains enjoyed by law officers typically came at a financial cost, a successful career in the law could also provide a certain measure of political independence. As Attorney General, Roundell Palmer made around £23,000 in 1865—said at the time to be more than any previous holder of that office—and even exceeded this in another year with income of more than £27,000.[182] Later, Lord Stanley cynically noted that Palmer's "refusal of office [in 1869] when the demolition of the Irish church was in progress, really involved no sacrifice, but on the contrary considerable pecuniary gain, he was adroit enough to make it appear a political martyrdom, and obtained unbounded sympathy from both sides."[183]

BARRISTERIAL-PARLIAMENTARY SPEECH

With respect to their oratorical standing in the House, barrister-MPs were seen as occupying a special position by virtue of their professional training and experience, but they were not viewed as contributing to either the eloquence or the efficiency of Parliament. For example, in a leader discussing the character of the Parliament of 1880, *The Times* attempted to interpret the consequences of the significantly increased proportion of lawyer-MPs, which it declared to be the new Parliament's salient feature. On one hand, *The Times* noted that "It is possible to have too much of a good thing, and a superabundance of legal talents does not necessarily promise well for the rapid despatch of business." On the other hand, "Large measures cannot be extemporized." Nevertheless, while raising these concerns over the consequences of more legal orators on parliamentary business and speech, the general sense of the leader was that more lawyers in Parliament was probably a good thing given the increasingly technical nature of legislation and administration.[184]

In practice, however, barrister-MPs were valued less for their ability to deal with technical bills, and far more for their courtroom-honed abilities in the cut and thrust of debate. If large measures could not be extemporized, responses to those measures could. A barrister who was successful in replying to the arguments of opposing counsel in the courts succeeded in the Commons to the extent that he could do the same to measures introduced from the opposing benches. When Hugh Cairns left the Attorney Generalship in 1866 to become Lord Justice of Appeal, the loss of his debating power on the Conservative side was deeply lamented. Lord Stanley recorded in his diary, "I do not see how without Cairns, we have the strength to get through the session."[185] Disraeli wrote that Cairns's removal to the bench "is a great blow for the party and mainly myself. For he was my right hand in debate and with him I was not afraid to encounter Gladstone and Roundell Palmer. Now I have got them both without the slightest assistance."[186] Later in the century, another barrister-MP noted for his speaking ability in both court and Parliament, Edward Clarke, was asked to perform the awesome task of replying to Gladstone's speech introducing the second Home Rule bill. It was felt by the Conservative leadership that Clarke's long experience of effective extemporaneous reply in courtroom debate would enable him to furnish an immediate (and therefore, in the parliamentary context, more effective) counter to Gladstone's program.[187]

Yet, while highly valued as debaters, barrister-MPs—even those who had been among the most successful courtroom speech-makers—rarely acquired a reputation for parliamentary eloquence. It appears to have been something of a commonplace that "There is undoubtedly a certain prejudice against lawyers in the House of Commons."[188] This prejudice can be observed particularly in the area of speaking. The barrister-MPs' seemingly paradoxical lack of oratorical success in the Commons was a fact of parliamentary life that experienced Parliament-watchers consistently remarked upon:

> It would be hard to say why, as a rule, lawyers are not successful, or at least are not popular, House of Commons debaters. It would be reasonable to expect precisely the reverse. A trained advocate endowed with natural gifts, strengthened and polished by daily training, appears to be the man of all others who should succeed in the Parliamentary arena. . . . This kind of dual life is lived at this day by some of the principal men at the Bar. In court, eloquent, brilliant, resourceful, and successful; in the House of Commons, prosy, artificial, tiresome, unconvincing.[189]

Two decades later, Lord Curzon attempted (somewhat unsuccessfully) to explain this phenomenon:

> There seems to be a general impression that lawyers are not generally successful or popular in the House of Commons, and that the abilities which may have won fame in cross-examining witnesses or winning verdicts from juries are not those suited to Parliamentary debate. . . . If there be such a law or even tendency, the explanation may perhaps lie in the fact that lawyers only come down to the House when their day's work is over and they are relatively tired. But it also lies in the different nature of the problems they approach and the audiences they address. The House of Commons dislikes that which is didactic and recoils from that which is dull. It never quite forgave hair-splitting even when it was Mr. Gladstone's foible. It will not accept it as the armoury of smaller men. Possibly also the House is a little suspicious of professions other than its own.[190]

These parliamentary prejudices reflected more than general suspicions of the advocate's arts. It was precisely those courtroom skills at which leading barristers excelled that worked against their reputations as parliamentary speakers. So, for example, according to an 1847 essay on parliamentary barristers, former Attorney General Frederick Thesiger "has not been successful in parliament. . . . Take up whatever subject he may,—a grave political question, a legal argument, an *ex officio* explanation, or a railway case,—he equally seems to speak as from a brief. He carries all the habits, gestures, and mode of treatment of the *nisi prius* [i.e. jury trial] advocate into parliament."[191] Former Solicitor General Fitzroy Kelly, was described as "a very effective speaker [in Parliament], but has never risen to a high rank as an orator. In hard argument, or ingenious special pleading, he excels, but he has not displayed declamatory power, nor can he successfully appeal to the feelings. The defects of his *nisi prius* advocacy follow him into the House of Commons."[192] According to another writer in the early 1870s, Roundell Palmer "is an admirable debater," but "is so careful not to go wrong, not to overstate or misjudge anything, that his speeches never have the impulse of genuine eloquence." Even Hugh Cairns "though almost a model debater, is not, to my thinking, either an orator or a statesman. . . . He is an able lawyer and an inestimable partisan—and nothing more." John Duke Coleridge "is really a great advocate, but I hardly think he shows to much advantage in the House of Commons."[193]

On one level, the unwillingness of MPs and parliamentary observers to believe that an advocate could be a great parliamentary orator stems from the antitheatrical/anti-legal prejudice. Commenting on the aftermath of a pitched battle between two parliamentary barristers, John Wodehouse (the future Lord Kimberley) wrote: "The learned Counsel who had been unsparing in their personal attacks on each other, informed us at the close that they were about to dine together at Greenwich. So much for the invectives of Counsel. They really acted their indignation very well."[194] On another level, the generally low oratorical reputation of barrister-MPs also resulted in part from the matters about which they typically spoke. Other than the issues of local concern that prompt most back-bench intervention, barrister-MPs addressed themselves mainly to questions where legal issues were involved, or bills of a highly technical nature. At first this seems peculiar because the success of a barrister in the courtroom generally depended more on his ability to undo the arguments of opposing counsel and win the sympathies of the jury than on his command of the law. However, although many successful barristers were not great lawyers, they knew more than the majority of non-legal MPs, and were in any case more familiar than most other MPs with the forms and language of the law.

Holding of one of the principal law offices seems to have been an oratorical damper, even for talented speakers. In 1850, Alexander Cockburn was a successful barrister but for the last three years an obscure MP. Nearly fifty years old, he acquired sudden parliamentary celebrity in the great Don Pacifico debate when he was asked by Palmerston to speak on the legal aspects of the matter in reply to Gladstone's condemnations. *The Times* recorded that it was "a speech of much power and eloquence with some lively and pointed sallies respecting the state of the parties."[195] So well-regarded was Cockburn's performance that "one-half of the treasury benches were left empty, while honourable members ran one after another, tumbling over each other in their haste, to shake hands with the honourable and learned member."[196] A few months after his great speech, Cockburn was appointed Solicitor General, and in early 1851 he was raised to Attorney General. Yet, although Cockburn continued to contribute to debates, he never again found the opportunity to repeat his oratorical triumph in the House. In the courtroom, however, it was a different story. In his capacity as Attorney General, Cockburn performed conspicuously—particularly in the two most sensational trials of the 1850s: the Palmer trial, and the Hopwood cause (a dispute over a great Lancashire property that involved a large number of aristocratic witnesses).

Cockburn's intervention in the Don Pacifico debate came to be something of a standard against which speeches by barrister-MPs were measured. For example, Henry James's 1872 speech on the Galway election controversy was warmly received by colleagues on both sides of the House (including the leader of the opposition, Disraeli). Like Cockburn, James was soon appointed Solicitor, then Attorney General. But also like Cockburn, James's intervention in the Galway election debate came to be viewed as the high point of his parliamentary speaking career. In its obituary of James *The Times* wrote: "In effect, in force of argument, and aptness of language, it was comparable to Cockburn's speech on the Don Pacifico case."[197]

Another notable example of a successful barrister who began his parliamentary career as a wide-ranging speaker, but who became far more narrow after accepting government office, is John Duke Coleridge. First elected to Parliament in 1865, he was asked to introduce the University Tests bill of 1866 for his maiden speech—a formidable feat, but Coleridge's qualifications as a solid Liberal, a known High Churchman, and a top speaker since his days at the Oxford Union made him an ideal candidate.[198] At first Coleridge declined, having "so keen a sense of the 'd___d lawyer' spirit of the House of Commons, as also a real feeling that it would be felt to be such unbecoming presumption on my part to take up such a measure in my first session."[199] Eventually, he was won over and his speech was much praised for its eloquence.

During his first session, Coleridge also made notable speeches on the second reading of the 1866 Reform bill (April 20, 1866) and the perennial bill to allow marriage to a deceased wife's sister (May 2, 1866). A year later, he spoke at length against disestablishment of the Church of Ireland (April 30, 1867). Yet, once Coleridge became a law officer (serving as Solicitor and Attorney General from 1868 until he was appointed Lord Chief Justice of England in 1873) his parliamentary utterances were largely confined to either wholly legal matters (e.g. state trials, criminal law, County Courts, the jury system, the role and remuneration of the law officers, law reform, and married women's property), or legal aspects of other issues before Parliament (e.g. corrupt practices, Army regulation, and supply).

Sir William Harcourt appears to prove the case in reverse, for his reputation as a parliamentary speaker tended to increase the farther his career moved from the well-trodden path of legal advancement through Parliament. Harcourt entered Parliament in 1869, and became Solicitor General in 1873. The turning point of his public life came when the Liberals regained the government in 1880 and he was offered the Home Secretaryship. Harcourt accepted, even though he had, after the traditional fashion, desired the Attorney Generalship with an eye on the Woolsack. A decade later, Henry Lucy wrote of Harcourt that, "It is curious . . . to note how a man drifting away from the practice of law succeeds with increasing force in becoming an acceptable Parliamentary debater."[200] Even so, although some of the lawyer's stigma wore off as he became Home Secretary and later Chancellor of the Exchequer, Harcourt was never regarded as a particularly eloquent speaker.[201] His set speeches tended to be over-prepared and over-elaborate. Instead, the growth of his parliamentary speaking reputation rested on his impromptu utterances in debate were lively and full of the brand of sarcastic humor that is well-received in the Commons. George Otto Trevelyan for one recalled how Harcourt in debate "overwhelmed his antagonist and convulsed the House by the humour and impetus of his onset, and having swept the field fell back on his prepared speech and sacrificed much of the impression his impromptu exordium had created."[202]

In part, the declining eloquence of law officers resulted from the nature of their parliamentary role. Outside of Parliament, it was the duty of the Attorney and Solicitor General to cross oratorical swords with the leading defense counsel. Indeed, one result of the creation of a Central Criminal Court in 1834 and the 1836 Prisoner's Counsel Act was that Attorneys and Solicitors General had to be more proficient courtroom speakers and debaters in order to be effective against the loosed forensic eloquence of defense counsel in the cockpit of the Old Bailey. In Parliament, however, Attorneys and Solicitors General were more or less constrained to speak on points of law for the government and for specific departments. Although in reality speaking in a partisan interest, law officers' speeches tend to adopt the independent tone of the legal expert. As Coleridge sought to remind the House (arguing against prohibiting private practice), a law officer

> has to advise the Government and the House itself on subjects of which the importance cannot be overstated; so that he must have judgement, which, as a rule, is the result of experience and the growth of time, and he must have ascertained and [*sic*] great professional position, so that he may not be overborne by the weight of greater authority in the House itself when he is called upon to speak on legal subjects; as to which, *if he does his duty, he will always remember that it is a real opinion, not a party argument, which the House is entitled to expect at his hands.*[203]

Regardless of the law officers' duties to the government and the Commons, however, there was clearly nothing to be gained, and potentially much to lose, by calling upon law officers to speak—even on legal questions—if they were not up to the task. It was also not unknown for a law officer to decline the requests of his superiors in government. In 1853, Gladstone, then Chancellor of the Exchequer, repeatedly called for the assistance of Attorney General Cockburn during the debate on the Succession Duty bill. Eventually, Cockburn sent back a message that he knew nothing about death duties and that the Chancellor had better look to the Solicitor General for help.[204]

Some have remarked upon how little nineteenth-century law officers spoke, even with respect to legal matters. Between the increasing demands of official business and private practice (even when curtailed), the ability of law officers to attend parliamentary sittings was often limited.[205] Even when they did attend, it was entirely possible that the law officers would not be called upon to speak—even upon legal matters. In 1842, for instance, Attorney General Pollock was never asked to speak on the highly complex Income Tax bill of that year. Instead, Peel assumed responsibility for carrying the measure through.[206] Of his experience as Solicitor General in 1866, William Bovill said that the law officers were only consulted in really important matters and were "not expected to attend ordinary divisions in the House of Commons unless specially summoned."[207]

The many roles of a law officer conflicted with one another: a request to appear in Parliament could take an Attorney or Solicitor General away from their intended appearance at a trial, leaving all in the hands of their junior.[208] The expectations for the law officer's attention to public business were greatly raised after the introduction of salaries in 1871, but the struggle was not fully resolved until the prohibition on their ability to engage in private practice in 1895.[209] Criticism of the law officers for neglecting their parliamentary role stands in contrast to some of the more general criticisms leveled at lawyer-MPs for not looking out for the interests of their profession. In 1852, for example, fearing the social degradation and financial immiseration of lawyers as a class that would result from the County Courts Extension bill, *The Law Times* wrote:

> It is greatly to be regretted that, although there are so many Lawyers in the House of Commons, there are none who look after the interests of the Profession. There are many earnest law reformers, and many who are hostile to all reform. Both of these parties are zealous in promoting or opposing changes in the law, but none makes it his care, while supporting improvements, to see that they are effected without utter disregard to the well-being of the Profession.[210]

Thus, in a number of ways, barrister-MPs were neither fish nor fowl—a fact clearly reflected in their overall reputation as parliamentary speakers. As a group, barrister-MPs seem to have been regarded as not particularly good, but occasionally useful speakers. It would also seem that even the best of them made only one or two notable speeches by parliamentary standards, although—the "'d____d lawyer' spirit of the House" notwithstanding—their barrister's powers of extemporaneous reply were valued. Legal advancement through Parliament appears to have come at an oratorical cost. Office-holders had to curtail both their parliamentary appearances and private practice in order to balance both against the increasing demands of other official duties. Additionally, the speeches of office-holders tended to become duller as the duties of office curtailed the scope, tone, and opportunity of speaking.

Conclusion

By the end of the nineteenth century, the law reforms of the preceding fifty years had given greater scope to legal oratory, but it was no longer the same free-wheeling speech evidenced by the generations of Charles Phillips and Charles Wilkins. In an elegiac summing up of this transformation, one historian of the Victorian bar has written:

> The early years of the Victorian Bar were peopled with personalities of a kind that was to disappear as the century progressed. They were relics of an earlier age, unmarked by the strict moral rectitude of their successors, less fearful of scandal, more profligate of money—and members of a school of advocacy that was to die out in the 1880s. Even in a profession that seemed to attract extroverts, to whom the stage was the nearest profession, they were larger than life and strutted through the Victorian scene with a panache and arrogance that was never to be repeated. Many of them lacked legal learning, but few of them lacked colour.[211]

The same trend was noticed by contemporaries, although the passing of the old days was less regretted by some. In the late 1880s, Fitzjames Stephen noted the restrained and prosaic character of speeches by counsel in even the most terrible of criminal cases. Although, as a public moralist seeking to promote greater respect for the law, Stephen perhaps went too far in claiming that attempts at eloquence are contemptible, ludicrous, and vulgar, or that most barristers "are justly afraid of being laughed at and looking silly if they aim at eloquence, and generally avoid it by keeping quiet."[212]

Another sign of the increasing respectability of barristers was the way in which the oratorical stock of barristers in Parliament experienced a considerable rise in the decades around the turn of the century. Perhaps this was because there was a greater number of barrister-MPs to assess their colleagues. Even so, the most obvious names are striking examples of parliamentary oratorical success at the highest level. The barristers H. H. Asquith, Rufus Isaacs, F. E. Smith, and John Simon were all regarded as being among the very best speakers in the House—Asquith rising to the premiership, Isaacs to Lord Chief Justice and Viceroy of India, and Smith and Simon to the Woolsack. Among barrister-MPs of the later nineteenth-century, only Roundell Palmer might have held an equal oratorical reputation. Not to be overlooked, the solicitor and advocate David Lloyd George also enjoyed a leading reputation as a parliamentary speaker, although he was often (like Gladstone) criticized for demagoguery.

If barristerial speech was viewed overall with considerable ambivalence in the nineteenth century, it reflects the somewhat ambivalent position of barristers themselves in Victorian public life. Indeed, beyond the ways in which the questions surrounding barristerial speech document the modernization of the legal profession during this period, questions of speech also lay close to the core of that modernizing process. In some ways, the case of barristerial speech reveals resistance to the overall expansion of oratorical production: the greater latitude afforded to barristerial speech in the first half of the century; followed by discipline imposed upon it in the second half through innovations like the Hardwicke Society, which cultivated common oratorical standards among young barristers, and the emphasis on improved legal knowledge at the expense of theatrical advocacy. As a sector of Victorian public life, the law and its courtroom practitioners adapted to new conditions and new attitudes. In an increasingly rationalized legal system as in an increasingly democratized legislature, the strongly negative cultural responses to barristers' oratory was a function of the larger role barristers came to play in both.

CHAPTER FIVE

The Platform

IN 1850, THOMAS CARLYLE published a pamphlet criticizing both the way in which British public life had become characterized by talking rather than doing, and the inflated value placed on the eloquence of public men. "Probably," he wrote, "there is not in Nature a more distracted phantasm than your commonplace eloquent speaker, as he is found on platforms, in parliaments, on Kentucky stumps, at tavern-dinners, in windy, empty insincere times like ours."[1] Adopting a Puritanical tone, Carlyle ends his piece with the call: "Be not a Public Orator, thou brave young British man, thou that art now growing up to be something: not a Stump Orator if thou canst help it."[2]

Carlyle, however, was on the wrong side of history. Public speech of many different kinds was on the rise in the second half of the nineteenth century—not least, platform speaking. Indeed, it is particularly significant that, around the same time as Carlyle's attack on the "stump orator," the nineteenth century's greatest public speaker had his first significant encounter with the mass platform. In October 1853, Gladstone visited Manchester for several days and made a number of speeches during his stay. The experience was not wholly novel: Gladstone had spoken to many audiences since his entry into public life, from election speeches to addresses before small religious societies. But Manchester in 1853 was different in two important respects. At that time, Gladstone had moved to the forefront of national public life through his much-publicized demolition of Disraeli's budget in 1852 followed in April 1853 by the promulgation of his own as Aberdeen's Chancellor of the Exchequer. At Manchester, he was treated as a great man. But not only was his relationship to his audience changed, the nature of his audience was also different. At the main event of his visit, the unveiling of the Peel Monument, Gladstone for the first time went before "a great assemblage—of *men* almost exclusively, & working men. There I spoke to the cracking of my voice." The novelty was repeated the following day when, laying a foundation for a new school, Gladstone "had again to speak to an assembly of the *people*."[3] Given his later history as an orator with an unprecedented command of the platform, and a politician who pioneered a new kind of mass politics centered on the platform, the speeches at Manchester are an important turning point—both for Gladstone himself,[4] and for the larger history of public speech and public life in nineteenth-century Britain.

The platform speaking about which Carlyle complained, if not exactly a new phenomenon in 1850, was nevertheless a fairly recent coinage. The "platform" as a term for a particular kind of public speaking is recorded as having come into currency around 1820.[5] As historical phenomena go, the emergence of the platform as an important vehicle of political communication is relatively self-evident. As a subject of historical inquiry, the platform has benefited from a number of notable studies over the last hundred years. The increasing trend of platform speaking was routinely commented upon (and often complained about) in the major journals of opinion in the late nineteenth century. The first full scholarly treatment of the platform as a political phenomenon is *The Platform: Its Rise and Progress*, written at the end of the nineteenth century by Henry Jephson.[6] As its title suggests, Jephson's is a highly narrative, highly Whiggish account of how the platform came to be incorporated into—and ultimately, in many ways, to dominate—formal politics as both cause and consequence of the progress of British democracy. Even though it is now over a century old, *The Platform* remains the only attempt at a comprehensive treatment of its subject. In fact, Jephson's work stands as a monument to the high-water mark of the utility of platform oratory in mainstream politics.

Writing a decade after Jephson, the political scientist Moisei Ostrogorski viewed the platform as an essential element in the creation of modern British democracy.[7] This view of the platform as a prominent feature of Britain's nineteenth-century democratic development was extended in the 1960s by John Vincent, who argued that the platform abilities of Bright, then Gladstone (combined with the new cheap popular press) harnessed mass support to the Liberal party, even though Liberal policy was framed to benefit the aristocratic members of the parliamentary party.[8] The increasing recourse of politicians to the platform in the second half of the nineteenth century has been further elucidated by H. C. G. Matthew, who viewed its political efficacy as dependent upon technical developments in the print media and the peculiarities of the extended, but still limited electoral franchise between 1867 and 1918.[9]

Despite the inherent limitations of some of these works, taken together they have covered the substantive and interpretive ground very thoroughly. Further, the term "platform" comprehends many varieties of public speaking and public speakers, and other scholars have shed considerable light on some of these specific aspects. A mere chapter cannot hope to take all of this into account, let alone match the comprehensive scope of Jephson's two large volumes. Nevertheless, platform oratory is indispensable to an account of the role of public speech in Victorian public life. Although many kinds of platform speaking will be noted and even discussed, the principal focus of this chapter (like its predecessors) will be *official* public life. For the platform, this means, in Matthew's words, the "growth of regular extra-parliamentary speech-making by leading politicians and by ordinary MPs."[10]

The Hustings

Because it overlaps with extra-parliamentary speech-making, it is important to make a few brief observations about hustings oratory. The word hustings has a variety of meanings, many of them relating to ancient local courts of law. More familiarly, it means the physical structure—the platform—erected for a public speaker. In its most particular usage, a hustings is the temporary structure from which the nomination of candidates was made before the Ballot Act of 1872, and from which the candidates addressed the electors. Here, therefore, hustings oratory is defined as speeches made by candidates to constituents during elections.

Making hustings speeches was a considerable ordeal for candidates. In *Middlemarch* (1871-72), George Eliot provides an agonizing depiction of a hustings *failure* when Mr. Brooke attempts to recommend himself to the electors of the town and ends up being ridiculed by the crowd and pelted with eggs.[11] As a number of historians have shown, elections were often more about carnival than candidature. Candidates' speeches were central to the local rituals of constituency politics. Frank O'Gorman and James Vernon in particular have produced valuable studies of hustings speeches as part of a broader interpretation of electoral political culture during the first two-thirds of the nineteenth century.[12] For both historians, the kind of platform speaking they discuss is part of an older set of political traditions which they see as essentially dying out by the middle of the nineteenth century. For O'Gorman, the emergence of national party organizations led to a supplanting of traditional local electoral culture by a new political culture centered on party politics. Among the consequences of this transition, O'Gorman observes a shift in the nature of speeches from the platitudinous to the party political. Vernon goes further to see that so-called "reform" legislation had the effect of curtailing the more democratic and libertarian forms of political expression in traditional electoral culture, thereby making the constitution less, rather than more democratic until the Second Reform Act.

Yet, while it may very well have been the case that electoral culture became far more regimented in the second half of the century,[13] this does not mean that the oratorical output at elections diminished. If anything, as Reform and redistribution acts placed an increasing number of constituencies at the disposal of an increasing electorate, it appears to have become increasingly incumbent on a candidate to speak. The declining number of uncontested elections—from more than 200 in the 1840s and 1850s to fewer than 100 in the 1880s and early 1890s—also exacerbated the need for candidates to say something to constituents.[14]

At the beginning of the century, there were a handful of notable "popular" urban constituencies—like the City, Middlesex, and Westminster—where the electorate was a relatively high proportion of the population, and candidates were expected to speak repeatedly and often during elections that were almost always contested. Other towns were also demanding on their candidates. In 1812, Henry Brougham described his grueling oratorical ordeal in Liverpool:

> You can have no idea of the nature of a Liverpool election; it is quite peculiar to the place. You have every night to go to the different clubs, benefit societies, etc., which meet and speechify. This is from half-past six to one in the morning at least; and you have to speak to each man who polls, at the bar, from ten to five. It lasted eight days. I began my canvass three whole days before, and had nine nights of the clubs, besides a regular speech each day at the close of the poll. I delivered in that time one hundred and sixty speeches and odd; and yesterday and to-day, after being beaten, I rallied and delivered regular speeches to the whole multitude. I had to close with one above an hour long, so you may guess how exhausted I am, especially as I never saw a popular election before. I knew nothing of it.[15]

By the end of the century, this kind of ordeal—once a local, urban peculiarity—had extended even to rural constituencies, as Richard Greville Verney discovered in 1895:

> The Rugby division of Warwickshire was a straggling rural constituency, about thirty miles long and fifteen broad, consisting of about ninety villages and the town of Rugby. In those days, there were no motor-cars, and the constituency was badly served in the matter of railways, so the distances had to be covered in carriages drawn by horses. . . . The county candidate or member is now [in the 1920s, with the benefit of a motor car] made to address two, three, four, five, or perhaps more meetings in a single night, and to keep on doing so; whereas in the days of horses and carriages he could only speak, as a general rule, at one meeting each evening. . . . As it was, [on election day] we started at eight o'clock in the morning, and drove with relays of horses between eighty and ninety miles.[16]

In terms of the production (and, implicitly, the consumption) of campaign oratory, then, it is possible to see that the traditions of a small number of more democratically minded constituencies were, by the end of the century, extended far more broadly across the political landscape—even if framed within the context of national parties and party factions. Hustings oratory itself relied (as indeed it continues to rely) on platitudinous flattery of both the locality and the locals (the beauty of the country and its women, the productivity of the town and its people), and promises to address a variety of local concerns if elected or reelected.

In the late eighteenth century, Edmund Burke is generally credited as a pioneer in using hustings speeches to go beyond flattery and platitudes and address substantial political issues. Standing as a candidate for Bristol in 1774, Burke delivered a brief speech in which he discussed the conflict with America and asserted his support of both constitution and commerce. Following his victory at the polls, Burke gave a more extensive speech on the nature of parliamentary representation. Six years later, during the general election of 1780, Burke again mounted the platform at the Guildhall in Bristol. In this speech—considered one of the masterpieces of British political oratory—Burke sought to explain his motivations and justify his actions as an MP with respect to a wide range of current political issues.[17]

Burke was, however, the exception that proved the rule for a considerable time. By the second half of the century, local appeal still remained at the forefront of hustings oratory, even when general elections were called over nationally divisive issues, such as Home Rule. In such cases, candidates were under no compulsion to speak to such matters unless it was a particular concern of the constituents and electors (e.g. if the constituency had a large Irish population). Thus, although the scope of hustings oratory expanded significantly in the nineteenth century, there was also a great deal of continuity in its general import.

Parallel Platform Developments

In the last third of the nineteenth century, major politicians increasingly went before the public to speak on the principal issues of the day. Although this occurred during elections as well as at other times, it was a far cry from the locally directed platitudes of the hustings tradition. For both speakers and audiences, this style of politics combined the techniques and experiences acquired from two major sources of activity over the preceding decades: experiments by a number of leading politicians in more public forms of address, and a linked succession of organized radical protest movements.

THE MINISTERIAL PLATFORM

Long before the extra-parliamentary platform became a routinely employed instrument of mainstream politics, there were a few notable instances of leading politicians who addressed large gatherings of people on political issues of the day. Charles James Fox is one of the earliest examples of a major political figure that engaged in a significant amount of extra-parliamentary speaking beyond the electoral hustings. Although Fox was a minister only briefly during his long political career, as the leader of the opposition in the Commons, he was, in a sense, a perpetual minister-in-waiting. In January 1780, he made his first speech outside the House of Commons at Wiltshire to a small meeting of the Association movement. It was in the following month, however, that Fox spoke to a really large audience when more than 3,000 people gathered to hear him at Westminster Hall. On both occasions, Fox urged his audiences to press the cause of their own liberties. Thereafter, on a variety of occasions, Fox continued to address crowds of his constituents either in Westminster Hall, or just outside in Palace Yard, almost always opposing government measures, or urging his audiences "to get the ministers out."[18]

Like Burke on the hustings, however, the extra-parliamentary speaking of Fox is best understood as arising out of political frustration. Both Burke and Fox had significant problems in the "proper" venue for politicians' speeches, the House of Commons. As already noted (p. 53), Burke was known as the parliamentary "dinner bell." His speeches at Bristol were like (but far less significant than) his practice of publishing his parliamentary speeches: a means to broadcast ideas that had gained little hearing in the House. Fox, although he had the ear of the House, had precious little support in it as leader of a small opposition against Pitt's patronage-fueled majorities. Therefore, he too had an interest in broadcasting his opposition more widely.

Perhaps the most significant precursor of the ministerial platform as it emerged in the later nineteenth century was Gladstone's boyhood hero, George Canning. Like Fox, Canning was one of the leading parliamentary orators of his day. Unlike Fox, however, Canning held ministerial and cabinet posts for substantial periods and eventually (albeit briefly) became Prime Minister. He spoke often to his constituents at Liverpool, and not only during elections. In his speeches, Canning often eschewed the usual local pieties in favor of fairly extensive accounts of his political opinions and policies. Writing in a laudatory mode, the publisher of Canning's Liverpool speeches asserted that:

> Mr. Canning is, so far as our recollection serves, the first British senator who has valued himself upon maintaining a constant intellectual intercourse with his constituents, and who has seized every opportunity of personally inculcating, with all the vigour of his commanding talents, those political opinions which he had invariably advocated, and with such splendid success, in the Commons' House of Parliament.[19]

As Canning himself said in January 1814 to more than 400 Liverpool men at a public dinner in his honor: "I know, Gentlemen, that it is your wish, and I feel it to be my duty, that I should now proceed to communicate to you my sentiments on the state of public affairs with all the same frankness which has hitherto distinguished all our intercourse with each other."[20] At this and on numerous similar occasions, the cabinet minister or ex-cabinet minister stated his views on current issues of foreign and domestic policy—first the conduct of the war; later, the Catholic emancipation and Reform questions. The novelty of Canning's actions was reflected in the disdain expressed by his Tory critics, who thought he made himself "more ridiculous than enough by going round the country *speechifying* & discussing the acts & intentions of the Government. This is quite a new system *among us* & excites great indignation."[21]

Although Canning was clearly unusual in his use of the platform to discuss government acts and intentions, this is not to say that he never indulged in the familiar platitudes of public address. What distinguished Canning from most of his contemporaries was his ability to mix platitudes with matters of policy. His speeches during the general election of 1818 are full of the standard election-time parochial issues, such as flattery of the local women. At the same time, however, he also used these speeches to declare his stand on a variety of national issues.[22] In October 1823, when being presented with the freedom of the borough of Plymouth, Canning praised the locality in the traditional manner; but the Foreign Minister also took the time to give "the right tone upon the issue of the Spanish war." It was a speech that took on national, and international importance. Using imagery directed at his Plymouth audience, Canning likened Britain's current "repose" to the nearby warships at anchor: "while apparently passive and motionless, she silently concentrates the power to be put forth on an adequate occasion. But God forbid that that occasion should arise!"[23]

Like his other platform speeches on foreign policy, the Plymouth speech was not (as the Austrian *chargé d'affaires* claimed) a diplomatic manifesto addressed to the world. But it was a significant instance of a high-ranking cabinet minister speaking out in public on larger political concerns. Canning's uniqueness in this regard can be seen most clearly in contrast to the situation immediately following his death in 1827. During the recess of 1828-29—while Reform and Catholic emancipation had been the subjects of much heated debate in Parliament and the causes of much popular platform agitation—*The Times* reports no speeches by even regular MPs except, as a matter of course, at the time of the general election.[24] Canning's published speeches provide further testimony to the way in which his extra-parliamentary speeches were viewed as extraordinary. As originally planned, the six-volume collection of his speeches was to be limited to Parliamentary speeches only—thereby replicating the printed monuments to Pitt and Fox. In the end, however, it was felt that justice could not be done to the statesman's eloquence without including his major efforts outside Parliament. In particular, his 1820 speech in the Liverpool Music Hall against Reform was viewed as having surpassed "both in power of eloquence and of argument, any speech which he ever delivered, either in or out of Parliament."[25] Hence, a section of major extra-parliamentary speeches was added to the end of volume six.

The use of platform speeches by political leaders to expound policy became a distinguishing feature of political life in the later nineteenth century. As in so many other things, Robert Peel was an innovator in this respect. Certainly, many of his policy pronouncements were made through speeches or written addresses to his Tamworth constituents—most notably the "Tamworth Manifesto" delivered at a constituency banquet in 1834. However, particularly during the late 1830s, Peel also delivered major statements of policy at a variety of public gatherings outside Tamworth. These efforts were viewed by contemporaries as extraordinary. As one of Peel's critics complained in 1835:

> During the last twelve months he has said more, in exposition of his political views, than probably any man ever did before in the same period of time. Besides taking the most frequent part in all the parliamentary debates of a very protracted session, he has written a letter to his constituents, spoken a long speech at the Mansion-house, made another to his constituents soon after, turned the Harrow dinner into a Tory meeting, and harangued the choicest Conservatives of London at Merchant Tailors' [Hall].[26]

To take the last named speech (at a dinner in his honor given by Conservative merchants, bankers, and traders of the City on May 11, 1835), Peel delivered what has been described as "the most significant public pronouncement outside the walls of Westminster which he had so far made."[27] Yet, freshly turned out of office, the former Prime Minister stated that he had only accepted the invitation because I believed that the object of the meeting was to express *public* feeling, and because I thought *public* interest might be promoted."[28] Further—a clear sign that the extra-parliamentary platform had not yet come into its own as a vehicle for the articulation of policy—Peel repeatedly insisted that he was not speaking as a "party-man."[29] These disclaimers notwithstanding, the substance of the speech was a clear assertion of partisan principles. The Conservative leader urged his audience to accept Reform, but not to permit interference with the mixed and balanced constitutional structure of King, Lords, and Commons. The desire to uphold and protect the Constitution in this form he defined as "Conservative Principles." The same ideas were repeated in a number of other platform speeches, such as at Glasgow in 1837 and Merchant Tailors' Hall in 1838.[30] In other extra-parliamentary speeches, Peel delivered detailed justifications of specific policies. In his last major extra-parliamentary effort, for example—at a dinner in his honor at Tamworth during the election campaign of 1841—he spoke for two hours about the Corn Laws and the sugar duties, citing a good deal of data on imports, exports, and other economic indicators.[31]

Like Canning, the contemporary importance attached to Peel's extra-parliamentary speaking efforts as both demonstrations of oratorical skill and articulations of political views is reflected in printed collections. The "official" collection of Peel's speeches, like those of Pitt's and Fox's speeches, was limited to those delivered in the Commons. However, when W. T. Haly "of the parliamentary galleries" published a collection of Peel's eloquence and opinions as articulated in his speeches, even though most of the extracts were from parliamentary speeches, many were from extra-parliamentary utterances. As Haly wrote in his introduction:

> it has been the object of the Editor to bring together all the finer passages of the Premier's orations—all the more important points of his official expositions—his opinions on the character and conduct of his cotemporaries [*sic*]—his personal explanations and defences—his views of public life and of public men;—in short, to collect from the hundreds of speeches he has delivered in parliament and without its walls, those passages which are likely to be considered of most interest by the general reader, and by which also future generations are likely to test the fame of Sir Robert Peel as an orator, a statesman, and a logician.[32]

On the Liberal side, Lord John Russell, like Peel, produced an exceptional amount of extra-parliamentary speech for his time on policy and party political philosophy. In December 1834, as a former cabinet minister, Russell made a very successful speech to his Devonshire constituents explaining the Whig position. The speech was placarded throughout the country and assisted Russell in becoming leader of the Whigs in the Commons.[33] In the fall of 1835, he made speeches at Plymouth and Bristol publicly criticizing the Lords for their resistance to reforming measures. After being returned for Stroud in 1837, Russell spoke at a banquet in his honor held by the local Liberals upholding his belief in measured progress.

Peel does not appear to have delivered a significant extra-parliamentary speech from 1841 until his accidental death in 1850. Russell, however, continued to speak from the platform throughout the 1850s and into the 1860s on issues of both foreign and domestic policy, as well as to vindicate his own political views. Yet, although both Peel and Russell in several respects strongly prefigured the great importance played by platform speaking in the last third of the century, their platform work did not revolutionize the technique of politics. First of all, both politicians delivered their most important speeches in the House of Commons. In practical terms—i.e. getting measures enacted—Peel and Russell viewed critical political issues such as repeal of the Corn Laws and a further measure of Reform within the confines of parliamentary politics. Although both benefited from broader popularity, given the realities of the time, there was no thought of "taking their case to the people." Both Peel and Russell used their extra-parliamentary speeches to spell out their political stances in the attempt to influence the direction of the nascent Conservative and Liberal parties, respectively. Peel's repeated defining of Conservative principles was an effort to promote a usable set of political tenets on which the party as a whole could act.[34] Similarly, Russell devoted much of his extra-parliamentary speaking to propounding his belief in steady, moderate reform.

Russell's performances can be contrasted to those of Lord Palmerston, who addressed a large number of public meetings in the 1850s and early 1860s. His use of the platform—particularly during his visits to large manufacturing towns, such as Sheffield in 1862 and Glasgow in 1863—was a crucial element in maintaining his popular appeal as Liberal leader.[35] By the 1850s, Palmerston was already a master of the electoral hustings, and his non-electoral speaking efforts tended to the platitudinous rather than the political.[36] His most significant non-electoral extra-parliamentary speaking efforts occurred during the later part of his career and life, and his appearances were generally patriotic venerations of the great elder statesman.

Palmerston's speeches on these occasions did not, in the main, articulate policies or seek to educate the audience on ministerial actions. At both Sheffield in 1862 and Glasgow in 1863, for instance, Palmerston made speeches upholding the principles of free trade, urging neutrality in the American Civil War, and stating the government's support for European democrats attempting to overthrow despotism.[37] This recital of known positions notwithstanding, the bulk of both speeches was devoted to praising the industriousness of the locals. At Sheffield, "Lord Cupid" also raised his glass to the charm and beauty of the town's women. Yet, although these visits always involved official dinners in Palmerston's honor given by the local worthies (at Sheffield, on one day's notice!), it is significant that a number of his speeches were intentionally given to predominantly working-class audiences. At Manchester in 1856, for example, he spoke at the Free Trade Hall to an audience of 4,000 members and friends of the Mechanics' Institution.[38] At Glasgow in 1863, he spoke at a soiree for the working classes at the City Hall. Of the 2,000 ticket-holders in attendance, it was claimed that 19 out of 20 actually belonged to the "industrious classes."[39] At a time when Gladstone was only just discovering audiences of "the people," Palmerston was successfully using the extra-parliamentary platform to maintain his base of popular support.

Conservative leaders in the third quarter of the century also began to put the platform to use. Generally, these speeches aimed to deliver important statements of policy to the party and the country. For example, at a banquet at Merchant Tailors' Hall on June 11, 1859, Lord Derby, then Prime Minister, announced that he found himself "compelled by circumstances to resign the great trust which his Sovereign has commanded to his hands."[40] He also used the opportunity to outline what would be his party's approach in opposition. Several months later, on October 29, the Conservatives of Liverpool threw a lavish banquet for the ex-ministry. Derby took this occasion to articulate the "doctrine of true Conservatism" with great feeling and eloquence:

> I do not mean of Conservatism falsely so-called, which would obstruct all useful changes, but I speak of that Conservatism which is not obstructive, but which is the best promoter of safe and gradual social improvements—of that Conservatism which, strenuously adhering to the old machinery of the Constitution, adapts from time to time the various parts of its mechanism to the real requirements and capacities of the age in which we live—of that Conservatism which would give to all orders and degrees of men within these realms their due weight, authority, and preponderance—of that Conservatism which loves the interests of the people at large, but will not be led away by the noisy denunciation of violent and blustering demagogues either to shrink at the voice of menace or timidly to concede rights and privileges to large bodies of men for the purpose of obtain-

> ing some amount of temporary popularity, when in our hearts we believe that the concession of those very coveted boons would be injurious rather than beneficial to the classes whom it is sought to benefit. (Cheers.)[41]

Through the early 1870s, perhaps the most significant examples of the ministerial platform were Disraeli's speeches in 1872 at the Manchester Free Trade Hall in April and at the Crystal Palace in June—"the first extra-parliamentary speeches by a former Prime Minister which had a really major impact."[42] These speeches not only helped Disraeli confirm his position as party leader, but also helped the party regain the political initiative. As speeches, they are among his most clever and memorable. At Manchester—despite several claims that he was not making a party speech—Disraeli defended the soundness of Conservative principles and sought to make the case for their benefit to the agricultural, laboring, and middle classes. This was the speech in which he famously stated that the motto of the party's social policy should be "*sanitas sanitatum, omnia sanitas*" (health health, all is health), and equally famously compared Gladstone and his ministers to a row of exhausted volcanoes.[43] At the Crystal Palace, to an audience of Conservative party loyalists, Disraeli criticized the party's exclusive tendencies, declaring that "the Tory party, unless it is a national party, is nothing."[44] He then went on to articulate three great objectives for the party: to maintain the traditional institutions of the country; to uphold the Empire; and to elevate the condition of the people.

THE PLATFORM OF PROTEST

Compared to the ministerial platform, the platform of protest enjoyed a far more vigorous existence during the first half of the century. As it developed, the platform of protest had two major variants, which could be crudely described as a "working class" type, and a "middle class" type in terms of structure, style, appeal, and aims. The "working class" type of the platform of protest is often described by its historians as the radical mass platform. Although there are significant instances of popular platform agitation in the late eighteenth century—such as the Wilkite demonstrations of the late 1760s and 1770s, and the monster protest meetings of the 1790s—these tended to be spontaneous and riotous crowd actions responding to immediate grievances. The radical mass platform of the mid-1810s through the late 1840s was novel in its attempt to coerce governmental action on a consistent set of radical political demands through demonstrating mass popular support. Beyond its consistent objectives, the principal defining feature of the radical mass platform was its fundamentally peaceful nature. By the early decades of the nineteenth century, popular protest had become far less violent, due in large part to the emergence of the "apparatus" of public meetings to display united will on a particular issue or set of issues.[45]

In late 1816 and early 1817, the new era in popular protest dawned with a series of mass meetings held at Spa Fields, London.[46] Holding sway over the vast crowds (perhaps as many as 100,000 people) was Henry "Orator" Hunt, a gentleman farmer turned radical spokesman. At Spa Fields, Hunt's fiery speeches advanced a vision of peaceful mass pressure as a constitutional means for securing popular constitutional rights. The radical mass platform thus called into being effectively supplanted earlier radical strategies of plots and conspiracies to produce an uprising, and provided the basic model for subsequent radical agitation throughout the rest of the first half of the century. Official repression, followed by the bloody breakup of the 1819 mass meeting over which Hunt presided at St. Peter's Field, Manchester, effectively put an end to mass platform demonstrations during much of the 1820s. Nevertheless, this new kind of mass protest—imbued with moral authority by its constitutionalist rhetoric—remained the model for working-class radicalism to the middle of the century.

The 1830s saw the radical mass platform resurgent. At the beginning of the decade, Hunt devoted his last years to leading popular protest demonstrations against the Reform bill for not extending political rights far enough. Most important, however, was the emergence of Chartism in the later 1830s. Chartism largely carried on Hunt's vision of peaceful external mass pressure as a constitutional means through which to coerce ministries into granting a greater degree of democracy. At the forefront of the Chartist movement was Feargus O'Connor, Hunt's successor as the leading radical platform demagogue.[47] Like Hunt, O'Connor was a talented popular orator and a commanding presence on the platform. (The continuity between the aims and methods of the two men was symbolically reinforced in the popular mind by banners displaying both their portraits.) By the late 1840s, however, the tactic of the mass platform had failed to bring about the radical program. In 1848, the machinery came to life once more to produce the last great Chartist platform agitation, but once more to no avail. The failure of 1848, and the subsequent assimilation of radicalism into the Liberal mainstream, marked the end of this strain of the platform of protest.

The life and death of the radical mass platform has benefited from far more incisive and nuanced scholarship than this brief sketch can indicate. The important point here is that, between the great Spa Fields meetings of 1816-17 and the last great Chartist demonstrations of 1848, new patterns of popular oratorical production and consumption were established. Meanwhile, as the brand of working-class populist radical protest pioneered by Hunt and continued by O'Connor entered its last phase in the 1840s, the largely middle-class Anti-Corn Law League also began to employ the technique of the platform to rally popular support for its cause.

The Anti-Corn Law League and all subsequent middle-class reforming campaigns were heavily influenced by the anti-slavery and anti-slave trade movements of the late eighteenth and early nineteenth centuries.[48] There is no need to provide a summary account of the League and its activities here. For the present purpose, it is enough to list the three most important aspects of the League as a phenomenon of public speaking. First, it successfully adapted for its own uses the kind of speaking outdoors to mass audiences that characterized the radical platform. Indeed, the League actively competed with the Chartists, and there was considerable tension when meetings were held nearby on the same day. Second, the League began to hold very large meetings centered around a slate of speakers at a variety of *indoor* venues—most notably the Free Trade Hall in Manchester which was built especially for the League's activities. In a further innovation, when the League mounted its great London campaign in 1843, it rented major theaters for its meetings. Third, the Anti-Corn Law cause was responsible for the "discovery" of John Bright, who first gained public speaking fame as the League's greatest platform exponent.

In recent years, historians have paid far more attention to the radical mass platform than the Anti-Corn Law League.[49] To the extent that the League has received attention, it has typically figured in arguments over how the kind of Liberal party platform activity that characterized the second half of the nineteenth century represented a continuity or a break with the radical platform of the 1810s through 1840s.[50] It was the League, however, that prefigured the shape of things to come as far as the platform is concerned for the next several decades. Although the Anti-Corn Law League employed the technique of the radical mass platform by arranging highly visible demonstrations of popular support, other elements were also vital to its success, such as the focus on a single (albeit extremely important and divisive) issue, and how the strongest platform advocates also had a voice in Parliament.[51] That the League's formulae should have been guides for the exertion of extra-parliamentary pressure in the decades after 1846 is not surprising. Unlike Chartism, the League had been a *success.* The Chartist movement collapsed in failure, and it took the better part of a century for the piecemeal granting of most of its demands. After only half a decade of active campaigning, the Anti-Corn Law League's mission was fulfilled when Peel and his supporters allied with the Whigs to repeal the Corn Laws in 1846.

The major platform exercises of the 1860s and 1870s, as will be shown, tended to follow the general pattern of the Anti-Corn Law campaign. Beyond the forms employed, however, one of the great pieces of continuity between the Anti-Corn Law League and platform activity in the third quarter of the nineteenth century was John Bright himself. After the repeal of the Corn Laws, the major cause to which Bright turned was the extension of suffrage. Yet, because the Chartist demonstrations had caused alarm, the guiding spirit behind the Anti-Corn Law League, Richard Cobden, believed that a new league for extending the franchise should not duplicate the kind of agitation that had characterized the struggle to repeal the Corn Laws.[52] For the next decade, Bright's principal oratorical venue was the Commons.

It was not until the Autumn and Winter of 1858, when a further measure of reform was "in the air," that Bright began to deliver major extra-parliamentary speeches in the great urban centers: Birmingham, Bradford, Edinburgh, Glasgow, London, and Manchester. These efforts abated when Lord Derby's Reform bill was defeated. By the time parliamentary reform came to the fore again in the mid-1860s, Bright had wearied of the platform and wished to limit his oratorical exertions to the Commons chamber.[53] Nevertheless, he once again mounted the platform to push for an ever-broader extension of the franchise. (During the early 1860s, Bright had made a number of important public speeches related to the U.S. Civil War, but although he sought to influence minds the speeches had not in any sense constituted a platform "campaign.") In the autumn of 1866, he spoke again to large assemblies in the major cities. Although these events typically involved mass outdoor gatherings during the day, "Bright had made it clear that he would not speak in the open air, but it was nevertheless clear that he was the great attraction."[54] Instead, he delivered speeches later on to smaller, but capacity crowds numbering several thousand in the towns' large public buildings: the Free Trade Hall in Manchester, the Town

Hall in Birmingham, St. James's Hall in London, and so on. At Glasgow on October 16, for example, a crowd of 150,000 assembled on Glasgow Green under the auspices of the Reform League. According to one observer, "it seemed as if nearly all the male population of the city were there."[55] In the evening, Bright delivered a lengthy speech at the City Hall, which was "crowded even to inconvenience."[56]

Beginning in the late 1860s, the National Education League consciously modeled itself and its methods on the Anti-Corn Law League. In addition to its parliamentary strategy and printed propaganda, the Education League dispatched speakers to address meetings in towns throughout the country. These activities even continued for a few years after the passage of the 1870 Education Act, which was more temperate than the Education League had wished for. Although the Education League ultimately failed to influence the shape of reform to its own satisfaction, it holds a special significance for marking the debut in public affairs of one who would become one of the century's most important and compelling platform speakers: Joseph Chamberlain. No less important (although beyond the scope of this study) is the fact that the creation in 1870 of school boards throughout the nation provided the first opportunity for women to enter elected public life and exercise their considerable powers of public oratory in an official capacity.[57]

Founded and headquartered in Chamberlain's Birmingham, the Education League was fundamentally a provincial movement: "No tribune of the people was established in the provinces to overshadow Chamberlain. The heroes of the last great age of Radicalism were gone or going. Cobden was dead, John Bright was ailing and had retired in 1870 from Gladstone's cabinet. Chamberlain moved on to a largely empty stage."[58] Nevertheless, the importance of Bright should not be downplayed. In addition to the Anti-Corn Law League serving as a model for the National Education League, it has also been observed that Bright, as member for Birmingham from 1857 to his death in 1889, had a great influence on the movement to improve the provision of elementary education, as well as on Chamberlain himself.[59] Ultimately, however, comparing his first great political cause to Bright's, Chamberlain recognized that the cry of "education for the ignorant" lacked the popular appeal of "bread for the starving."[60]

The radical mass platform in the first half of the century had been led by gentlemen whose social status and financial independence were key elements in their credibility as leaders.[61] To the extent that they involved platform speaking, the Anti-Corn Law League, the campaign to extend the franchise, and the National Education League had all involved representatives of advanced middle-class opinion motivated by a combination of altruism and self-interest—always seeking to benefit those lower down on the socio-economic scale while also preserving the bases for the peace and prosperity of their own class. Although the goals of these campaigns were essentially economic, political, and social, the rhetoric was strongly moralistic. Indeed, mid-nineteenth-century religious sensibilities were the explicit basis of these movements' appeal. In a private letter of 1841, Cobden wrote of the Anti-Corn Law League that "henceforth we will grapple with the religious feelings of the people. Their veneration for God shall be our leverage to upset their reverence for the aristocracy."[62] The influence of Nonconformity can not be overestimated. Besides Bright's Quaker background, a number of ministers took active parts in these platform campaigns, such as Birmingham's R. W. Dale, who played a prominent role in the work of the Education League.

Beyond rhetoric and tone, moral concerns came to the fore with the great platform campaign of the mid-1870s against the pro-Turkish orientation of Disraeli's foreign policy. The "Bulgarian atrocities" agitation of 1876 failed in its objective to redirect the Government's foreign policy, but nevertheless represents an important development of the platform.[63] Although the Bulgarian atrocities agitation was like the earlier platform campaigns centered on a single issue, its focus on foreign policy rather than domestic reform was novel. It was also different because its purpose was not to push for a single piece of legislation. Although specific measures to be taken against Turkey were advocated, the agitation was essentially an organized expression of moral indignation that sought to instill the same kind indignation in the nation at large. Further, the rhetoric of the agitation was explicitly above party. It was also above religious denomination. The Bulgarian atrocities agitation differed from earlier campaigns by virtue of the active participation and leadership of Church of England clergymen of various stripes, including some of the most notable preachers (see pp. 153–54). As opposed to a campaign like the Education League, which appealed to Nonconformist self-interest by proposing to remove the Church of England's monopoly on state-funded schooling, the violent oppression of Christian subjects within the Ottoman Empire caused concern across the sectarian spectrum.

The agitation was also important for bringing Gladstone back—somewhat ambivalently at first—from retirement, and placing him most prominently upon the platform. As it was treated at the time and recalled by later witnesses, the climactic event of the Bulgarian agitation was Gladstone's September 1876 speech to an audience of around 10,000 people at Blackheath. By the mid-1870s, extra-parliamentary speaking by Cabinet-level ministers and ex-ministers was no longer a novelty, although it was still somewhat unusual. The holding of mass demonstrations at which thousands gathered to hear speeches in support of a particular cause was also becoming a well-worn technique. In 1876, in the person of Gladstone, the ministerial platform and the popular platform began to converge.[64] It was the beginning of a process that would produce a new style of oratorical dynamism in politics.

Gladstone and the Platform

At the end of 1879, Gladstone observed in his diary:

> For the last 3½ years I have been passing through a political experience which I believe is without example in our Parliamentary history. I profess it to believe it has been an occasion, when the battle to be fought was a battle of justice humanity freedom law, all in their first elements from the very root, and all on a gigantic scale. The word spoken was a word for millions, and for millions who themselves cannot speak.[65]

Despite his early and sustained interest in rhetoric and oratory,[66] and his early admiration for both Canning and Peel, Gladstone did not do very much extra-parliamentary speaking until later in his life. By 1865, however, it could be reported that "He goes down to make a great speech at the Free Trade Hall just as another man goes to eat his lunch."[67] The growth of Gladstone's extra-parliamentary speaking beginning in the 1860s is indicated by the references in his diary, which note seven speeches through the 1850s, and 123 after 1860.[68] The more comprehensive index of Gladstone's speech-making compiled by Arthur Tilney Bassett shows that Gladstone averaged 1.3 extra-parliamentary speeches per year from 1833 to 1859, and 10.2 from 1860 to 1896.[69] Through his speeches in the 1860s—and the often verbatim reports of them in the press which, as Chancellor of the Exchequer in the 1850s and 1860s, he had liberated from stamp and paper duties—Gladstone cultivated for himself a national, and popular political following. Just as Palmerston had used public appearances and speeches to boost his popularity, Gladstone, through efforts such as his great speaking tours of Tyneside in 1862 and Lancashire in 1864, became "The People's William."

In the general election of 1865, after his rejection at Oxford University, Gladstone sought election for the new, third seat in South Lancashire. Because tradition precluded candidates for the University from making speeches to the electors, it had been eighteen years since Gladstone had delivered an election speech.[70] Speaking to a "dense throng" of around 5,000 people at the Manchester Free Trade Hall, he said: "at last my friends I am come among you—('hear, hear,' and cheers)—and I am come, to use an expression which has become very famous and is not likely to be forgotten, I am come among you unmuzzled."[71] In 1866, with the Reform bill in trouble thanks to Robert Lowe and the "Adullamites," the Chancellor of the Exchequer made two speeches in Liverpool, in which he took the unprecedented (and to some scandalous) step of appealing, as a current Cabinet minister, to the public on behalf of a bill currently before the Commons.[72] In the 1868 general election, Gladstone continued to use the platform to a great extent. In October and November he covered a tremendous amount of ground, speaking (often twice, generally about the disestablishment of the Irish Church) at no fewer than 14 towns around Great Britain.

Once in office, however, this copious flow of platform speaking dried up almost completely. During his first ministry, taken up as it was with many sweeping measures of reform, Gladstone spoke constantly, but almost never outside of Parliament. Consistent with the political behavior of the time, since the election had given him his mandate to govern and endowed with a large majority in the House, it was seen as unnecessary to continue cultivating popular support. In the autumn of 1871, he made a few extra-parliamentary speeches on policy, most notably at the end of October to his Greenwich constituents at Blackheath, but appears to have agreed with his Foreign Secretary, Lord Granville, that it was both wearisome and a distraction. On October 14, Gladstone wrote: "We certainly have over-stumped, or shall have over-stumped. But you cannot help it; nor can I. I have had much difficulty and *labour* in fighting off all manner of invitations. I think Glasgow cost me seven or eight letters."[73] He did not give a major speech outside Parliament again until the general election of 1874.

Despite Gladstone's slow start with respect to extra-parliamentary speech-making in the 1870s, he delivered around 60 percent of his political platform speeches in the 1870s and 1880s. His 1876 speech at Blackheath on the Bulgarian atrocities commenced the three-and-a-half-year "political experience" about which he wrote in his diary. The ex-Premier began to speak more frequently on public affairs to a variety of audiences. He spoke often on the Eastern Question, but also on other issues of public concern, such as Ireland and Imperial affairs. Through these speeches, Gladstone broadened his scope from the Bulgarian atrocities to a more general condemnation of Conservative policies. The culmination of this movement was the famous Midlothian campaigns—two great speaking tours of Scotland in November and December 1879 (anticipating the dissolution of Parliament) and March 1880 (during the general election campaign).

The first two Midlothian campaigns are among the great events of nineteenth-century British politics and have been described and analyzed at length.[74] Particular importance is attached to the first, 1879 campaign for its picture of a former Prime Minister—no longer even the leader of his party—"stumping" with high visibility against the policies of the government before Parliament was dissolved. Between November 25, when he arrived at Carlisle, and December 8, when he returned to Hawarden, Gladstone reckoned that he addressed a total of 87,000 people in 30 speeches ranging from six to eight minutes in length to one and three-quarters hours (an estimated total of 15½ hours).[75] Generally, Gladstone delivered more than one speech per day. On December 1, he spoke on five separate occasions. December 5 was another "overpowering day":

> At 12 delivered the inaugural Address [as Rector of Glasgow University] to 5000. . . . Then went to Academical luncheon, where I spoke. Away at 4. At 5.15 off to St Andrew's Hall. Spoke 1½ hour to 6500 or 7000. Finally at 9 to the City Hall; spoke again to 3000. Did not God of His mercy wonderfully bear me through?[76]

Testimony to how extraordinary Gladstone's speaking efforts during the first Midlothian campaign were viewed, *Punch* published a cartoon depicting him as "The Colossus of Words."[77]

In the Midlothian campaigns of 1879 and 1880, Gladstone successfully brought together the two major platform trends that had heretofore developed in parallel. The fact that he was an ex-Prime Minister and still (even if not currently party leader) a party heavyweight, made Gladstone's unprecedented production of extra-parliamentary speeches represent the attainment of a new level for the ministerial platform. However, the substance and tone of the speeches, although discussing a broad range of foreign and domestic policy issues, owes far more to the kind of platform speaking seen in the single-issue campaigns from the Anti-Corn Law League to the Bulgarian atrocities agitation. Gladstone's critique of "Beaconsfieldism" was rendered in moral terms. Thus, Disraeli's foreign policy was based upon the "untrue, arrogant, and dangerous assumption that we were entitled to assume for ourselves some dignity, which we should also be entitled to withhold from others, and to claim on our part authority to do things which we would not permit others to do";[78] and his laxity in fiscal matters encouraged "jobbery and minute waste and extravagance."[79] The religious qualities of the Midlothian campaign—at times revivalesque, at times churchly—were not lost on contemporaries. Joseph Chamberlain, for example, later described the Midlothian speeches as no "mere farrago of barren criticism," but rather "the whole body of Liberal faith and doctrine."[80]

In considering the religious qualities of Gladstone's platform performances, it is important to bear in mind that the popularity of religious oratory at this time existed across a broad range of styles (see chapter 3). As indicated by Chamberlain's comment, Gladstone's appeals aimed more for minds than for hearts. In 1919, discussing "the force of demagogic speech" in politics, Max Weber wrote:

> Its character has changed since the time speakers like Cobden addressed themselves to the intellect, and Gladstone who a mastered the technique of apparently 'letting sober facts speak for themselves.' At the present time, often purely emotional means are used—the means the Salvation Army also exploits in order to set the masses in motion.[81]

In this respect, it is not surprising that Gladstone's extra-parliamentary speeches would be more akin to the analytical but hugely popular sermons of his fellow High Churchman, Canon Liddon, than to those of more evangelically inclined preachers.

In the course of the first Midlothian campaign, a *Times* leader criticized Gladstone for being more demagogue than statesman, and making his political appeals to the "mob" rather than to the "Senate."[82] It was, however, the shape of things to come. Like the Anti-Corn Law League, the first two Midlothian campaigns provided a compelling model of success. After the 1880 election, *The Times* reported that, "it was remarked as a curious coincidence, that at every halting-place where Mr. Gladstone made a speech, the Liberals gained a seat."[83] To contemporaries, the Midlothian campaign took on symbolic meanings. The very word "Midlothian" was subsequently used to mean a major, or a series of major political speeches outside of Parliament. (The term could also be used with irony, such as the critical report of Lord Randolph Churchill's June 1886 speech to a loyal Tory audience in a riding stable at Paddington, dubbed by the *Pall Mall Gazette* as "The Midlothian of the Metropolis."[84]) The example set by Gladstone at Midlothian proved to be well-suited to the political conditions of the last two decades of the nineteenth century.

"The Battle of the Platforms"

Writing about the politics of the 1880s and 1890s in which her father, the Marquis of Salisbury, was a leading protagonist, Lady Gwendolen Cecil described the period as a prolonged "battle of the platforms."[85] It was the culmination of the development of the platform as a mainstream political force. Regular speaking tours became "the rule for most MPs, and for any MP who expected any sort of national prominence."[86] As described by Lord Curzon in 1913,

> No Parliamentary reputation, however great, will avail in the future to secure for a statesman the confidence of his party or the support of the nation unless it is confirmed by the verdict of the platform. It is there that the shrillest war-cries are uttered; there that the gauge of oratorical combat is thrown down. Lord Randolph Churchill would never have become leader of the House of Commons but for his platform triumphs.[87]

Despite his belief in the deleterious effects of the "rise" of the platform on both politics and parliamentary eloquence, Curzon was also prepared to take a more historically minded view of these developments, recognizing that a new standard and type of political oratory was in the process of being made: "This is undoubtedly the case, and the waning of one form of the art is accompanied, if it is not counterbalanced by the growth of another."[88]

Although the battle of the platform was joined in full beginning in the mid-1880s, the vigorous recourse of leading politicians to the platform was already well in evidence, and well-remarked upon during the general election of 1880. After the dissolution of Parliament, the *Annual Register* estimated that "more speeches had been made by Cabinet ministers than in all the recesses of other Parliaments put together."[89] During the campaign, there had been 15 major speeches from Gladstone, 24 from Lord Hartington, and six apiece from Bright, W. H. Smith, Sir Stafford Northcote, and Sir William Vernon Harcourt, in addition to numerous minor speeches.[90] The novelty of all this is reflected in the derisive nickname given by *Blackwood's* to the new government: "The Stump Ministry."[91]

In terms of gross oratorical production, the general election of 1885 exceeded that of 1880, and was also less one-sided. According to one contemporary investigator, in the six weeks preceding the election, the total number of platform speeches by politicians of sufficient importance to be reported in the daily newspapers was 157. Of the total, members of the Gladstone's victorious Liberal government had made 44 speeches, while members of the defeated minority Conservative government had made 68. The major contributors to these figures were Chamberlain, who made 14 speeches, Hartington with 13, Goschen with nine.[92] Gladstone, however, did not repeat his epic output of 1880; during the 1885 campaign he delivered only five major political speeches. Salisbury, for his part, delivered only three speeches.

In addition to the increasing volume of platform oratory during elections, extra-parliamentary speaking by both government and opposition politicians became an increasingly routine part of the regular political calendar. As Gladstone had delivered an extended public critique of the current government's policies in 1879, so now the Conservatives took to the platform to criticize Gladstone's policies. Joseph Chamberlain, for one, while still a loyal Gladstonian, found Conservative platform efforts a good object for public ridicule. In 1882 he (along with Bright) addressed a capacity crowd at the Birmingham Town Hall and described the recent "oratorical bombardment of the Liberal position":

> The London Season was hardly over when the leaders of the Opposition went north, south, east, and west on provincial tours. The

> Marquess of Salisbury—(hisses)—assisted by Sir Stafford Northcote—(hisses)—went on a starring expedition into the North of England. (Laughter.) Lord Randolph Churchill—(laughter)—fearful, no doubt, that he should be overlooked—(renewed laughter)—followed suit, and, assisted by nobody—(renewed laughter)—made a most successful exhibition of himself at Hull and elsewhere. Sir Richard Cross demonstrated all by himself in Lancashire. . . . It is enough to say that almost every member of the Conservative party, from the highest to the lowest, contributed to this unusual display.[93]

In particular, Chamberlain enjoyed pointing out how the Conservatives were now resorting to the tactics upon which they once looked askance:

> Lord Salisbury and his friends still denounce the agitation which preceded the last general election. But everywhere they are doing their best to imitate it. The Midlothian campaign is at once the object of their most virulent invective, and the model which they assiduously endeavour to copy.[94]

However hypocritical his platform efforts in the early 1880s seemed to Chamberlain, Salisbury had been a regular user of the platform from the beginning of his political career and came to rely on extra-parliamentary speaking quite heavily. As an Oxford undergraduate from 1848 to 1850, he had been an active member of the Union—delivering at least 12 speeches[95]—and served as its Secretary in 1848 and Treasurer in 1849-50. In 1854, as Lord Robert Cecil, he took his seat in the Commons and quickly established a reputation as a fluent speaker and a coming man. In addition to his parliamentary efforts, however, Salisbury was already using the platform—both during elections and at other times—to articulate his political views in public. Between 1853 and taking his place in the House of Lords in 1868, he made no fewer than 12 major extra-parliamentary speeches.[96] During the 1870s and early 1880s, both in office and out, Salisbury delivered a number of important political speeches outside of Parliament. In opposition. he was a leading critic of Gladstone's governments, as at Hertford in 1873, Taunton in 1880, Newcastle in 1881, and Liverpool in 1882, to name a few examples. As a member of Disraeli's cabinet, he was a leading defender of government policy, as at Bradford in 1877 and Manchester in 1879.[97]

That Salisbury was keenly aware of the importance of the platform is evident in a number of statements. At Liverpool in 1882, for example, he spoke about how Parliament existed in a different relation to the people as a representative institution: "This great meeting is proof of it. The people are taking a more direct influence in, and assuming a more direct control of, their own affairs."[98] In the general elections of 1885 and 1886, during which he campaigned until the eve of voting, Salisbury "shattered the convention which prohibited a peer from intervening personally in an election after the issue of the writs."[99] Further testimony to Salisbury's belief in the necessity and efficacy of the platform, he is estimated to have delivered between 60 or 70 platform speeches during his ministry of 1886-92.[100] Although he disliked the appearance of pandering to the public and eschewed Gladstone's "whistle-stop" style in favor of organized rallies, Salisbury's average of more than ten major extra-parliamentary speeches per year while Prime Minister compares favorably to Gladstone's statistics around this time. [101] In a political world in which platform speaking had become a fact of life for major politicians, Salisbury's substantial output of extra-parliamentary speeches may reflect the fact that, governing from the Lords, he required a greater degree of public exposure or more useful venues in which to articulate his views.

In general, the political conditions of the 1880s and 1890s favored the growth of platform speaking by leading politicians. The broadened electoral franchises of 1867 and 1884, combined with the introduction of the secret ballot in 1872, left the traditional forms of party discipline and election management increasingly ineffective. Platform speaking, like the new national party organizations founded in the 1870s, helped to answer the need for a new, more broad-based techniques of voter appeal. At the same time, the franchise, even after 1884, was still limited to "responsible citizens" to which a "respectable," non-demagogical style of platform speaking could be addressed.[102] Yet, if platform speaking was encouraged by a certain kind of stability within the electorate, it was also encouraged by the political instability caused by a number of other issues (e.g. Gladstone's refusal to retire) that led to the fracturing of the Liberal party and, with Home Rule, broke it. One historian has recently argued that, Gladstone's demagogical populism led him to diverge from the political values of traditional Liberalism and thus split the party.[103] If this was indeed the case, it is interesting to observe that, after the schism, the Liberal party devolved into a number of factions, each headed by its own leading platform performer: most notably Gladstone, Chamberlain, and Lord Hartington. At the same time, after his resignation from Salisbury's government in 1886, Lord Randolph Churchill became an independent platform force on the Conservative side. In terms of substance, as Lady Gwendolen Cecil recalled of her father, Lord Salisbury, "the subject which occupied the greater part of his platform oratory—as it did that of all his contemporaries—was the Irish controversy in its least fruitful aspects."[104] In the "Irish controversy," as in other matters, Chamberlain and Churchill were two of the most active and exciting platform speakers. Even a brief examination of their extra-parliamentary speaking careers helps reveal the ways in which the platform functioned within the political structures of their times.

Joseph Chamberlain's development as a platform speaker took place within the context of Birmingham municipal politics. Arriving in Birmingham in 1854, Chamberlain joined the Birmingham and Edgbaston Debating Society (see pp. 46–47).[105] He had no natural gift for public speaking and it "took a long time before he could think on his feet, and fifteen years before he could speak well."[106] It was perhaps fortunate for him that, beyond boasting a vigorous debating society, Birmingham in Chamberlain's time was rich in models of public speaking. Indeed, Birmingham could well lay claim to having been Victorian Britain's oratorical second city. During Chamberlain's political apprenticeship the town was home to the great preacher-orator George Dawson, and parliamentary home to the "Tribune of the People," John Bright. (Later, in addition to Chamberlain himself, Birmingham's complement of great orators included the Congregationalist minister, R. W. Dale.) Dawson's renowned preaching and speaking have been mentioned already (see p. 125), and his propounding of the "civic gospel" influenced Chamberlain's actions as a municipal leader. Although Bright did not reside in Birmingham, he visited the city every year. Chamberlain "had personally listened to all the major speeches which Bright had delivered in Birmingham since his election in 1857. When Chamberlain was twenty-two he heard Bright's first speech to his constituents and it made a lasting impression on him."[107]

Despite his inauspicious oratorical beginnings, Chamberlain became an avid speaker. As his son, Austen, wrote: "To him, as to Chatham, speech was a form of action. He valued the triumphs of the platform and of Parliament only as they formed opinion and led to action. And so the speech was the man—simple, direct, sincere, courageous, prompt in decision and resolute in action."[108] Platform speaking became an inseparable element in Chamberlain's political career. In the introduction to an 1885 collection of his speeches, the parliamentary reporter Henry Lucy devotes a great deal of space to Chamberlain's attainments as a parliamentary speaker. Only when noting how rarely a platform orator is successful in the House does Lucy briefly pay tribute to Chamberlain's abilities as an extra-parliamentary speaker. Tellingly, however, only one speech reprinted in the volume was delivered in the House of Commons.[109] Chamberlain firmly believed that platform speaking was not only politically efficacious, but also a duty. In 1885, in the wake of the Third Reform Act, he wrote to Gladstone:

> Popular government is inconsistent with the reliance which official etiquette formerly imposed on speakers, & which was easily borne as long as the electorate was a comparatively small & privileged class, & the necessity of consulting it at hustings infrequent & limited.
>
> Now, the Platform has become one of the most powerful & indispensable instruments of Government, & any Ministry which neglected the opportunities offered by it wold speedily lose the confidence of the People. A new public duty and personal labour has thus come into existence, which devolves to a great extent & as a matter of necessity, on those members of a Government who may be considered specially to represent the majority who are to be appealed to.[110]

Chamberlain's assertions about the efficacy of the platform were not mere words. Yet, despite his great popularity as a platform orator, Chamberlain's history demonstrates the limits to platform success. For him, the limits were those tending to be characteristic of the platform of protest. Chamberlain, perhaps more than any other leading politician of his time, sought to achieve specific political ends through the platform. This was not only expressive of his background as a municipal leader; it was also partially the result of a considerable amount of political frustration that marked his career.

Each of Chamberlain's major platform efforts as a leading national politician was accompanied by some degree of political fracture. In January 1885, while President of the Board of Trade, he delivered a series of three speeches advocating a kinder, gentler socio-economic order in somewhat inflammatory language. Significantly, the substance of these speeches had been articulated first in 1883 as articles in the *Fortnightly Review*. It was, however, the speeches that made the great impact—so much so that their message was dubbed the "Radical Programme of 1885."[111] As a prominent cabinet minister, Chamberlain's attempt to push the government in the direction of his brand of radicalism caused considerable friction. The "Radical Programme" became the "Unauthorized Programme." During the general election of 1885, Chamberlain delivered the ultimatum that he would not join a ministry that excluded his program. Even so, he accepted a post in Gladstone's third government, but later resigned over the first Home Rule bill. From 1886 to the defeat of the second Home Rule bill in 1893, Chamberlain was a leading platform proponent of imperial unity. The pattern of political fracture continued in 1903 when Chamberlain resigned his position as Colonial Secretary in Balfour's Unionist ministry over the issue of tariff reform. Having failed to win over the government to his notions of replacing free trade with imperial preference, Chamberlain once again sought—and failed—to shape policy from without.

Lord Randolph Churchill's career as a platform orator was relatively brief—lasting only from 1880 to the early 1890s—but, like the rest of his political career, strongly marked the age. Although Churchill was an effective Commons debater and parliamentary maneuverer, his position within the Conservative party was an ambivalent one for most of his career (he held cabinet office for a total of only 11 months). It was, in fact, his platform work that maintained him as a front-rank politician. He was extremely popular and effective as an extra-parliamentary speaker, and attained a greater national reach than Chamberlain: in the mid-1880s, the "only one man in the country who could at all be matched, on any platform outside the midlands, against Mr. Gladstone."[112] Like other leading platform speakers, Churchill addressed audiences ranging from a few hundred to tens of thousands. By far his greatest single audience (or probably anyone else's, except those on the platform with him) was at the great Conservative demonstration in Manchester on August 9, 1884 where he addressed "an assembly admitted by all to number close upon 100,000 people."[113]

In his speeches—delivered with "superabundant gestures and now and again wildly melodramatic attitudes"[114]—Churchill's favorite target was Gladstone and "Gladstone received his most severe verbal lambasting since the days of Disraeli."[115] Because it was the central issue of those decades, the Irish question was naturally the subject of most of his speeches. A contemporary wrote that Churchill "first won the ear of the country" with his speech to a large audience at Hull on October 31, 1881.[116] Although the speech was, in the main, a vigorous condemnation of Gladstone's Irish policies, at the end, Churchill turned the force of his invective on to Gladstone himself. Contrasting him to the recently deceased Disraeli (whose memory and ministerial record, he said, would be cherished by generations of grateful Britons), and likening him to Herod, Churchill claimed that, if Gladstone was permitted to continue,

> we shall soon be within a measurable distance of the day when, with an empire disintegrated at home and tottering abroad, with our commerce waning, with our industries decayed, dependent for all the necessaries of life on the bounty or on the cupidity of the foreigner; with the mass of our labour, skilled and unskilled, driven by free imports to other lands; with our armies defeated, our flag disgraced, with the spectres of revolution and communism hovering over this once peaceful country, his name will never be uttered by any patriotic Englishman without deep and bitter condemnation, and upon him will be pronounced the irrevocable and avatal verdict that, throughout his long career, in spite of his great opportunities, in spite of his marvelous gifts, he was animated by no true love of country, by no real loyalty to the Throne, not even by any fidelity to party.[117]

Whether in or out of office, Gladstone could count on every aspect of his domestic, foreign, and imperial policies, as well as his personal character, being the subject of Churchill's platform invective. More constructively, Churchill also used platform speeches to develop and articulate his notion of what came to be called "Tory Democracy"—the attempt to once and for all shake the Conservative party free of its exclusivist nature and place it on a basis of genuinely popular support. "Trust the People" became Churchill's motto.[118] This attempt to "dish" the Radicals culminated during the recess of 1886, while Churchill was Chancellor of the Exchequer, with the "Dartford Programme"—named for his speech at Dartford in October.[119] As envisioned by Churchill, an important facet of Tory Democracy was public economy, which developed into a major platform theme in its own right after he resigned as Chancellor of the Exchequer in January 1887.

Like Chamberlain, Churchill's career also reveals some limitations on platform speaking, albeit different ones. In Churchill's case, these limits are those that tend to characterize the ministerial platform, particularly the Tory variety. Most of Churchill's major extra-parliamentary speeches were delivered to some kind of Conservative group. Indeed, it was part of his Tory Democracy mission to promote the growth of

Conservative party organizations. Yet, however large these groups were, their selective nature precluded him working his platform magic on the unconverted. Given the relative brevity of Churchill's standing as a politician of national dimensions, it is hard to say how he might have used his considerable abilities over a longer course. As it was, once outside of government, the rhetorical brilliance and savagery of his oratory lacked the necessary conduits to turn policy ideas into legislation. The 1892 invitation for him to sit on the Conservative front bench was a sop, and by that time, for the diseased and increasingly incoherent Lord Randolph, it was too late anyway.

Despite their outstanding careers as extra-parliamentary speakers, both Chamberlain and Churchill were ultimately unable to realize their major political projects. In this light, Gladstone's use of the platform from 1876 to 1880 to reverse "Beaconsfieldism" and re-install himself as Liberal leader and Prime Minister appears to be a unique, if temporary achievement. Later, however, all his heroic platforming could not save his ministries from foundering in Irish waters. Salisbury, while an extremely adept platform practitioner, was no insurgent. His rise to the Conservative leadership was based on parliamentary politics. For him, the platform served as a vehicle through which to make his party—so anachronistically led from the Lords—dynamically relevant in a more democratic age. In this sense, therefore, Salisbury could perhaps be seen as the victor in the battle of the platforms.

The Experience and Techniques of Platform Oratory

Platform speeches were very different affairs from speeches in Parliament. To begin with, in order to succeed, platform speakers had to engage their various audiences. In Parliament, however, stimulating oratory was rarely the object, and indeed was frowned upon from any but a handful of speakers. MPs had the luxury, if not the duty, of being dull speakers. At Westminster, it was necessary to speak within the established forms of the House and within a structure of opportunity regulated by the parties and by the Speaker. MPs spoke to a limited, if not necessarily consistent, number of people whom they either knew or knew of. The partisan sentiment of the parliamentary audience was manifested in seating arrangements. On the platform, how speeches were produced and consumed had to respond to the particular circumstances—the place of delivery, the nature of the occasion, the size and character of the audience, the type of message to be conveyed.

INDOORS AND OUTDOORS

One of the most important aspects of platform speaking were the physical conditions under which the speeches were delivered. By definition, parliamentary and barristerial oratory occurred in the Houses of Parliament and the courtroom, respectively. In churches and chapels religious oratory had formal space devoted to it but much preaching also took place in other venues—indoors and outdoors, permanent and makeshift (see chapter 3). With no venues formally devoted to extra-parliamentary oratory, platform speaking was, in terms of space, perhaps the most pragmatic form of public speech. As extra-parliamentary speeches became an accepted and necessary practice for politicians, platform speaking created, occupied, and redefined space for its own purposes.

Because of the variety of spaces that were used or adapted for platform speaking, it is a difficult subject to discuss with any thoroughness. However, a number of representative examples can suggest the range. One of the more spectacular early instances of the creation of space for a platform speech occurred in 1837 after Peel's inauguration as Lord Rector of Glasgow University. For the great public dinner held in Peel's honor two days later, no public building in Glasgow was large enough to handle the 3,400 people who subscribed 25 shillings each to be present. Instead, a temporary, yet "princely" structure was constructed out of wood and cloth in the garden of a private house, complete with a 32-foot ceiling and a gallery held up by large wooden columns decorated with Corinthian capitals and painted to look like Sienna marble. This highly flammable structure of wood, cloth, and paint was lit by a series of gas lustres containing more than 3,000 burners. As the preface to the official account of the speech stated, the structure's "vast dimensions, its classic and commodious proportion, the splendour of its decorations, and the unprecedentedly short time in which the whole has been completed, we hesitate not to pronounce it the most magnificent *hospitium* in which a British subject was ever entertained by his admiring and confiding countrymen."[120]

In the second half of the century, however, the creation of such lavish temporary structures became far less necessary as an increasing number of large, permanent, public buildings were erected throughout the country. To judge from the most comprehensive list of these structures available, the rate at which they were erected appears to have started increasing in the late 1840s, and a particularly large number of town halls, assembly rooms, corn exchanges, and so forth were commenced in the 1860s and 1870s.[121] These provincial town halls and similar buildings became the standard venues for platform oratory outside the metropolis. Two of the most notable structures were Manchester's Free Trade Hall and Birmingham's Bingley Hall.

Like many municipal halls, the Manchester Free Trade Hall went through several iterations. The first Free Trade Hall was a temporary wooden pavilion erected on the site of the Peterloo massacre by 100 men in 11 days in January 1840. It could hold about 5,000 people.[122] As its name suggests, the purpose of the Hall was to house Anti-Corn Law meetings. Thus, in symbolic terms, the Free Trade Hall was a monumental fusion of the popular and middle-class varieties of protest. It was also, therefore, a monument to platform oratory. The growth of the Anti-Corn Law movement soon necessitated a larger building. Completed in February 1843, the new Free Trade Hall (built on the same site as the old) was made of brick, included galleries, and had a maximum capacity of around 8,000 people. Between 1854 and 1856, a third and still larger Free Trade Hall made of stone was erected. The Free Trade Hall became one of the major provincial venues for platform speaking. Although the Hall's existence was an enduring expression of Free Trade radicalism (including relief carvings depicting the Anti-Corn Law struggle), it came to be used not only by Liberals, but also Conservatives. It is, therefore, both ironic and a sign of the increasing prominence of platform speaking in public life that Disraeli, the man who effectively broke Peel over his conversion to Free Trade, would in 1872 produce what many then and since have argued was his greatest extra-parliamentary performance (the *sanitas sanitatum*/exhausted volcanoes speech) at the Free Trade Hall.

Birmingham's Bingley Hall also began as a makeshift building. The original structure was "a temporary building of immense dimensions, in the grounds of Bingley House, Broad Street"[123] erected in 1849 to house an exhibition of manufactures from Birmingham and the Midlands counties. In 1850, this was replaced by a more permanent structure. Especially when compared to the grand classical edifice of Birmingham's Town Hall (begun 1832), Bingley Hall was no monument to civic pride. It was a functional building, architecturally unprepossessing. According to one author writing in the 1860s, "Bingley Hall is . . . a building of great capacity and utility, especially for annual exhibitions of cattle, sheep, horses, pigs, and poultry."[124] If he had written his account a decade or two later, the author would probably have added politicians to this list, for Bingley Hall became the setting for a considerable amount of platform activity, and at one point or another most of the leading extra-parliamentary speakers spoke there.

Perhaps Bingley Hall's greatest moment as an oratorical venue occurred during Birmingham's June 1883 celebration of Bright's 25th anniversary as its MP. The three-day affair organized by the Birmingham Liberal Association culminated in a speech by the great Tribune of the People himself (as well as one by Chamberlain) at Bingley Hall. Anticipating a vast attendance, the Committee went to considerable trouble and expense to expand the capacity of the Hall (which normally accommodated around 20,000 people) while still attempting to ensure that every person would be able to hear and see the speakers. In addition to the seating available from the Hall's permanent galleries, additional seating for 8,000 people was created on platforms and galleries especially built for the occasion. The town notables and holders of 10*s.* tickets sat on tiers of seats placed on the deep speakers' platform. On the south and north sides of the Hall, other platforms were constructed for the members of the various ward committees and the 5*s.* ticket-holders. Opposite the speakers' platform was an ascending gallery from floor to roof for the holders of 2*s.* 6*d.* tickets. For the general public, the floor was opened without charge to an estimated 15,000 people.[125]

Although municipal town halls were the sites for a great deal of extra-parliamentary speaking, spaces of all kinds were used for platform events. For example, when the Conservatives of Liverpool wished to honor Lord Derby and his ex-ministry in 1859, they held a great banquet at the Philharmonic Hall—naturally, a more exclusive site than Liverpool's Town Hall. Covers were laid for around 600 people, and the upper galleries were filled with Conservative supporters who had been unable to obtain tickets for the dinner.[126] In 1872, the Crystal Palace (moved to Sydenham in 1854) became the site of one of Disraeli's most famous speeches, either inside or outside of the House of Commons. The speech was delivered to 1,500 people at a banquet held in the room usually set aside for Saturday afternoon concerts. It must have made a striking backdrop for Disraeli's striking performance. In fact, the Crystal Palace seems to have become something of a Conservative party room. On March 3, 1886, for example, Lord Salisbury addressed more than 1,300 noblemen and gentlemen there at a great banquet to celebrate recent Conservative victories in Lambeth.

One of the most risible examples of the adaptation of space for platform speaking is when, in June 1886, Lord Randolph Churchill addressed the Tory Party Caucus of Paddington at a riding school. The obscurity of this location was derisively reported on by the *Pall Mall Gazette*: "The school is not even in the street. It is hidden at the bottom of a slight decline which leads to the mews of which the school forms one side. . . . What with the smell and the distribution of seats, a sight seer ignorant of the occasion would have thought he was going to a circus."[127]

While greater amounts of space were created or adapted for platform speaking, speeches were also delivered outdoors. For those who spoke outdoors, the great hazard was, of course, the weather. In the event of rain, a speaker was fortunate if he spoke from a covered temporary platform, but such accommodation was not always available. Since parliamentary sessions typically ran from February to the beginning of August, outdoor speeches made after the prorogation ran a greater risk of bad weather. Dissolutions, however, tended to occur during fair weather months. This was certainly the case for most of the "battle of the platforms" years: March 1880, June 1886, June 1892, and July 1895. Only the dissolution of November 1885 occurred in a non-spring or summer month.

With respect to out-of-door speeches, conditions were perhaps never as bad as those during Gladstone's speech at Blackheath after the dissolution of January 1874. "What an afternoon it was!" recalled one member of the audience. "Rain fell incessantly, and the weather was cold and raw. I suppose there could not have been a worse afternoon for an open-air demonstration."[128] Despite the weather, however, a great crowd turned up to hear the Prime Minister. When Gladstone arrived at the covered wagon from which he was to deliver a speech of over an hour in length, the "grand old statesman was drenched with rain, but his ardour was clearly in no wise dampened."[129]

Two years later, in September 1876, Gladstone again addressed his Greenwich constituents at Blackheath in a heavy rainfall—this time on the Bulgarian atrocities.[130] In planning for the speech—perhaps recalling the conditions of two years before—Gladstone had "inclined to an indoor meeting."[131] Nevertheless, it was decided to hold the meeting outdoors. Mindful of the weather, the organizers of the event selected a flat and dry spot at the northeast corner of the heath, and a platform was formed from a number of wagons covered by a pent roof of planks, with a small rostrum projecting from the center. Fortunately for Gladstone (but not for his audience), the heavy rains fell before and after his speech, but abated during it.

Given these conditions, it is remarkable to think that between 10,000 and 15,000 people stood in the pouring rain before and during speeches lasting for over an hour. With respect to the speaker in question, it may be that the diluvian experiences of 1874 and 1876 contributed to the infrequency of Gladstone's outdoor speaking while representing Greenwich (or at least made him glad he spoke there so seldom). Yet, he had to contend with bad weather in other locations, such as at Exeter on July 13, 1877, when he made a speech from a hotel balcony under cover of an umbrella. Despite the rain, noted *The Times*, "the numbers of those in the Square were not perceptibly reduced."[132] Gladstone was clearly prepared to deliver his speeches regardless of what the weather had to offer. During the Midlothian campaign of November 1879, in addition to his major indoor speeches, Gladstone made a number of incidental speeches out of doors "delivered hatless in the frosty air."[133] It seems, however, that Exeter was the last outdoor speech delivered in bad weather. Understandably, he was grateful for this. In 1888, speaking outdoors at Hawarden to a deputation from the Staffordshire Liberal Association, he observed:

> The pleasure of meeting you is enhanced by the improved aspect of the weather. I do not know whether I have been more fortunate than other people, but in the last no very great number of years—say, perhaps, eight or ten years—in the course of which I have had to address my fellow-countrymen many scores of times, I can gratefully record, what perhaps you may think extraordinary, that I have never once, since a certain evening in the town of Exeter twelve years ago, been interfered with or incommoded by the weather.[134]

EVENTS AND AUDIENCES

The nature of various types of platform events and the nature of the audiences that attended them were closely connected. A speech at a party banquet, for instance, would have a smaller audience of party notables and loyalists, while a platform speech made in more general circumstances would be heard by a larger and more diverse crowd. Very often, audiences for the latter type of event—both indoor and outdoor—are reported to have been "respectable." At Gladstone's 1876 Blackheath speech, for example, the "Assemblage was large & respectable. Not Rags but people in Cloth Coats & Top Hats."[135] Nevertheless, accounts of this and other platform events make clear that the working classes were present at the outdoor events and also (when areas of free or very cheap admission were provided) at indoor events. Working men became a greater presence in platform audiences in the 1880s, particularly after large numbers of them had been enfranchised by the 1884 Reform Act. During the campaign of 1885, as one historian has written, "Even the Conservative candidates appear to have been surprised at the large crowds of working-men who attended their meetings, and disquieting reports began to pour into the liberal headquarters from agitated urban candidates."[136]

Those who have examined the platform-speaking phenomenon often make a distinction between Conservative and Liberal events. It is generally asserted that Conservatives tended to address meetings of their supporters, with ticketing and admission under strict control of party operatives.[137] Certainly, Disraeli's great speeches at the Manchester Free Trade Hall and the Crystal Palace in 1872 were delivered to audiences of the party faithful. Similarly, in 1886, Lord Randolph spoke to the well-heeled Tories of his Paddington South constituency. The attendance was strictly controlled by party bouncers—described as "gentlemen" in evening dress—who prevented people from entering unless they had proper tickets. "The whole audience," recorded the *Pall Mall Gazette*, "was eminently respectable and well-to-do, composed chiefly of that middle class whose vanity Lord Randolph tickled late in the evening."[138] Nevertheless, although audiences were regulated at such events, it was not unusual for disruptive elements to be present. For example, when speaking to a Conservative party meeting at Perth in 1889, Lord Randolph had to contend with people answering the wrong way to his rhetorical questions, and shouts of "Grand Old Man" when he started in on Gladstone. Lord Randolph chose to respond to nearly all of these interruptions and, as is required for all great platform speakers, used the heckling to display the quickness and sharpness of his wit.[139]

Although it is generally asserted that Liberals tended to address "open" audiences, with no controls on admission, this was not always the case. Like the Conservatives, Liberals also attempted to restrict platform audiences to their supporters. When Gladstone spoke at Blackheath in 1871, the local Liberal committee making arrangements for the event erected a series of zig-zag barriers on the common in order to admit only those who were issued tickets—an inner enclosure (20 yards x 12 yards) in front of the platform for about 1,000 people, and an outer enclosure providing space for 10,000 more. Greenwich's Conservative paper advised its readers that such restrictions of movement on public grounds was illegal and encouraged all who wished to question their representative to assert their constitutional rights and attend despite the obstacles.[140] After the event, Greenwich's Liberal paper claimed that a great many Conservative leaders and Conservative working men had been present—some even in the front enclosure.[141] Regarding a different occasion, none other than Lord Randolph happily pointed out the restricted nature of Gladstone's audience. In a speech at Birmingham during the general election of 1885, Churchill told his audience how, at Edinburgh, Gladstone had spoken to "carefully packed and chosen audiences, and no inconvenient questions which could possibly be stopped, or which had not been subjected to the most rigourous censorship, were allowed to be put to him."[142]

The presence of women became an increasingly significant feature of platform events, and the nature of their presence changed over time. It had been a common practice for women to be seated in a separate area. This was especially the case at political dinners, where women were typically relegated to a gallery, overlooking the men who dined and spoke below. For instance, when the Conservative MPs gave a dinner for Peel at Merchant Tailors' Hall in 1838, "At each end of the hall is a light but capacious gallery, in which were seated the ladies who attended to witness the proceedings."[143] A somewhat more spectacular display of Conservative women occurred at the 1859 dinner for the late Derby ministry at the Liverpool Philharmonic Hall. On this occasion, the ladies were seated in the boxes and orchestra so that, above the banqueters, "there was a circle of Englishwomen, all dressed in the Tory uniform of red and blue."[144] Political banquets were highly formalized, symbolic affairs.[145] It takes little imagination to see that the placement of women in these events reflected their supposed role in the political scheme of things: above politics, but keen observers of their men's work from a distance.

As extra-parliamentary platform activity became more prevalent in the last quarter of the century, women became more directly involved. Not only was Gladstone a pioneer in the political use of platform speaking, but his wife, Catherine, was also something of a pioneer with respect to the presence of women at platform events. During the first Midlothian campaign, women "attended the meetings in quite large numbers, encouraged by Mrs Gladstone who broke precedent by sitting by her husband in the centre of the platform, rather than in a special 'ladies' section'."[146] Yet, Catherine Gladstone did not attend these occasions merely out of spousal duty or concern. She was an eager participant in her husband's platform work. Even before Midlothian, her desire to be on the platform was evidently strong enough that she did not let the bad weather dissuade her from being at Gladstone's side for the rainy Blackheath speeches of 1874 and 1876. During the 1879 Midlothian campaign, Catherine Gladstone sat by her husband throughout the tour. And even though the considerable strain of this activity caused her to collapse and take to her bed on returning to Hawarden, she would not be left behind when it came time for Gladstone to return to Midlothian in March 1880.[147]

Gladstone's former Parliamentary Private Secretary provides a wonderful description of Catherine Gladstone playing a tender, if overprotective Sancho Panza to her husband's platform Quixote during the general election of 1880. When Gladstone arrived at Newman Hall off Oxford Street for a speaking engagement, the lack of a side door forced him to wade through the eager throng that packed the Hall. Behind him followed

> a simply-clothed woman, who busies herself in warding off the hands of enthusiasts eager to touch him, or pat his back, or help him forward. That is Mrs. Gladstone, with the soft face, high-coloured like a girl's, and tremulous in mouth; intent on one thing only in this life—her husband. They step up to the platform by a reporter's stool. A dozen willing hands would aid him, but it is hers which grasps his ankle to steady him lest in his eagerness he slip. . . . She begs a seat immediately behind him. Forth he stands and begins at once: 'Mr. Chairman.' She pulls at his overcoat, and one sleeve comes free. Impatiently he stops, while she tugs at the other sleeve; and the coat has scarcely gone from him ere he is flourishing in our faces his free hand. . . . Two more sentences, and we were fairly launched upon a sea of passion, regardless of Mrs. Gladstone, who sat behind, placidly folding her husband's overcoat.[148]

Jennie Churchill was also a highly visible presence on the platform with her husband. The display of her beauty and fine dress was both an asset to Lord Randolph and an added attraction for audiences. More independently than Mrs. Gladstone, however, Lady Randolph was also very active in public during her husband's campaigns—both canvassing for him and making campaign speeches to groups of voters.[149] As the daughter of an American plutocrat, Jennie Churchill may have had fewer inhibitions than British gentlewomen about engaging in political activity.[150] Recalling Lord Randolph's 1885 reelection for Woodstock, she wrote: "From the window of the

Bear Hotel I made a little speech to the crowd and thanked them 'from the bottom of my heart' for returning my husband for the third time. I surpassed the fondest hopes of the Suffragettes, as though I was duly elected, and I certainly experienced all the pleasure and gratification of being a successful candidate."[151]

AUDIBILITY AND EXPERIENCE

In considering the way in which politicians addressed thousands of people in large halls or out-of-doors without any amplification beyond that which their own lungs and throats could provide, the question of how audible these speakers really were naturally arises. In 1876, for example, the *Daily Telegraph* wrote: "In the open air, it is questionable whether more than 1000 to 1500 persons, in a gathering which may possibly exceed 30,000, will catch all that is said; but the mere assemblage is in itself an eloquent utterance of popular feeling; and, as all present will be assured, the next morning's papers are certain to contain full reports."[152] Indoors, conditions might be little better. Gladstone described Bingley Hall, where he spoke to an audience of 25,000, as being "of no acoustical merit."[153]

Yet, unamplified platform speeches might not have been as inaudible as this suggests. When large indoor gatherings were anticipated, organizers took great pains to insure the visibility and audibility of the speakers—for instance, the preparations already discussed for the great John Bright celebration at Bingley Hall. At outdoor meetings too, it is possible that audibility was better than recent analysts have assumed. Take as examples Gladstone's three speeches at Blackheath. There is, in fact, evidence suggesting that the audibility of the 1871 speech was quite good. When preparations were being made for the 1876 speech, the local committee in charge of arrangements deliberately selected a site close to that of 1871 "when it was found that the right hon. gentleman, and even less powerful speakers had no difficulty in making themselves heard throughout an assembly of twenty thousand persons."[154] Some of the views about bad audibility outdoors might be in part attributed to bad weather. Nevertheless, of the rainy Blackheath speech of 1874, Montagu Williams later recalled that "An extraordinary effect was produced when Mr. Gladstone began to speak. That great crowd of many thousands became, on the instant profoundly silent. You might actually have heard the proverbial pin drop."[155] (It should be noted, however, that Williams was standing close to the speaker.) According to one historian, at the 1876 Blackheath speech, "between ten and fifteen thousand people were present, but little could be heard of the speech for the rain on the umbrellas."[156] The local reports, however, state that the rain ceased five minutes before Gladstone arrived and held off until he was gone, after which the torrent resumed.[157]

What must certainly have been true was that the effort of speakers to be heard by as many as possible of those assembled was a great strain. Of the 1871 Blackheath speech, for example, Gladstone recorded in his diary: "I spoke 1h. 50 min.; too long yet really not long enough for a full development of my points: physically rather an excess of effort."[158] Again, when speaking to a capacity audience at Bingley Hall in 1877, "the strain was excessive."[159] The physical toll of orating to large audiences has already been observed in the discussion of preachers (chapter 3), and platform speaking must have had similar effects. Further, although railway travel enabled politicians to deliver speeches all over the country, the travel could have only added to the strain of speaking. Beyond the extreme physical demands of platform speaking, there was also the mental strain. As Gladstone wrote in his review of Jephson: "Nay, the demands made upon the speaking powers of members increased to such a point that, if continued at the present rate, they threaten the enormous mischief of extinguishing their opportunities of study and reflection."[160]

By 1885, Lord Randolph Churchill was expressing his feelings in both public and private over the political and personal toll exacted by platform speaking. This is hardly surprising considering the great amount of his platform activity during the previous five years. To the Cambridge University Carlton Club, he cited platform duties as one cause of the modern politician's lack of time for thought: "The ordinary member of Parliament has perpetually to fly up to the House of Commons, or down to a public meeting, where he is supposed to discuss an illimitable range of British interests with the Government's policy towards them." Of the great politicians of the past—Canning, Grey, Peel, Russell, Disraeli—he said that he did not believe that "in the whole course of their career, attended half a dozen of those public meetings of the nature which some of us have to attend every week, or every month."[161] A few months later, he wrote in a letter:

> I find . . . that addressing these large meetings is such anxious and exciting work that for a day or two afterwards I am quite useless and demoralised. . . . I have made up my mind to give up almost entirely

> attendance at these public meetings. It is simply killing and the constant necessity of trying to say something new makes one a driveling idiot.[162]

If the effects of platform oratory on the speakers were considerable, far more important were the effects on the hearers. It was in large part from Gladstone's spectacular use of the political platform, and the publicity he generated therefrom, that the "cult of Gladstone" emerged. "It was frequently implied that he hypnotised his audiences and put them under some sort of spell through his oratory, his gestures, and his facial appearance."[163] One contemporary described this effect as being "Gladstonised."[164] The persuasive power of Gladstone's platform speaking in 1874 left an indelible impression upon Montagu Williams. Williams was a staunch Conservative and a top-ranked barrister. He was, therefore, not only antagonistic to Gladstone's politics, but also well-versed in the arts of oratorical persuasion. Nevertheless, even he joined the many who had fallen under the "spell" (to use one of the many metaphors drawn from the black arts that were routinely used by contemporaries) of Gladstone's oratory.

> I had come to Blackheath [in 1874] strongly prejudiced against the speaker's opinions. I was under the impression that I should disagree with everything that Mr. Gladstone said. What judges we are of ourselves! The reverse of what I had expected took place. I had heard all the finest orators of the day in my profession, and I had heard many great speakers hold forth from the hustings; but never in the whole course of my life, had I listened to a speech that carried me away so completely as the one Mr. Gladstone now delivered.[165]

By the time that Gladstone concluded, "the magician's power had succeeded, and that, as I walked away from Blackheath, my political opinions, at all events with regard to the Straits of Malacca, had undergone a complete change."[166]

Yet, although Gladstone had the reputation of Mesmer, a number of other leading platform speakers exerted extraordinary emotional and psychological power over their audiences. On hearing Joseph Chamberlain speak, the somewhat besotted Beatrice Potter wrote:

> Into the tones of his voice he threw the warmth of feeling which was lacking in his words, and every thought, every feeling, the slightest

> intonation of irony and contempt was reflected on the face of the crowd. It might have been a woman listening to the words of her lover! Perfect response, unquestioning receptivity. Who *reasons* with his mistress?[167]

Lord Randolph Churchill's powers of persuasion were noted by The *Pall Mall Gazette* in its amused report of his 1886 speech to the Tory Caucus held at a riding school in Paddington. "The villadom of Paddington, some two thousand of whom were thrilled by Lord Randolph's eloquence and fascinated by Lady Randolph's magnificent bonnet, would swear at Lord Randolph's bidding—aye, and believe they were swearing the truth—if he had told them that Paddington was situated in Yorkshire, and that Yorkshire was in South Africa."[168]

The spellbinding qualities of the major speakers, and the large audiences who came to hear them, made platform events a very special kind of experience. The great era of platform oratory in the last quarter of the nineteenth century must be understood alongside the changing nature of public diversion—including the quasi-secular popularity of "star" preachers (see chapter 3), the increasing respectability of theatrical entertainment (see pp. 203–4), and the emergence of spectator sports. In this context, platform events must be viewed not only as political communication, but also as a cultural experience: "for the audience present, a speech by a Party Leader was often as much an occasion—a 'happening'—as a detailed examination of the issues."[169] A very small number of platform speakers were able to match the great preachers and actors of the day by becoming the happening themselves. It could not be said of Chamberlain and Churchill, for instance, what one historian has written of Bright's speeches: "it was not the politics or the morality that mattered, but Bright himself. He was the experience."[170]

Gladstone's speeches had a similar effect, and masses of people turned out—even in the rain—to hear his thunder. For outdoor speeches, like outdoor concerts, good weather extended the nature of the happening by providing a greater variety of ways in which the speech could be experienced. Gladstone's 1871 speech at Blackheath, for example, took place on

> the loveliest of autumn afternoons, the sun shone brightly, the breeze was bracing but not chilly, the "half-holiday" gave the opportunity to multitudes to repair to "the heath" and make it a part of their afternoon's amusement to see the "People's William". . . . It was, therefore,

> not strange that a crowd, which has been variously estimated at from 8,000 to 15,000 people, but which it is safe to compute at 10,000, of all shades of politics, and of all sexes and ages, should assemble to hear, or rather to see the Prime Minister of England on an occasion which had been so widely advertised.[171]

An illustration of this event (figure 9) shows the variety of activities that could take place around a speaking event. Gladstone speaks from the covered hustings to a dense throng of people. Away from this press of people, in the middle-ground of the picture, a number of gentlemen and ladies on horseback and in carriages have either stopped to listen to the speech or have merely paused in the course of their ride. Meanwhile, in the foreground, numerous vendors and entertainers ply their trades to people who are paying little or no attention to the speech.

Indoor events featuring the leading speakers of the day were happenings too—full of the kind of energy generated by large numbers of closely packed people. To read about them now, they were also happenings over which a significant shadow of danger loomed. "The audience used to be packed so tight, when Bright was advertised to speak, that it was impossible for men to get their hands up if once they had them down. The heat for those on the floor would have been considered unendurable in any less cause than listening to Bright."[172] In 1877, Gladstone spoke at Birmingham's Bingley Hall. The Hall's estimated capacity of 20,000 was exceeded by an additional 10,000 people and glass had to be removed from the ceiling to let in more air. "But once Gladstone started to talk, even men who fainted struggled back to their feet to catch his words."[173] During the first Midlothian campaign, Gladstone spoke for only 20 or so minutes at the Waverley Market to an audience of 20,000. Even though the Market was, in his words, an "enormous building,"[174] he recorded in his diary that, "People were continually handed out over the heads who had fainted and were as if dead."[175]

Thus, despite the (certainly by today's standards) generally rational appeals of the major platform speakers, there was a strong element of irrationality to all this and the conditions common to major indoor platform events were potentially a recipe for disaster. No major platform speaker appears to have experienced what happened to Spurgeon at the Surrey Gardens Music Hall, when someone shouted "fire" and the resulting stampede of his 12,000-strong audience caused several fatalities and many serious injuries (see p. 129). Even so, the crowd conditions of platform events could result in tragedies that anticipate the rock concerts and sports matches of today. Take, for example, Jennie Churchill's description of an 1886 speech delivered by Lord Randolph at the Manchester Drill Hall:

> Eighteen thousand people filled the place to suffocation—no singer that ever lived can command the audience of a popular politician. If the building had held 40,000 or 50,000, it would still have been crowded. Most of the people had been standing for two hours before we arrived. . . . Randolph's speech lasted for two hours. The heat was great, and on leaving the building the crowd pressed round the carriage to such an extent that two men were killed.[176]

Historians have noted the religious sensibilities underlying the appeal and the experience of both Gladstone and Bright on the platform.[177] As already discussed, Gladstone enjoyed significant personal and political support from a number of the great preachers of his time (pp. 150–62), and Bright incorporated many religious elements into his oratorical style (p. 91). Platform events blended revivalist boisterousness with churchly seriousness. In the Midlothian campaigns, Gladstone's thunderous speeches heaping moral condemnation upon the Conservatives and their policies were delivered to an audience warmed up by singing Liberal songs set to the tune of hymns.[178] Occasionally, speeches were even delivered in churches, such as when, on March 19, 1880, Gladstone made a political speech in the Free Church at Davidson's Maine near Edinburgh.[179]

Certainly, the rise of preaching celebrity from Wesley and Whitefield on did much to condition audiences to stirring oratory. Indeed, through blending the intimate and the spectacular, the growing number and popularity of preachers in the nineteenth century in some senses created the kind of stable, receptive audience—an audience of what could be termed "civic strangers"—for the political platform of the 1880s and 1890s. But the religious resonance of major platform figures went considerably beyond incorporating of pulpit rhetoric or paralleling the patterns of nonconformist preaching.[180] As Curzon wrote of Gladstone and Bright, "what appealed to the crowd would seem to have been not so much the rolling sentences, or the majestic mien of the orator, as the spectacle of righteous fervour, invoking the moral sense of the community to storm some citadel of ancestral privilege or to redress an unexpiated wrong."[181]

PLATFORM AND PRESS

So far, the widespread practice of platform speaking in the last quarter of the century has been explored as a technique and an experience—the ways in which it changed the conduct of politics in space, in feeling, in meaning. In a very reductive sense, the "battle of the platforms" era can be understood as supply crudely attempting to meet—and exploit—new democratic demand. In this light, it is important to explore platform oratory not merely from the perspective of technique, but also from the perspective of technology.

The second half of the nineteenth century was marked by a massive growth in the production and circulation of a cheap, but still "respectable" press. These developments were facilitated by a series of fiscal reforms enacted during Gladstone's terms as Chancellor of the Exchequer, and Gladstone later reaped political dividends from the support of Liberally inclined newspapers like the *Daily Telegraph*.[182] The abolition of the duty on advertisements in 1852, the repeal of the stamp duty in 1855, and the elimination of the paper duty in 1861 fundamentally altered the economics of newspaper publishing. In 1821, *The Times* and the *Manchester Guardian* both cost 7*d.* per issue; in 1861, their prices had dropped to 3*d.* and 1*d.*, respectively.[183] Increased circulation went hand-in-hand with lower prices. By 1864, London weeklies enjoyed a total circulation of more than 2 million copies per week, and London dailies enjoyed a total circulation of nearly 250,000 per day. At the same time, provincial dailies and weeklies came near to doubling the circulation figures of the London papers.[184] Throughout the second half of the century, new papers were launched. The total number of newspapers in the United Kingdom grew from 795 in 1856 to 2,093 by 1886—a nearly threefold growth in the space of thirty years.[185]

Beginning in the later 1850s, the economically liberated newspapers developed a new kind of political influence in tandem with the concurrent growth of national party organizations. Accordingly, in the ensuing decades, newspapers were employed on an "unprecedented scale to formulate party programmes, to implement political strategies, and to serve personal ambitions."[186] The Conservatives lagged somewhat behind the Liberals in their exploitation of the press. By 1884, advocates of party modernization like Lord Randolph Churchill could opine that "the Conservative provincial press was for many years, and up to a very recent date, badly behindhand. I think it is waking up now."[187] A few years later, the Conservatives began to benefit from the wholesale defection of the national press from its general support of the Liberal party.

If the rise of national party organizations was the primary impetus for the development of a modern political press, it was politicians' speeches that in large measure provided the substance to be printed. And by the 1880s and 1890s, it was the platform speech rather than the parliamentary speech in which the bases of partisan politics were most clearly articulated. There was, however, a symbiotic relationship between the platform and the press. The growth and effectiveness of extra-parliamentary oratory was, in many respects, the consequence of technical and organizational innovations in newspaper reporting.[188]

The tangible residue of the increasing volume of platform speaking was the increasing volume of newsprint devoted to covering it. Party leaders were, of course, the first and greatest beneficiaries of press coverage. During 1868 general election, Gladstone could rely upon verbatim, or near-verbatim reports of his speeches. *The Times* devoted five columns to printing his speech at Liverpool, four to his speech at Newton, and seven for his speeches at Ormskirk and Southport.[189] In the general election of 1880, *The Times* complained that "if the Midlothian campaign continues as it has begun, the newspapers will have no opportunity of allowing anyone else to be heard."[190] By the general election of 1885, the press was covering an unprecedented number of platform speeches by a wider range of politicians. A statistical inquiry into the "gross production of political oratory" during the six weeks immediately preceding the general election of 1885 found that the "aggregate reports of all the electioneering oratory amounts to no less than two hundred and eighty-five columns of the *Times*. And this in a space of six weeks of six working days each!"[191] According to this study, the reports of speeches averaged 49 columns per week and 1,500 lines per day. While no comparable data for previous elections is presented, the reader is assured that a "glance at the newspaper file of the earlier year [1880], and the most rapid comparison of its electioneering reports with those of last October and November, is enough to show that the stump orator of 1885 has beaten him of 1880 by as much as 'mules distance oxen in the furrow'."[192]

All of this required a significant reporting apparatus. Bright normally drew about 50 reporters to his provincial meetings, and more than 70 reporters were on hand for his Reform speeches of the 1860s.[193] In 1871, Gladstone's speech at Blackheath was covered by nearly 100 reporters from the London and provincial press seated immediately in front of the platform.[194] Similarly, provision was made for 100 reporters at the 1876 Blackheath speech.[195] In 1887, Chamberlain went on a speaking tour of the Western Isles of Scotland, along with a corps of reporters from the national press. Although his following in the Commons was relatively small, "judged by the press he attracted, his influence in the country was second only to Gladstone's and Salisbury's."[196]

In terms of press coverage of political speeches, the turning point occurred around 1870. By 1852, the telegraph connected every major city in Britain. In 1870, the telegraph lines were purchased by the state and the responsibility for their operation transferred to the Post Office. It was around this time that the new central news agencies were formed, such as the Press Association (1868) and the Exchange Telegraph (1872). These developments led to the creation of an effective "trade in great men's speeches" managed along professional and profitable lines. How this trade worked is spelled out in an article from 1899.[197] The market in great men's oratory was a wholesale market, and the news agencies were the wholesale merchants. On Saturday, the agencies provided newspapers throughout the country with a list of the week's upcoming events. Based upon the interest of the speech and the politics of the paper, local editors selected the kind of report they wanted to purchase: "verbatim," "full" (both written in the first person), or "summary" (written in the third person). The charge to the client newspapers, including the cost of telegraphing, was 10*s.* per column (reckoned at 2,000 words). The Telegraph Act of 1868 gave news agencies privileged access to the wires through favorable rates. The Post Office charged the news agencies £1 per column for the first report, but charged only 3*s.* 4*d.* per column for all subsequent reports. Agencies' profits increased as more papers bought more columns. Accordingly, it was to the great advantage of the Press Association and other news agencies to have someone like Gladstone on the scene—someone who routinely spoke at great length and whose speeches created such interest that local editors would want to print at least "full" reports of them. Further, Gladstone's commanding position meant that his speeches set the agenda for the cycle of extra-parliamentary oratory. A Gladstone speech catalyzed both allies and opponents to make speeches of their own—the profits from this additional oratorical output accruing to the news agencies.

Yet, while all of this is testimony to the expanding reach and power of the press, it needs to be assessed very carefully with respect to the role of public speech in Victorian public life. It is wrong to see great men's speeches as a creature of the press. Press coverage was a very important aspect of extra-parliamentary speaking, but its importance did not lie primarily in (literally) spreading the word. As they were delivered to different audiences throughout the country, the speeches of leading politicians involved a great deal of repetition. Even when speeches were (on the model of Midlothian) planned as a series in which different themes were elaborated upon at each successive event, platform speakers generally reiterated their positions on a finite set of issues. Although the emphasis might shift from speech to speech, the basic themes remained the same—and were often articulated in nearly the same words. In this light, the function of press reports was more akin to political advertising than to political communication: the reports compounded the repetitions of the speeches. Newspaper readers, if they read accounts of each platform speech by a given politician, would be reading essentially the same points (and even much of the same language) over and over again. Thus, the most important aspect of press coverage was not necessarily the substance of a given speech, but rather that the speech had been given.

Further, one should not lose sight of the role of the individual. In the trade in great men's speeches, only a handful of speakers ranked as major commodities. Verbatim reporting extended only to Gladstone, Salisbury, Chamberlain, and Churchill around 1885; and to Salisbury, Rosebery, Balfour, and Chamberlain around 1897.[198] (Other leading politicians, were relegated to second-shelf of "full" reporting—still profitable for the news agencies, but doubtless galling to the individuals thus reported.) In particular, it was argued, the extraordinary nature of Gladstone's extra-parliamentary performances were instrumental in generating both supply and demand. "Mr. Gladstone, whether as Prime Minister or whether as seated in the cold shade of Opposition, kept up values by inspiring platform and recessional discussion."[199] After his retirement, it was perceived, the market fell off.

That Gladstone's speeches were typically rooted in the details of policy meant that opponents like Lord Randolph Churchill had also to speak to the details. When, for example, Gladstone led his audiences through the reasons why Home Rule was both wise and just, Lord Randolph was obliged to lay out for his audiences all the ways that it would work against the national interest. In terms of the press, Gladstone's success at setting the nation's political agenda—achieved in no small measure through his platform activities—is revealed by the fact that no political newspaper could do without a more or less full report of a Gladstone speech. Further, no paper opposed to his views could do without a reply.

In terms of speeches, no politicians during this period made their reputations based upon newspaper readership alone. Innovations in the technology and organization of communications notwithstanding, oral delivery and aural reception were still the most important factors. The oratorical reputation of a politician had to be made in front of live audiences before newspaper reports of his speeches could become an item of interest to readers, and a worthwhile commodity for the news agencies. Far more people read Bright's speeches in print than even the large audiences that actually heard him speak. "The first and the most profound, quasi-religious, effect of [his] oratory was, however, aural and immediate."[200] In Gladstone's case, although he was clearly one of the greatest beneficiaries of the widespread dissemination of his speeches through the press, some contemporary critics asserted the primacy of the oral over the printed:

> His [Gladstone's] oratory is peculiarly of that type which requires to be listened to, and depends for its charm upon the presence and personal characteristics of the orator. When read, the speeches turned out to be in substance a mere *réchauffé* of what we have been accustomed to in previous lucubrations, and in articles in the 'Nineteenth Century.'[201]

Ultimately, one did not become "Gladstonised" through reading newspapers.

Conclusion

Without following Jephson down the path of excessive Whiggishness, it seems fair to characterize the history of the platform in nineteenth-century Britain as both a "rise" and a "progress." This is especially evident in the way that politicians increasingly perceived the need to exert themselves as speakers outside of Parliament. Yet, viewed in terms of results, the platform's record—despite its increasing prevalence—was in fact a very mixed one. It seems unlikely that platform speeches by Anti-Corn Law League orators played a decisive role in getting the Corn Laws repealed. The phenomenon of Gladstone's first two Midlothian campaigns maintain their historical interest because of their unique features—most notably, their success. Afterwards, powerful speakers like Chamberlain and Churchill tried to use platform speaking to carry them to the top of the greasy pole, but failed in the attempt. Further testimony to the limits to the platform's rise and progress is how, after Gladstone, Chamberlain, and Churchill passed from the political scene, the newspapers seem to have found the economics of great men's oratory increasingly unrewarding. The conclusion that can be drawn from these observations is that the rise and progress of the platform says far more about political style than political substance. It also says more about political personalities than political parties.

It might be possible to contend that the increasing prevalence of the extra-parliamentary platform from the mid-1870s, and the use of the platform by politicians to change personal or political destinies in Parliament, was in fact a means of disciplining the increasingly politicized masses in an era of economic discontent within the existing structures of politics. Yet there is no evidence that such an intent existed. If anything, Gladstone, Chamberlain, and Churchill, each in his own way, used the platform to stir up mass sentiment against the *status quo*—and nowhere more so than within their own political parties. For them, the platform was a technique of political insurgency. Nor would these politicians have thought of their platform efforts as a means of disciplining the masses. Churchill sought with Tory Democracy to reinvigorate and modernize the Conservative Party in spite of itself. Chamberlain, however much he eventually soured, never fully escaped his civic gospel concern for the harmonious relations between the working and middle classes. Gladstone, although he was an extremely shrewd political calculator, attributed his political success to a divinely inspired sense of "right-timing" and he viewed his innovative use of the platform was a manifestation of this instinct (see p. 161).

Certainly, it can be seen that the platform was "in the air." The heyday of the extra-parliamentary platform in the last quarter of the nineteenth century coincided with a wide diffusion of unofficial platform activities. In 1872 (coincidentally, the same year the Ballot Act was passed), Speakers' Corner in Hyde Park was officially designated as a permanent popular platform.[202] A few years later, even though one cannot make a direct connection between the two, it is surely significant that the period of platform activity ushered in by the Bulgarian atrocities agitation and the Midlothian campaign coincided with the onset of what came to be called the Great Depression. Worsening economic conditions led to the establishment of several socialist organizations, notably The Social Democratic Federation (1881) and the Fabian Society (1884), which sponsored platform-speaking events in order to revive the popular radicalism that appeared to have died with Chartism in 1848. Recalling his speaking efforts as a Fabian, George Bernard Shaw wrote how, for a period of twelve years beginning in the mid-1880s,

> I sermonized on Socialism at least three times a fortnight average. I preached whenever and wherever I was asked. It was first come first served with me: when I got an application for a lecture I gave the applicant the first date I had vacant, whether it was for a street-corner, a public-house parlor, a market place, the economic section of the British Association, the City Temple, a cellar or a drawing room. My audiences varied from tens to thousands.[203]

Viewed in this context, the extra-parliamentary platform was part of a more general impetus toward public speaking prevalent in society. Questions of "right timing" aside, leading platform orators were able to capitalize upon, and generate even further demand. The extraordinary popularity of the extra-parliamentary platform is in no way better demonstrated than by the vast crowds that consistently turned out to hear speeches in all manner of uncomfortable, and even dangerous conditions. Certainly, the leading speakers were charismatic enough. Entertainment value alone, however, cannot fully account for either the appeal of the platform, or its tactical, if not always strategic successes. In a period in which the momentum for progressive extensions of the franchise was clear, but manhood (let alone universal) suffrage still unachieved, large platform speaking events provided political as well as experiential satisfactions to non-electors. In the age of Samuel Smiles, the relative decorum of the "respectable" electorate was generally emulated by those who did not have the vote. Even heckling as a form of political expression became domesticated through the routinization of platform activity. Ultimately there is no way to determine whether supply begat demand or demand begat supply. Nevertheless, what does seem clear is that, regardless of its efficacy, the extra-parliamentary platform provided an intimate form of mass politics for a society that had only barely become a mass polity.

Conclusion

IN THE PARISH CHURCH at Hughenden, Queen Victoria erected a monument to her favorite Prime Minister, Benjamin Disraeli, who had died in April 1881. Below the image of Disraeli's profile, carved in relief from pure white Carrara marble, the Queen placed a tablet bearing this inscription:

TO
THE DEAR AND HONOURED MEMORY
OF
BENJAMIN EARL OF BEACONSFIELD
THIS MEMORIAL IS PLACED BY
HIS GRATEFUL SOVEREIGN AND FRIEND
VICTORIA R. I.
"Kings love him that speaketh right."
PROVERBS, xvi. 13.[1]

While this could be viewed as little more than a monument to Disraeli's considerable powers of royal flattery, the sentiment also holds a more general meaning. As the preceding chapters have shown, the ability to "speak right" was valued not only by the Queen, but also by a great number of her subjects.

By the time that Victoria erected her memorial to Disraeli, more people were producing more public speech than during any previous period in British history. In addition, more people were hearing and reading those orations. Certainly, speeches in the House of Commons, from the pulpit, in the courtroom, and from the platform differed from each other with respect to form, tradition, style, audience, and intended outcomes. Even so, the practices of public speaking in politics, religion, and law experienced similar developments in a number of important respects which reveal much about the broader culture of public life in the nineteenth century.

Summary: Nineteenth-Century Developments

If it were possible to characterize a "typical" (that is, in-season) week in British public life during the last quarter of the nineteenth century, the description would have to include, at minimum, something like of 40 hours of parliamentary debate (including several lengthy speeches by Gladstone and others),[2] around 38,000 sermons,[3] speeches by counsel (and judges) in London and provincial courtrooms, platform orations of various kinds, and the weekly activities of trainees for public life in university, professional, and local debating societies. In each area of public life discussed here, internal developments created new structures of public speaking that responded to, but also helped to condition, broader structural changes in British society and culture.

The changing nature of parliamentary business and the increasingly public function of members, the concern over the spiritual well-being of the expanding and urbanizing population, and legal reforms all created new demands that stimulated Britain's gross oratorical productivity. And certainly, more public speaking was not the path of least resistance. Rather, it both reflected and manifested the extraordinary energy unleashed by Victorian society. The expanding domain of public speech placed new and formidable demands upon both speakers and hearers. Even so vigorous a man and an orator as Gladstone found his great speeches to be a considerable exertion. It was no less of a strain for other politicians, preachers, and barristers. Audience stamina was also high. In their thousands, people from all classes listened to lengthy orations in hot and ill-ventilated halls, in packed churches, in cold and drafty cathedrals, in cramped courtrooms, in downpours, and in frost. For many the audibility and the visibility of the speaker were poor. Even so, the often boisterous but usually peaceable audiences gathered and remained for the events.

But public speech was not merely the beneficiary of developments within the political, religious, and legal worlds. The relationship between public speech and public life became dynamic: the increased production and consumption of oratory shaped at the same time that it was shaped by the course of nineteenth-century public life. From the early decades of the century, prospective orators organized and enjoyed the benefits of societies devoted to the improvement of their abilities as public speakers: the Oxford and Cambridge Unions, the Church Homiletical Society, the Forensic Society, the Hardwicke Society, as well as numerous local debating societies and later the local parliament movement. To varying degrees these societies were all premised upon the idea that the improvement of public speaking was not only a useful, but also now a necessary attainment for public life. Thus, the increasing frequency of groups organized for oratorical self-improvement manifested how crucially important speech was perceived to be for the transaction of the business of public life, while the groups and their activities also perpetuated the idea of that importance.

Other manifestations were equally telling. The construction of new churches and chapels, courthouses, and public halls together with novel uses of old arenas expanded the number and variety of venues for public speaking. Thus, to the extent that the physical life of modern Britain—in particular, its *public* physical life—came into being during the nineteenth-century, oratory played an important role in shaping it. Public speaking moved into new kinds of space: cathedral naves, theaters, and nearly any indoor space that could fit a speaker and an audience (such as the riding school in which Lord Randolph Churchill addressed his Paddington constituents). Further, the practice of delivering speeches and sermons "out-of-doors"—once seen as a radical and evangelical excess—was adopted as a technique of mainstream public life.

In the realm of print, too, public speech played a central defining part. The removal of financial strictures on print media—the "taxes on knowledge"—permitted the reach of oratory to extend far beyond the time and the place in which a speech was originally delivered. MPs, preachers, barristers, and platform speakers could all increasingly rely upon their words being carried in newspapers—national and provincial, religious and secular—or other forms of publication aimed at a mass audience (e.g. *The Penny Pulpit*). A significant proportion of what the increasingly literate British public read was printed oratory.

The dynamic relationship between public speech and public life is especially evident when considering two of the nineteenth century's defining innovations in the technology of communication. The rapidly expanding railway network enabled politicians, preachers, and lawyers to speak at points that were considerably distant from their "home bases" in London or elsewhere. Railways also brought audiences to speakers, such as the tourists who went to see the great London preachers, or the people who traveled to hear Gladstone and other leading figures make platform speeches. Where railways facilitated the immediate, synchronous connection between speakers and hearers, the creation of a national telegraph network by the 1860s provided the means for virtual, asynchronous connections by enabling national and provincial newspapers to furnish their readership with texts of speeches delivered throughout the country.

While developments in politics, religion, and law encouraged the expansion of public speech, and while oratorical practices both created and filled new spaces in the shifting structure of public life, it also seems clear that there was increased demand from the consumers of speeches. The nature of the historical record is such that explaining why audiences of unprecedented size gathered with unprecedented frequency requires some degree of measured inference. Certainly, the Victorian audiences' prototypes were those associated with the evangelical movement and the radical mass platform of the late eighteenth and early nineteenth centuries. Even so, the audiences that emerged in the second half of the nineteenth century—the amassing of "civic strangers" that constituted the consuming body for Victorian oratory—created something new. The willingness of audiences to listen to often quite complicated speeches and sermons for hours at a time in less than comfortable conditions was certainly conducive to the increased supply of oratory. The relationship between the supply of, and the demand for, public speech can be seen most clearly in the new kinds of celebrity that was attached to the notable orators of the period.

In summing up the developments and dynamics of the nineteenth century, it is also important to at least mention that the increased production of public speech was hardly confined to the areas of public life covered in this study. The urbanization and embourgeoisment of British society produced an efflorescence of public speaking for a variety of public and semi-public occasions. Speeches marked the meetings of the many intellectual, literary, and professional societies formed in the course of the century. The same was true for the many organizations created for the edification of the working classes. Public lectures of all sorts drew in large numbers from many walks of life. The middle and late nineteenth century also saw the proliferation of institutions for the public good—hospitals, libraries, museums—the dedication ceremonies for which were invariably the occasion for speeches. In provincial towns, reflecting trends in national public life, speeches by local and invited notables took on a new importance in civic rituals.[4] How and why public speaking functioned in all of these areas (and more) require further study. The point here is that even a quick glance reveals how, on both the large and the small scales, the culture of public life in the second half of the nineteenth century became ever more suffused with public speech.

Lloyd George and the Legacy of Victorian Rhetorical Culture

The impact of public speech on the culture of public life in the nineteenth century endured well into the twentieth century, as exemplified by the early career of David Lloyd George.[5] Born in 1863, Lloyd George was raised in a Wales where the normally vigorous religious life and preaching culture had been recently energized further by the great revival of 1858–60. As a young man he held the sermons of his uncle Lloyd in great esteem, and would later credit the Nonconformist chapels of his youth as the formative influence on his oratorical style. In a culture with a strong tradition of lay preaching, the 18-year-old Lloyd George even temporarily filled a chapel pulpit, and according to some made his public speaking reputation as a Temperance orator.

Like may of his late-Victorian contemporaries, Lloyd George was a dedicated sermon-taster, even after he ceased to be religious.[6] In 1881, when in London to sit for a law exam, he attended services at St. Paul's and heard Joseph Parker.[7] On his honeymoon in London in 1888, he and his new bride attended sermons by famous preachers. Later, as a newly elected MP, he continued to attend the services of the great preachers, including Spurgeon and Liddon. Spurgeon, he wrote, "was very inspiring—he almost galvanized my dead faith into something like a transient somnolence, if not life."[8] His life-long interest in great preachers was akin to his avid consumption of drama—from both the pulpit and the stage he derived lessons in public speech.

But the shaping of Lloyd George's famous powers of public speaking did not stop with the influence and practice of preaching. As a youth, he acquired experience in arguing the political questions of the day in informal debating groups of young men such as the ones that gathered at Hugh Jones's smithy in Llanystumdwy (which later he affectionately called his first parliament), and later at John Roberts's candle shop in

Portmadoc. He gained more structured experience beginning in 1887 when he joined the Portmadoc Debating Society. The Society's membership consisted of a select group of two or three dozen local professional men. Eighteen years old when he joined, Lloyd George was its youngest member. The Society was organized along parliamentary lines and its proceedings were regularly reported in the *North Wales Observer and Express* published in Carnarvon. Despite his relative youth, Lloyd George rapidly established himself as a leader in the Society's debates.[9] Later, he became a leading speaker in the Criccieth Debating Society.

At the time he joined the Portmadoc Debating Society, Lloyd George was on his way to entering the local professional elite. He had been articled to a firm of solicitors in 1878 and was formally admitted to the Roll of Solicitors in 1884. At the end of that year, he established his own firm. Although he was not a barrister, the 1846 County Courts Act had given solicitors the right of address in the new lower courts, and Lloyd George quickly acquired a substantial reputation as a courtroom orator. A year after his first courtroom performance he was enjoying the benefits of a widespread practice. He became particularly notable for his cross-examinations and his zealous advocacy on behalf of accused poachers. The 1888 Llanfrothen burial trials—in which the recently granted right of Nonconformists to hold their own funeral rites in the parish graveyard was upheld—made Lloyd George a regional hero and a good prospect for adoption as a parliamentary candidate. As a kinsman later wrote:

> he never lost sight of his overriding ambition to become a public speaker who could surpass his contemporaries by the force of his eloquence and the cogency of his arguments. Each court case was judged [by Lloyd George] not so much on its legal and factual merits, but in light of the opportunity it provided him to test and improve his style of speech.[10]

By the time of the Llanfrothen trials, Lloyd George had entertained parliamentary ambitions for some time. His growing involvement in politics was marked by his increasingly prominent presence on Welsh platforms. He became a crusading Liberal, and identified far more with the rising young Joseph Chamberlain than the grand old Gladstone (although, not surprisingly, it turned out that the Welshman had far more natural sympathy for Home Rule than "Radical Joe"). Lloyd George was an energetic, and sometimes inflammatory platform speaker in the general elections of 1885 and 1886, as well as in his own victorious by-election campaign of 1890. Of a meeting in Portmadoc in November 1885, he recorded in his diary, "I raised alternate roars of laughter and rounds of cheering. John Roberts in proposing the vote of thanks to the speakers singled me out as a future MP. The audience cheered."[11]

When not platforming for parliamentary contests, he made public speeches on a variety of issues, such as the abolition of the Church tithe. After winning a seat in the House of Commons, Lloyd George was in even greater demand as a platform speaker within Wales, and his speaking activities expanded into England. In May 1890, he spoke at a meeting of the Liberation Society held at the Metropolitan Tabernacle, but his platform credentials in England were fully established in the following month when he appeared before several thousands packed into the Manchester Free Trade Hall. As one biographer has written: "Lloyd George's first important speeches as an MP were made from public platforms, not in the House of Commons. Indeed, he had established himself in England as an orator before he delivered his maiden speech."[12]

Thus, by the time that Lloyd George delivered his maiden speech in the Commons (after prudently observing its forms for a period) he was able to bring to bear on his parliamentary career many of the main developments that had placed oratory at the center of public life in later nineteenth-century Britain—debate club training, a close study and even some practice of preaching, the forensic theatrics of the courtroom, and years of activity on the platform. Nevertheless, where the decade-younger Winston Churchill would steep his oratory in the orotundity of the past, Lloyd George's speaking style was much more in tune with the times. He spoke as a figure of modernity rather than an upholder of tradition.

Lloyd George admired the self-made men and great public speakers of American politics such as Henry Clay and Abraham Lincoln. As it had been for them, oratory was the vehicle of his own political self-creation. Indeed, there is no better demonstration of the centrality of oratory in public life than Lloyd George's determined cultivation of his speech-making abilities. With the near-democratic Reform and Redistribution Acts of 1884–85, the infrastructure was in place to permit the Nonconformist, provincial, Celtic, lower-middle-class solicitor—in no small measure through his oratorical (many claimed demagogical) powers honed in the chapel, in the debating society, in the courtroom, and on the platform—to be able not only to climb to the top of the greasy pole, but also to pick up Gladstone's mantle of rhetorical leadership.[13]

Into the Twentieth Century

Lloyd George's early career demonstrates the ways in which, by the closing decades of the nineteenth century, public speech had become a pervasive force in public life. It also shows the extent to which access to public life through oratory had been expanded. But at the same time that Lloyd George was a great beneficiary of these developments, in many ways he also symbolizes their end. His rhetorical leadership coincided with the destruction of the nineteenth-century world in the Great War, and afterwards was imbricated with the decline of the Liberal Party that had animated the political culture of the second half of the nineteenth century. Indeed, it seems clear that there was a close affinity, if not exactly a direct connection, between Britain's oratorical heyday and its great age of Liberalism.

Already by the turn of the twentieth century, commentators remarked upon the diminished importance of public speech in the culture of public life. Some attributed the growing lack of public interest in oratory to the fact that most of the great public speakers discussed in the preceding chapters had died or retired.[14] With hindsight, this "supply side" explanation does not seem quite fair. Along with Lloyd George, many notable orators who began their careers in the age of Gladstone ascended to the top rungs of public life in the Edwardian era and beyond: Asquith, Balfour, Birkenhead, Clarke, Curzon, Simon, to name a few. All of these figures and others were able to use their powers of public speech to good advantage. It is also true, however, that oratorical ability did not work for them to the extent that it had for their predecessors. By the end of the nineteenth century, the contexts in which public speaking was produced and consumed were being transformed. Where material and structural developments in the mid-nineteenth century encouraged the expansion of public speech, developments in the late nineteenth and early twentieth centuries served to attenuate the connections between oratory and public life.

In Parliament, earlier nineteenth-century beliefs about middle-class influence were finally realized. The traditional landed elite in the Commons at last became a minority. The social composition of the House broadened, with MPs increasingly coming from the business and professional classes (particularly lawyers), joined by the first handfuls of genuinely working-class representatives.[15] As already demonstrated, however, the changing social and educational profile of the membership cannot fully explain the changing character of parliamentary oratory. Given the prevalent nineteenth-century view that great political eloquence could only be fully realized under an aristocratic constitution, it is somewhat ironic that the emergence of the Labour Party possibly did the most to keep the spirit of nineteenth-century political oratory alive deep into the twentieth century through figures like Aneurin Bevan and Neil Kinnock (both, significantly, Welshmen).[16] In what some have taken to calling the "conservative century," it seems likely that the association of oratory with the Labour Party ultimately did the cause of public speaking little good. Yet, despite the orators it produced, Labour's advent also contributed to the blunted tone of parliamentary discourse. As T. P. O'Connor, who first took a seat in 1880, observed in 1909: "as an old member of the House of Commons I am bound to say that the Labour Party has given to parliament a seriousness, a strenuousness, and an effectiveness, which rarely if ever existed in that assembly before."[17]

Perhaps because he had dominated the House of Commons so absolutely for so long, when Gladstone passed from the parliamentary scene there was no one (able or willing) to take his place as "Old Man Eloquent." But Gladstone's oratory, like Gladstone himself, was increasingly a survivor of an earlier age. He was nearly 60 on becoming Prime Minister for the first time, and 85 when he resigned the premiership for the last time. All the while the Grand Old Man held sway over the Commons, young men were entering Parliament, getting on their legs, and reflecting the new styles of their generation in their speeches. The younger generations of MPs also viewed Gladstone's oratory differently from their predecessors. In his long prime, Gladstone had been known as a man who could captivate the Commons with a five-hour budget speech. Toward the end of his career, however, the rising generation of parliamentarians saw more in his formidable powers of debate than in his virtuoso performances in set-piece speeches. Lloyd George, for example, described Gladstone as "far and away the best Parliamentary speaker I have ever heard. He was not so good in exposition. He was very long and he often bored you, but in debate, when he was attacked, he was superb."[18]

The changing tone of parliamentary speech-making by the 1890s could be ascribed, in part, to new sources of unease about Britain's position in the world. By the time of Victoria's Diamond Jubilee in 1897, the bases of Britain's nineteenth-century greatness—agriculture, industry, free trade, navy, empire—were meeting with increasing challenges.[19] These external challenges introduced new levels of anxiety, shrillness, and outright fear into British public discourse.[20] Yet, although these developments obviously comprise a highly significant structural context, it is difficult to make direct connections between the beginnings of Britain's "relative decline" and the fact that the great parliamentary speech all but went out of fashion.

It is also possible to observe how someone like Stanley Baldwin, one of the most successful politicians of the early twentieth century, abstained from using his reputedly considerable powers of oratory and instead adopted a speaking style of cultivated plainness while at the same time the magniloquent Winston Churchill was a "study in failure." But such observations do not provide the kind of structural explanation necessary to account for the new character of and values associated with parliamentary speech-making. One pithy but cogent analysis comes from the pen of that keen contemporary observer, Virginia Woolf:

> Wit, invective, passion, are no longer called for. Mr. [Ramsay] MacDonald is addressing not the small separate ears of his audience in the House of Commons, but men and women in factories, in shops, in farms on the [South African] veldt, in Indian villages. He is speaking to all men everywhere, not to us sitting here. Hence the clarity, the gravity, the plain impersonality of his statement.[21]

Before the special combination of intimacy and reach made possible by television, the broadening of audience was accompanied by a flattening of style. Yet there is also a politics, not just a utility to style. In this vein, it is important to understand the phlegmatic speech-making of Baldwin and other successful interwar politicians like Neville Chamberlain as on some levels a reaction against the emotive political styles that were increasingly in evidence. At home, the country had experienced two decades of Lloyd George. Abroad, there were the examples of Lenin, Mussolini, and Hitler.

Along with the changing nature of parliamentary oratory at the beginning of the twentieth century, the political efficacy and the cultural significance of extra-parliamentary speech-making declined. When Gladstone died, the Press Association claimed that it lost £400 a year in revenues as a result. And although figures like Joseph Chamberlain continued to depend on press coverage of his speeches to disseminate his dissenting views, even he could not get verbatim reporting during his 1903 tariff campaign.[22] By the 1900s, the market for great men's speeches was clearly drying up.

In the 1890s, the individual platform speaking of the previous thirty years began to diminish in importance with the rise of the centralized party "programmes" on which approved candidates were to run. During the First World War, the development of vigorous censorship and propaganda regimes, along with the general curtailing of civil liberties (not least freedom of speech) under the Defence of the Realm Act, largely suspended extra-parliamentary speech-making as a vehicle of national political debate. After the granting of manhood, and partial womanhood suffrage in 1918, party leaders and back benchers alike had even more cause to court the voters. But even with the electorate more than doubled, socio-economically diversified, and including both sexes, "the complex structure of extra-parliamentary national debate . . . never recovered its rude, late-Victorian health."[23] In general, although leading politicians like Lloyd George and MacDonald seemed to save their best performances for the platform, the old combination of speaking and reporting had ceased to produce the kind of political dividends that Gladstone and others had reaped.

At the beginning of the twentieth century, speech-making continued to be a feature of public culture, but political life came to be shaped far more by action. Despite the abundance of their rhetorical and symbolic productivity, direct action was the hallmark of the troublesome triad of suffragette, labor, and Irish militancy. ("Deeds not Words" was the slogan of Emmeline Pankhurst's Women's Social and Political Union.) More broadly, the First World War not only eliminated a generation of political leadership, the War experience and its aftermath (promises of "homes fit for heroes" and the like) also produced a lasting public cynicism about politics—particularly with respect to what politicians say.

In the interwar period, political life appeared to many as characterized by inaction—and dynamic speech-making by men of action like Oswald Mosley and Winston Churchill hardly served to fill the void. In the politics of the second half of the nineteenth century, speech *was* action. To the extent that there were political speakers in the first half of the twentieth century who could have functioned well in the age of Gladstone, they, and their hearers were becoming ever fewer in number.

In the realm of religious oratory, something of how the popular interest in preaching was significantly dampened by the early decades of the twentieth century was amusingly illustrated by P. G. Wodehouse in his 1923 story, "The Great Sermon Handicap." Bertie Wooster wagers on the longest sermon to be preached among a number of country curates.

Wooster's money is on Old Heppenstall, and he encourages the aged clergyman to revive a particularly lengthy sermon from his younger days. Heppenstall fears that the sermon will be too long, and notes that, in these restless times, "brevity in the pulpit is becoming more and more desiderated by even the bucolic churchgoer." The new sensibility is summed up by Heppenstall's young nephew: a sermon "should be a bright, brisk, straight-from-the-shoulder address, never lasting more than ten or twelve minutes."[24]

Brevity in the pulpit was one of many manifestations of the secularization of British society that became evident in the early years of the twentieth century. One historian has described the Victorian era as "a paradox of manifest vitality [in religion] and latent secularization."[25] In the late nineteenth century and into the twentieth, the extent of secularization was masked through religion's "inherited social prominence and continuing involvement in mainstream politics."[26] It was also masked by preaching.

The importance of preaching can be read in the figures for church membership. In the early decades of the nineteenth century, membership in Nonconformist churches grew by leaps and bounds, while membership in Anglican churches grew by less than a tenth of the Nonconformist rate. Beginning in the 1840s, however, the Nonconformist growth rate slowed while the Anglican growth rate accelerated. For the rest of the century, increases in Anglican membership equaled those for Nonconformist churches—and both grew faster than the population at large.[27] These comparative growth rates of church membership indicate how the Anglican church, through its church-building and subsequent preaching-enhancement campaigns that took hold in the middle decades of the century, was able to compete more effectively against the Nonconformist churches.

By examining what was going on *inside* the churches and chapels in the later nineteenth century, it is possible to observe how the broad popularity of preaching—particularly the ecumenicism with which the pulpit celebrities of the day were heard by a sermon-tasting public—served to disguise the underlying cultural secularization. In the twentieth century, particularly after the First World War, the secularization became overt. Although British culture continued to be marked by a generalized Christian moral sensibility, an ever smaller minority actually participated in organized religion.[28] As the importance of religious practice declined, the enormous popularity that preaching had enjoyed during the time of Spurgeon and Liddon could not be sustained.

Compared to politics and religion, the law in the twentieth century enjoyed a far greater degree of oratorical continuity. The law continued to capture public interest with dramatic trials centered upon horrific crimes and scandalous personal behavior, as documented so well in numerous volumes of the *Notable British Trials* series. Yet, this continuity can be understood best as a function of how, in the words of one legal historian, the "modern Bar, with its distinctive blend of old and new ideas, was largely the creation of Victorian advocates."[29] Further, some have remarked upon the enduring oratorical Victorianism of the English bar. While dining in the Middle Temple, the playwright David Hare noted: "I am not sure if it is the surroundings or the Master Treasurer's own natural manner which has us all discoursing in an orotund, High Victorian style of speech."[30]

Despite these continuities, however, the structural and cultural position of barristerial oratory was changing by the close of Victoria's reign. Barristerial oratory had become a far more sober affair by the last decades of the nineteenth century. According to Max Beerbohm, lamenting young Harry Irving's decision to ply his theatrical talents on the stage instead of in the courtroom, "The tone of the Old Bailey had already [by the 1890s] been dulcified to that pitch of suavity and ruth which is the key-note of our modern life."[31] In structural terms, after the right of prisoners to give testimony under oath was granted by the 1898 Criminal Evidence Act, speeches by barristers ceased to be the principal focus of the courtroom's oratorical drama.

The relationship between courtroom oratory and newspaper reporting also changed. The beginnings of what would be called the "new journalism" led new publishing ventures in the later decades of the nineteenth century to move away from the lengthy accounts of courtroom proceedings of the kind that filled the pages of *The Times*. Instead, increasing stress was laid upon the sensational details of crime and scandals for the approbation of the broad reading public. For example, the *Star*, founded in 1888, benefited greatly in its early years from the Jack the Ripper murders with headlines like: "The Ripper Again / Surpasses himself in fiendish mutilations / His victim found in Cable Street Archway / The legs cut off and Carried away"—a headline that helped the circulation for that day reach 360,598.[32]

Just as in the nineteenth century, new developments in the practices and technology of communications in the early twentieth century had an enormous impact on the culture of public life. Also like the nineteenth century, these new developments had important effects on the functions of public speaking in public life. In the nineteenth century, the role of public oratory was strongly conditioned by the rise of the railroads that carried audiences to speakers and speakers to audiences, the newspapers that filled their growing number of columns with printed speeches, and the telegraphy that enabled the wide dissemination of speeches throughout the nation. In the twentieth century, new developments in communications and media radically expanded the potential to reach people. But where the nineteenth-century developments had contributed to broadening the domain of public speaking, the forms and applications of the twentieth-century developments served to curtail it.

In print journalism, the years around 1900 witnessed the emergence of a new breed of popular half-penny dailies that brought the new journalism to full flower. The model for these papers was Alfred Harmsworth's *Daily Mail* (founded in 1896), which sought to present "all the news in the smallest space."[33] The *Daily Mail* was an enormous commercial success, and by 1912 it had attained a circulation of more than a million.[34] The numerous cheap dailies that followed the *Daily Mail*'s formula also enjoyed large readerships. Antithetical to the new formula were things like full reports of political speeches and courtroom orations. The *Daily Mail* (and by extension its imitators) "maintained a high political content, but it packaged politics in a way that verbatim speech reporting could not do."[35] The anti-oratorical bent of the new journalism was perhaps summed up best by one of Harmsworth's henchmen, who went so far as to credit the *Daily Mail* with having done "more . . . than anything else to reduce parliamentary proceedings and the speeches of politicians to their right proportions in the daily prints."[36]

The potential of the wireless to be a great disseminator of oratory was limited by policy. In the 1920s, the Post Office, in charge of the fledgling BBC, refused to permit the broadcast of anything that could be considered controversial. "The Derby and political speeches alike were taboo."[37] The one major exception to this ban occurred during the general election of 1924, when the BBC was permitted to broadcast a speech by each of the three party leaders, MacDonald, Baldwin, and Asquith. The general ban on political speeches also applied to debates. The Post Office refused the BBC permission either to broadcast debates (such as that of the Oxford Union on the King's speech in 1925), or to stage its own debates. In addition to the extremely cautious approach to broadcasting political speeches, some leading politicians, like MacDonald and Neville Chamberlain, failed to perceive the potential of the wireless. Yet, even for those like Baldwin who were keenly interested in using the new medium to best advantage, the wireless was never destined to be a Midlothian of the air. The BBC attempted to keep political broadcasts short. Baldwin's 1924 election broadcast, for example, was a mere twenty minutes long.[38]

While it provided only limited scope for political speech-making, the wireless, as A. J. P. Taylor has written, had broad effects on the place of oratory in political culture:

> Men and women heard the voices of leading statesmen in their own homes. They ceased to attend political meetings, except those held by the advocates of minority views [like Mosley] which were denied expression over the air. Public opinion could no longer be gauged by public demonstrations. New, supposedly more scientific tests had to be used. The character of oratory changed. Broadcasting demanded a gentler, more intimate style. The oldtimers, trained on audiences, could not manage this. Lloyd George and Ramsay Macdonald, once great magicians, were both ineffective on the air. Baldwin came into his own.[39]

Religious oratory on the wireless was subject to fewer strictures than political speech-making, but it was also quite limited in the early days of the BBC.[40] The rise of the BBC coincided with the post-Victorian overt secularization of British society. The principal broadcasting of religious oratory consisted of addresses by popular preachers in the middle of orchestral concerts. At the beginning of 1924, the BBC began to broadcast a series of non-denominational services from St. Martin in the Fields. (The first service broadcast from a church other than St. Martin's was from the Metropolitan Tabernacle. One can only imagine what use that great communicator Spurgeon could have made of the wireless!) Ultimately, however, all religious programming occupied as little as one percent of the total weekly broadcasting hours.[41]

These are only the most direct and obvious ways in which the domain of public speech contracted in the early twentieth century. It also bears noting that as the discourses of public life became both more pithy and (in politics at least) more shrill, private life became more diverse and diverting. In the second half of the nineteenth century, public speech certainly provided entertainment value—the active entertainment of the debating club or local parliament; the more passive, but probably no less strenuous activity of sermon tasting; or even simply turning up in the park on a nice day to hear a platform celebrity. By the early twentieth century, public culture had come to be strongly marked by the many new amusements and secular recreations that had originated during the heyday of public speech: seaside resorts, the music hall, and "respectable" theater. Later, the wireless and the cinema would prove at least equally popular. Spectator sports were another major, and highly compelling, late-nineteenth-century development that took off in the early years of the twentieth century. As a 1915 account of railway workers observed: "Politics, religion, the fates of empires and governments, the interest of life and death itself must yield to the supreme fascination and excitement of football."[42]

The case of public speech helps us to see how unlike twentieth-century Britain Victorian Britain was. In the later nineteenth century, oratory was deeply connected to, and materially embodied in the substance and institutions of society. Public speech did not simply float over the surface of life and events. It was an integral part of the newspaper you read, the buildings and open spaces you walked past. For some, it was a significant aspect of their education or self-education. For a great many, it formed the content of their leisure time. In these ways and others described here, oratory was an important factor in structuring both time and space. By bringing and holding together large numbers of people with surprisingly minimal amounts of strife and disruption, public speech was an implicit organizing principle of social behavior. It is by looking at how oratory interacted with, and at times helped shape the material and the structural developments of the nineteenth century, that we see how public speech—its theatricality, sense of occasion, and sheer verbosity—must be understood as nothing less than a key defining characteristic of British public life in the Victorian era.

In 1924, Virginia Woolf made the famous observation that "on or about December 1910 human character changed."[43] The rapidly diminishing place of public speech in British political culture was certainly one important aspect of this change. By the time Woolf penned these lines, in the words of Isaiah Berlin, "not only rhetoric but even noble eloquence seemed outrageous hypocrisy."[44] New circumstances, new technologies, and new sensibilities demanded new approaches to the mediation and articulation of public life. For a generation after his death, "Mr. Gladstone" may have been spoken of in terms of a sage. In the unsettled times of the early twentieth century, however, public speech as practiced in the age of Gladstone came to be understood as old-fashioned and, pejoratively, "Victorian."

NOTES

Abbreviations in Notes

BL Add. MS	British Library Additional Manuscript.
DNB	*The Dictionary of National Biography* (including supplements).
DD 1	*Disraeli, Derby and the Conservative Party: Journals and Memoirs of Edward Henry, Lord Stanley, 1849–1869*. John Vincent, ed. Hassocks: Harvester, 1987.
DD 2	*A Selection from the Diaries of Edward Henry Stanley, 15th Earl of Derby (1826–93) Between September 1869 and March 1878*. John Vincent, ed. *Camden Fifth Series*, vol. 4 (1994).
GD	*The Gladstone Diaries* (14 vols.). M. R. D. Foot and H. C. G. Matthew, eds. Oxford: Oxford University Press, 1968–94.
HP: 1754–1790	*The History of Parliament: The House of Commons, 1754–1790* (3 vols.). Lewis Namier and John Brooke, eds. London: HMSO, 1964.
HP: 1790–1820	*The History of Parliament: The House of Commons, 1790–1820* (5 vols.). R. G. Thorne, ed. London: Secker & Warburg, 1986.
M&B	William Flavelle Monypenny and George Earle Buckle. *The Life of Benjamin Disraeli, Earl of Beaconsfield* (6 vols.). London: Murray, 1910–20.
Parl. Deb., NS / 3s / 4s	*Parliamentary Debates*, New Series / 3rd Series / 4th Series
PP	Parliamentary Papers.
TT	*The Times*

INTRODUCTION

1. Quoted in George Watson, *The English Ideology: Studies in the Language of Victorian Politics* (London: Allen Lane, 1973), p. 141.

2. Walter Bagehot, "Mr. Gladstone" (1860), *The Collected Works of Walter Bagehot*, vol. 3, ed. Norman St John-Stevas (London: Economist, 1968), p. 429.

3. G. S. R. Kitson Clark, "The Romantic Element—1830–1850," in *Studies in Social History: A Tribute to G. M. Trevelyan*, ed. John Harold Plumb (London: Longmans Green, 1955), p. 213.

4. Robert T. Oliver, *Public Speaking in the Reshaping of Great Britain* (Newark, DE: University of Delaware Press, 1987), p. 212.

5. Karen J. Musolf, *From Plymouth to Parliament: A Rhetorical History of Nancy Astor's 1919 Campaign* (New York: St. Martin's Press, 1999). See her introduction for an overview of the genre of rhetorical history.

6. John Morley, *The Life of William Ewart Gladstone*, 3 vols. (London: Macmillan, 1903), 2: 589–90.

7. Gareth Stedman Jones, *Languages of Class: Studies in English Working Class History, 1832–1982* (Cambridge: Cambridge University Press, 1983), pp. 23–24.

8. Patrick Joyce, *Visions of the People: Industrial England and the Question of Class* (Cambridge: Cambridge University Press, 1991), p. 27.

9. Joyce, *Visions of the People*, p. 43.

10. See Raymond Williams, *Culture and Society, 1780–1950* (London: Chatto & Windus, 1958).

11. Jürgen Habermas, *The Structural Transformation of the Public Sphere: An Inquiry into a Category of Bourgeois Society*, tr. Thomas Burger (Cambridge, MA: MIT Press, 1989), p. 203.

12. Habermas, *Public Sphere*, p. 16.

13. Walter J. Ong, *Orality and Literacy: The Technologizing of the Word* (London: Routledge, 1989), pp. 41, 109, 115, 158.

14. H. G. C. Matthew, "Rhetoric and Politics in Great Britain, 1860–1950," *Politics and Social Change in Britain: Essays Presented to A. F. Thompson*, ed. P. J. Waller (Hassocks: Harvester, 1987), pp. 34–58. See also Colin Matthew, ed., *The Nineteenth Century* (Oxford: Oxford University Press, 2000), pp. 106–8.

15. In contrast to the historical literature on Britain, a significant (if unconnected) body of recent work analyzes the rhetorical culture of nineteenth-century American public life. Particularly notable are Kenneth Cmiel, *Democratic Eloquence: The Fight Over Popular Speech in Nineteenth-Century America* (New York: Morrow, 1990); Robert A. Ferguson, *Law and Letters in American Culture* (Cambridge, MA: Harvard University Press, 1984); Wayne Fields, *Union of Words: A History of Presidential Eloquence* (New York: Free Press, 1996); Frances Lea McCurdy, *Stump, Bar, and Pulpit: Speechmaking on the Missouri Frontier* (Columbia: University of Missouri Press, 1969); and Garry Wills, *Lincoln at Gettysburg: The Words that Remade America* (New York: Simon & Schuster, 1992).

16. See, e.g., Paul Langford, *Englishness Identified: Manners and Character, 1650–1850.* (Oxford: Oxford University Press, 2000), pp. 203–12.

17."On Eloquence," *The Eton Miscellany* 2 , no. 8 (1827): 107–8.

18. Keith Robbins, *Nineteenth-Century Britain: Integration and Diversity. The Ford Lectures Delivered in the University of Oxford, 1986–1987* (Oxford: Clarendon, 1988), p. 181.

19. Raymond Cocks, *Foundations of the Modern Bar* (London: Sweet & Maxwell, 1983), p. 27.

20. See Walter L. Arnstein, "Queen Victoria Opens Parliament: The Disinvention of Tradition," *Historical Research* 63, no. 151 (1990): 178–94; and "Queen Victoria's Speeches from the Throne: A New Look," in *Government and Institutions in the Post-1832 United Kingdom*, ed. Alan O'Day (Lewiston: Mellen, 1995), pp. 127–53.

21. Lytton Strachey, *Eminent Victorians: Cardinal Manning, Florence Nightingale, Dr. Arnold, General Gordon* (London: Chatto & Windus, 1918), p. 308.

22.Quoted in M&B, 6: 356–57.

CHAPTER 1: SCHOOLS FOR PUBLIC SPEAKING

1. See *TT,* October 23, 1873, p. 5; October 24, 1873, p. 5. In his memoirs, Selborne recalled that, "The dinner itself was tedious and ill-managed, perhaps unavoidably on account of the great number of guests; but the interest of the proceedings was great." Roundell Palmer, Earl of Selborne, *Memorials: Personal and Political, 1865–1895*, 2 vols. (London, 1898), 1: 325.

2. See Donna T. Andrew, *London Debating Societies, 1776–1799* (London: London Record Society, 1994).

3. The standard history of the Oxford Union is Herbert Arthur Morrah, *The Oxford Union, 1823–1923* (London: Cassell, 1923). (Morrah was President of the Oxford Union in 1894.) Christopher Hollis, *The Oxford Union* (London: Evans Brothers, 1965) brings the story up to the 1960s. See also David Walter, *The Oxford Union: Playground of Power* (London: Macdonald, 1984).

4. Loren Reid, *Charles James Fox: A Man for the People* (Columbia, MO: University of Missouri Press, 1969), p. 14.

5. "On Eloquence," *The Eton Miscellany* 2, no. 8 (1827): 114. On Gladstone's experience in Pop, see John Morley, *The Life of William Ewart Gladstone*, 3 vols. (London: Macmillan, 1903), 1: 34–37.

6. Ernest Hartley Coleridge, *Life & Correspondence of John Duke Lord Coleridge, Lord Chief Justice of England*, 2 vols. (London: Heinemann, 1904), 1: 48.

7. Earl Curzon of Kedleston, "Eton," *Subjects of the Day: Being a Collection of Speeches and Writings*, ed. Desmond M. Chapman-Huston (London: George Allen & Unwin, 1915), p. 85.

8. Curzon, "Eton," p. 86.

9. See Sheldon Rothblatt, "The Student Sub-culture and the Examination System in Early 19th Century Oxbridge," in *The University and Society*, ed. Lawrence Stone, 2 vols. (Princeton: Princeton University Press, 1974), vol. 1, esp. pp. 252–56.

10. Wendy Hinde, *George Canning* (London: Collins, 1973), p. 15.

11. See Linda Colley, *Britons: Forging the Nation, 1707–1837* (New Haven: Yale University Press, 1992), ch. 8.

12. My discussion of the historical background of the Cambridge Union is drawn largely from Percy Cradock, *Recollections of the Cambridge Union, 1815–1939* (Cambridge: Bowes & Bowes, 1953), and the preface to The Cambridge Union Society, *Inaugural Proceedings* (London, 1866), published to commemorate the opening of the Union's new buildings.

13. See D. A. Winstanley, *Early Victorian Cambridge* (Cambridge: Cambridge University Press, 1940), pp. 25–28.

14. On the relationship of the Apostles to the Cambridge Union, see Peter Allen, *The Cambridge Apostles: The Early Years* (Cambridge: Cambridge University Press, 1978), especially chs. 1–3, and pp. 233, 234–35.

15. Quoted in Allen, *Cambridge Apostles*, p. 45.

16. See "Note on the Property of the Society" appended to the "Financial Statement" of The Cambridge Union Society, *Annual Report*, 1907 (Cambridge: Fabb & Tyler, 1907).

17. Reproduced in Cambridge Union, *Inaugural Proceedings*, p. 44.

18. *Laws and Transactions of the United Debating Society, Oxford* [reprint] (Oxford, 1872), p. 10.

19. *Laws and Transactions of the United Debating Society*, p. [4].

20. Quoted in *Laws and Transactions of the United Debating Society*, p. [2]. See also *Rules and Regulations of the Oxford Union Society, Corrected to October 1st, 1908, With a List of Former Officers* (Oxford: Bryan, 1908), p. 3.

21. Oxford Union, *Rules and Regulations . . . 1908*, p. 8.

22. See *Catalogue of the Library of the Oxford Union Society*, 3rd ed. (Oxford, 1852).

23. Oxford Union, *Rules and Regulations . . . 1908*, p. 8.

24. *Demosthenes Demobilized: A Record of the Cambridge Union Society Debates February, 1919–June, 1920* (Cambridge: Heffer, 1920), p. v.

25. Quoted in A. G. Gardiner, *The Life of Sir William Harcourt*, 2 vols. (New York: Doran, [1923?]), 1: 36.

26. Viscount Birkenhead, "Oxford Union Society," *Points of View*, 2 vols. (London: Hodder and Stoughton, [1923]), 1: 80.

27. Significantly, the period that saw the founding of the Union Societies, the 1820s, was also the time when competitive team sports became firmly established at Oxford and Cambridge. See Rothblatt, "The Student Sub-culture," p. 258. Birkenhead notes that, in Oxford society, presidency of the Union was subordinate in prestige and power to leadership in athletics. He recalls that Lord Ampthill was the only person to combine the offices of captain of the Boat Club and president of the Union. "The combination must have represented the nearest approach to the apotheosis of which our degenerate age is capable." Further, he expresses regret over never being able to get his Wadham colleague, C. B. Fry (captain of cricket, football, and athletics) interested in the Union. "This grieved me, because he was by far the most important person of his day at Oxford. Even Heads of Houses and Vice-Chancellors used to bow to him in the street." Birkenhead, "Oxford Union Society," pp. 80–81.

28. A. M. M. Steadman, *Oxford: Its Life and Schools* (London, 1887), p. 135.

29. Simon's extended recollections of the Union are included in Morrah, *Oxford Union*, pp. 292–96. This quotation from p. 293.

30. *Rules and Regulations of the Oxford Union Society, Corrected to October, 1858* (Oxford, 1858), p. 52.

31. Birkenhead, "Oxford Union Society," p. 83.

32. Birkenhead, "Oxford Union Society," p. 84.

33. Earl of Birkenhead, *Frederick Edwin Earl of Birkenhead: The First Phase,* (London: Butterworth, 1933), pp. 55–56. In his later recollections, Birkenhead describes this score against his rival as "somewhat unworthy." Birkenhead, "Oxford Union Society," p. 82.

34. Quoted in Cradock, *Recollections,* p. 68.

35. John Smith, *Sketches of Cantabs* (London, 1849), pp. 39–40.

36. Smith, *Sketches of Cantabs,* p. 41. Smith also provides a parody of a "typical" Union debate in which all matters of substance are avoided in favor of airy generalizations and crude syllogisms.

37. William Everett, *On the Cam: Lectures on the University of Cambridge in England* (Cambridge, 1865), pp. 183–84.

38. The societies at Edinburgh and Dublin grew out of debating clubs founded in the late eighteenth and early nineteenth centuries. Evidently, the society at Durham did not last for very long since its successor, the Durham Union Society was formed around 1842. See Durham University Library Archives and Special Collections Handlist, p. 5; and J. T. Fowler, "The Durham Union Society," *Durham University Journal* 20 (1912): 204–7.

39. Cambridge University Library, Manuscripts Department, Cambridge Union Society Minute Books, vol. 11.

40. In Morrah, *Oxford Union,* p. 294.

41. Smith, *Sketches of Cantabs,* p. 37.

42. Leslie Stephen, the first editor of the *DNB,* had been a member of the Cambridge Union Society.

43. Quoted in Birkenhead, "Oxford Union Society," p. 83.

44. In Morrah, *Oxford Union,* p. 295.

45. Birkenhead, "Oxford Union Society," p. 80.

46. Reproduced in Cambridge Union, *Inaugural Proceedings,* p. 45.

47. Birkenhead, "Oxford Union Society," p. 80.

48. Cambridge Union, *Inaugural Proceedings,* p. 21. With characteristic acerbity, Raymond Asquith, President of the Oxford Union in 1900, described the Cambridge Union "a detestable place to speak in, and the Cambridge orators are as repulsive a crew as I have ever seen." John Jolliffe, *Raymond Asquith: Life and Letters* (London: Collins, 1980), p. 68.

49. *The Gladstone Papers,* ed. A. Tilney Bassett (London: Cassell, 1930), p. 94.

50. Morley, *Gladstone,* 1: 72.

51. Birkenhead, "Oxford Union Society," p. 89.

52. *Proceedings of the Oxford Union Society on Thursday, May 19th, 1898, Being the Day of Mr. Gladstone's Death* (Oxford, 1898), p. 7.

53. *GD,* 4: 464.

54. After Gladstone's defeat at Oxford in 1865 (with the exception of one by-election in 1878), neither seat for the University was contested until 1918. See H. C. G. Matthew, *Gladstone,* 2 vols. (Oxford: Clarendon, 1986–95), 1: 129.

55. Quoted in Morley, *Gladstone,* 1: 360.

56. Matthew, *Gladstone,* 1: 129.

57. According to Morrah: "This was not a political gathering. Yet the Union had become identified with political feelings, and it is a significant fact that the partisanship rife

in England at that time manifested itself more than once during the evening." Morrah, *Oxford Union*, pp. 236–37.

58. "After enumerating other eminent members of the Union, the Lord Chancellor remarked that the assemblage was not what it ought to be in the absence of Mr. Gladstone —a man not behind Pitt or Canning in eloquence. (Cheers and expressions of dissent.) He reminded those who interrupted that he was referring not to the opinions, but to the eloquence and the genius of the present Premier, who while a young member of that society, gave the promise of that distinction he had so fully attained." *TT,* October 23, 1873, p. 5.

59. See *GD*, 8: 291 n. 4.

60. The late Colin Matthew was kind enough to speculate on this matter in correspondence with the author.

61. *GD*, 8: 403.

62. Gordon Campbell, letter to the editor, *TT,* October 25, 1873, p. 7.

63. In Morrah, *Oxford Union*, p. 295.

64. Oxford Union, *Mr. Gladstone's Death*, p. 4. Also quoted in Birkenhead, *Frederick Edwin Earl of Birkenhead*, pp. 57–58. The biographer, Birkenhead's son, states that the news of Gladstone's death had been received on that day, and that Smith's speech was delivered impromptu. Nevertheless, since it was Smith's habit at this time to carefully prepare and elaborately rehearse his speeches, it is safe to assume that he did not speak without some preparation. Indeed, Birkenhead's speaking style was characterized one obituary as "concocted impromptu" (p. 56). Not all who heard F. E. 's speech were equally impressed. Raymond Asquith wrote: "The debate here last Thursday wh. was supposed to have been of a humorous description was postponed in consequence of Gladstone's death: in private business funeral orations were delivered by F. E. Smith and Simon . . . F. E. made a thoroughly bad artificial speech which took in most of the audience: Simon was more sincere and a great deal better." Jolliffe, *Asquith*, p. 39.

65. Birkenhead, "Oxford Union Society," p. 83.

66. By limiting the analysis to the Unions' presidents, this examination obviously misses many Union members who did not assume the presidency, but nevertheless later attained great stature in public life. Lord Robert Cecil, who served as Secretary (1848) and Treasurer (1849–50) of the Oxford Union, became, as Lord Salisbury, the Prime Minister. Further, since the analysis ends at 1873, it misses some important figures that filled the presidency in subsequent years. If extended by one year, for instance, the analysis it would include the future Prime Minister H. H. Asquith, who served as President of the Oxford Union in 1874.

67. T. J. H. Bishop and Rupert Wilkinson, *Winchester and the Public School Elite: A Statistical Analysis* (London: Faber and Faber, 1967), p. 128.

68. Information on the honors gained by individual students at Oxford can be obtained more readily than for students at Cambridge. *The Historical Register of the University of Oxford: Being a Supplement to the Oxford University Calendar with an Alphabetical Record of University Honours and Distinctions, Completed to the End of Trinity Term, 1900* (Oxford: Clarendon, 1900) lists honors alphabetically by name, so that for each person, all honors garnered conveniently appear together. *The Historical Register of the University of Cambridge: Being a Supplement to the Calendar with a Record of University Offices Honours and Distinctions to the Year 1910*, ed. J. R. Tanner (Cambridge: Cambridge University Press,

1917), however, lists honors by examination by year, making it very difficult to produce a comprehensive list of honors for each Cambridge Union president.

69. The figures in this paragraph are taken from M. C. Curthoys, "The Careers of Oxford Men," in *The History of the University of Oxford*, vol. 6, *Nineteenth Century Oxford, Part I*, ed. M. G. Brock and M. C. Curthoys (Oxford: Clarendon, 1997), Appendix Tables 14. A1 and 14. A2, pp. 503–4.

70. In at least one case, however, a life was noteworthy for its negative achievements. William Scott O'Brien (President of the Cambridge Union, 1831), after serving a few sessions as an MP for Irish constituencies, became a revolutionist in 1848. He was arrested, tried, and sentenced to death, subsequently commuted to transportation.

71. Roundell Palmer, Earl of Selborne, *Memorials: Family and Personal, 1766–1865*, 2 vols. (London, 1896),1: 140–41.

72. Gemma Bailey, ed., *Lady Margaret Hall: A Short History* (London: Oxford University Press, 1923), p. 48.

73. Quoted in Pauline Adams, *Somerville for Women: An Oxford College, 1879–1993* (Oxford: Oxford University Press, 1996), p. 128. See also Penny Griffin, ed., *St Hugh's: One Hundred Years of Women's Education in Oxford* (London: Macmillan, 1986), pp. 45–46 n. 34.

74. Ann Phillips, ed., *A Newnham Anthology* (Cambridge: Cambridge University Press, 1979), p. 29.

75. Newnham College Club, *Cambridge Letter &c.*, 1883, pp. 5–6.

76. Newnham College Club, *Cambridge Letter &c.*, 1883, pp. 11–12; 1884, pp. 14–15.

77. Newnham College Club, *Cambridge Letter &c.*, 1883, p. 11.

78. Mary Agnes Hamilton, *Newnham: An Informal Biography* (London: Faber and Faber, 1936), p. 162.

79. Newnham College Club, *Cambridge Letter &c.*, 1883, p. 11.

80. Newnham College Club, *Cambridge Letter &c.*, 1888, pp. 7–8.

81. Newnham College Club, *Cambridge Letter &c.*, 1884, pp. 17–18.

82. Newnham College Club, *Cambridge Letter etc.*, 1894, p. 10.

83. Newnham College Club, *Cambridge Letter &c.*, 1887, p. 9.

84. Newnham College Archives, Newnham College Political Society Minute Books.

85. Phillips, *Newnham Anthology*, p. 29.

86. Alice Gardner, *A Short History of Newnham College Cambridge* (Cambridge: Bowes & Bowes, 1921), p. 125.

87. Phillips, *Newnham Anthology*, p. 29.

88. Newnham College Club. *Cambridge Letter &c.*, 1886.

89. Phillips, *Newnham Anthology*, p. 29; Gardner, *Short History of New*nham, p. 125.

90. Adams, *Somerville*, p. 135.

91. Old Newnham Students Club, *Cambridge Letter and List of Members*, 1881, p. 10.

92. Patricia Hollis, *Ladies Elect: Women in English Local Government, 1865–1914* (Oxford: Clarendon, 1987), p. 2. See also Appendix B, p. 486.

93. See e. g. Hollis, *Ladies Elect*, p. 137.

94. To take Newnham as an example, alumnae from the College's early years became local politicians, such as Florence Ada Brown (Newnham 1878–80) the first woman on the Cambridge Town Council and later Alderman and Mayor. For more instances, see *Newnham College Register*, vol. 1, *1871–1923*, 2nd ed. (Cambridge: Newnham College, 1979).

95. George Macaulay Trevelyan, *The Life of John Bright* (Boston: Houghton Mifflin, 1914), p. 24.

96. John Alfred Langford, *Modern Birmingham and its Institutions: A Chronicle of Local Events, from 1841 to 1871*, 2 vols. (Birmingham: Downing, [1873–77]), 2: 247. For the year-to-year activities of the Birmingham and Edgbaston Debating Society, see pp. 235–48.

97. For a detailed analysis of Birmingham's nineteenth-century local elite, see E. P. Hennock, *Fit and Proper Persons: Ideal and Reality in Nineteenth-Century Urban Government* (London: Arnold, 1973). Regrettably, Hennock does not examine the role of the Birmingham and Edgbaston Debating Society in the creation of that elite.

98. Peter T. Marsh, *Joseph Chamberlain: Entrepreneur in Politics* (New Haven: Yale University Press, 1994), p. 15.

99. Jonathan Parry, *The Rise and Fall of Liberal Government in Victorian Britain* (New Haven: Yale University Press, 1993), p. 221.

100. An incisive discussion of the local parliament movement can be found in H. C. G. Matthew, "Rhetoric and Politics in Great Britain, 1860–1950," *Politics and Social Change in Britain: Essays Presented to A. F. Thompson*, P. J. Waller, ed. (Hassocks: Harvester, 1987), pp. 36–38.

101. Blanchard Jerrold, "On the Manufacture of Public Opinion," *The Nineteenth Century* 13, no. 76 (1883): 1085–86.

102. *Eastbourne Gazette*, December 26, 1883, n. p.

103. M. Ostrogorski, *Democracy and the Organization of Political Parties*, tr. Frederick Clarke, 2 vols. (New York: Macmillan, 1922), 1: 417. None of the sources I have consulted mentions whether any women were members of local parliaments.

104. Ross McKibbin, *The Ideologies of Class: Social Relations in Britain, 1880–1950* (Oxford: Clarendon, 1990), pp. 22–23; H. A. Taylor, *The Strange Case of Andrew Bonar Law* (London: Paul, [1932]), pp. 27–33.

CHAPTER 2: THE HOUSE OF COMMONS

1. *The Works of Lord Macaulay Complete*, ed. Lady Trevelyan, 8 vols. (London, 1871), 7: 378.

2. Winston S. Churchill, *My Early Life: A Roving Commission* (1930; London: Cooper, 1989), p. 48.

3. My discussion of Churchill's oratorical development is based upon Robert Rhodes James, "The Young Tribune, 1897–1914," *Winston S. Churchill: His Complete Speeches, 1897–1963*, ed. Robert Rhodes James, 8 vols. (New York: Chelsea House, 1974), vol. 1, esp. pp. 10–12; and David Cannadine, "Introduction," *Blood, Toil, Tears and Sweat: The Speeches of Winston Churchill* (Boston: Houghton Mifflin, 1989).

4. See Robert Rhodes James, *Churchill: A Study in Failure, 1900–1939* (Harmondsworth: Penguin, 1973), pp. 29–40.

5. As Edward R. Murrow wrote on the occasion of Churchill's 80th birthday. Quoted in Asa Briggs, *The History of Broadcasting in the United Kingdom*, 5 vols. (Oxford: Oxford University Press, 1995), 3: 4.

6. Earl Curzon of Kedleston, *Modern Parliamentary Eloquence: The Rede Lecture Delivered Before the University of Cambridge, November 6, 1913* (London: Macmillan , 1913), p. 47.

7. See "Political Orators and Writers of Pamphlets" in *The Cambridge History of English Literature*, vol. 14, *The Nineteenth Century III*, ed. A. W. Ward and A. R. Waller (Cambridge: Cambridge University Press, 1917), pp. 131–151.

8. It is not only space that precludes a discussion of the House of Lords, but also the very different structures, functions, and history of the upper house. Already by the close of the eighteenth century, the Commons had become the principal chamber of legislative power and deliberation, even when the Prime Minister sat in the "other place." Additionally, although many notable speakers made many notable speeches in the House of Lords during the period under examination, most had previously gained oratorical renown in the Commons. The oratorical functions of the lords spiritual and the Lord Chancellor are noted in chapters 3 and 4, respectively.

9. Quoted in Stanley Ayling, *The Elder Pitt, Earl of Chatham* (London: Collins, 1976), p. 427. See Henry Montagu Butler, *Lord Chatham as an Orator* (Oxford: Clarendon, 1912); and Robert T. Oliver, *The Influence of Rhetoric in the Shaping of Great Britain* (Newark, DE: University of Delaware Press, 1986), esp. ch. 8.

10. John Morley, *Burke* (London, 1897), p. 208.

11. Horace Walpole, *Journal of the Reign of King George the Third from the Year 1771 to 1783*, 2 vols. (London, 1859), 1: 84.

12. Morley, *Burke*, p. 209.

13. Useful studies of parliamentary oratory include: Robert Craig, *A History of Oratory in Parliament*, 1213 to 1913 (London: Heath, Cranton & Ouseley, [1913]); Curzon, *Parliamentary Eloquence*; T. H. S. Escott, "The House of Commons: Its *Personnel* and its Oratory," *Fraser's Magazine* (New Series) 10, no. 58 (October 1874): 504–17; George Henry Francis, "Contemporary Orators" (16 parts), *Fraser's Magazine* 31, no. 84 (April 1845) to 34, no. 104 (December 1846); Abraham Hayward, "The British Parliament: Its History and Eloquence," *The Quarterly Review* 132, no. 264 (April 1872), pp. 450–95; Frederic George Kenyon, *Comparison of Ancient and Modern Political Oratory. The Chancellor's Essay, 1889* (Oxford: Blackwell, 1889).

14. Earl Stanhope, *Life of the Right Honourable William Pitt*, 3rd ed., 4 vols. (London, 1867), 1: 8–9. Pitt's early training in extemporaneous translation was manifested in his adult life on at least several occasions that have been recorded. Lord John Russell relates a story that, while waiting for Pitt in the library of his country house one day, Lords Harrowby and Grenville were perusing Thucydides and came to a passage that they could not make out. When Pitt arrived, he construed the passage on the spot "with the greatest facility." *Memorials and Correspondence of Charles James Fox*, ed. Lord John Russell, 4 vols. (London, 1853), 2: 3. On another occasion, a sentence from Tacitus's *De Oratoribus* was quoted in Pitt's presence. Someone opined that the sentence, "*Magna eloquentia sicut flamma materiâ alitur et motibus excitatur et urendo clarescit*," was untranslatable, to which Pitt immediately replied, "No; I should translate it thus: 'It is with eloquence as with a flame. It requires fuel to feed it, motion to excite it, and it brightens as it burns.'" Samuel Rogers, *Recollections* (London, 1859), p. 178.

15. Stanhope, *Pitt*, 1: 9.

16. George Tomline, *Memoirs of the Life of the Right Honourable William Pitt*, 4th ed., 3 vols. (London, 1822), 1: 5, n.

17. *The Speeches of the Right Honourable William Pitt in the House of Commons*, 4 vols. (London, 1806), 2: 83.

18. Stanhope, *Pitt,* 2: 145–46. For an example of how the legend endured, see Earl of Birkenhead, "Eloquence," *Law Life and Letters,* 2 vols. (New York: Doran, 1927), 2: 120–21. Pitt's definitive modern biographer states that it is a shame to question so well-known a story, but he has discovered no conclusive evidence to support it. John Ehrman, *The Younger Pitt: The Years of Acclaim* (New York: Dutton, 1969), p. 401, n. 1.

19. George Otto Trevelyan, *The Early History of Charles James Fox,* 3rd ed. (London, 1881), p. 50.

20. According to the best recent account of Fox as an orator: "Descriptions of eighteenth-century speaking suggest that many members of the House of Commons employed a style of public address that was pompous, dignified, studied, rehearsed, formalized, groomed-and-tailored. In sharp contrast, Fox developed a style that was natural, simple, unaffected, conversational. Part of this style resulted from the self-assurance that he had developed at Eton and elsewhere, part from his continual discussion of politics with young and old friends, part from his accumulation not merely of classical gems but of an ample store of contemporary fact and example, part from an analytical mind that allowed him to follow an argument closely from beginning to end, part from the habit of sharp listening to what the other people were actually saying, part from an unusual memory that would allow him to prepare a reply as he listened." Loren Reid, *Charles James Fox: A Man for the People* (Columbia, MO: University of Missouri Press, 1969), pp. 14–15.

21. Pitt, *Speeches,* 1: 21.

22. *The Speeches of the Right Honourable Charles James Fox in the House of Commons,* 6 vols. (London, 1815), 3: 124.

23. *The Historical and the Posthumous Memoirs of Sir Nathaniel William Wraxall, 1772–1784,* ed. Henry B. Wheatley, 5 vols. (London, 1884), 3: 225.

24. Linda Colley, *Britons: Forging the Nation, 1707–1837* (New Haven: Yale University Press, 1992), p. 152. See also *HP: 1790–1820,* 1: 331–32.

25. See Hayward, "British Parliament," p. 475; also Escott, "House of Commons," pp. 515–16.

26. For the limitations of Pitt, *Speeches,* see Ehrman, *Pitt,* pp. 671–72. Similar reservations must certainly apply to Fox, *Speeches.*

27. Pitt, *Speeches,* 1: 164.

28. *Memorials and Correspondence of. . . Fox,* 1: 31.

29. Wraxall, *Memoirs,* 3: 12.

30. Escott, "House of Commons," pp. 515–16.

31. Craig, *History of Oratory in Parliament,* p. 12.

32. A number of scholars have sought to anatomize the ways in which the classical civilizations were interpreted and used in British culture generally. Particularly useful accounts of the general influence of the classics on British culture are R. M. Ogilvie, *Latin and Greek: A History of the Influence of the Classics on English Life from 1600 to 1918* (Hamden, CT: Archon, 1964); Richard Jenkyns, *The Victorians and Ancient Greece* (Cambridge, MA: Harvard University Press, 1980); Frank Miller Turner, *The Greek Heritage in Victorian Britain* (New Haven: Yale University Press, 1981); some of the essays in Turner's *Contesting Cultural Authority: Essays on Victorian Intellectual Life* (Cambridge: Cambridge University Press, 1993); and Norman Vance, *The Victorians and Ancient Rome* (Oxford: Blackwell, 1997). Also instructive are studies of the enduring uses of classical rhetoric, such as Martin

J. Svaglic, "Classical Rhetoric and Victorian Prose," *The Art of Victorian Prose*, ed. George Levine and William Madden (London: Oxford University Press, 1968), pp. 268–88.

33. *Disraeli's Reminiscences*, ed. Helen M. Swartz and Marvin Swartz (New York: Stein and Day, 1976), pp. 97–98. The first part of this document is almost identical to a passage in Disraeli's last complete novel, *Endymion* (1880), ch. 76, in which the unwritten rules of quotation in parliamentary speeches are attributed to Charles James Fox.

34. Curzon, *Parliamentary Eloquence*, p. 11.

35. Curzon, *Parliamentary Eloquence*, p. 8.

36. Curzon, *Parliamentary Eloquence*, p. 12.

37. Kenyon, *Political Oratory*, p. 33.

38. Kenyon, *Political Oratory*, p. 18.

39. Curzon, *Parliamentary Eloquence*, p. 8.

40. Kenyon, *Political Oratory*, p. 15.

41. See, e. g., S. F. Wooley, "The Personnel of the Parliament of 1833," *The English Historical Review* 53, no. 210 (April 1938): 240–62.

42. Norman Gash, *Politics in the Age of Peel: A Study in the Technique of Parliamentary Representation, 1830–1850* (London: Longmans, 1953), p. x.

43. See, e.g., James Vernon, *Politics and the People: A Study in English Political Culture, c. 1815–1867* (Cambridge: Cambridge University Press, 1993).

44. William Henry Whiteley, "The Social Composition of the House of Commons, 1868–1885" (Ph.D. diss., Cornell University, 1960).

45. See, e. g., W. L. Guttsman, *The British Political Elite* (New York: Basic Books, 1963).

46. Ian R. Christie, *British 'Non-Élite' MPs, 1715–1820* (Oxford: Clarendon, 1995), esp. pp. 66 and 108.

47. See Martin J. Wiener, *English Culture and the Decline of the Industrial Spirit, 1850–1980* (Cambridge: Cambridge University Press, 1981). For the "patterns of advancement" of new men in Parliament during the eighteenth century, see Christie, *Non-Élite MPs*, ch. 5.

48. Hayward, "British Parliament," p. 474.

49. Escott, "House of Commons," p. 515–16.

50. John Cannon, *Aristocratic Century: The Peerage of Eighteenth-Century England* (Cambridge: Cambridge University Press, 1984), pp. 34–59.

51. Lawrence Stone, "The Size and Composition of the Oxford Student Body 1580–1910," in *The University in Society*, ed. Lawrence Stone, 2 vols. (Princeton, Princeton University Press, 1974), vol. 1 esp. pp. 37–60.

52. *HP: 1754–1790*, 1: 111; *HP: 1790–1820*, 1: 293.

53. Christie, *Non-Élite MPs*, pp. 136–40.

54. The term "public life" itself was effectively a creation of the eighteenth century that achieved common currency in the middle 1700s. See Paul Langford, *Public Life and the Propertied Englishman, 1689–1798* (Oxford: Clarendon, 1991), p. vi.

55. Cannon, *Aristocratic Century*, p. 43.

56. Cannon, *Aristocratic Century*, p. 34. On the ideological component of public school and university education in this period, see Colley, *Britons*, pp. 167–70.

57. See Francis G. Hutchins, *The Illusion of Permanence: British Imperialism in India* (Princeton: Princeton University Press, 1967), pp. 143–50.

58. Report of Her Majesty's Commissioners Appointed to Inquire into the Revenues and Management of Certain Colleges and Schools, and the Studies Pursued and Instruction Given Therein [hereafter Clarendon Commission Report], PP, 1864, 20: 13.

59. Clarendon Commission Report, 21: 188.

60. Roundell Palmer, Earl of Selborne, *Memorials: Family and Personal, 1766–1865*, 2 vols. (London, 1896), 1: 100–103.

61. Clarendon Commission Report, 20: 28.

62. In the 1770s, students at Christ Church read Sophocles, Herodotus, Thucydides, Xenophon, Cicero, Caesar, Livy, Sallust, Virgil, Lucretius, Horace, and the New Testament (in Greek). P. Quarrie, "The Christ Church Collection Books," in *The History of the University of Oxford*, vol. 5, *The Eighteenth Century*, ed. L. S. Sutherland and L. G. Mitchell (Oxford: Clarendon, 1986), pp. 493–506. In the 1780s, Greek readings even exceeded Latin.

63. See D. J. Palmer, *The Rise of English Studies: An Account of the Study of English Language and Literature from its Origins to the Makings of the Oxford English School* (London: Oxford University Press, 1965); and Reba N. Soffer, *Discipline and Power: The University, History, and the Making of the English Elite, 1870–1930* (Stanford: Stanford University Press, 1994).

64. John Morley, *The Life of William Ewart Gladstone*, 3 vols. (London: Macmillan, 1903) 1: 50.

65. In his 1831 degree examination, Gladstone was questioned on Aristotle, Plato, Homer, Virgil, Persius, Aristophanes, Herodotus, and Thucydides. He was prepared for, but not questioned on Hellenics, Livy, Polybus, Select Orations, Horace, Juvenal, Aeschylus, and Sophocles. *GD*, 1: 393 (November 17, 1831).

66. See M. L. Clarke, *Classical Education in Britain, 1500–1900* (Cambridge: Cambridge University Press, 1959), ch. 8.

67. See Clarke, *Classical Education*, ch. 12.

68. See, e.g., *Report of the Committee Appointed by the Prime Minister to Inquire into the Position of the Classics in the Educational System of the United Kingdom* (London: HMSO, 1921).

69. Stone, "Oxford Student Body," p. 37.

70. Stone, "Oxford Student Body," p. 95.

71. These figures are taken from the *Historical Registers* for Oxford and Cambridge. For both universities, I have used the figures for the second year in which the exams were given, the novelty of the exams rendering the first-year figures significantly lower than those of subsequent years.

72. Quoted in Rhodes James, "Young Tribune," p. 10.

73. P. D. G. Thomas, *The House of Commons in the Eighteenth Century* (Oxford: Clarendon, 1971), p. 127.

74. M. H. Port, ed. *The Houses of Parliament* (New Haven: Yale University Press, 1976), Appendix II, p. 312.

75. Port, *Parliament*, p. 182; and Roland Quinault, "Westminster and the Victorian Constitution," *Transactions of the Royal Historical Society*, 6th Series, vol. 2 (1992), p. 90.

76. Port, *Parliament*, pp. 1, 94.

77. *The New Palace of Westminster*, 15th ed. (London, 1858), p. 43.

78. William White, *The Inner Life of the House of Commons*, 2 vols. (London, 1897), 1: 70.

79. Churchill, *Speeches*, 8: 7104.

80. Thomas, *Commons*, pp. 229–30.

81. *HP: 1790–1820*, 1: 344.

82. Thomas, *Commons*, p. 231.

83. Related in Curzon, *Parliamentary Eloquence*, p. 9.

84. Thomas, *Commons*, p. 123.

85. Wraxall, *Memoirs*, 3: 225.

86. Thomas, *Commons*, p. 221–22.

87. DD 1, pp. 150–51.

88. DD 1, p. 122. The tally of speeches for 1847–8 and 1852–3 counts all questions and answers recorded in the *Parliamentary Debates*. The two sessions analyzed were among the lengthiest of the nineteenth-century: 1847–8 lasted 170 days and 1852–3 lasted 160 days.

89. Thomas, *Commons*, p. 230.

90. J. Guinness Rogers, "Chatter Versus Work in Parliament," *The Nineteenth Century* 16, no. 91 (September 1884): 397–99, 401. In the session of 1883, after the 98 MPs who were members of the government, officials and ex-officials, or Parnellites are deducted, 67 percent of the remaining members made a total of 9,515 contributions to debates. Again excluding the 98 government, official, and Parnellite members, 56 members spoke more than 50 times contributing 62 percent of the 9,515 speeches; 24 members spoke more than 100 times contributing 39 percent .

91. Earl Grey, "The House of Commons," *The Nineteenth Century*, 15, no. 85 (March 1884): 519.

92. Curzon, *Parliamentary Eloquence*, p. 13.

93. *Parl. Deb.*, 3s, vol. 285, cols. 106–7 (February 28, 1884).

94. See Michael MacDonagh, *The Reporters' Gallery* (London: Hodder and Stoughton, [1913]); and A. Aspinall, "The Reporting and Publishing of the House of Commons' Debates, 1771–1834," in *Essays Presented to Sir Lewis Namier*, ed. Richard Pares and A. J. P. Taylor (London: Macmillan, 1956), pp. 227–57.

95. Between 1831 and 1836, Charles Dickens made his living as a reporter for *The Mirror of Parliament* (1828–41), which for a time successfully rivaled *Hansard's Parliamentary Debates* (the successor to Cobbett). In 1877, Gladstone paid a retrospective tribute to the fullness of the *Mirror's* reporting as compared to that of *Hansard*. See *The Letters of Charles Dickens*, vol. 1, ed. Madeline House and Graham Storey (Oxford: Clarendon, 1965), p. 10n.

96. In his review of Henry Hallam's *Constitutional History of England*. Thomas Babington Macaulay, *Critical and Historical Essays Contributed to* The Edinburgh Review, 2 vols. (London, 1856), 1: 95.

97. William Fraser, *Disraeli and His Day* (London, 1891), p. 386.

98. See William Law, *Our Hansard, or the True Mirror of Parliament* (London: Pittman, 1950), esp. ch. 3.

99. Matthew Engel, *Tickle the Public: 100 Years of the Popular Press* (London: Gollancz, 1996), p. 24.

100. MacDonagh, *Reporters' Gallery*, p. 415.

101. Alfred Kinnear, "Parliamentary Reporting," *The Contemporary Review* 87 (March 1905): 372. Cf. A. P. Nicholson, "Parliamentary Reporting—A Reply," *The Contemporary Review* 87 (April 1905): 577–82.

102. *Parl. Deb.*, NS, vol. 20, col. 1596 (March 30, 1829).

103. *The Speeches of the Late Right Honourable Sir Robert Peel, Bart., Delivered in the House of Commons*, 4 vols. (London, 1853). This comprehensive collection reveals a total of 43 Latin quotations (excluding a variety of Latin phrases) and a total of 32 English quotations. On a number of occasions Latin and English quotations are in the same speech. Some of the quotations, both English and Latin, are repetitions of quotations used by former statesmen (e.g. Pitt), and some are repetitions of quotations used by Peel in earlier speeches on the same subject.

104. George Henry Francis, "Contemporary Orators," no. i, *Fraser's Magazine* 31, no. 84 (April 1845): 389.

105. For differing views on when accents became a social issue see Lynda Mugglestone, *'Talking Proper': The Rise of Accent of Social Symbol* (Oxford: Clarendon, 1995) on the early eighteenth century; Keith Thomas, "The Place of Laughter in Tudor and Stuart England," *The Times Literary Supplement*, January 21, 1977, p. 77 on the Tudor period; and P. J. Waller, "Democracy and Dialect, Speech and Class," in *Politics and Social Change in Britain: Essays Presented to A. F. Thompson*, ed. P. J. Waller (Sussex: Harvester, 1987), pp. 1–33 on the middle and later nineteenth century.

106. Quoted in Donald Read, *Peel and the Victorians* (London: Blackwell, 1987), p. 22.

107. François Guizot, *Memoirs of Sir Robert Peel* (London, 1857), p. 25.

108. Hayward, "British Parliament," p. 480.

109. Curzon, *Parliamentary Eloquence*, p. 8. Canning himself came to find his position as the leading parliamentary orator to be a dubious distinction. His powers as a speaker notwithstanding, Canning's ambition to become first minister was continually frustrated by both his politics and his personality. In 1821, reflecting on his political failures, Canning lamented to his wife, "And what does the reputation of being the First Speaker in the H of C do for me? Nothing. It only leads people to believe that *first speaking* is not necessary for carrying on the affairs of the government—that it is very well to have—very delightful to witness—but that business can go on very well without it. And so it can." Quoted in J. E. Cookson, *Lord Liverpool's Administration: The Crucial Years, 1815–22* (Hamden, CT: Archon, 1975), p. 310.

110. Edward Bulwer Lytton, *England and the English*, ed. Standish Meacham (1833; Chicago: University of Chicago Press, 1970), pp. 384–85.

111. Norman Gash, *Sir Robert Peel: The Life of Sir Robert Peel After 1830* (London: Longman, 1972), p. 659. The appendix is on pp. 717–22.

112. Peel, *Speeches*, 1: 3.

113. See Read, *Peel and the Victorians*, ch. 7.

114. On Peel's statue, see Richard Jenkyns, *Dignity and Decadence: Victorian Art and the Classical Inheritance* (London: HarperCollins, 1991), pp. 111–12.

115. For an insightful account of Gladstone's political career organized around his major parliamentary speeches see Peter Stansky, *Gladstone: A Progress in Politics* (Boston: Little, Brown, 1979).

116. *GD*, 14 indexes Gladstone's vast reading—around 21,000 titles (including periodicals) and more than 4,500 authors. Although the largest entries (after immediate contemporaries such as Newman) are those for Scott and Shakespeare, the entries for classical authors reveal Gladstone's continued reading of Greek and Latin works throughout his life.

117. Roy Jenkins, *Gladstone* (London: Macmillan, 1995), p. 455.

118. Jenkins, *Gladstone*, pp. 455–56, 590.

119. Gladstone Papers, BL Add. MS 44649, f. 11.

120. Gladstone Papers, BL Add. MS 44649, f. 16b.

121. Jenkins, *Gladstone*, p. 262.

122. George Henry Francis, "Contemporary Orators," no. xvi, *Fraser's Magazine* 34, no. 104 (December 1846): 660.

123. Escott, "House of Commons," p. 515.

124. *Parl. Deb.*, 3s, vol. 115, col. 594 (March 25, 1851). Six years earlier, Russell, speaking against Britain's enduring anti-Catholic prejudices, had paraphrased this passage as follows: "We all recollect the beautiful passage in Virgil, in which he supposes that in future time the husbandman will dig up the remains of the arms of those who fell in the civil wars of Rome, and that he will find the spears covered with rust and the empty helmets worn in some forgotten battle." *Parl. Deb.*, 3s, vol. 79, col. 1010 (April 18, 1845).

125. *Parl. Deb.*, 3s, vol. 183, col. 130 (April 27, 1866). Peel used the same quotation in a speech on January 31, 1840, which Gladstone certainly heard. See *GD*, 3: 6. That Gladstone was able to use the same quotation for a very different purpose and in a very different spirit than Peel (to charge Macaulay with hypocrisy) says something about the fund of quotations with which diligent schoolboys came to be equipped. This is but one of many examples in the history of Parliament of the same quotation appearing in a number of different speeches.

126. *Parl. Deb.*, 3s, vol. 278, col. 1192 (April 26, 1883). See also Morley, *Gladstone*, 3: 20: "The House, though but few perhaps recollected their Lucretius or had ever even read him sat, as I well remember, with reverential stillness hearkening from this born master of moving cadence and high sustained modulation, 'to the rise and long roll of the hexameter,'—to the plangent lines that have come down across the night of time to us from great Rome."

127. H. C. G. Matthew, *Gladstone*, 2 vols. (Oxford: Oxford University Press, 1986–95), 2: 392.

128. Pitt, *Speeches*, 3: 323.

129. Gladstone's budget speech of April 18, 1853 is reprinted in Arthur Tilney Bassett, *Gladstone's Speeches: Descriptive Index and Bibliography* (London: Methuen, 1916), pp. 182–252.

130. DD 1, p. 106. Gladstone's hackneyed Virgilian quotation was given by way of apologizing for the great length of his speech: "All I can say in apology is, that I have endeavoured to keep closely to the topics which I had before me— . . . *immensum spatiis confecimus æquor, / Et jam tempus equam fumantia solvere colla.*" Bassett, *Gladstone's Speeches*, p. 251. The passage from *Georgics* (Book II, 541–42) is translated (in full): "But in our course we have traversed a mighty plain, and now it is time to unyoke the necks of our smoking steeds." At Cambridge, Lord Stanley had ranked in the first class of the Classical Tripos, so he knew a Virgilian chestnut when he heard one.

131. *Reminiscences of Lord Kilbracken* (London: Macmillan, 1931), pp. 147. Cf. John Morley, *Recollections*, 2 vols. (London: Macmillan, 1917), 1: 197.

132. See Matthew, *Gladstone*, 1: 121.

133. Pitt, *Speeches*, 3: 361–403.

134. Gladstone's speech on the first Home Rule bill is reprinted in Bassett, *Gladstone's Speeches*, pp. 601–44.

135. Introducing the budget on April 18, 1853; Bassett, *Gladstone's Speeches*, p. 252.

136. Speech of July 30, 1878; Bassett, *Gladstone's Speeches*, p. 549.

137. Introducing the first Home Rule bill on April 8, 1886; Bassett, *Gladstone's Speeches*, p. 606.

138. Quoted in George Macaulay Trevelyan, *The Life of John Bright* (Boston and New York: Houghton Mifflin, 1914), pp. 13–14.

139. Quoted in Ernest Hartley Coleridge, *Life and Correspondence of John Duke Coleridge, Lord Chief Justice of England*, 2 vols. (London: Heinemann, 1904), 2: 137.

140. George Henry Francis, "Contemporary Orators," no. xi, *Fraser's Magazine* 34, no. 199 (July 1846): 102–3.

141. Henry Lucy, *Men and Manners in Parliament* (London: Unwin, 1919), p. 32.

142. See Patrick Joyce, *Democratic Subjects: The Self and the Social in Nineteenth-Century England* (Cambridge: Cambridge University Press, 1994), pp. 93–97.

143. John Bright, *Speeches on Questions of Public Policy*, ed. James E. Thorold Rogers, 2 vols. (London, 1868), 1: 490.

144. Bright, *Speeches*, 2: 482. Translation by Jennifer McBride.

145. Trevelyan, *Bright*, p. 404. Trevelyan had this story on good authority from Lord George Hamilton, who witnessed the event.

146. Keith Robbins, *John Bright* (London: Routledge & Kegan Paul, 1979), p. 262.

147. Bright, *Speeches*, 2: 144.

148. Bright's critique of the idleness of the House of Lords on March 13, 1865. Bright, *Speeches*, 1: 130.

149. *Parl. Deb.*, 3s, vol. 182, col. 219 (March 13, 1866). The lines are from Thomas Gray's "Elegy in a Country Churchyard," a long-time favorite of parliamentary quotation. Bright, in his parodic version, substitutes "office" and "Treasury," respectively, for the original's "being" and "cheerful day." The first substitution cleverly changes the meaning of the word "resigned."

150. Hayward, "British Parliament," p. 487.

151. Hayward, "British Parliament," p. 488.

152. See Joyce, *Democratic Subjects*, p. 143: "The 'tribunes' of 'olden times' were identified as those in ancient Rome chosen from among themselves by a people made angry by tyranny."

153. M&B, 1: 26.

154. Robert Blake, *Disraeli* (London: Eyre & Spottiswoode, 1966), pp. 17–18.

155. *Disraeli's Reminiscences*, p. 98.

156. *Parl. Deb.*, 3s, vol. 86, col. 674.

157. *Parl. Deb.*, 3s, vol. 106, col. 1171 (July 2, 1849).

158. *Parl. Deb.*, 3s, vol. 68, col. 949 (April 25, 1843).

159. *Parl. Deb.*, 3s, vol. 83, col. 119 (January 22, 1846).

160. Robert Blake, *Disraeli and Gladstone: The Leslie Stephen Lecture, 1969* (Cambridge: Cambridge University Press, 1969), p. 9.

161. Anthony Trollope, *Can You Forgive Her?* (1864–65), ch. 42.

162. *Parl. Deb.*, 3s, vol. 39, col. 807 (December 7, 1837). Tityrus and Daphnis (not Daphne as recorded) are both shepherds who appear in Roman literature, Tityrus in Virgil's *Eclogues.* A Daphnis is one who is fond of rural employments. The Latin phrases are from Terence, *Andria* (Act III, scene iii), but it is more likely they came to Disraeli via the *Eton Latin Grammar.*

163. See Blake, *Disraeli*, p. 149; and M&B, 2: 14. An extended and picturesque account of Disraeli's maiden speech can be found in André Maurois, *Disraeli: A Picture of the Victorian Age*, tr. Hamish Miles (New York: Appleton, 1928), pp. 119–131.

164. Sheil's advice is quoted in a letter from Disraeli to his sister, reproduced in M&B, 2: 14.

165. Curzon, *Parliamentary Eloquence*, pp. 28–29.

166. Lucy, *Men and Manners*, p. 24.

167. Blake, *Disraeli*, pp. 77–78, 212–13.

168. M&B, 5: 507.

169. In 1851, Disraeli brought forward a motion for relieving agricultural distress and produced the following encomium on the land of England, "that land to which we owe so much of our power and of our freedom; that land which has achieved the union of those two qualities for combining which a Roman Emperor was deified, *Imperium et Libertas.*" *Parl. Deb.*, 3s, vol. 114, col. 414 (February 11, 1851). Later, in his Guildhall speech of 1879, Disraeli revived this phrase, this time to characterize the program of his ministry.

170. During his speech on the Public Worship Regulation Bill; *Parl. Deb.*, 3s, vol. 221, col. 1342 (August 5, 1874).

171. Escott, "House of Commons," p. 508.

172. Quoted in David Cannadine, *G. M. Trevelyan: A Life in History* (New York: Norton, 1993), p. 109. Other twentieth-century scholars who have considered classical quotation in Parliament include C. A. Vince, "Latin Poets in the British Parliament," *The Classical Review* 46, no. 3 (1932): 97–104; George Watson, *The English Ideology: Studies in the Language of Victorian Politics* (London: Allen Lane, 1973), pp. 117–120; and Christopher Stray, *Classics Transformed: Schools, Universities, and Society in England, 1830–1960* (Oxford: Clarendon, 1998), pp. 65–68.

173. *Parl. Deb.*, 3s, vol. 182, col. 59 (March 12, 1866).

174. *Parl. Deb.*, 3s, vol. 182, cols. 163–4 (March 13, 1866). Virgilian lots is the practice of using a randomly-selected passage from Virgil as a source of oracular wisdom. See Sir Philip Sydney, A *Defence of Poetry* (1595), ed. J. A. van Dorsten (London: Oxford University Press, 1966), pp. 21–2.

175. *Parl. Deb.*, 3s, vol. 182, cols. 1148–9 (April 12, 1866).

176. *Parl. Deb.*, 3s, vol. 182, cols. 2117–8 (April 26, 1866). The passage is from the *Aeneid*, Book II, 328–31.

177. Herbert Paul, "The Decay of Classical Quotation" (1896), *Men and Letters* (London: Lane, 1901), p. 50. See also Sir Edward Cook, "The Classics in Daily Life," *More Literary Recreations* (London: Macmillan, 1919), pp. 42–45.

178. Bright, *Speeches*, 2: 135.

179. *Parl. Deb.*, 3s, vol. 112, col. 444 (June 25, 1850). For an interesting discussion of the classical issues at stake in this episode, see Vance, *Victorians and Ancient Rome*, pp. 225–28.

180. DD 1, p. 22.

181. Churchill, *My Early Life*, p. 37.

182. Churchill, *My Early Life*, p. 36. See also Darrell Holley, *Churchill's Literary Allusions: An Index to the Education of a Soldier, Statesman, and Litterateur* (Jefferson, NC: McFarland, 1987), p. 38. Holley's analysis is limited to Churchill's written oeuvre. Regrettably, he does not consider the speeches (even though the complete speeches were published more than a decade before his study). In Churchill's writings, the Bible is alluded to most frequently, followed by the classics.

183. Powell won all the classical prizes at Cambridge, authored various works of classical scholarship and translation, and for a time was a professor of Greek at the University of Sidney.

184. Trevelyan, *Fox*, p. 102.

185. Curzon, *Parliamentary Eloquence*, p. 9.

186. Turner, "Virgil in Victorian Contexts," *Contesting Cultural Authority*, p. 284.

187. Michael Bentley, *Politics Without Democracy: Great Britain, 1815–1914. Perception and Preoccupation in British Government* (Oxford: Blackwell, 1985), p. 88.

188. Peel, *Speeches*, 1: 1.

189. *The Parliamentary Diaries of Sir John Trelawny, 1858–1865*, ed. T. A. Jenkins, Camden Fourth Series, vol. 40 (1990); and "The Parliamentary Diaries of Sir John Trelawny, 1868–1873," ed. T. A. Jenkins, *Camden Miscellany XXXII*, Camden Fifth Series, vol. 3 (1994).

190. See, e.g., "Bagehot: The Golden Age of the Commons," *The Economist*, January 10, 1998, p. 50; James Landale, "Never Mind the Quality of Speeches—Feel the Brevity," *TT*, April 1, 1999, p. 33.

CHAPTER 3: RELIGION

1. This chapter deals almost exclusively with Protestant Christianity. Non-Protestant, non-Christian, and even non-religious groups made up a small percentage of the British population for most of the century. Around the middle of the century, according to a recent analysis, roughly 60 percent of the population of England and Wales considered themselves Anglicans, and 30 percent Nonconformists; Roman Catholics constituted roughly 5 percent, and Jews and all other groups the remaining 5 percent. Hugh McLeod, *Religion and Society in England, 1850–1914* (New York: St. Martin's, 1996), pp. 11–12.

2. Population of Great Britain, 1851: Religious Worship in *England* and *Wales*, PP, 1852–53, 89: 152–54.

3. Census of Great Britain, 1851: Religious Worship, and Education, Scotland, PP, 1854, 59: ix. On the shortcomings of the Scottish census, see Callum G. Brown, *Religion and Society in Scotland Since 1707* (Edinburgh: Edinburgh University Press, 1997), pp. 43–44.

4. A. Eubule Evans, "A Discourse Upon Sermons," *Macmillan's Magazine* 57, no. 337 (November 1887): 58.

5. Based on the average of 1881 and 1891 census figures for England, Wales, and Scotland.

6. See Ian Bradley, *The Call to Seriousness: The Evangelical Impact on the Victorians* (Lon-

don: Cape, 1976), pp. 22–33; Geoffrey Best, "Evangelicalism and the Victorians," in *The Victorian Crisis of Faith*, ed. Anthony Symondson (London: SPCK, 1970), pp. 38–39; and David Englander, "The Word and the World: Evangelicalism in the Victorian City," in *Religion in Victorian Britain*, vol. 2, *Controversies*, ed. Gerald Parsons (Manchester: Manchester University Press, 1988), pp. 18–23.

7. For the role played by bishops in the House of Lords, see E. A. Smith, *The House of Lords in British Politics and Society, 1815–1911* (London: Longman, 1992), pp. 82–89. Some of the Lords Spiritual, such as William Connor Magee, Bishop of Peterborough and later Archbishop of York, gained particular renown as parliamentary orators.

8. From Robert Currie, Alan Gilbert, and Lee Horsley, *Churches and Churchgoers: Patterns of Church Growth in the British Isles Since 1700* (Oxford: Clarendon, 1977), Appendix D, pp. 196–212.

9. Alan D. Gilbert, *Religion and Society in Industrial England: Church, Chapel, and Social Change, 1740–1914* (London: Longman, 1976), p. 131.

10. Growth in clergy calculated from data in Currie, et al., *Churches and Churchgoers,* Appendix D, pp. 196–212.

11. A Report of His Majesty's Commissioners Appointed by Virtue of an Act of Parliament Passed in the Fifty-Eighth Year of the Reign of His Late Majesty King Geo. III c. 45; Intutled "An Act for Building and Promoting the Building of Additional Churches in Populous Parishes", PP, 1821, 10: 7.

12. M. H. Port, *Six Hundred New Churches: A Study of the Church Building Commission, 1818–1856, and its Church Building Activities* (London: SPCK, 1961), pp. 34–35.

13. Port, *Six Hundred New Churches*, pp. 125–26.

14. Calculated from data in Currie, et al., *Churches and Churchgoers*, p. 213.

15. The question of how the new churches would be maintained was resolved in 1835 when Peel established the Ecclesiastical Commission (into which the Church Building Commission was dissolved in 1856), empowered to reallocate Church resources more rationally. See G. F. A. Best, *Temporal Pillars: Queen Anne's Bounty, the Ecclesiastical Commission, and the Church of England* (Cambridge: Cambridge University Press, 1964), esp. ch. 9.

16. Gilbert, *Religion and Society*, p. 130, Table 6.1; Returns Showing the Number of Churches (Including Cathedrals) in Every Diocese in *England* Which Have Been Built or Restored at a Cost Exceeding £. 500 Since the Year 1840, PP, 1876, 58: 657–58.

17. Ultimately, something like 60 percent of the new sittings were free, but, as constructed, they were quite cramped. Far more spacious were the sittings available for rent. See Owen Chadwick, *The Victorian Church*, 2 vols. (Oxford: Oxford University Press, 1966–70), 1: 330, n. 6.

18. Chadwick, *Victorian Church*, 2: 238.

19. Mark Smith, *Religion in Industrial Society: Oldham and Saddleworth, 1740–1865* (Oxford: Clarendon, 1994), p. 69.

20. Returns Showing the Number of Churches . . . Built or Restored . . . Since the Year 1840, p. 39.

21. Quoted in James Obelkevich, *Religion and Rural Society: South Lindsey, 1825–1875* (Oxford: Clarendon, 1976), p. 111.

22. See Smith, *Religion in Industrial Society*, pp. 73–77.

23. See Religious Worship, *England* and *Wales*, p. 144, Table 17.

24. Based on data in Gilbert, *Religion and Society*, p. 31, Table 2.2.

25. Based on data in Currie, et al., *Churches and Churchgoers*, p. 213 and n. 7.

26. Brown, *Religion and Society in Scotland*, p. 103.

27. Religious Worship and Education, Scotland, p. 3.

28. Simon Eliot, *Some Patterns and Trends in British Publishing, 1800–1919* (London: The Bibliographical Society, 1994), pp. 46–50, 127–128 (Tables C1–C4). The number of religious publications increased in most decades of the century but declined as a percentage of all publications, losing ground mainly to fiction. For the period 1814–46, at 20 percent of all titles religious books were the largest category; by 1899 they had dropped to 9.2 percent. Fiction, which had been 16 percent of all titles in 1814–46, overshadowed all other categories by 1899 at 34 percent of all titles.

29. See Joseph L. Altholz, *The Religious Press in Britain, 1760–1900* (Westport, CT: Greenwood, 1989), p. 135.

30. See Patrick Scott, "The Business of Belief: The Emergence of 'Religious' Publishing," *Studies in Church History* 10 (Oxford: Blackwell, 1973), pp. 215–17.

31. See L. E. Elliott-Binns, *Religion in the Victorian Era* (London: Lutterworth, 1936), pp. 331–37.

32. Eliot, *British Publishing*, pp. 86–87, 150 (Table E6). Like religious books, religious magazines also experienced relative decline. In 1864, clearly religious magazines represented 36 percent of all periodical titles; by 1900, they had dropped to 23 percent.

33. *The Homilist: A Monthly Pulpit Review*, Editor's Series, 12 (1877): iv.

34. Francis Hitchman, "The Penny Press," *Macmillan's Magazine* 43, no. 257 (March 1881): 388.

35. Lytton Strachey, *Eminent Victorians* (London: Chatto & Windus, 1918), p 11. Ellipsis in original.

36. Quoted in Randall Thomas Davidson and William Benham, *Life of Archibald Campbell Tait, Archbishop of Canterbury*, 3rd ed., 2 vols. (London, 1891), 1: 253.

37. D. N. Hempton, "Bickersteth, Bishop of Ripon: The Episcopate of a Mid-Victorian Evangelical," in *Religion in Victorian Britain*, vol. 4, *Interpretations*, ed. Gerald Parsons (Manchester: Manchester University Press, 1988), p. 43.

38. Palmerston's motives in appointing Tait are unknown. Shaftesbury had suggested Tait, but only for one of the less important sees. Queen Victoria, the head of the Church, had Latitudinarian views and like many in society had been moved by Tait's recent personal tragedy when, in 1856, five of his children died in a scarlet fever epidemic. See P. T. Marsh, *The Victorian Church in Decline: Archbishop Tait and the Church of England, 1868–1882* (London: Routledge, 1969), p. 16. Although Marsh believes that the decision to elevate Tait would have ultimately rested with Palmerston, Victoria exerted a decisive influence in ecclesiastical appointments. Later on, even Disraeli had to defer to her wish to make Tait Archbishop of Canterbury. See Dudley W. R. Bahlman, "The Queen, Mr. Gladstone, and Church Patronage," *Victorian Studies* 3, no. 4 (June 1960): 349–80.

39. See Davidson and Benham, *Tait*, 1: 44–46; and Edward B. Nicholson, "The Oxford Union," *Macmillan's Magazine* 28, no. 168 (October 1873): 570–73.

40. Davidson and Benham, *Tait*, 1: 255.

41. Quoted in Davidson and Benham, *Tait*, 1: 252.

42. *A Charge, Delivered in November MDCCCLVIII, to the Clergy of the Diocese of London, at his Primary Visitation, by Archibald Campbell, Lord Bishop of London* [hereafter Tait, *Charge*, 1858], 7th ed. (London, 1858), p. 70.

43. Tait, *Charge*, 1858, p. 26.

44. Tait, *Charge*, 1858, pp. 70–71.

45. *A Charge, Delivered in December 1862, to the Clergy of the Diocese of London, at his Visitation, by Archibald Campbell, Lord Bishop of London* [hereafter Tait, *Charge*, 1862] (London, 1862), p. 79.

46. Tait, *Charge*, 1862, p. 80.

47. Tait, *Charge*, 1862, p. 83.

48. Tait, *Charge*, 1862, p. 84.

49. The rules of the Church Homiletical Society are contained in a pamphlet appended to *The Clergyman's Magazine: Conducted by Members of the Church Homiletical Society* 12, no. 67 (January 1881); quotation from p. 5 of the pamphlet.

50. *The Clergyman's Magazine* 12, no. 67 (January 1881), supplementary "Advertiser" section, p. 4.

51. Charles Kingsley, *Yeast: A Problem* (1851), ch. 17.

52. See J. G. Davies, "The Role of a Cathedral in the Past," in *Cathedral & Mission*, ed. Gilbert Cope (Birmingham: Birmingham Institute for the Study of Worship and Religious Architecture, [1969]), esp. pp. 7–12.

53. *TT*, June 8, 1857, p. 11.

54. See e.g. the letter from "A Parochial Clergyman" in *TT*, June 4, 1857, p. 9.

55. *TT*, January 4, 1858, p. 10

56. *TT*, November 29, 1858, p. 6.

57. Chadwick, *Victorian Church*, 1: 525.

58. See *TT*, December 6, 1858, p. 10.

59. Quoted in Elliott-Binns, *Religion in the Victorian Era*, p. 434.

60. Chadwick, *Victorian Church*, 2: 381.

61. Elliott-Binns, *Religion in the Victorian Era*, p. 433.

62. Archibald Campbell, Archbishop of Canterbury, "Address to the Members of the Cathedral Body," *The Church of the Future* (London, 1880), pp. 181–82.

63. William Hanna, *Memoirs of the Life and Writings of Thomas Chalmers, D.D., LL.D.*, 4 vols. (Edinburgh, 1849–52), 1: 418.

64. Quoted in Hanna, *Chalmers*, 2: 5. On Chalmers's preaching at its peak, see pp. 148–164; and A. C. Cheyne, *Studies in Scottish Church History* (Edinburgh: Clark, 1999), pp. 81–87.

65. Stewart J. Brown, *Thomas Chalmers and the Godly Commonwealth in Scotland* (Oxford: Oxford University Press, 1982), p. 106.

66. Hanna, *Chalmers*, 2: 148–49.

67. Hanna, *Chalmers*, 2: 160.

68. Brown, *Chalmers*, p. 108.

69. Quoted in Hanna, *Chalmers*, 2: 100. For Chalmers's eventful visit to London, see pp. 98–105.

70. See Hanna, *Chalmers*, 2: 146; and Brown, *Chalmers*, pp. 115–16.

71. William Garden Blaikie, *The Preachers of Scotland from the Sixth to the Nineteenth Century* (Edinburgh, 1888), pp. 281–82.

72. The major nineteenth-century biography of Irving is Mrs. [Margaret] Oliphant, *Minister of the National Scotch Church, London, Illustrated by his Journals and Correspondence*, 2nd ed., Revised, 2 vols. (London, 1862).

73. Blaikie, *Preachers of Scotland*, p. 290.

74. The major biographical treatment of Robertson is Stopford A. Brooke, *Life and Letters of Frederick W. Robertson*, 2 vols. (London, 1865). See also Chadwick, *Victorian Church*, 2: 135–36.

75. Brooke, *Robertson*, 1: 154–55.

76. See R. W. Dale, "George Dawson: Politician, Lecturer, and Preacher," *The Nineteenth Century* 2, no. 4 (August 1877): 44–61.

77. Dale, "Dawson," p. 48.

78. Asa Briggs, *Victorian Cities* (New York, Harper & Row, 1965), pp. 197–98.

79. Dale, "Dawson," p. 47.

80. David K. Guthrie and Charles K. Guthrie, *Autobiography of Thomas Guthrie, D.D. and Memoir by his Sons*, Popular Edition (London, 1877), p. 128.

81. Quoted in Guthrie, *Autobiography*, p. 506.

82. Quoted in Guthrie, *Autobiography*, p. 535.

83. J. Vyrnwy Morgan, *The Church in Wales in the Light of History: A Historical and Philosophical Study* (London: Chapman & Hall, 1918), p. 135.

84. See, e.g., Owen Jones, *Some of the Great Preachers of Wales* (London, 1885).

85. As many as 70 percent of the Welsh people spoke the native tongue until educational reforms hastened the spread of English beginning in the 1870s. Don M. Cregier, *Bounder from Wales: Lloyd George's Career Before the First World War* (Columbia, MO: University of Missouri Press, 1976), p. 5. On the importance of the Welsh language in the Welsh ministry, see Ieuan Gwynedd Jones, *Mid-Victorian Wales* (Cardiff: University of Wales Press, 1992), p. 65.

86. Other historians have equated Spurgeon and Liddon. For example: "The sermons of Liddon, the most celebrated Anglican preacher of his day, were something of a national institution, almost on the same level as C. H. Spurgeon's in the Baptist Metropolitan Tabernacle." R. T. Shannon, *Gladstone and the Bulgarian Agitation, 1876*, 2nd ed. (Hassocks: Harvester, 1975), p. 61.

87. Spurgeon's sermons continue to be studied as evidenced by the continuing stream of faculty publications, student theses, and websites (e.g. www.spurgeon.org). His enduring influence is perhaps greatest in the United States, with its large Baptist population.

88. Of the numerous accounts of Spurgeon's life and work that appeared during his lifetime and shortly after his death, most can be said to at least verge on the hagiographic. The classic biography is W. Y. Fullerton, *C. H. Spurgeon: A Biography* (London: Williams and Norgate, 1920). The most recent full-scale treatment is Lewis Drummond, *Spurgeon: Prince of Preachers* (Grand Rapids, MI: Kregel, 1992). The most historically analytical work is Patricia Stallings Kruppa, *Charles Haddon Spurgeon: A Preacher's Progress* (New York: Garland, 1982).

89. See *The Autobiography of Charles H. Spurgeon, Compiled from his Diary, Letters, and Records by his Wife and his Private Secretary*, 4 vols. (London, 1897–1900), 1: ch. 11.

90. Fullerton, *Spurgeon*, p. 52.

91. "Men of the Day. No. 16. The Rev. Charles Spurgeon," *Vanity Fair*, December 10, 1870.

92. Quoted in Fullerton, *Spurgeon*, p. 83.

93. Letter from "A Parochial Clergyman," *TT*, June 4, 1857, p. 9.

94. Letter from Charles Haddon Spurgeon, April 10, 1880: Dr. Williams's Library, London, Henry Allon Papers, MS 24.110/317. The author thanks the Trustees of Dr. Williams's Library for permission to quote from the collection.

95. See Drummond, *Spurgeon*, p. 286.

96. C. Maurice Davies, *Unorthodox London: Or, Phases in the Religious Life of the Metropolis*, 2nd. ed. (London, 1876), p. 67.

97. *The Hornet*, April 4, 1878, p. 918.

98. *The George Eliot Letters*, ed. Gordon S. Haight, vol. 5 (New Haven: Yale University Press, 1955), p. 121.

99. *South London Press*, August 17, 1878.

100. Fullerton, *Spurgeon*, p. 231.

101. See Charles Ray, *A Marvelous Ministry: The Story of C. H. Spurgeon's Sermons, 1855–1905* (London: Passmore and Alabaster, 1905); and Spurgeon, *Autobiography*, 2, ch. 47.

102. Spurgeon, *Autobiography*, 2: 154.

103. A "row of reporters below the footlights gave the utterances of this original and powerful preacher to the press." *Vanity Fair*, December 10, 1870.

104. Ray, *Marvelous Ministry*, pp. 35–36.

105. Quoted in Ray, *Marvelous Ministry*, p. 20.

106. Ray, *Marvelous Ministry*, p. 28.

107. W. Harvey, "Spurgeon as Preacher," no. I, *The Preacher and Homiletic Monthly* 5, no. 9 (June 1881): 527.

108. *The Hornet*, August 14, 1878, p. 918.

109. *Eliot Letters*, 5: 121.

110. Lewis O. Brastow, *Representative Modern Preachers* (London: Macmillan, 1905), ch. 9

111. John Stanford Holme, "Mr. Spurgeon: His Variety, Freshness, and Power as a Preacher," *The Preacher and Homiletic Monthly*, 5, no. 2 (November 1880): 111.

112. Holme, "Spurgeon," p. 112.

113. Kruppa, *Preacher's Progress*, p. 1.

114. Gilbert, *Religion and Society*, pp. 37–39.

115. Quoted in *The Hornet*, August 14, 1878, p. 918.

116. See Kruppa, *Preacher's Progress*, ch. 6.

117. *Weekly Dispatch*, November 9, 1879.

118. See, for example, James Douglas, *The Prince of Preachers: A Sketch; A Portraiture; and a Tribute* (London, 1893), p. 77: "The very build of this man, as in the case of John Bright, marks him out as a man of the people." In an exception to this rule, Charles Greville in his diaries describes Spurgeon as "in face rather resembling a smaller Macaulay." See *The Greville Diary, Including Passages Hitherto Withheld from Publication*, ed. Philip Whitwell Wilson, 2 vols. (Garden City, NY: Doubleday, 1927), 2: 295.

119. *Letters of Matthew Arnold*, 2 vols., ed. George W. E. Russell (London, 1895–96), 1: 342.

120. *Daily Telegraph*, February 23, 1874.

121. *Daily Chronicle*, February 1, 1892.

122. *Leeds Mercury*, November 15, 1879; quoted in Fullerton, pp. 148–49.

123. *The Speaker*, February 6, 1892.

124. *The Figaro*, April 22, 1874.

125. *DNB* (Henry Parry Liddon). That both Spurgeon and Liddon played church is also noted in Kruppa, *Preacher's Progress*, p. 28.

126. Bodleian Library, Cuddesdon College MSS, Box 3.

127. Quoted in G. W. E. Russell, *Dr. Liddon* (London: Mowbray, 1905), p. 4.

128. According to his biographer, only one entry in Liddon's diary "mentions being present at a debate at the Union; and that with the remark 'Disgusted.'" John Octavius Johnston, *Life and Letters of Henry Parry Liddon, D.D., D.C.L., L.L.D.* (London: Longmans, 1904), p. 8. But Liddon's loyalty to the Union was either greater than this would indicate, or else it appreciated over time. Not only did he attend the Union's 1873 Jubilee, he proposed the toast to "Literature." Rising after midnight and after many over-long speeches, Liddon's eloquence stirred the weary gathering back to life. See Henry Scott Holland, "Books of the Month: Life and Letters of Henry Parry Liddon" [review of Johnston], *The Commonwealth: A Christian Social Magazine* 10, no. 1 (January 1905): 30.

129. Quoted in *TT*, September 10, 1890, p. 9.

130. Johnston, *Liddon*, p. 42.

131. Pusey House, Oxford, Liddon Diaries, June 2, 1864.

132. Uncataloged letter from Liddon to Louisa Liddon, Thursday in 10th Week, 1853: Bodleian Library, Cuddesdon College MSS, Box 2.

133. Johnston, *Liddon*, pp. 52–53.

134. Liddon Diaries, January 2, 1859.

135. Liddon Diaries, April 5, 1863.

136. Quoted in Russell, *Liddon*, p. 32.

137. Liddon Diaries, June 2, 1861.

138. Liddon Diaries, April 19, 1863.

139. Liddon Diaries, April 17, 1870.

140. Johnston, *Liddon*, p. 137.

141. Liddon Diaries, September 11, 1870.

142. *DNB* (Henry Parry Liddon).

143. Evans, "Discourse Upon Sermons," p. 62.

144. James Richards, "Preachers of the Day," *Temple Bar* 70 (April 1884): 485.

145. Tait, "Address to Members of the Cathedral Body," p. 177.

146. Johnston, *Liddon*, p. 302.

147. Frederick Wedmore, *Memories*, 2nd ed. (London: Methuen, 1912), p. 220.

148. Notes for sermons from Liddon's most peripatetic phase of preaching, 1862–69, are in the Bodleian Library, MS. Eng. th. e. 170.

149. Johnston, *Liddon*, p. 54.

150. BL Add. MS 41667, f. 5.

151. From the 1873 sermon, "The Glory of the Gospel" (on I Timothy 1: 2) in H. P. Liddon, *Advent in St. Paul's: Sermons Bearing Chiefly on the Two Comings of Our Lord*, 2nd ed., revised, 2 vols. (1889), 1: 128.

152. Wedmore, *Memories*, p. 220.

153. *The Manchester Guardian*, September 10, 1890, p. 5.

154. Quoted in Russell, *Liddon*, p. 34.

155. Arthur Christopher Benson, *The Life of Edward White Benson, Sometime Archbishop of Canterbury*, 2 vols. (London, 1899), 1: 403.

156. See Reginald Farrar, *The Life of Frederic William Farrar, D.D., F.R.S., etc., Sometime Dean of Canterbury*, New and Revised ed. (London: Nisbet, 1905).

157. See Lawrence Pearsall Jacks, *Life and Letters of Stopford Brooke*, 2 vols. (London: Murray, 1917); Fred L. Standley, "Stopford Augustus Brooke: Studies Toward a Biography" (Ph.D. diss., Northwestern University, 1964); and Standley, *Stopford Brooke* (New York: Twayne, 1972).

158. See Joseph Parker, *A Preacher's Life: An Autobiography and an Album* (Boston, 1899); and William Adamson, *The Life of Joseph Parker, Pastor of the City Temple, London* (London: Revell, [1902]).

159. See Frederic W. Macdonald, *The Life of William Morley Punshon, LL.D.* (London, 1887).

160. On May 5, 1867, the first time he preached at Westminster Abbey, Brooke estimated that the audience was around 2,500, and described feeling "that strange electricity of a mass of men." Reprinted in Jacks, *Brooke*, p. 221. The record of Brooke's subsequent appearances at the Abbey is unclear, but in 1869 he preached to what he described as "an enormous congregation," and in 1871, "there was not even standing room in any part of the place." Quoted in Standley, "Brooke," p. 116.

161. Richards, "Preachers of the Day," p. 489.

162. Quoted in Jacks, *Brooke*, 1: 104.

163. Quoted in Jacks, *Brooke*, 1: 213.

164. Quoted in Adamson, *Parker*, p. 132.

165. Parker, *A Preacher's Life*, p. 363.

166. *William Morley Punshon: Preacher and Orator, 1824–1881* (London, 1881), p. 5.

167. Wedmore, *Memories*, pp. 211–12.

168. Adamson, *Parker*, pp. 123–26, 138–41.

169. Quoted in Macdonald, *Punshon*, p. 42.

170. Hitchman, "Penny Press," p. 388.

171. On Brooke's non-preaching activities, see Standley, *Brooke*.

172. See Deborah M. Valenze, *Prophetic Sons and Daughters: Female Preaching and Popular Religion in Industrial England* (Princeton: Princeton University Press, 1985).

173. See Olive Anderson, "Women Preachers in Mid-Victorian Britain: Some Reflexions on Feminism, Popular Religion and Social Change," *The Historical Journal* 12, no. 3 (1969): 467–84.

174. Quoted from the *Dunstable Borough Gazette* in Mrs. Grattan Guinness, *"She Spake of Him." Being Recollections of the Loving Labours and Early Death of the Late Mrs. Henry Denning*, 6th ed. (Bristol, 1873), p. 60.

175. Quoted from the *Western Daily Mercury* in Guinness, *"She Spake of Him,"* p. 76.

176. Obelkevich, *Religion and Rural Society*, pp. 212–13.

177. Guinness, *"She Spake of Him,"* p. 41.

178. To note the major treatments very briefly: John Morley, *The Life of William Ewart Gladstone*, 3 vols. (London: Macmillan, 1903) deliberately avoided the religious dimension almost completely. D. C. Lathbury's *Mr. Gladstone* (London: Mowbray, 1907), a volume in

the Leaders of the Church series, filled in Morley's blanks in to some extent. Ever since, historians and biographers have sought to join the religious and the secular. Phillip Magnus, *Gladstone: A Biography*, (London: Murray, 1954), and to a somewhat lesser extent Richard Shannon, *Gladstone*, vol. 1 (London: Hamilton, 1982) and *Gladstone: Heroic Minister, 1865–1898* (London: Penguin, 1998), attempt to place religious motivations at the forefront of Gladstone's public life. H. C. G. Matthew, *Gladstone*, 2 vols. (Oxford: Oxford University Press, 1986–95) provides the most nuanced treatment yet of the intertwined evolution of Gladstone's religious and political views. David Bebbington, *William Ewart Gladstone: Faith and Politics in Victorian Britain* (Grand Rapids, MI: Erdmans, 1993), a volume in the Library of Religious Biography series, provides a compact analysis of Gladstone as a Christian statesman. Roy Jenkins, *Gladstone* (London: Macmillan, 1995) acknowledges the religious side but is mainly concerned with politics.

179. Matthew, *Gladstone*, 1: 27–29, 54, 72.

180. Matthew, *Gladstone*, 2: 42. Cf. Perry Butler, *Gladstone: Church, State, and Tractarianism. A Study of His Religious Ideas and Attitudes, 1809–1959* (Oxford: Clarendon, 1982).

181. Gladstone Papers, BL Add. MS 44127, f. 368.

182. The connection between and Spurgeon and Gladstone is usually considered as no more than the paths of two great figures briefly crossing on a few occasions. This is even the case to some extent in Kruppa, *Preacher's Progress*, which uses the Gladstone connection to document Spurgeon's Liberalism and the various political issues with which he became actively involved.

183. Gladstone Papers, BL Add. MSS 44456, f. 338; 44476, f. 64; 44477, f. 150; 44497, f. 294.

184. The letter, and the glowering photographic portrait Gladstone sent along with it, is in a scrapbook in the Heritage Room at Spurgeon's College, London. A draft of the letter is in the Gladstone Papers, BL Add. MS 44486, f. 279.

185. Parker, *A Preacher's Life*, esp. ch. 15. See also Joseph Parker, "Mr. Gladstone Close at Hand: A Personal Sketch," *The New Review* 4, no. 22 (March 1891): 204–12.

186. Parker, *A Preacher's Life*, p. 278.

187. See D. W. Bebbington, "Gladstone and the Nonconformists: A Religious Affinity in Politics," *Studies in Church History* 12 (Oxford: Blackwell, 1975), pp. 369–82.

188. Richards, "Preachers of the Day," p. 502.

189. Gladstone Papers, BL Add. MSS 44420, ff. 124, 133.

190. Liddon Diaries, August 13, 1876.

191. On Liddon's central role in making the Eastern Question a crisis of British conscience, see Shannon, *Bulgarian Agitation*.

192. Quoted in Shannon, *Bulgarian Agitation*, p. 190.

193. Reproduced in Standley, "Brooke," p. 443.

194. Introducing the first Home Rule bill on April 8, 1886; Arthur Tilney Bassett, *Gladstone's Speeches: Descriptive Index and Bibliography* (London: Methuen, 1916), p. 606.

195. Parker, *A Preacher's Life*, p. 287–89.

196. *GD*, 12: 32 (May 11, 1887).

197. Quoted in Shannon, *Bulgarian Agitation*, pp. 67–8.

198. Spurgeon's College, Heritage Room, Scrap Book no. 12.

199. Quoted in Johnston, *Liddon*, p. 337. Johnston mis-dates the letter from 1885 according to Russell, *Liddon*, p. 163.

200. Quoted in Johnston, *Liddon*, p. 372.

201. *The Prime Ministers' Papers: W. E. Gladstone, vol. 1: Autobiographica*, ed. John Brooke and Mary Sorenson (London: HMSO, 1971), p. 27. The occasion was so memorable for Gladstone primarily because, from his vantage point in the luxurious gallery pew, he spotted his Eton headmaster, Dr. Keate, among the seething mass packed on the floor below.

202. Quoted in W. Forbes Gray, "Chalmers and Gladstone: An Unrecorded Episode," *Records of the Scottish Church History Society* 10 (1948): 9. Gladstone also heard Chalmers a few months earlier. See Gladstone, *Autobiographica*, p. 217. Chalmers had become acquainted with John Gladstone in 1817. See Hanna, *Chalmers*, 2: 105.

203. *GD*, 5: 427 (September 25, 1859).

204. Gladstone Papers, BL Add. MS 44779–44781. See Magnus, *Gladstone*, pp. 51, 123; and Matthew, *Gladstone*, 1: 54.

205. Parker, *A Preacher's Life*, pp. 285–86.

206. "Mr. Gladstone on Preaching," *TT*, March 23, 1877, p. 10.

207. Letter to Archbishop Benson dated September 1, 1885, reproduced in *GD*, 11: 273.

208. Parker, "Gladstone Close at Hand," p. 207.

209. *GD*, 9: 430.

210. Gladstone Papers, BL Add MS 44471, f. 98.

211. *GD*, 10: 189.

212. Gladstone Papers, BL Add MS 44474, f. 14.

213. *GD*, 10: 191.

214. *The Daily Telegraph*, January 10, 1882. The sermon on "The Touch" is printed in C. H. Spurgeon, *The Metropolitan Tabernacle Pulpit*, vol. 28 (1882), pp. 41–48.

215. *GD*, 10: 196.

216. See Spurgeon's College, Heritage Room, Scrap Book no. 5, pp. 128–137.

217. "Ministerial Dis-Appointments," *Moonshine*, 14 March 1885.

218. *South London Chronicle*, January 14, 1882.

219. *GD*, 6: 559 (November 24, 1867).

220. *GD*, 9: 132 (June 11, 1876).

221. Quoted in Jacks, *Brooke*, 2: 367.

222. Reproduced in Standley, "Brooke," p. 493.

223. *GD*, 9: 32 (April 25, 1875).

224. See Shannon, *Bulgarian Agitation*, p. 28; Matthew, *Gladstone*, 2: 58; and John Coffey, "Democracy and Popular Religion: Moody and Sankey's Mission to Britain, 1873–1875," in *Citizenship and Community: Liberals, Radicals and Collective Identities in the British Isles, 1865–1931*, ed. Eugenio F. Biagini (Cambridge: Cambridge University Press, 1996), pp. 117–18.

225. Fullerton, *Spurgeon*, p. 112.

226. Quoted in Coffey, "Democracy and Popular Religion," p. 103. Coffey does not, however, explore Spurgeon's influence on Moody.

227. James F. Findlay, Jr., *Dwight L. Moody: American Evangelist, 1837–1899* (Chicago: University of Chicago Press, 1969), p. 146.

228. *GD*, 9: 471 (December 28, 1879).

229. See Magnus, *Gladstone*, p. 401; Matthew, *Gladstone*, 2: 80.

230. Russell, *Liddon*, p. 163.

231. Gladstone Papers, BL Add. MS 44420, f. 133.

232. Gladstone Papers, BL Add. MS 44513, f. 69.

233. See Chadwick, *Victorian Church*, 1: 409, 518; 2: 309–19.

234. Smith, *Religion in Industrial Society*, p. 4.

235. The trend toward preaching as entertainment in the second half of the nineteenth century can be seen, for instance, among the Methodist preachers of rural South Lindsey, who, after 1850, "went furthest in providing villagers with entertainment. Inevitably this was at the expense of a blurring of religious content." Obelkevich, *Religion and Rural Society*, p. 213.

236. See Horton Davies, *Worship and Theology in England*, vol. 4, *From Newman to Martineau, 1850–1900* (Princeton: Princeton University Press, 1962), p. 283; Brown, *Religion and Society in Scotland*, pp. 113–14.

237. See Davies, *Worship and Theology*, 4: 283–84.

238. Quoted in Adamson, *Parker*, p. 132.

239. Richards, "Preachers of the Day," pp. 484–85.

240. Adapted from *The British Weekly: A Journal of Social and Christian Progress*, March 18, 1887, pp. 11, 14.

241. *Great Thoughts*, September 3 and 24, 1887.

242. John Morley, *Recollections*, 2 vols. (London: Macmillan, 1917), 1: 293.

243. Davies, *Worship and Theology*, 4: 286.

CHAPTER 4: LAW

1. Sir James Fitzjames Stephen, *A History of the Criminal Law of England*, 3 vols. (London, 1893), 3: 424.

2. See *TT*, May 15, 1865, p. 7; *Annual Register* 1856, p. 287.

3. The proceedings of the entire trial, with supplemental materials, are reproduced in *The Trial of William Palmer*, 3rd. ed., ed. George H. Knott, rev. Eric R. Watson (London: Hodge, 1952).

4. Stephen, *Criminal Law*, 3: 424.

5. *Trial of William Palmer*, p. 128.

6. *TT*, May 28, 1856, p. 9.

7. Although a comparison of barristerial oratory in the separate legal systems of England, Scotland, and Ireland would make an excellent study, this chapter considers only the English system. Fortunately, this in no way means that the Scots and Irish are absent from the discussion, for they contributed significantly to the life and lore of the nineteenth-century English bar.

8. John Morrison and Philip Leith, *The Barrister's World, and the Nature of Law* (Milton Keynes: Open University, 1992), p. 208.

9. Women could not be called to the bar until after the 1919 Sex Disqualification (Removal) Act. The first woman barrister was called in 1921, followed by thirty more of "our new Portias" the following year. Robert Graves and Alan Hodge, *The Long Week-End: A Social History of Great Britain, 1918–1939*, 2nd ed. (New York: Norton, 1963), p. 46.

10. The most important works are Raymond Cocks, *Foundations of the Modern Bar* (London: Sweet & Maxwell, 1983), W. R. Cornish and G. de N. Clark, *Law and Society in England, 1750–1950* (London: Sweet & Maxwell, 1989), and Daniel Duman, *The English and Colonial Bars in the Nineteenth Century* (London: Croom Helm, 1983). The story is made particularly colorful (but maddeningly bereft of notes) in J. R. Lewis, *The Victorian Bar* (London: Hale, 1982). See also the sociological studies Brian Abel-Smith and Robert Stevens, *Lawyers and the Courts: A Sociological Study of the English Legal System, 1750–1965* (London: Heinemann, 1967), Abel-Smith and Stevens, *In Search of Justice: Society and the Legal System* (London: Lane, 1968), and Alan Harding, *A Social History of English Law* (Gloucester, MA: Smith, 1973).

11. "The State of the Profession," *The Law Review and Quarterly Journal of British and Foreign Jurisprudence* 3 (August 1845–May 1846): 348–49.

12. Duman, *English and Colonial Bars*, pp. 6–8.

13. [James Fitzjames Stephen], "The Bars of France and England," *The Cornhill Magazine* 10, no. 60 (December 1864): 674.

14. Duman, *English and Colonial Bars*, pp. 148–49.

15. *DNB* (William Schwenck Gilbert).

16. W. S. Gilbert and Arthur Sullivan, *The Complete Plays of Gilbert and Sullivan* (New York: Modern Library, [1936]), p. 47.

17. See Cocks, *Foundations of the Modern Bar*, and Lewis, *Victorian Bar.*

18. For a description of the old circuit life, see e.g. Mr. Serjeant [Benjamin C.] Robinson, *Bench and Bar: Reminiscences of One of the Last of an Ancient Race*, 4th ed. (London, 1894), pp. 27–30; and "On Circuit," *Chambers's Journal of Popular Literature*, August 16, 1856, pp. 97–100.

19. See William Wesley Thomas Pue, "The Making of the English Bar: Metasomatism in the Nineteenth Century" (D. Jur. thesis, York University [Canada], 1989).

20. Cornish and Clark, *Law and Society*, p. 562.

21. "When they [prisoners] were allowed to have counsel cross-examine, but not speak for them, the cross-examination tended to become a speech thrown into the form of questions, and it has ever since retained this character to a greater or lesser extent." James Fitzjames Stephen, *A General View of the Criminal Law of England*, 2nd ed. (London, 1890), p. 169.

22. See John Hostettler, *The Politics of Criminal Law Reform in the Nineteenth Century* (Chichester: Rose, 1992), ch. 4.

23. Based on the Judicial Statistics for 1858 reprinted in A. H. Manchester, *Sources of English Legal History: Law, History, and Society in England and Wales, 1750–1950* (London: Butterworths, 1984), pp. 211–12.

24. "The Prisoners' Counsel Bill," *The Law Magazine, or Quarterly Review of Jurisprudence* 15, no. 2 (May 1836): 398.

25. *Parl. Deb.*, 3s, vol. 34, col. 768 (June 23, 1836).

26. Bernard W. Kelly, *Famous Advocates and Their Speeches: British Forensic Eloquence, from Lord Erskine to Lord Russell of Killowen, with an Historical Introduction* (London: Sweet & Maxwell, 1921), p. 22.

27. See Sir William Holdsworth, *A History of English Law*, vol. 15, ed. A. L. Goodhart and H. G. Hanbury (London: Methuen, 1966), pp. 111–12.

28. "Law Reform in the Late Parliament," *The Law Magazine and Law Review: or, Quarterly Journal of Jurisprudence* 20, no. 39 (November 1865): 51.

29. See Holdsworth, *English Law,* 15: 158.

30. J. H. Baker, *An Introduction to English Legal History,* 2nd ed. (London: Butterworths, 1979), p. 80.

31. See B. R. Mitchell, *British Historical Statistics* (Cambridge: Cambridge University Press, 1988), pp. 783–84.

32. Abel-Smith and Stevens, *Lawyers and the Courts,* p. 35.

33. Cocks, *Foundations of the Modern Bar,* p. 9.

34. Andrew Swann Rowley, "Professions, Class and Society: Solicitors in 19th Century Birmingham" (PhD diss., University of Aston in Birmingham, 1988), p. 136. Although, in this example, a tight clique of solicitors appears to have had a near monopoly on County Court advocacy, it is also true that other solicitors outside this group had substantial practices in local courts. Indeed, advocacy in the County and other local courts (e.g. magistrate's and police courts) was a means by which a number of solicitors made their professional name, secured increased income, and sometimes became local notables.

35. H. W. Arthurs, "Special Courts, Special Law: Legal Pluralism in Nineteenth Century England," in *Law, Economy and Society, 1750–1914: Essays in the History of English Law,* ed. G. R. Rubin and David Sugarman (Abingdon: Professional Books, 1984).

36. *GD,* 6: 306 (October 14, 1864).

37. *TT,* February 11, 1867, p. 12.

38. See David Brownlee, *The Law Courts: The Architecture of George Edmund Street* (New York: Architectural History Foundation, and Cambridge, MA: MIT Press, 1984).

39. William Ballantine, *Some Experiences of a Barrister's Life,* 6th ed. (London, 1890), p. 318.

40. W. Eden Hooper, *The History of Newgate and the Old Bailey* (London: Underwood, 1935), pp. 17–8

41. See Katherine Fischer Taylor, *In The Theater of Criminal Justice: The Palias de Justice in Second Empire Paris* (Princeton: Princeton University Press, 1993), p. 13.

42. Brownlee, *Law Courts,* p. 334.

43. Joseph Kinnard, "G. E. Street, the Law Courts, and the 'Seventies," in *Victorian Architecture,* ed. Peter Ferriday (London: Cape, 1963), p. 234.

44. William Forsyth, *Hortensius: or, the Advocate. An Historical Essay* (London, 1849), p. 384.

45. Stephen, "Bars of France and England," p. 681.

46. Montagu Williams, *Later Leaves* (London, 1891), p. 121.

47. Edward W. Cox, *The Advocate: His Training, Practice, Rights, and Duties* (London, 1852), p. 177.

48. *The Law Times* 42 (December 1, 1886): 83.

49. On the two-way traffic of upper and middle classes in the law, see David Cannadine, *The Decline and Fall of the British Aristocracy* (New Haven: Yale University Press, 1990), pp. 250–55.

50. Cox, *Advocate,* p. 177.

51. Frederick Pollock, *Personal Remembrances of Sir Frederick Pollock, Second Baronet, Sometime Queen's Remembrancer,* 2 vols. (London, 1887), 1: 106.

52. Reports of the Joint Committee [of the Inns of Court] on Legal Education 1851–63, Gray's Inn, Holker Library MSS G(b)12.

53. *The Lord Chief Baron Nicholson: An Autobiography* (London, [1860]), p. 287.

54. *Mr. & Mrs. Bancroft On and Off Stage, Written by Themselves,* 4th ed., 2 vols. (London, 1888), 1: 208.

55. The interest in forming debating societies was not confined to the Inns of Court. In the mid-1830s, the Law Students' Debating Society was established at the Law Institution for aspiring and new solicitors. Although it continued to hold regular debates after its founding, the Society was not notably successful in generating interest in its activities until after the 1846 County Courts Act gave solicitors the right of address in the new courts. "Law Students' Debating Society," *The Law Times,* April 6, 1850, p. 36.

56. Beyond a few stray references, information on the Forensic Society is hard to come by. My statement that the Society originated at the beginning of the nineteenth century is based on the Forensic's *List of Members, December 1832* (London, 1832), which claims Serjeant John Adams, called to the bar in 1812, as an original member. For other members, the earliest listed date of admission to the Society is 1809.

57. Cox, *Advocate,* pp. 187–97. Cox also mentions a New Forensic Society holding debates on a different night of the week than the original Forensic, and recommended that students join this Society as well. Like the Forensic, however, there is little information on the New Forensic.

58. The origins of the Hardwicke are difficult to reconstruct. Even the Hardwicke's own materials cannot produce the names of the Society's officers from its first decade. The Hardwicke Society, *Rules and List of Members* (London: Straker, 1922), p. 2 n. This describes 1858–59 as "The first year of extant records."

59. Hardwicke Society, *Rules,* p. 5.

60. "The Hardwicke. In the Old Court of Chancery," *Morning Post,* April 17, 1920. After the First World War, the Hardwicke moved its meetings to the Middle Temple. The barristers' common room still holds the most comprehensive set of the Hardwicke's publications, as well as the Society's "Library of Advocacy" collection begun around 1917. I am grateful to the Honourable Society of the Middle Temple for access to the barristers' common room and permission to examine these materials.

61. "The Hardwicke. In the Old Court of Chancery."

62. See, e.g. *TT,* March 10, 1893, p. 7; and *The Law Times,* May 4, 1895, pp. 13–16.

63. Edward Clarke, *The Story of My Life* (London: Murray, 1918), p. 61. Clarke also dedicated a volume of his speeches to the Hardwicke, "in recognition of the fact that in the meetings of that Society I found my best training for the work of the Bar." *Speeches by Sir Edward Clarke, Q.C., M.P.: Second Series, Chiefly Forensic* (London, [1894]).

64. See, e.g. *The Law Times,* February 26, 1898, pp. 390–91; May 6, 1899, pp. 18–19; April 28, 1900, p. 615; June 8, 1901, p. 137. Clarke's feelings about the Hardwicke were fully reciprocated by the Society. After his call to the bar in 1864, he spent four years as the Hardwicke's Honorary Secretary, followed by another four years as its first elected president (previously, the Society was presided over by a committee). In 1904, on the fortieth anniversary of his call to the bar, the Hardwicke showed its appreciation of Clarke by throwing him a great banquet. See Hardwicke Society, *Dinner to Sir Edward Clarke, July 22, 1904* (London: Spottiswoode, 1904).

65. See William Ralph Douthwaite, *Gray's Inn: Its History and Associations, Compiled from Original and Unpublished Documents* (London, 1886), pp. 80–86.

66. See the evidence of Lord Campbell in the Report from the Select Committee on Legal Education; Together with the Minutes of Evidence, Appendix and Index, PP, 1846, 10: 289.

67. The most thorough examination of this subject to date is Bege Bowers Neel's unpublished doctoral dissertation "Lawyers on Trial: Attitudes Toward the Lawyer's Use and Abuse of Rhetoric in Nineteenth-Century England" (PhD diss., University of Tennessee, Knoxville, 1984). While the emphasis of (as she is now known) Professor Bowers's dissertation is significantly different from that of this section, I discuss some of the same issues and materials, and gratefully acknowledge my debt to her study.

68. See Forsyth, *Hortensius*, pp. 428–30; and Neel, "Lawyers on Trial," pp. 3–13.

69. Stefan Collini, *Public Moralists: Political Thought and Intellectual Life in Britain, 1850–1930* (Oxford: Clarendon, 1991), p. 282.

70. Collini, *Public Moralists*, p. 284.

71. Peter Gay, *The Bourgeois Experience: Victoria to Freud*, vol. 1. *Education of the Senses* (Oxford: Oxford University Press, 1984), p. 421.

72. Thomas H. Huxley, "Universities: Actual and Ideal" [Rectorial Address, Aberdeen University], *Science and Education* (New York, 1895), p. 205.

73. Jeremy Bentham, *Rationale of Judicial Evidence Specially Applied to English Practice* (1827), *The Works of Jeremy Bentham*, ed. John Bowring, 11 vols. (Edinburgh, 1843–46), 6: 350. See also the extended editorial comment by John Stuart Mill in vol. 8, esp. p. 479. Another Utilitarian, John Austin, was closer in theoretical terms to the realities of barristerial practice by arguing that the law must be de-coupled from religious and moral precepts. John Austin, *The Province of Jurisprudence Determined* (London, 1832). Significantly, when first published, this treatise attracted little notice, when it was posthumously reissued in the early 1860s, it became highly influential.

74. See Harold Perkin, *The Origins of Modern English Society* (London: Routledge & Kegan Paul, 1969).

75. See *Speeches of Charles Phillips, Esq. Delivered at the Bar and on Various Public Occasions in Ireland and England*, 2nd ed. (London, 1822).

76. *DNB* (Charles Phillips); Robinson, *Bench and Bar*, p. 45.

77. Daniel O'Connell criticized Phillips's testimony and accused him of only seeking to further his own emoluments. O'Connell retracted his accusation during the debate on the second reading of the bill. *Parl. Deb.*, 3s, vol. 31, cols. 1150–2 (March 21, 1836).

78. The most thorough modern treatment of the trial and its aftermath is David Mellinkoff, *The Conscience of a Lawyer* (St. Paul, MN: West, 1973).

79. *TT*, June 19, 1840, p. 5. See also Robinson, *Bench and Bar*, pp. 48–9.

80. Ballantine, *Experiences*, p. 61.

81. *TT*, June 22, 1840, p. 6.

82. *The Examiner*, June 28, 1840, p. 411; quoted in Neel, "Lawyers on Trial," p. 43.

83. *TT*, June 22, 1840, pp. 6–7.

84. See Neel, "Lawyers on Trial," pp. 47–52.

85. Ballantine, *Experiences*, p. 62.

86. Indeed, Phillips's performance at the Courvoisier trial quickly became a classic "case

study" in barristerial practice. In this capacity, Phillips's name has carried on well into the twentieth century. See, for example, Richard du Cann, *The Art of the Advocate* (Harmondsworth: Penguin, 1964), p. 41.

87. [James Fitzjames Stephen], "The Morality of Advocacy," *Cornhill Magazine* 3, no. 16 (April 1861), p. 453.

88. Cox, *Advocate*, p. 65.

89. *The Law Times*, November 19, 1864, p. 25.

90. *Speeches by Henry Lord Brougham*, 4 vols. (Edinburgh, 1838), 1: 105.

91. All quotations from *The Law Times*, November 19, 1864, p. 25.

92. See *The Law Times*, December 10, 1864, pp. 61; September 30, 1865, p. 575.

93. This is the principal conclusion of Neel's dissertation: "Essentially, the concept of the purse-squeezing, truth-dodging, browbeating pleader . . . derived from popular tradition seems to have survived the [nineteenth] century. Without forcing the point, I would suggest, however, that the portraits of the barristers generally seem to be grimmer and the attacks on the profession seem to be more vicious in those works that were written after 1840—when Charles Phillips' controversial and much-publicized defense of Courvoisier gave substance once and for all to the fears and suspicions that had for so long been associated with professional advocacy." Neel, "Lawyers on Trial," p. 224.

94. Philip Collins, *Dickens and Crime*, 2nd ed. (London: Macmillan, 1965), p. 174; see also p. 190.

95. Charles Dickens, *The Old Curiosity Shop. A Tale* (London, 1841), p. 152. *The Old Curiosity Shop* was published serially between April 25, 1840 and February 6, 1841. The trial of Kit Nubbles, from which this quotation is taken, was published (and most likely composed) after the Courvoisier revelations in June 1840. In May 1840, when the Courvoisier trial was taking place, Dickens had written up to chapter 5; this quotation is from chapter 63. That Dickens, keen observer of London life, was not miraculously unaware of the Courvoisier proceedings is attested to by the fact of his documented determination to witness the hanging of the condemned valet. See Peter Ackroyd, *Dickens* (London: Sinclair-Stevenson, 1990), pp. 312–14.

96. The great popularity of Dickens's "Trial from Pickwick" readings is observed throughout Reymund Fitzsimons, *The Charles Dickens Show: An Account of His Public Readings, 1858–1870* (London: Bles, 1970).

97. Ballantine, *Experiences*, pp. 94–5.

98. Gilbert and Sullivan, *Complete Plays*, p. 245.

99. Gilbert and Sullivan, *Complete Plays*, pp. 47–8.

100. Herbert Paul, "The Victorian Novel" (1897), *Men & Letters* (London: Lane, 1901), p. 142.

101. Donald A. Smalley, ed., *Trollope: The Critical Heritage* (London: Routledge & Kegan Paul, 1969), pp. 4–5.

102. Anthony Trollope, *The Eustace Diamonds* (1873; Oxford: Oxford University Press, 1973), 2: 302.

103. Anthony Trollope, *The Life of Cicero*, 2 vols. (London, 1880), 1: 29; 2: 333; 1: 30.

104. Anthony Trollope, *Orley Farm* (1861–62; London: The Trollope Society, 1993), p. 305. See R. D. McMaster, "Chaffanbrass for the Defence: Trollope and the Old Bailey Tradition," *Trollope and the Law* (London: Macmillan, 1986).

105. *The Three Clerks* (1858), *Orley Farm*, and *Phineas Redux* (1874).

106. Trollope, *Orley Farm*, p. 514. That Chaffanbrass works with solicitors who are Jewish (always a bad thing in Trollope) is intended to make the barrister seem all the more disreputable and his motives all the more mercenary.

107. Trollope, *Orley Farm*, p. 686.

108. Anthony Trollope, *Phineas Redux* (1874; Oxford: Oxford University Press, 1973), 2: 180.

109. J. H. Baker, "History of the Gowns Worn at the English Bar," *Costume*, no. 9 (1975), p. 15. Barristers' robes were in fact adopted by the junior bar in 1685 after the death of Charles II and never abandoned. The small hood hanging from the left shoulder is a mourning hood.

110. Edward Abbott Parry, *The Drama of the Law* (London: Unwin, 1924), p. 19.

111. Cicero, *Brutus*, LXXXIV, 290.

112. See James Stirling, "Advocacy and Acting," *Verdict* 2, no. 1 (Hilary, 1966): 7–8.

113. George Pleydell Bancroft, *Stage and Bar* (London: Faber, 1939), pp. 237–38.

114. See Jonas Barish, *The Antitheatrical Prejudice* (Berkeley: University of California Press, 1981), pp. 67, 305–17.

115. For example, a lawyer has compared the adversary trial to *Hamlet* and *Oedipus Rex*: "An adversary trial is a dramatic thing put to legal use. It is not a legal thing any more than a book or a wig or a bench or a robe is a legal thing. As a dramatic thing, it has dramatic attributes, such as dramatic form, dramatic substance and, most significantly, dramatic effect" Richard Harbinger, "Trial by Drama," *Judicature* 55, no. 3 (October 1971): 122. Sociologists and criminologists—generally influenced by Erving Goffman's theories of performance in everyday life—have turned some attention to the dramaturgical aspects of courtroom procedure. See Pat Carlen, "The Staging of Magistrates' Justice," *The British Journal of Criminology* 16, no. 1 (January 1976): 48–55; and Carlen, *Magistrates' Justice* (London: Robertson, 1976), esp. pp. 32–38. For a critique of these and other similar analyses of legal procedure, see J. Maxwell Atkinson and Paul Drew, *Order in Court: The Organisation of Verbal Interaction in Judicial Settings* (Atlantic Highlands, NJ: Humanities Press, 1979), esp. ch. 1.

116. E. P. Thompson, *Customs in Common* (London: Penguin, 1993), pp. 45, 83.

117. Taylor, *Theater of Criminal Justice*, p. 10.

118. Taylor, *Theater of Criminal Justice*, p. 13.

119. Stephen, "Bars of France and England," p. 674.

120. For the historical background to the Criminal Evidence Act, see Graham Parker, "The Prisoner in the Box—The Making of the Criminal Evidence Act, 1898," in *Law and Social Change in British History: Papers Presented to the Bristol Legal History Conference, 14–17 July 1981*, ed. J. A. Guy and H. G. Beale (London: Royal Historical Society, 1984), pp. 156–75.

121. Of his desire to witness the hanging of Courvoisier in 1840, Dickens said: "Just once, I should like to watch a scene like this, and see the end of the Drama." Quoted in Ackroyd, *Dickens*, p. 313.

122. See Thomas W. Laqueur, "Crowds, Carnival and the State in English Executions, 1604–1868," in *The First Modern Society: Essays in English History in Honour of Lawrence Stone*, ed. A. L. Beier, et al. (Cambridge: Cambridge University Press, 1989), pp. 305–55.

123. William Charles Macready, *Macready's Reminiscences, and Selections from his Diaries and Letters*, ed. Frederick Pollock, 2 vols. (London, 1875), 1: 26.

124. William Charles Macready, *The Diaries of William Charles Macready, 1833–1851*, ed. William Toynbee, 2 vols. (London: Chapman and Hall, 1912), 2: 292, n. 2.

125. Macready, *Reminiscences*, 1: 15.

126. A bitterness clearly expressed in his *Reminiscences*, e.g. 1: 26–27. On one occasion, when asked for his views on the stage, Macready replied that he "would sooner see a son of mine coffin'd at my feet than that he should take to acting and the stage." Quoted in Michael Sanderson, *From Irving to Olivier: A Social History of the Acting Profession in England, 1880–1983* (London: Athlone, 1984), p. 10.

127. See Max Beerbohm, "H. B. Irving as a Young Man" (1914), *The Incomparable Max* (London: Icon, 1964), pp. 281–86.

128. Perhaps the fullest—though by no means wholly accurate—account of Wilkins's life is the chapter on him in Humphrey William Woolrych, *Lives of Eminent Serjeants-at-Law of the English Bar*, 2 vols. (London, 1869), 2: 850–88. Particularly useful for Wilkins's early life is "Local Recollections of Serjeant Wilkins (from a Birmingham paper)," *The Law Times*, August 4, 1857, pp. 23–24. According to the author of this piece, while attempting to run a school in Birmingham in the late 1820s, Wilkins joined the Methodists and "preached two or three impressive sermons at the Cherry-street Chapel," and also joined a local debating society that met at a tavern: "I shall never forget the effect, not so much of his speeches as his speaking, upon my youthful mind. I thought I never heard so eloquent a man as the poor schoolmaster."

129. "Local Recollections of Serjeant Wilkins," p. 23.

130. The definitive account of James's life and career is J. R. Lewis, *Certain Private Incidents: The Rise and Fall of Edwin James QC., MP.* (Newcastle-upon-Tyne: Templar North, 1980).

131. Responding to a comment that neither Wilkins nor James possessed the right looks to make it on the stage, the great actor Charles Kemble is reported to have said, "Figure has very little to do with it, so that there is the talent, which they both had." Quoted in Cyrus Jay, *The Law: What I Have Seen, What I Have Heard, and What I Have Known* (London, 1869), p. 298.

132. "Local Recollections of Serjeant Wilkins," p. 23.

133. Quoted in Lewis, *Victorian Bar*, p. 14.

134. *TT*, April 17, 1858, p. 12. According to this report, "Distinct clapping of hands and other symptoms of approval were manifested by a portion of the audience at the conclusion of the learned counsel's address, and it was some time before the ordinary aspect of the court was restored."

135. Augustine Birrell, *Sir Frank Lockwood: A Biographical Sketch* (London, 1898), pp. 42–45. There were also apparently unfounded rumors that Lockwood made subsequent appearances on the boards acting under a pseudonym (pp. 45–46).

136. See Montagu Williams, *Leaves of a Life*, 2 vols. (London, 1890), 1: ch. 5.

137. Williams, *Leaves*, 1: 61.

138. Squire Bancroft, *Empty Chairs* (New York: Stokes, 1925), ch. 4.

139. Birrell, *Lockwood*, p. 45.

140. Ballantine, *Experiences*, p. 96.

141. Bancroft, *Empty Chairs*, pp. 61–62.

142. Ballantine, *Experiences*, p. 186.

143. Ballantine, *Experiences*, p. 147. See ch. 18.

144. See, e.g., Williams, *Leaves*, 1: 61.

145. Nicholson, *Autobiography*, p. 286.

146. Nicholson, *Autobiography*, p. 286.

147. Nicholson, *Autobiography*, p. 314.

148. Nicholson, *Autobiography*, p. 294.

149. Frederic Boase, *Modern English Biography*, 6 vols. (Truro: Netherton and Worth, 1892–1921), 2: 1143.

150. See Cocks, *Foundations of the Modern Bar*, ch. 8; and Pue, "Making of the English Bar."

151. See Sanderson, *From Irving to Olivier*, ch. 1. Gladstone had recommended Irving for a knighthood in 1883 but the actor declined the honor. See Glynne Wickham, "Gladstone, Oratory and the Theatre," *Gladstone*, ed. Peter J. Jagger (London: Hambledon, 1998), pp. 1–31.

152. Over the years, the Tichborne case has received extended treatment in a number of works. J. B. Atlay, *The Tichborne Case* (1899; London: Hodge, 1912) faithfully adheres to the case successfully presented against the Claimant. Atlay also wrote the entry for the Claimant ("Arthur Orton") in the *DNB*. Atlay's account was superseded by Lord Maugham, *The Tichborne Case* (London: Hodder & Stoughton, 1936), which also generally follows the anti-Claimant line. A far more thorough and (as far as possible) balanced account is Douglas Woodruff, *The Tichborne Claimant: A Victorian Mystery* (New York: Farrar, Straus, and Cudahy, 1957). Additionally, the various lawyers and judges involved give substantial space in their memoirs to the case.

153. Ballantine, *Experiences*, p. 318.

154. See the account of the cross-examination in H. Montgomery Hyde, *Famous Trials: Oscar Wilde* (Harmondsworth: Penguin, 1962), pp. 105–40.

155. Woodruff, *Tichborne Claimant*, p. 199.

156. Quoted in Ernest Hartley Coleridge, *Life & Correspondence of John Duke Lord Coleridge, Lord Chief Justice of England*, 2 vols. (London: Heinemann, 1904), 2: 185, n. 1.

157. For a discussion of the political dimensions and ramifications of the Tichborne case, see Michael Roe, *Kenealey and the Tichborne Cause: A Study in Mid-Victorian Populism* (Carlton: Melbourne University Press, 1974), esp. chs. 5, 7; and Rohan McWilliam, "Radicalism and Popular Culture: The Tichborne Case and the Politics of 'Fair Play', 1867–1886," in *Currents of Radicalism: Popular Radicalism, Organised Labour and Party Politics in Britain, 1850–1914*, ed. Eugenio F. Biagini and Alastair J. Reid (Cambridge: Cambridge University Press, 1991).

158. Undated clipping (c. January 1872) from the *Saturday Review* in an album of Tichborne Case Newspaper Cuttings, Lincoln's Inn Library manuscript collection, Misc. 788.

159. "The Tichborne Trial: Seventy-First Day," *Daily News*, January 16, 1872, p. 5.

160. *Daily News*, January 16, 1872, p. 5.

161. *Daily News*, January 16, 1872, p. 5.

162. According to Jean Cruppi, criminal trials in London were conducted "in cramped courtrooms, where a grand gesture was unthinkable because the speaker might knock the very wig off a colleague!" Quoted in Taylor, *Theater of Criminal Justice*, p. 13.

163. In Tichborne Case Newspaper Cuttings, Lincoln's Inn Library manuscript collection, Misc. 788.

164. John Vincent, *The Formation of the Liberal Party, 1857–1868* (London: Constable, 1966), pp. 39–40.

165. *HP: 1754–1790*, 1: 126, 128.

166. *HP: 1790–1820*, 1: 300.

167. Based on 1,964 MPs in the 1754–1790 period, and 2,143 in the 1790–1820 period. An analysis of legal membership in Parliament during the period between 1680 and 1730 estimates the percentage of practitioners rising from 7 percent to 9 percent. See David Lemmings, *Gentlemen and Barristers: The Inns of Court and the English Bar, 1680–1730* (Oxford: Clarendon, 1990), pp. 182–83.

168. Duman, *English and Colonial Bars*, pp. 169–70. However, these figures do not distinguish between practicing and non-practicing barristers. Nor do they represent a consistent data set (the figures for the early years of the series include solicitors, while figures for the later years exclude Irish barristers).

169. The doubling of Irish lawyer-MPs in 1874 is primarily attributable to the election of Home Rule lawyers. The election of nationalist lawyers also contributed to the increasing number of lawyer-MPs from Wales. In England, the 33 percent increase in lawyer-MPs in 1880 is part of the greater level of "middle class" representation generally. See William Henry Whiteley, "The Social Composition of the House of Commons, 1868–1885" (PhD diss., Cornell University, 1960), pp. 555–56. The proportion of practicing lawyer-MPs for English and Scottish constituencies between 1868 and 1885 was less than the proportion of English and Scottish parliamentary seats, while the proportion practicing lawyer-MPs for Welsh and Irish constituencies was greater than the proportion of Welsh and Irish seats. It is important to note, however, that these proportions do not necessarily correspond to the nationality of the lawyer-MPs themselves. Scottish and Irish barristers represented a significant number of English constituencies throughout the century. In England, the legal circuit provided London-based barristers the opportunity to develop their electoral potential outside the metropolis. By the 1860s, barristers "were already carpet-bagging, in a modified form, among the towns of their circuit—and with a success which anticipated the enormous growth of non-local representation after 1885." Vincent, *Liberal Party*, p. 40.

170. *The History of Parliament: The House of Commons, 1660–1690*, ed. Basil Duke Henning, 3 vols. (London: Secker & Warburg, 1983), 1: 9; *HP: 1754–1790*, 1: 126; *HP: 1790–1820*, 1: 302.

171. Duman, English and Colonial Bars, pp. 172–73.

172. Practicing barrister-MPs tended to enter the House at a later age than members from other groups. Between 1790 and 1820, the average ages of entry for English, Scottish, and Irish barristers were 38, 39, and 45, respectively, compared to the overall average for all MPs of 33. *HP: 1790–1820*, 1: 300. According to another study, of MPs who entered the House between 1734 and 1832, lawyers (including practicing and non-practicing barristers, solicitors, and attorneys) first entered at an average age of almost 39, over four years later than the overall average. Gerritt P. Judd, IV, *Members of Parliament, 1734–1832* (New Haven: Yale University Press, 1955), p. 52. Between 1885 and 1905, something like 60 percent of barrister-MPs entered Parliament at ages of 41 and older, compared to 50 percent for all members. In this period, more than two-thirds of the MPs from the landed classes (around 40 percent of the total membership) entered Parliament before the age of 40. J. P. Cornford, "The Parliamentary Foundations of the Hotel Cecil," in *Ideas and Institutions*

of Victorian Britain: Essays in Honour of George Kitson Clark, ed. Robert Robson (London: Bell, 1967), p. 311.

173. Bodleian Library, MS Bryce 442, f. 95. I am grateful to John Seaman for this quotation.

174. Anthony Trollope, *Phineas Finn* (1869; Oxford: Oxford University Press, 1973), 2: 225.

175. See Duman, *English and Colonial Bars*, p. 171.

176. [George Nathaniel] Earl Curzon of Kedleston, *Modern Parliamentary Eloquence: The Rede Lecture, Delivered before the University of Cambridge, November 6, 1913* (London: Macmillan, 1913), p. 66.

177. See, generally, J. Ll. J. Edwards, *The Law Offices of the Crown* (London: Sweet & Maxwell, 1964).

178. Henry W. Lucy, *A Diary of Two Parliaments: The Disraeli Parliament, 1874–1880*, 2nd ed. (London, 1885), p. 97.

179. For an analysis of the background and careers of these law officers, see Joseph S. Meisel, "Public Speech and the Culture of Public Life in the Age of Gladstone" (Ph.D. diss, Columbia University, 1999), pp. 354–56. For the eighteenth century, cf. R. A. Melikan, "Mr Attorney General and the Politicians," *The Historical Journal* 40, no. 1 (1997): 41–69.

180. *Parl. Deb.*, 3s, vol. 211, col. 259 (May 3, 1872).

181. From testimony given by Jervis to the Select Committee on Official Salaries, quoted in Edwards, *Law Officers*, p. 76.

182. DD 1, p. 247; Palmer Papers, Lambeth Palace Library MSS 2851, f. 48.

183. DD 2, p. 118. Cf. Roundell Palmer, Earl of Selborne, *Memorials: Personal and Political, 1865–1895*, 2 vols. (London, 1898), 1: 131–34.

184. *TT*, May 1, 1880, p. 11.

185. DD 1, p. 274. See also p. 269.

186. DD 1, p. 377, n. 49.

187. Derek Walker-Smith and Edward Clarke, *The Life of Sir Edward Clarke* (London: Butterworth, 1939), p. 235.

188. "Lawyers in Parliament," *The Saturday Review*, January 14, 1888, p. 45.

189. Henry W. Lucy, *A Diary of the Salisbury Parliament, 1886–1892* (London, 1892), pp. 252–53. Occasionally, lawyers got some of their own back: "I venture to think that a young barrister of twelve months' practice at sessions, would in a case involving no law and depending entirely on facts, defend a prisoner with a better chance of success than either Mr. Gladstone or Lord Beaconsfield could have done it, notwithstanding their enormous powers of oratory." Robinson, *Bench and Bar*, p. 77.

190. Curzon, *Modern Parliamentary Eloquence*, pp. 66–67.

191. [George Henry Francis], "A Batch of Parliamentary Barristers," *Fraser's Magazine* 36, no. 213 (September 1847): 311–12.

192. Francis, "Parliamentary Barristers," p. 319.

193. Justin McCarthy, "Some Great English Lawyers," *The Galaxy* 14, no. 6 (December 1872): 793, 795.

194. *The Journal of John Wodehouse, First Earl of Kimberley for 1862–1902*, ed. Angus Hawkins and John Powell, *Camden Fifth Series*, vol. 9 (London: The Royal Historical Society, 1997), p. 71. The long half-life of this attitude is evident in a recent account of Michael

Howard: "'He sounded too much like a barrister.' He was so fluent and smooth that his audience began to doubt whether he believed what he was saying." Matthew Parris, "Political Sketch: Howard Finds Eloquence No Asset in the Credibility Game," *TT*, March 3, 1999, p. 4.

195. *TT*, June 29, 1850, p. 6.

196. Quoted in *DNB* (Alexander Cockburn).

197. *TT*, August 19, 1911, p. 9.

198. See Coleridge, *Life & Correspondence of . . . Lord Coleridge*, 2: 40–41.

199. Quoted in Coleridge, *Life & Correspondence of . . . Lord Coleridge*, 2: 59.

200. Lucy, *Salisbury Parliament*, p. 254.

201. For the general assessment of Harcourt's speech-making, see A. G. Gardiner, *The Life of Sir William Harcourt*, 2 vols. (New York: Doran, [1923?].), 1: 211, 351.

202. Quoted in Gardiner, *Harcourt*, 1: 351.

203. *Parl. Deb.*, 3s, vol., 211 cols. 256–57 (May 3, 1872). Emphasis added.

204. See Edwards, *Law Officers*, p. 48, n. 76.

205. The courtroom burdens of the law officers were somewhat alleviated by the establishment in 1879 of the new office of Director of Public Prosecutions, directly responsible to the Attorney General.

206. Lord Hanworth, *Lord Chief Baron Pollock: A Memoir by his Grandson* (London: Murray, 1929), pp. 77–78.

207. Recalled in Viscount Alverstone, *Recollections of Bar and Bench*, (London: Arnold, 1914), pp. 137–38.

208. This evidently happened to Alexander Cockburn when he was Attorney General. See Robinson, *Bench and Bar*, pp. 88–89.

209. See Edwards, *Law Officers*, pp. 49–51, 101–5.

210. *Law Times*, June 19, 1852, p. 89.

211. Lewis, *Victorian Bar*, p. 62.

212. Stephen, *General View of the Criminal Law*, pp. 169–70.

CHAPTER 5: THE PLATFORM

1. Thomas Carlyle, "The Stump Orator" (1850), *Latter-Day Pamphlets* (London, 1858), pp. 160–61.

2. Carlyle, "Stump Orator," p. 188.

3. *GD*, 4: 562 (October 12 and 13, 1853). The account of the proceedings in the *Manchester Guardian* (October 15, 1853, p. 8) does not give an estimate of the size of the crowd that gathered for the inauguration of the Peel monument. The *Times* account (October 14, 1853, p. 6) states that "the spectators were the populace of the largest manufacturing city in the world; the place their busiest thoroughfare; and the time their dinner hour."

4. Richard Shannon lays great stress on the 1853 Manchester speeches as a transformative moment in Gladstone's career. Shannon, *Gladstone*, vol. 1 (London: Hamilton, 1982), pp. 276–77. See also H. C. G. Matthew, *Gladstone*, 2 vols. (Oxford: Clarendon, 1986–95), 1: 102.

5. *Oxford English Dictionary*, "platform," definition 9a.

6. Henry L. Jephson, *The Platform: Its Rise and Progress*, 2 vols. (London, 1892). The book was reviewed (favorably) by Gladstone in *The Nineteenth Century* 31, no. 182 (April 1892): 686–89. Despite its extreme Whiggishness, *The Platform* remains a remarkably thorough treatment of the subject and an unsurpassed trove of citations. About Jephson himself, little is known.

7. M. Ostrogorski, *Democracy and the Organization of Political Parties*, tr. Frederick Clarke, 2 vols. (London: Macmillan 1922), esp. vol. 1, pt. 3, ch. 2.

8. John Vincent, *The Formation of the British Liberal Party, 1857–1868*, 2nd ed. (Hassocks: Harvester, 1976).

9. H. C. G. Matthew, "Rhetoric and Politics in Great Britain, 1860–1950," in *Politics and Social Change in Britain: Essays Presented to A. F. Thompson*, ed. P. J. Waller (Sussex, UK: Harvester, 1987).

10. Matthew, "Rhetoric and Politics," p. 39.

11. George Eliot, *Middlemarch* (Oxford: Oxford University Press, 1986), pp. 410–14.

12. Frank O'Gorman, "Campaign Rituals and Ceremonies: The Social Meaning of Elections in England, 1780–1860," *Past & Present* 135 (May 1992), esp. pp. 88, 99–100, 113; James Vernon, *Politics and the People: A Study in English Political Culture, c. 1815–1867* (Cambridge: Cambridge University Press, 1993), esp. pp. 117–31.

13. The vigorous endurance of local electoral traditions customs in the later nineteenth century can be seen in the way that, when Gladstone was on his way to make a speech at Woolwich in 1874, a "party of enthusiastic supporters met the Premier's carriage (in which were Mrs. and Miss Gladstone) at a short distance from the hustings, and removing the horses drew it in triumph to Beresford-square." *Kentish Independent*, February 7, 1874, n.p. At Birmingham in 1884, Lord Randolph Churchill's carriage was also unhorsed and drawn into the city by a large and enthusiastic crowd. *The Life and Speeches of Lord Randolph Henry Spencer-Churchill*, ed. Frank Banfield (London, [1884]), p. 85.

14. Chris Cook and Brendan Keith, *British Historical Facts, 1830–1900* (London: Macmillan, 1975), p. 143.

15. *The Life and Times of Henry Lord Brougham, by Himself*, 3 vols. (Edinburgh, 1871), 2: 62.

16. Richard Greville Verney, Lord Willoughby de Broke, *The Passing Years* (London: Constable, 1924), pp. 178–79.

17. *The Works of the Right Honourable Edmund Burke, a New Edition*, vol. 3 (London, 1803), pp. 1–22 and 353–427.

18. See Loren Reid, *Charles James Fox: A Man for the People* (Columbia, MO: University of Missouri Press, 1969), esp. pp. 104–6.

19. *Speeches of the Right Hon. George Canning Delivered on Public Occasions in Liverpool*, ed. Thos. Kaye (Liverpool, 1825), p. xiv.

20. Canning, *Speeches . . . in Liverpool*, p. 87.

21. Quoted in Jonathan Parry, *The Rise and Fall of Liberal Government in Victorian Britain* (New Haven: Yale University Press, 1993), p. 40.

22. See Canning, *Speeches . . . in Liverpool*, pp. 157–236.

23. *The Speeches of the Right Honourable George Canning, with a Memoir of his Life*, ed. R. Thierry, 6 vols. (London, 1828), 6: 424.

24. Jephson, *Platform*, 2: 162.

25. Canning, *Speeches*, 6: 319.

26. The Editor of the *Globe, Sir Robert Peel and His Last Tamworth Oration Shortly Considered* (Edinburgh, 1835), p. 2.

27. Norman Gash, *Sir Robert Peel: The Life of Sir Robert Peel After 1830* (London: Longman, 1972), p. 129.

28. *Speech of the Right Hon. Sir Robert Peel, Bart. M.P., Delivered at the Dinner Given to Him by the Merchants, Bankers, and Traders of the City of London, at Merchant Tailors' Hall, on Monday, the 11th of May, 1835* (London, [1835]), p. 5. Italics in original.

29. Peel, *Speech . . . at Merchant Tailors' Hall*, pp. 7, 10.

30. *Speech of Sir R. Peel, Bart., M.P., at Glasgow, January 13, 1837* (Glasgow, [1837]); *Speeches of the Rt. Hon. Sir Robert Peel, Bart., Lord Stanley, and Sir James Graham, Bart., at Merchant Tailors' Hall, May 12, 1838* (London, 1838).

31. *Tamworth Election: Speech of Sir Robert Peel, June 28, 1841* (London, 1841).

32. W. T. Haly, *The Opinions of Sir Robert Peel, Expressed in Parliament and in Public* (London, 1843), p. v.

33. Spencer Walpole, *The Life of Lord John Russell*, 2 vols. (London, 1889), 1: 211–12.

34. See Norman Gash, "Peel and the Party System, 1830–50," *Transactions of the Royal Historical Society*, 5th series, vol. 1 (1950), pp. 47–69.

35. Antony Taylor, "Palmerston and Radicalism, 1847–1865," *Journal of British Studies* 33, no. 2 (April 1994): 177–78. Taylor's attempt to rehabilitate Palmerston's reputation as an extra-parliamentary speaker can be contrasted to the way in which Jephson, in his compendious study of *The Platform*, mentions Palmerston only once, and then only in passing.

36. Palmerston's secretary provides "characteristic" examples of hustings speeches at Tiverton. Evelyn Ashley, *The Life and Correspondence of Henry John Temple Viscount Palmerston*, 2 vols. (London, 1879), 1: 409; 2: 238–45.

37. See *TT*, August 11, 1862, p. 6; April 1, 1863, p. 9.

38. See *The Manchester Guardian*, November 7, 1856, pp. 3–4.

39. *TT*, April 1, 1863, p. 9.

40. *TT*, June 13, 1859, p. 6.

41. *TT*, October 31, 1859, p. 4.

42. Matthew, "Rhetoric and Politics," p. 41.

43. *Speech of the Right Hon. B. Disraeli, M. P., at the Free Trade Hall, Manchester, April 3, 1872* (London, [1872]), pp. 19, 22.

44. *Report of the Proceedings at the National Conference, Held at the Westminster Palace Hotel and of the Banquet at the Crystal Palace, on Monday, June 24th, 1872, Together with the Speeches of the Duke of Abercorn, the Right Hon. B. Disraeli, M. P., etc. etc.* (London, [1872]), p. 16.

45. Charles Tilly, *Popular Contention in Great Britain*, 1758–1834 (Cambridge, MA: Harvard University Press, 1995), pp. 8, 341–44.

46. John Belchem, *'Orator' Hunt: Henry Hunt and English Working-Class Radicalism* (Oxford: Clarendon, 1985), pp. 58–70. See also Belchem, *Popular Radicalism in Nineteenth-Century Britain* (New York: St Martin's, 1996), pp. 41–42.

47. My discussion of O'Connor is drawn from James Epstein, *The Lion of Freedom: Feargus O'Connor and the Chartist Movement, 1832–1842* (London: Croom Helm, 1982),

esp. ch. 3; and John Belchem, "1848: Feargus O'Connor and the Collapse of the Mass Platform," in *The Chartist Experience: Studies in Working-Class Radicalism and Culture, 1830–60*, ed. James Epstein and Dorothy Thompson (London: Macmillan, 1982), pp. 269–310.

48. See Brian Harrison, "The Rhetoric of Reform in Modern Britain: 1780–1918," *Peaceable Kingdom: Stability and Change in Modern Britain* (Oxford: Clarendon, 1982), pp. 378–443. For Harrison's use of "middle-class" to describe these protests, see pp. 385–86.

49. Although the League features prominently in works about Cobden and Bright, the last full study of the League in its own right is Norman McCord, *The Anti-Corn Law League* (London: Allen and Unwin, 1958). The most recent assessment is Paul A. Pickering and Alex Tyrrell, *The People's Bread: A History of the Anti-Corn Law League* (London: Continuum, 2000), published as this study was in final preparation.

50. For an account of the various positions of historians on this issue and an argument, see John Belchem and James Epstein, "The Nineteenth-Century Gentleman Leader Revisited," *Social History* 22, no. 2 (May 1997): 174–93.

51. One nineteenth-century analyst answered the question "Was the Repeal of the Corn Laws the Effect of Oratory?" (the title of his first chapter) in the negative. Rather, he believed, the League's strong organization and the large amount of money at the disposal of the League's council to support various activities were the decisive factors. However, by oratory, the author was referring specifically to parliamentary, not platform, oratory; and he concludes his chapter by asserting that "Free discussion at public meetings, a free press, and a free Parliament, although a vast amount of nonsense and worse than nonsense may be uttered or printed, are inseparable from a free people." Andrew Bisset, *Notes on the Anti-Corn Law Struggle* (London, 1884), p. 33.

52. Herman Ausubel, *John Bright, Victorian Reformer* (New York: Wiley, 1966), p. 33.

53. Keith Robbins, *John Bright* (London: Routledge & Kegan Paul, 1979), p. 172.

54. Robbins, *Bright*, p. 186.

55. *Speeches on Questions of Public Policy by John Bright, M. P.*, ed. James E. Thorold Rogers, 2 vols. (London, 1868), 2: 199.

56. *TT*, October 17, 1866, p. 7. See also George Macaulay Trevelyan, *The Life of John Bright* (Boston and New York: Houghton Mifflin, 1914), p. 362, n. 1.

57. For a thorough account of women's powerful oratorical presence as members of school boards, see Patricia Hollis, *Ladies Elect: Women in English Local Government, 1865–1914* (Oxford: Clarendon, 1987), chs. 2–3.

58. Peter T. Marsh, *Joseph Chamberlain: Entrepreneur in Politics* (New Haven: Yale University Press, 1994), p. 50; see generally ch. 3.

59. Roland Quinault, "John Bright and Joseph Chamberlain," *The Historical Journal* 28, no. 3 (1985), esp. pp. 626, 629–31.

60. In a letter to John Morley; cited in Quinault, "John Bright and Joseph Chamberlain," p. 630.

61. Belchem and Epstein, "Gentleman Leader Revisited."

62. Quoted in Harrison, "Rhetoric of Reform," p. 386.

63. My discussion of the Bulgarian atrocities agitation is drawn from R. T. Shannon, *Gladstone and the Bulgarian Agitation, 1876*, 2nd. ed. (Hassocks: Harvester, 1975).

64. See Matthew, *Gladstone*, 2: 41–46; Eugenio F. Biagini, *Liberty, Retrenchment and Reform: Popular Liberalism in the Age of Gladstone, 1860–1880* (Cambridge: Cambridge Uni-

versity Press, 1992), pp. 385–425; and A. J. P. Taylor, *The Trouble Makers: Dissent Over Foreign Policy, 1792–1939* (1957; London: Panther, 1969), pp. 63–64.

65. *GD*, 9: 47 (December 28, 1879).

66. Evidenced by his essay "On Eloquence," *The Eton Miscellany* 2, no. 8 (1827): 107–115; and an unpublished essay on "Public Speaking" written in the 1830s, later published with commentary by Loren Reid as "Gladstone's Essay on Public Speaking," *The Quarterly Journal of Speech* 39, no. 3 (October 1953): 265–72.

67. Quoted in Walter Bagehot, "Oxford and Mr. Gladstone" (1865), *The Collected Works of Walter Bagehot*, vol. 3, ed. Norman St John-Stevas (London: Economist, 1968), p. 443.

68. Calculated from *GD*, 14: 830–31.

69. Calculated from Arthur Tilney Bassett, *Gladstone's Speeches: Descriptive Index and Bibliography* (London: Methuen, 1916), pp. 6–90. For a detailed quantitative analysis of Gladstone's speech-making, see Joseph S. Meisel, "Words by the Numbers: A Quantitative Analysis and Comparison of the Oratorical Careers of William Ewart Gladstone and Winston Spencer Churchill," *Historical Research* 73, no. 182 (2000): 262–95.

70. As a *Times* leader observed: "It is the etiquette of the University of Oxford that its candidates shall observe the most rigorous silence towards it both before and during the election. They may not even approach the place while the seat is vacant; and when, after a decent interval, they venture to tread that most sacred ground, it must only be to pay formal visits and leave cards of thanks." *TT*, July 20, 1865, p. 8.

71. *The Manchester Guardian*, July 19, 1865, p. 3.

72. See Matthew, *Gladstone*, 1: 141.

73. *The Political Correspondence of Mr. Gladstone and Lord Granville, 1868–1871*, ed. Agatha Ramm, *Camden Third Series*, vol. 82 (1952): 274. Granville's letter complaining about stumping is on p. 266.

74. In addition to the treatments in the Magnus, Matthew, and Jenkins biographies, see also M. R. D. Foot's introduction to the reprint of W. E. Gladstone, *Midlothian Speeches, 1879* (New York, Humanities Press, 1971); Richard T. Shannon, "Midlothian: 100 Years After," Gladstone, *Politics and Religion: A Collection of Founder's Day Lectures Delivered at St. Deiniol's Library, Hawarden, 1967–83*, ed. Peter J. Jagger (London: Macmillan, 1985), Shannon, *Gladstone: Heroic Minister, 1865–1898* (London: Lane, 1999), chs. 6, 7; and Biagini, *Liberty, Retrenchment and Reform*, pp. 405–16.

75. *GD*, 9: 466.

76. *GD*, 9: 464.

77. *Punch*, December 13, 1879.

78. Speech at West Calder, November 27, 1879; Gladstone, *Midlothian Speeches, 1879*, p. 124.

79. Speech at the Edinburgh Corn Exchange, November 29, 1879; Gladstone, *Midlothian Speeches*, p. 148.

80. Speech at Birmingham, March 30, 1883; *Speeches of the Right Hon. Joseph Chamberlain, M. P., with a Sketch of his Life*, ed. Henry W. Lucy (London, 1885), p. 38.

81. Max Weber, "Politics as a Vocation" (1919), *From Max Weber: Essays in Sociology*, ed. H. H. Gerth and C. Wright Mills (New York: Oxford University Press, 1958), p. 107.

82. *TT*, November 29, 1879, p. 9.

83. *Annual Register*, 1880, p. 45.

84. "The Midlothian of the Metropolis: Lord Randolph at the Tory Caucus," *Pall Mall Gazette*, June 28, 1886; reprinted as Appendix 3 in R. F. Foster, *Lord Randolph Churchill: A Political Life* (Oxford: Clarendon, 1981), p. 410–11.

85. Lady Gwendolen Cecil, *Life of Robert Marquess of Salisbury*, 4 vols. (London: Hodder & Stoughton, 1922–32), 4: 165.

86. Matthew, "Rhetoric and Politics," p. 41.

87. Earl Curzon of Kedleston, *Modern Parliamentary Eloquence: The Rede Lecture Delivered Before the University of Cambridge, November 6, 1913* (London: Macmillan, 1913), p. 15.

88. Curzon, *Parliamentary Eloquence*, p. 15.

89. Quoted in Jephson, *Platform*, 2: 519.

90. William Saunders, *The New Parliament, 1880* (London, [1880]), p. 38.

91. "The Stump Ministry: Its First Session," *Blackwood's Magazine* 128, no. 780 (October 1880): 515–34.

92. H. D. Traill, "The Plague of Tongues," *The National Review* 6, no. 35 (January 1886): 620.

93. Speech at Birmingham, January 3, 1882; *Before Joseph Came into Egypt* [speeches by Joseph Chamberlain and others reprinted from newspaper accounts], ed. William Sykes (London, 1898), p. 49.

94. Speech at Birmingham, March 30, 1883; *Speeches of . . . Chamberlain*, p. 38.

95. A descriptive list of Salisbury's Union speeches appears in Appendix Two of Michael Pinto-Duschinsky, *The Political Thought of Lord Salisbury, 1854–68* (London: Constable, 1967), pp. 191–92.

96. Listed in Appendix Two of Pinto-Duschinsky, *Political Thought of . . . Salisbury*, p. 192.

97. See, F. S. Pulling, *The Life and Speeches of the Marquis of Salisbury, K. G.*, 2 vols. (London, 1885), 1: 178–85, 254–60, 2: 37–54, 71–74, 116–19, and 156–58. On Salisbury's "apprenticeship in platform oratory," see Peter Marsh, *The Discipline of Popular Government: Lord Salisbury's Domestic Statecraft, 1881–1902* (Hassocks: Harvester, 1978), p. 42.

98. Pulling, *Speeches of . . . Salisbury*, 2: 117. See also Colin Matthew, ed., *The Nineteenth Century* (Oxford: Oxford University Press, 2000), pp. 106–8.

99. Marsh, *Popular Government*, p. 187.

100. Cecil, *Salisbury*, 4: 162.

101. See Meisel, "Words by the Numbers," p. 278.

102. See Matthew, "Rhetoric and Politics," pp. 35–38.

103. Parry, *Liberal Government*, pp. 289–90, 302–3, 305–6.

104. Cecil, *Salisbury*, 4: 164.

105. For information on the origins, development, membership, and activities of the Birmingham and Edgbaston Debating Society, see John Alfred Langford, *Modern Birmingham and its Institutions, a Chronicle of Local Events from 1841 to 1871*, 2 vols. (Birmingham, [1873–77]), 1: 235–48.

106. Marsh, *Chamberlain*, p. 15.

107. Quinault, "John Bright and Joseph Chamberlain," p. 626.

108. *Mr. Chamberlain's Speeches*, ed. Charles W. Boyd, 2 vols. (London: Constable, 1914), 1: xiii.

109. *Speeches of . . . Chamberlain.*

110. Chamberlain to Gladstone, February 7, 1885. Gladstone Papers, BL Add. MS 44126, f. 65b.

111. Marsh, *Chamberlain*, p. 184.

112. T. H. S. Escott, *Randolph Spencer-Churchill, as a Product of his Age: Being a Personal and Political Monograph* (London, 1895), p. 195.

113. *Speeches of the Right Honourable Lord Randolph Churchill, M. P.*, ed. Louis J. Jennings, 2 vols. (London, 1889), 1: 201. In his speech on the same occasion, Salisbury stated that 120,000 tickets had been taken for the demonstration. *TT*, August 11, 1884, p. 7. The managers of the meeting produced a (doubtless inflated) estimate of 150,000 to 200,000. *Annual Register*, 1879, p. 112.

114. Escott, *Churchill*, p. 302.

115. Robert Rhodes James, *Lord Randolph Churchill* (London: Weidenfeld and Nicolson, 1959), p. 246.

116. Escott, *Churchill*, p. 296.

117. *Speeches . . . of Lord Randolph Churchill*, p. 52.

118. See his April 16, 1884 speech at Birmingham in *Speeches of . . . Lord Randolph Churchill*, 1: 131–40.

119. See *Speeches of . . . Lord Randolph Churchill*, 2: 68–86.

120. Peel, *Speech . . . at Glasgow*, p. 3. Details of the structure from pp. 3–4, and from Gash, *Peel*, 2: 154–55.

121. Colin Cunningham, *Victorian and Edwardian Town Halls* (London: Routledge & Kegan Paul, 1981), Appendix III: "a Chronological List of Town Halls, 1820–1914," pp. 252–99. According to Cunningham, although his list cannot be considered exhaustive, it includes "all the major buildings of the period and the majority of other typical buildings" (p. 252).

122. George Macaulay Trevelyan, *The Life of John Bright*, (Boston and New York: Houghton Mifflin, 1914), p. 85, n. 2; Asa Briggs, *Victorian Cities* (New York: Harper & Row, 1965), p. 123; Donald Read, *Cobden and Bright: A Victorian Political Partnership* (London: Arnold, 1967), p. 45.

123. *The Builder*, September 8, 1849, p. 429.

124. Elihu Burritt, *Walks in the Black Country and its Green Border-Land* (London, 1869), p. 85.

125. Birmingham Liberal Association, *John Bright Celebration, June 11th, 13th, & 14th, 1883: The Official Programme* (Birmingham, [1883]), p. 11.

126. *TT*, October 31, 1859, pp. 4, 6.

127. "Midlothian of the Metropolis," in Foster, *Churchill*, p. 411.

128. Montagu Williams, *Leaves of a Life*, 2 vols. (London, 1890), 2: 24. At least one press report differed from Williams's recollections, noting only that the weather "was not quite pleasant on Blackheath: there was a mist and a drizzle of rain." *The Illustrated London News*, February 7, 1874, p. 134.

129. Williams, *Leaves*, 2: 25.

130. *Kentish Mercury*, September 16, 1876, p. 5; *Kentish Independent*, September 16, 1876, n.p.

131. *GD*, 9: 153, n. 4.

132. *TT*, July 14, 1877, p. 13.

133. Magnus, *Gladstone*, p. 265. Morley writes of Gladstone speaking "With bare head in the raw air." Morley, *Gladstone*, 2: 588.

134. *The Treatment of the Irish Members and the Irish Political Prisoners. A Speech Delivered by the Right Hon. W. E. Gladstone, M. P., to the Staffordshire Liberals, at Hawarden Castle, August 20, 1888* (London, 1888), p. 3.

135. Quoted in Shannon, *Bulgarian Agitation*, p. 115.

136. Rhodes James, *Churchill*, p. 213.

137. See, e.g., Matthew, "Rhetoric and Politics," pp. 40–41.

138. "The Midlothian of the Metropolis," in Foster, *Churchill*, p. 411.

139. These disruptions are recorded in *Speech Delivered by Lord Randolph Churchill, M. P., at the Meeting of the Conservative Party at Perth, on the 5th of October, 1889* (London, 1889).

140. *Kentish Mercury*, October 28, 1871, pp. 4, 5; see also November 4, 1871, pp. 4, 6.

141. *Kentish Independent*, November 4, 1871, n.p.

142. *Speeches of . . . Lord Randolph Churchill*, 1: 334.

143. Peel, *Speeches . . . at Merchant Tailors' Hall*, p. 2.

144. *TT*, October 31, 1859, pp. 4, 6.

145. See Peter Brett, "Political Dinners in Early Nineteenth-Century Britain: Platform, Meeting-Place and Battleground," *History* 81, no. 264 (October 1996): 527–52.

146. Matthew, *Gladstone*, 2: 58.

147. Magnus, *Gladstone*, p. 265.

148. *Reminiscences of Lord Kilbracken* (London: Macmillan, 1931), pp. 110–11.

149. See Rhodes James, *Churchill*, p. 213.

150. A wealthy American background also helped Nancy Astor to be an effective campaigner. See Karen J. Musolf, *From Plymouth to Parliament: A Rhetorical History of Nancy Astor's 1919 Campaign* (New York: St. Martin's, 1999), p. 2.

151. Mrs. George Cornwallis-West, *The Reminiscences of Lady Randolph Churchill* (London: Arnold, 1908), p. 126.

152. *Daily Telegraph*, September 8, 1876; quoted in Matthew, "Rhetoric and Politics," p. 42.

153. *GD*, 9: 223 (May 31, 1877).

154. *Kentish Independent*, September 9, 1876, n.p.

155. Williams, *Leaves*, 2: 25–26.

156. Matthew, "Rhetoric and Politics," p. 41.

157. *Kentish Independent*, September 16, 1876, n.p.; *Kentish Mercury*, September 16, 1876, p. 5.

158. *GD*, 8: 53 (October 28, 1871).

159. *GD*, 9: 223 (May 31, 1877).

160. Gladstone, "Platform," p. 689.

161. *Speeches of . . . Lord Randolph Churchill*, 1: 255–56.

162. Quoted in Matthew, "Rhetoric and Politics," p. 45.

163. D. A. Hamer, "Gladstone: The Making of a Political Myth," *Victorian Studies* 22, no. 1 (1978): 35. See also Alison Winter, *Mesmerized: Powers of Mind in Victorian Britain* (Chicago: University of Chicago Press, 1998), pp. 333–41.

164. Kilbracken, *Reminiscences*, p. 112.

165. Williams, *Leaves,* 2: 26.

166. Williams, *Leaves,* 2: 28.

167. *The Diary of Beatrice Webb,* ed. Norman and Jeanne MacKenzie, vol. 1 (Cambridge, MA: Harvard University Press, 1982), p. 108.

168. "Midlothian of the Metropolis," in Foster, *Churchill,* p. 411.

169. Matthew, "Rhetoric and Politics," p. 41.

170. Patrick Joyce, *Democratic Subjects: The Self and the Social in Nineteenth-Century England* (Cambridge: Cambridge University Press, 1994), p. 98.

171. *Kentish Mercury,* November 4, 1871, p. 4.

172. Trevelyan, *Bright,* p. 269, n. 1.

173. Marsh, *Chamberlain,* p. 120.

174. Gladstone, *Midlothian Speeches,* p. 163.

175. *GD,* 9: 463 (November 29, 1879).

176. Cornwallis-West, *Reminiscences of Lady Randolph Churchill,* pp. 132–33.

177. See Matthew, *Gladstone,* 2: 58; and Joyce, *Democratic Subjects,* p. 98.

178. Matthew, *Gladstone,* 2: 58.

179. *TT,* March 20, 1880, p. 12. According to the report, "The Church was crowded, a large portion of the audience being ladies."

180. Cf. Eugenio F. Biagini, "Marshall's 1873 'Lectures to Women,'" *Quaderni di Storia dell'Economica Politica* 9, nos. 2–3 (1991), esp. pp. 338–39, 344–45.

181. Curzon, *Parliamentary Eloquence,* pp. 16–17.

182. See Matthew, *Gladstone,* 1: 135–37.

183. Cook and Keith, *British Historical Facts, 1830–1900,* p. 214.

184. Figures cited in Vincent, *Liberal Party,* p. 59.

185. H. Whorlow, *The Provincial Newspaper Society, 1836–1886* (London, 1886), p. 38.

186. Stephen Koss, *The Rise and Fall of the Political Press in Britain*: vol. 1, *The Nineteenth Century* (London: Hamilton, 1981), p. 1.

187. Inaugural speech to the Birmingham Conservative Club, October 17, 1884, *Speeches of . . . Lord Randolph Churchill,* 1: 204.

188. See Matthew, "Rhetoric and Politics," pp. 43–48.

189. Jephson, *Platform,* 2: 473, n. 1.

190. Quoted in *Annual Register,* 1880, p. 48.

191. Traill, "Plague of Tongues," p. 618.

192. Traill, "Plague of Tongues," p. 619.

193. Vincent, *Liberal Party,* p. 60; Matthew, "Rhetoric and Politics," p. 43.

194. *Kentish Mercury,* November 4, 1871, p. 6.

195. *Kentish Independent,* September 9, 1876, n.p.

196. Marsh, *Chamberlain,* p. 269.

197. Alfred Kinnear, "The Trade in Great Men's Speeches," *Contemporary Review* 75 (March 1899): 439–44; see also Matthew, "Rhetoric and Politics," p. 45.

198. Matthew, "Rhetoric and Politics," p. 46.

199. Kinnear, "Great Men's Speeches," p. 439.

200. Joyce, *Democratic Subjects,* p. 98.

201. "Mr Gladstone's Pilgrimage," *Blackwood's Magazine* 127, no. 771 (January 1880): 125.

202. See Michael Peel, "The Lost Voice of Public Speaking," *Financial Times*, January 10–11, 1998, p. xxii.

203. Bernard Shaw, "How I Became a Public Speaker," *Sixteen Self Sketches* (London: Constable, 1949), p. 59.

CONCLUSION

1. See *TT*, April 20, 1882, p. 8.

2. Based upon statistics for Parliament's sessional average time of daily sitting in Chris Cook and Brendan Keith, *British Historical Facts, 1830–1900* (London: Macmillan, 1975), pp. 102–3.

3. Based upon the estimate of 2 million sermons per year preached in the 1880s in A. Eubule Evans, "A Discourse Upon Sermons," *Macmillan's Magazine* 57, no. 337 (November 1887): 58.

4. See David Cannadine, *Lords and Landlords: The Aristocracy and the Towns, 1774–1967* (Leicester: Leicester University Press, 1980), pp. 73, 341, 344–45; and Cannadine, "The Transformation of Civic Ritual in Modern Britain: The Colchester Oyster Feast," *Past & Present* 94 (1982): 107–30.

5. The section draws primarily upon Don M. Cregier, *Bounder from Wales: Lloyd George's Career Before the First World War* (Columbia, MO: University of Missouri Press, 1976), chs. 1–3; John Grigg, *The Young Lloyd George* (London: Eyre and Methuen, 1973); and W. R. P. George, *The Making of Lloyd George* (London: Faber & Faber, 1976).

6. On Lloyd George's sermon-tasting, see William George, *My Brother and I* (London: Eyre & Spottiswoode, 1958), p. 79; and George, *Making*, pp. 117–18.

7. George, *Making*, p. 101.

8. Quoted in George, *Making*, p. 118.

9. See George, *Brother and I*, pp. 117–18.

10. George, *Making*, p. 123.

11. Quoted in George, *Making*, p. 127.

12. Grigg, *The Young Lloyd George*, p. 99.

13. For a useful discussion of Lloyd Geroge's oratory when a leading politician, see Roy Jenkins, *The Chancellors* (Londonn: Macmillan, 1998), pp. 181–82.

14. See, e.g., Alfred Kinnear, "The Trade in Great Men's Speeches," *The Contemporary Review* 75 (March 1899): 439–44; and Kinnear, "Parliamentary Reporting," *The Contemporary Review* 87 (March 1905): 369–75.

15. William Henry Whiteley, "The Social Composition of the House of Commons, 1865–1885" (Ph.D. diss., Cornell University, 1960), pp. 566–69; see also David Cannadine, *The Decline and Fall of the British Aristocracy* (New Haven: Yale University Press, 1990), pp. 184–95.

16. On Bevan's powers of oratory, see Michael Foot, *Aneuran Bevan: A Biography*, vol. 2 (London: Davis-Poynter, 1973), pp. 244–49. For a considerably less appreciative assessment of Kinnock's "prolix oratory" and "windbaggery," see Richard Heffernan and Mike Marqusee, *Defeat from the Jaws of Victory: Inside Kinnock's Labour Party* (London: Verso, 1992), pp. 105–6.

17. Quoted in Keith Hutchison, *The Decline and Fall of British Capitalism* (New York: Scribner, 1950), p. 89.

18. *Lord Riddell's War Diary, 1914–1918* (London: Nicholson & Watson, 1933), p. 67.

19. See Aaron L. Friedberg, *The Weary Titan: Britain and the Experience of Relative Decline, 1895–1905* (Princeton: Princeton University Press, 1988).

20. See, e.g., A. J. A. Morris, *The Scaremongers: The Advocacy of War and Rearmament, 1896–1914* (London: Routledge & Kegan Paul, 1984).

21. Virginia Woolf, "This Is the House of Commons" (1932), *The London Scene: Five Essays by Virginia Woolf* (London: Hogarth, 1982), p. 43.

22. Alan J. Lee, *The Origins of the Popular Press in England,* 1855–1914 (London: Croom Helm, 1976), p. 123.

23. H. C. G. Matthew, "Rhetoric and Politics in Great Britain, 1860–1950," in *Politics and Social Change in Britain: Essays Presented to A. F. Thompson,* ed. P. J. Waller (Sussex, UK: Harvester, 1987), p. 54.

24. P. G. Wodehouse, "The Great Sermon Handicap" (1923), *The Inimitable Jeeves* (London: Penguin, 1953), p. 135.

25. Alan D. Gilbert, *Religion and Society in Industrial England: Church, Chapel, and Social Change, 1740–1914* (London: Longman, 1976), p. viii.

26. Alan D. Gilbert, *The Making of Post-Christian Britain: A History of the Secularization of Modern Society* (London: Longman, 1980), p. 78.

27. Calculated from data in Robert Currie, Alan Gilbert, and Lee Horsley, *Churches and Churchgoers: Patterns of Church Growth in the British Isles Since 1700* (Oxford: Clarendon, 1977), Table 2.3, "Decennial British Church Membership Totals, 1800–1970," p. 25; and B. R. Mitchell, *British Historical Statistics* (Cambridge: Cambridge University Press, 1988), pp. 11–13.

28. See Ross McKibbin, *Classes and Cultures: England 1918–1951* (Oxford: Oxford University Press, 1998), ch. 7.

29. Raymond Cocks, *Foundations of the Modern Bar* (London: Sweet & Maxwell, 1983), p. 5.

30. David Hare, *Asking Around: Background to the David Hare Trilogy,* ed. Lyn Haill (London: Faber and Faber, 1993), p.130.

31. Max Beerbohm, "H. B. Irving as a Young Man" (1914), *The Incomparable Max* (London: Icon: 1964), p. 284.

32. John Goodbody, "The *Star*: Its Role in the Rise of the New Journalism," in *Papers for the Millions: The New Journalism in Britain, 1850s to 1914,* ed. Joel H. Wiener (New York: Greenwood, 1988), p. 150.

33. *DNB* (Alfred Harmsworth).

34. *DNB* (Alfred Harmsworth).

35. Matthew, "Rhetoric and Politics," p. 53.

36. Quoted in Stephen Koss, *The Rise and Fall of the Political Press in Britain,* vol. 1 (London: Hamilton, 1981), p. 358.

37. Asa Briggs, *The Birth of Broadcasting* (Oxford: Oxford University Press, 1995), p. 244.

38. Briggs, *Broadcasting,* p. 248.

39. A. J. P. Taylor, *English History, 1914–1945* (Oxford: Oxford University Press, 1965), p. 235.

40. See Briggs, *Broadcasting*, pp. 248–51.

41. Briggs, *Broadcasting*, p. 251.

42. Quoted in Ross McKibbin, *The Ideologies of Class: Social Relations in Britain, 1880–1950* (Oxford: Clarendon, 1990), p. 148.

43. Quoted in Peter Stansky, *On or About December 1910: Early Bloomsbury and its Intimate World* (Cambridge, MA: Harvard University Press, 1996), p. 2.

44. Isaiah Berlin, *Mr. Churchill in 1940* (1949; London: Murray, [1964]), p. 9.

BIBLIOGRAPHY

Outline

I. Manuscript and Archival Collections
II. Printed Primary Sources
- A. Speeches, Sermons, and Trials
- B. Diaries, Correspondence, Memoirs
- C. Parliamentary Papers
- D. Official Reports and Publications
- E. Contemporary Journalism and Pamphlets
- F. Major Newspapers and Periodicals
- G. Contemporary Fiction

III. Secondary Sources
- A. Biographies
- B. Books, Articles, and Theses
- C. Reference Works

I. Manuscript and Archival Collections

Bodleian Library, Oxford: Cuddesdon College MSS; MS Eng. th. e. 170.
British Library: Gladstone Papers.
Cambridge University Library: Cambridge Union Record Books.
Dr. Williams's Library, London: Henry Allon Papers.
Greenwich Local History Library: Gladstoniana.
Holker Library, Gray's Inn.
Lambeth Palace Library: Tait Papers; Palmer/Selborne Papers.
Lincoln's Inn Library.
Middle Temple Library.
Newnham College, Cambridge: Newnham College Debating Society Minute Books; Political Society Minute Books.

Oxford Union Society Library: Oxford Union Record Books.
Pusey House Library, Oxford: Liddon Diaries.
Spurgeon's College, London: Heritage Room Collection.

II. Printed Primary Sources

A. SPEECHES, SERMONS, AND TRIALS

Atlay, J. B. *The Tichborne Case.* London: Hodge, 1912.

[Bright, John.] *Speeches on Questions of Public Policy by John Bright, M. P.* (2 vols.). James E. Thorold Rogers, ed. London, 1868.

[Brougham, Henry.] *Speeches by Henry Lord Brougham* (4 vols.). Edinburgh, 1838.

[Burke, Edmund.] *The Works of the Right Honourable Edmund Burke, a New Edition*, vol. 3. London, 1803.

[Canning, George.] *Speeches of the Right Hon. George Canning Delivered on Public Occasions in Liverpool.* Thos. Kaye, ed. Liverpool, 1825.

[———.] *The Speeches of the Right Honourable George Canning, with a Memoir of His Life* (6 vols.). R. Thierry, ed. London, 1828.

[Chamberlain, Joseph.] *Speeches of the Right Hon. Joseph Chamberlain, M. P., with a Sketch of His Life.* Henry W. Lucy, ed. London, 1885.

[———.] *Mr. Chamberlain's Speeches* (2 vols.). Charles W. Boyd, ed. London: Constable, 1914.

[———, et al.] *Before Joseph Came into Egypt.* William Sykes, ed. London, 1898.

[Churchill, Lord Randolph.] *The Life and Speeches of Lord Randolph Henry Spencer-Churchill.* Frank Banfield, ed. London, [1884].

[———.] *Speeches of the Right Honourable Lord Randolph Churchill, M. P.* (2 vols.). Louis J. Jennings, ed. London, 1889.

[———.] *Speech Delivered by Lord Randolph Churchill, M. P., at the Meeting of the Conservative Part at Perth, on the 5th of October, 1889.* London, 1889.

[Churchill, Winston S.] *Winston S. Churchill: His Complete Speeches, 1897–1963* (8 vols.). Robert Rhodes James, ed. New York: Chelsea House, 1974.

Clarke, Edward. *Speeches by Sir Edward Clarke, Q. C., M. P.: Second Series, Chiefly Forensic.* London, [1894].

[Disraeli, Benjamin.] *Speech of the Right Hon. B. Disraeli, M. P. At the Free Trade Hall, Manchester, April 3, 1872.* London, [1872].

[———.] *Report of the Proceedings at the National Conference, Held at the Westminster Palace Hotel and of the Banquet at the Crystal Palace, on Monday, June 24th, 1872, Together with the Speeches of the Duke of Abercorn, the Right Hon. B. Disraeli, M. P., etc., etc.* London, [1872].

[———.] *Selected Speeches of the Late Right Honourable the Earl of Beaconsfield* (2 vols.). T. E. Kebbel, ed. London, 1882.

[Fox, Charles James.] *The Speeches of the Right Honourable Charles James Fox in the House of Commons* (6 vols.). London, 1815.

[Gladstone, William Ewart.] *Midlothian Speeches, 1879.* 1879. New York: Humanities Press, 1971.
[———.] *The Treatment of the Irish Members and the Irish Political Prisoners. A Speech Delivered by the Right Hon. W. E. Gladstone, M. P., to the Staffordshire Liberals, at Hawarden Castle, August 20, 1888.* London, 1888.
[———.] *Gladstone's Speeches: Descriptive Index and Bibliography.* Arthur Tilney Bassett, ed. London: Metheun, 1916.
———. "A Recording for Thomas Edison's Phonograph 1889." *Great Political Speeches: Selected from over 100 Years of Archive Recording.* Hodder Headline Audiobooks (HH660), 1996.
Haly, W. T. *The Opinions of Sir Robert Peel, Expressed in Parliament and in Public.* London, 1843.
Hyde, H. Montgomery. *Famous Trials: Oscar Wilde.* Harmondsworth: Penguin, 1962.
Kelly, Bernard W. *Famous Advocates and their Speeches: British Forensic Eloquence, from Lord Erskine to Lord Russell of Killowen, with an Historical Introduction.* London: Sweet & Maxwell, 1921.
Knott, George H., ed. *The Trial of William Palmer,* 3rd ed. Revised by Eric R. Watson. London: Hodge, 1952.
Liddon, H. P. *Some Elements of Religious Life: Lent Lectures, 1870,* 5th and cheaper ed. London, 1885.
———. *Advent in St. Paul's: Sermons Bearing Chiefly on the Two Comings of Our Lord,* 2nd ed., revised (2 vols.). London, 1889.
Parliamentary Debates. New Series. 3rd Series. 4th Series.
[Peel, Robert.] *Speech of the Right Hon. Sir Robert Peel, Bart. M. P., Delivered at the Dinner Given to Him by the Merchants, Bankers, and Traders of the City of London, at Merchant Tailors' Hall, the 11th of May, 1835.* London, [1835].
[———.] *Speech of Sir R. Peel, Bart. M. P., at Glasgow, January 13, 1837.* Glasgow, [1837].
[———.] *Speeches of the Rt. Hon. Sir Robert Peel, Bart., Lord Stanley, and Sir James Graham, Bart., at Merchant Tailors' Hall, May 12, 1838.* London, 1838.
[———.] *Tamworth Election: Speech of Sir Robert Peel, June 28, 1841.* London, 1841.
[———.] *The Speeches of the Right Honourable Sir Robert Peel, Bart., Delivered in the House of Commons* (4 vols.). London, 1853.
[Phillips, Charles.] *Speeches of Charles Phillips, Esq. Delivered at the Bar and on Various Public Occasions in Ireland and England,* 2nd ed., 1822.
[Pitt, William.] *The Speeches of the Right Honourable William Pitt in the House of Commons* (4 vols.). London, 1806.
Pulling, F. S. *The Life and Speeches of the Marquis of Salisbury, K. G.* (2 vols.). London, 1885.
Spurgeon, Charles H. *The New Park Street Pulpit* (6 vols.). London, 1855–60.
———. *The Metropolitan Tabernacle Pulpit* (57 vols.). London, 1861–1917.
[Tait, Archibald Campbell.] *A Charge, Delivered in November MDCCCLVIII, to the Clergy of the Diocese of London, at His Primary Visitation, by Archibald Campbell, Lord Bishop of London,* 7th ed. London, 1858.
[———.] *A Charge, Delivered in December 1862, to the Clergy of the Diocese of London, by Archibald Campbell, Lord Bishop of London.* London, 1862.
———. *The Church of the Future.* London, 1880.

B. DIARIES, CORRESPONDENCE, MEMOIRS

Alverstone, Viscount. *Recollections of Bar and Bench.* London: Arnold, 1914.

Arnold, Matthew. *Letters of Matthew Arnold* (2 vols.). George W. E. Russell, ed. London, 1895–96.

Ballantine, William. *Some Experiences of a Barrister's Life,* 6th ed. London, 1890.

Bancroft, George Pleydell. *Stage and Bar.* London: Faber, 1939.

[Bancroft, Squire and Marie.] *Mr. & Mrs. Bancroft On and Off Stage, Written by Themselves,* 4th ed. (2 vols.). London, 1888.

Bancroft, Squire. *Empty Chairs.* New York: Stokes, 1925.

[Brougham, Henry.] *The Life and Times of Henry Lord Brougham, by Himself* (3 vols.). Edinburgh, 1871.

Churchill, Winston S. *My Early Life: A Roving Commission.* 1930. London: Cooper, 1989.

Clarke, Edward. *The Story of My Life.* London: Murray, 1918.

Cornwallis-West, Mrs. George. *The Reminiscences of Lady Randolph Churchill.* London: Arnold, 1908.

[Dickens, Charles.] *The Letters of Charles Dickens,* vol. 1. Madeline House and Graham Storey, eds. Oxford: Clarendon, 1965.

[Disraeli, Benjamin.] *Disraeli's Reminiscences.* Helen M. Swartz and Marvin Swartz, eds. New York: Stein and Day, 1976.

[Eliot, George.] *The George Eliot Letters,* vol. 5. Gordon S. Haight, ed. New Haven: Yale University Press, 1955.

Everett, William. *On the Cam: Lectures on the University of Cambridge in England.* Cambridge, 1865.

Gladstone, William Ewart. *The Gladstone Diaries* (14 vols.). M. R. D. Foot and H. C. G. Matthew, eds. Oxford: Oxford University Press, 1968–94.

[———.] *The Gladstone Papers.* [A. Tilney Bassett, ed.] London: Cassell, 1930.

[———.] *The Political Correspondence of Mr. Gladstone and Lord Grenville, 1868–1871.* Agatha Ramm, ed. Camden Third Series, vol. 82 (1952).

[———.] *The Prime Ministers' Papers: W. E. Gladstone,* vol. 1: *Autobiographica.* John Brooke and Mary Sorenson, eds. London: HMSO, 1971.

Greville, Charles. *The Greville Diary, Including Passages Hitherto Withheld from Publication* (2 vols.). Philip Whitwell Wilson, ed. Garden City, NY: Doubleday, 1927.

[Godley, Arthur, Lord Kilbracken.] *Reminiscences of Lord Kilbracken.* London: Macmillan 1931.

Guthrie, David K. and Charles K. Guthrie. *Autobiography of Thomas Guthrie, D.D. and Memoir by his Sons,* Popular Edition. London, 1877.

Jay, Cyrus. *The Law: What I Have Seen, What I have Heard, and What I Have Known.* London, 1869.

Macready, William Charles. *Macready's Reminiscences, and Selections from his Diaries and Letters* (2 vols.). Frederick Pollock, ed. London, 1875.

———. *The Diaries of William Charles Macready, 1833–1851* (2 vols.). William Toynbee, ed. London: Chapman and Hall, 1912.

Morley, John. *Recollections* (2 vols.). London: Macmillan, 1917.

[Nicholson, Renton.] *The Lord Chief Baron Nicholson: An Autobiography.* London, [1860].

Palmer, Roundell, Earl of Selborne. *Memorials: Family and Personal, 1766–1865* (2 vols.). London, 1896.

———. *Memorials: Personal and Political, 1865–1895* (2 vols.). London, 1898.

Parker, Joseph. *A Preacher's Life: An Autobiography and an Album.* Boston, 1899.

Phillips, Ann, ed. *A Newnham Anthology.* Cambridge: Cambridge University Press, 1979.

Pollock, Frederick. *Personal Remembrances of Sir Frederick Pollock, Second Baronet, Sometime Queen's Remembrancer* (2 vols.). London, 1887.

[Riddell, George Allardice, Baron.] *Lord Riddell's War Diary, 1914–1918.* London: Nicholson & Watson, 1933.

Robinson, Mr. Serjeant [Benjamin C.] *Bench and Bar: Reminiscences of One of the Last of an Ancient Race,* 4th ed. London, 1894.

Rogers, Samuel. *Recollections.* London, 1859.

Shaw, Bernard. "How I Became a Public Speaker." *Sixteen Self Sketches.* London: Constable, 1949.

Smith, John. *Sketches of Cantabs.* London, 1849.

[Spurgeon, Charles H.] *The Autobiography of Charles H. Spurgeon, Compiled from his Diary, Letters, and Records by his Wife and his Private Secretary* (4 vols.). London, 1897–1900.

[Stanley, Edward Henry, 15th Earl of Derby.] *Disraeli, Derby and the Conservative Party: Journals and Memoirs of Edward Henry. Lord Stanley, 1849–1869.* John Vincent, ed. Hassocks: Harvester, 1987.

[———.] *A Selection from the Diaries of Edward Henry Stanley, 15th Earl of Derby (1826–93) Between September 1869 and March 1878.* John Vincent, ed. *Camden Fifth Series,* vol. 4 (1994).

[Trelawny, John.] *The Parliamentary Diaries of Sir John Trelawny, 1858–1865.* T. A. Jenkins, ed. *Camden Fourth Series,* vol. 40 (1990).

[———.] "The Parliamentary Diaries of Sir John Trelawny, 1868–1873." T. A. Jenkins, ed. *Camden Fifth Series,* vol. 3 (1994).

Verney, Richard Greville, Lord Willoughby de Broke. *The Passing Years.* London: Constable, 1924.

Walpole, Horace. *Journal of the Reign of King George the Third from the Year 1771 to 1783* (2 vols.). London, 1859.

Webb, Beatrice. *The Diary of Beatrice Webb,* vol. 1. Norman and Jeanne MacKenzie, eds. Cambridge, MA: Harvard University Press, 1982.

Wedmore, Frederick. *Memories,* 2nd ed. London: Methuen, 1912.

White, William. *The Inner Life of the House of Commons* (2 vols.). London, 1897.

Williams, Montagu. *Leaves of a Life* (2 vols.). London, 1890.

———. *Later Leaves.* London, 1891.

[Wodehouse, John, 1st Earl of Kimberley.] *The Journal of John Wodehouse, First Earl of Kimberley, for 1862–1902.* Angus Hawkins and John Powell, eds. *Camden Fifth Series,* vol. 9 (1997).

Wraxall, Nathaniel W. *The Historical and Posthumous Memoirs of Sir Nathaniel William Wraxall, 1772–1784* (5 vols.). Henry B. Wheately, ed. London, 1884.

C. PARLIAMENTARY PAPERS

Census of Great Bitain, 1851: Religious Worship, and Education, Scotland. PP, 1854, vol. 59.

Population of Great Britain, 1851: Religious Worship in *England* and *Wales*. PP, 1852–3, vol. 89.

Report from the Select Committee on Legal Education; Together with the Minutes of Evidence, Appendix and Index. PP, 1846, vol. 10.

Report of Her Majesty's Commissioners Appointed to Inquire into the Revenues and Management of Certain Colleges and Schools, and the Studies Pursued and Instruction Given Therein. PP, 1864, vols. 20–21.

A Report of His Majesty's Commissioners Appointed by Virtue of an Act of Parliament Passed in the Fifty-Eighth Year of the Reign of His Late Majesty King Geo. III c. 45; Intutled "An Act for Building and Promoting the Building of Additional Churches in Populous Parishes." PP, 1821, vol. 10.

Report of the Committee Appointed by the Prime Minister to Inquire into the Position of the Classics in the Educational System of the United Kingdom. London: HMSO, 1921.

Returns Showing the Number of Churches (Including Cathedrals) in Every Diocese in *England* Which Have Been Built or Restored at a Cost Exceeding £. 500 Since the Year 1840. PP, 1876, vol. 58.

D. OFFICIAL REPORTS AND PUBLICATIONS

Birmingham Liberal Association. *John Bright Celebration, June 11th, 13th, & 14th, 1883: The Official Programme.* Birmingham, [1883].

Cambridge Union Society. *Annual Report.* Cambridge: Fabb & Tyler, 1907.

[———.] *Demosthenes Demobilized: A Record of the Cambridge Union Society Debates February, 1919 - June, 1920.* Cambridge: Heffer, 1920.

———. *Inaugural Proceedings.* London, 1866.

Forensic Society. *List of Members, December 1832.* London, 1832.

Hardwicke Society. *Dinner to Sir Edward Clarke, July 22, 1904.* London: Spottiswoode, 1904.

———. *Rules and List of Members.* London: Straker, 1922.

The New Palace of Westminster, 15th ed. London, 1858.

[Newnham College, Cambridge.] *Newnham College Register,* vol. 1, *1871–1923,* 2nd ed. Cambridge: Newnham College, 1979.

Newnham College Club. *Cambridge Letter &c.* Various years.

[Oxford Union Society.] *Catalogue of the Library of the Oxford Union Society,* 3rd ed. Oxford, 1852.

[———.] *Proceedings of the Oxford Union Society on Thursday, May 19th, 1898, Being the Day of Mr. Gladstone's Death.* Oxford, 1898.

[———.] *Rules and Regulations of the Oxford Union Society, Corrected to October, 1858.* Oxford, 1858.

———. *Rules and Regulations of the Oxford Union Society, Corrected to October 1st, 1908.* Oxford: Bryan, 1908.

[United Debating Society, Oxford.] *Laws and Transactions of the United Debating Society, Oxford* [reprint]. Oxford, 1872.

[University of Cambridge.] *The Historical Register of the University of Cambridge: Being a Supplement to the Calendar with a Record of University Offices Honours and Distinctions to the Year 1910*. J. R. Tanner, ed. Cambridge: Cambridge University Press, 1917.

[University of Oxford.] *The Historical Register of the University of Oxford: Being a Supplement to the Oxford University Calendar with an Alphabetical Record of University Honours and Distinctions, Completed to the End of Trinity Term, 1900*. Oxford: Clarendon, 1900.

E. CONTEMPORARY JOURNALISM AND PAMPHLETS

Walter Bagehot. "Mr. Gladstone" (1860). *The Collected Works of Walter Bagehot*, vol. 3. Norman St John-Stevas, ed. London: Economist, 1968.

———. "Oxford and Mr. Gladstone" (1865). *The Collected Works of Walter Bagehot*, vol. 3. Norman St John-Stevas, ed. London: Economist, 1968.

C., E. G. "Law Reform in the Late Parliament." *The Law Magazine and Law Review: or, Quarterly Journal of Jurisprudence* 20, no. 39 (November 1865): 38–51.

Carlyle, Thomas. "The Stump Orator" (1850). *Latter-Day Pamphlets*. London, 1858.

Dale, R. W. "George Dawson: Politician, Lecturer, and Preacher." *The Nineteenth Century* 2, no. 6 (August 1877): 44–61.

Editor of the *Globe*. *Sir Robert Peel and his Last Tamworth Oration Shortly Considered*. Edinburgh, 1835.

Escott, T. H. S. "The House of Commons: Its *Personnel* and its Oratory." *Fraser's Magazine* (New Series) 10, no. 58 (October 1874): 504–17.

Evans, A. Eubule. "A Discourse Upon Sermons," *Macmillan's Magazine* 58, no. 337 (November 1887): 58–63.

Francis, George Henry. "Contemporary Orators" (16 parts). *Fraser's Magazine* 31, no. 184 (April 1845) to 34, no. 204 (December 1846).

[———.] "A Batch of Parliamentary Barristers." *Fraser's Magazine* 36, no. 213 (September 1847): 310–24.

[Gladstone, William Ewart.] "On Eloquence." *The Eton Miscellany* 2, no. 8 (1827): 107–15.

———. "The Platform: Its Rise and Progress" [review of Jephson, *The Platform*]. *The Nineteenth Century* 31, no. 182 (April 1892): 686–89.

Grey, [Henry George, 3rd] Earl. "The House of Commons." *The Nineteenth Century* 15, no. 85 (March 1884): 507–36.

Harvey, W. "Spurgeon as Preacher" (2 parts). *The Preacher and Homiletic Monthly* 5, no. 9 (June 1881): 527–29; 5, no. 11 (August 1881): 655–58.

Hayward, Abraham. "The British Parliament: Its History and Eloquence." *The Quarterly Review* 132, no. 264 (April 1872): 450–95.

Hitchman, Francis. "The Penny Press." *Macmillan's Magazine* 43, no. 257 (March 1881): 385–98.

Holland, Henry Scott. "Books of the Month: Life and Letters of Henry Parry Liddon." *The Commonwealth: A Christian Social Magazine* 10, no. 1 (January 1905): 30.

Holme, John Stanford. "Mr. Spurgeon: His Variety, Freshness, and Power as a Preacher." *The Preacher and Homiletic Monthly* 5, no. 2 (November 1880): 111–12.

Jerrold, Blanchard. "On the Manufacture of Public Opinion." *The Nineteenth Century* 13, no. 76 (1883): 1080–92.

Kinnear, Alfred. "The Trade in Great Men's Speeches." *The Contemporary Review* 75 (March 1889): 439–44.

———. "Parliamentary Reporting." *The Contemporary Review* 87 (March 1905): 369–75.

"Local Recollections of Serjeant Wilkins (from a Birmingham paper)." *The Law Times*, August 4, 1857, pp. 23–24.

Lucy, Henry W. *A Diary of Two Parliaments: The Disraeli Parliament, 1874–1880*, 2nd ed. London, 1885.

———. *A Diary of the Salisbury Parliament, 1886–1892*. London, 1892.

———. *Men and Manners in Parliament.* London: Unwin, 1919.

McCarthy, Justin. "Some Great English Lawyers." *The Galaxy* 14 , no. 6 (December 1872): 787–97.

"Men of the Day, No. 16: The Rev. Charles Spurgeon." *Vanity Fair*, December 10, 1870.

"Mr. Gladstone's Pilgrimage." *Blackwood's Magazine* 127, no. 771 (January 1880): 124–38.

Nicholson, A. P. "Parliamentary Reporting—A Reply." *The Contemporary Review* 87 (April 1905): 577–82.

Nicholson, Edward B. "The Oxford Union." *Macmillan's Magazine* 28, no. 168 (October 1873): 567–76.

"On Circuit." *Chambers's Journal of Popular Literature.* August 16, 1956, pp. 97– 100.

Parker, Joseph. "Mr. Gladstone Close at Hand: A Personal Sketch." *The New Review* 4, no. 22 (March 1891): 204–12.

Paul, Herbert. "The Victorian Novel" (1897). *Men & Letters.* London: Lane, 1901.

"The Prisoners' Counsel Bill." *The Law Magazine, or Quarterly Review of Jurisprudence* 15, no. 2 (May 1836): 394–402.

Richards, James. "Preachers of the Day." *Temple Bar* 70 (April 1884): 484–502.

Rogers, J. Guinness. "Chatter Versus Work in Parliament." *The Nineteenth Century* 16, no. 91 (September 1884): 396–411.

"The State of the Profession." *The Law Review and Quarterly Journal of British and Foreign Jurisprudence* 3 (1845–46): 348–49.

[Stephen, James Fitzjames.] "The Morality of Advocacy." *The Cornhill Magazine* 3 , no. 16 (April 1861): 446–59.

[———.] "The Bars of France and England." *The Cornhill Magazine* 10, no. 60 (December 1864): 672–82.

"The Stump Ministry: Its First Session." *Blackwood's Magazine* 128, no. 780 (October 1880): 515–34.

Traill, H. D. "The Plague of Tongues." *The National Review* 6, no. 35 (January 1886): 616–30.

F. MAJOR NEWSPAPERS AND PERIODICALS

(Other newspapers and periodicals, largely drawn from volumes of clippings, are cited in the notes.)

The Annual Register.
The Clergyman's Magazine.
The Homelist.
Kentish Independent.
Kentish Mercury.
The Law Journal.
The Law Times.
The Law Review, or Quarterly Journal of Jurisprudence.
The Manchester Guardian.
The Penny Pulpit.
The Times.

G. CONTEMPORARY FICTION

Dickens, Charles. *The Pickwick Papers.* 1836–37.
———. *The Old Curiosity Shop. A Tale.* 1840–41.
Eliot, George. *Middlemarch.* 1871–72.
Gilbert, W. S. and Arthur Sullivan. *The Complete Plays of Gilbert and Sullivan.* New York: Modern Library, [1936].
Kingsley, Charles. *Yeast: A Problem.* 1851.
Trollope, Anthony. *Barchester Towers.* 1857.
———. *The Three Clerks.* 1858.
———. *Orley Farm.* 1861.
———. *Can You Forgive Her?* 1864–65.
———. *Phineas Finn.* 1869.
———. *The Eustace Diamonds.* 1873.
———. *Phineas Redux.* 1874.
Wodehouse, P. G. "The Great Sermon Handicap." 1923.

III. Secondary Works

A. BIOGRAPHIES

Ackroyd, Peter. *Dickens.* London: Sinclair-Stevenson, 1990.
Adamson, William. *The Life of Joseph Parker, Pastor of the City Temple, London.* London: Revell, [1902].
[Anonymous.] *William Morley Punshon: Preacher and Orator, 1824–1881.* London, 1881.
Ashley, Evelyn. *The Life and Correspondence of Henry John Temple Viscount Palmerston* (2 vols.). London, 1879.
Ausubel, Herman. *John Bright, Victorian Reformer.* New York: Wiley, 1966.
Ayling, Stanley. *The Elder Pitt, Earl of Chatham.* London: Collins, 1976.

Bebbington, D. W. *William Ewart Gladstone: Faith and Politics in Victorian Britain.* Grand Rapids, MI: Erdmans, 1993.

Beerbohm, Max. "H. B. Irving as a Young Man" (1914). *The Incomparable Max.* London: Icon, 1964.

Belchem, John. *'Orator' Hunt: Henry Hunt and English Working-Class Radicalism.* Oxford: Clarendon, 1985.

Benson, Arthur Christopher. *The Life of Edward White Benson, Sometime Archbishop of Canterbury* (2 vols.). London, 1899.

Berlin, Isaiah. *Mr. Churchill in 1940.* 1949. London: Murray, [1964].

Birrell, Augustine. *Sir Frank Lockwood: A Biographical Sketch.* London, 1898.

Blake, Robert. *Disraeli.* London: Eyre & Spottiswoode, 1966.

Brooke, Stopford A. *Life and Letters of Frederick W. Robertson* (2 vols.). London, 1865.

Brown, Stewart J. *Thomas Chalmers and the Godly Commonwealth in Scotland.* Oxford: Oxford University Press, 1982.

Butler, Henry Montagu. *Lord Chatham as an Orator.* Oxford: Clarendon, 1912.

Cannadine, David. *G. M. Trevelyan: A Life in History.* New York: Norton, 1993.

Cecil, Lady Gwendolen. *Life of Robert Marquess of Salisbury* (4 vols.). London: Hoder & Stoughton, 1922–32.

Coleridge, Ernest Hartley. *Life & Correspondence of John Duke Lord Coleridge, Lord Chief Justice of England* (2 vols.). London: Heinemann, 1904.

Cregier, Don M. *Bounder from Wales: Lloyd George's Career Before the First World War.* Columbia, MO: University of Missouri Press, 1976.

Davidson, Randall Thomas and William Benham. *Life of Archibald Campbell Tait, Archbishop of Canterbury*, 3rd ed. (2 vols.) London, 1891.

Douglas, James. *The Prince of Preachers: A Sketch; A Portraiture; and a Tribute.* London, 1893.

Drummond, Lewis. *Spurgeon: Prince of Preachers.* Grand Rapids, MI: Kregel, 1992.

Ehrman, John. *The Younger Pitt: The Years of Acclaim.* New York: Dutton, 1969.

Epstein, James. *The Lion of Freedom: Feargus O'Connor and the Chartist Movement, 1832–1842.* London: Croom Helm, 1982.

Escott, T. H. S. *Randolph Spencer-Churchill, as a Product of his Age: Being a Personal and Political Monograph.* London, 1895.

Farrar, Reginald. *The Life of Frederic William Farrar, D.D., F.R.S., etc., Sometime Dean of Canterbury*, Revised ed. London: Nisbet, 1905.

Findlay, James F., Jr. *Dwight L. Moody: American Evangelist, 1837–1899.* Chicago: University of Chicago Press, 1969.

Foot, Michael. *Aneuran Bevan: A Biography*, vol. 2. London: Davis-Poynter, 1973.

Foster, R. F. *Lord Randolph Churchill: A Political Life.* Oxford: Clarendon, 1981.

Fraser, William. *Disraeli and His Day.* London, 1891.

Fullerton, W. Y. *C. H. Spurgeon: A Biography.* London: Williams and Norgate, 1920.

Gardiner, A. G. *The Life of Sir William Harcourt* (2 vols.). New York: Doran, [1923?].

Gash, Norman. *Sir Robert Peel: The Life of Sir Robert Peel After 1830.* London: Longman, 1972.

George, W. R. P. *The Making of Lloyd George.* London: Faber & Faber, 1976.

George, William. *My Brother and I.* London: Eyre & Spottiswoode, 1958.

Grigg, John. *The Young Lloyd George*. London: Eyre and Methuen, 1973.
Guinness, Mrs. Grattan. *"She Spake of Him." Being Recollections of the Loving Labours and Early Death of the Late Mrs. Henry Denning*, 6th ed. Bristol, 1873.
Guizot, Francois. *Memoirs of Sir Robert Peel*. London, 1857.
Hanna, William. *Memoirs of the Life and Writings of Thomas Chalmers, D.D., LL.D.* (4 vols.). Edinburgh, 1849–52.
Hanworth, Lord. *Lord Chief Baron Pollock: A Memoir by his Grandson*. London: Murray, 1929.
Hinde, Wendy. *George Canning*. London: Collins, 1973.
Jacks, Lawrence Persall. *Life and Letters of Stopford Brooke* (2 vols.). London: Murray, 1917.
Jenkins, Roy. *Gladstone*. London: Macmillan, 1995.
Johnston, John Octavius. *Life and Letters of Henry Parry Liddon, D.D., D.C.L., L.L.D.* London: Longmans, 1904.
Jolliffe, John. *Raymond Asquith: Life and Letters*. London: Collins, 1980.
Kruppa, Patricia Stallings. *Charles Haddon Spurgeon: A Preacher's Progress*. New York and London: Garland 1982.
Lathbury, D. C. *Mr. Gladstone*. London: Mowbray, 1907.
Lewis, J. R. *Certain Private Incidents: The Rise and Fall of Edwin James QC., MP.* Newcastle-upon-Tyne: Templar North, 1980.
Macdonald, Frederic W. *The Life of William Morley Punshon, LL.D.* London, 1887.
Magnus, Phillip. *Gladstone: A Biography*. London: Murray, 1954.
Marsh, Peter T. *Joseph Chamberlain: Entrepreneur in Politics*. New Haven: Yale University Press, 1994.
Matthew, H. C. G. *Gladstone* (2 vols.). Oxford: Oxford University Press, 1986–95.
Maurois, André. *Disraeli: A Picture of the Victorian Age*. Hamish Miles, tr. New York: Appleton, 1928.
Monypenny, William Flavelle and George Earle Buckle. *The Life of Benjamin Disraeli, Earl of Beaconsfield* (6 vols.). London: Murray, 1910–20.
Morley, John. *Burke*. London, 1897.
———. *The Life of William Ewart Gladstone* (3 vols.). London: Macmillan, 1903.
Oliphant, Mrs. [Margaret]. *Minister of the National Scotch Church, London, Illustrated by his Journals and Correspondence*, 2nd ed., revised (2 vols.). London, 1862.
Read, Donald. *Cobden and Bright: A Victorian Political Partnership*. London: Arnold, 1967.
———. *Peel and the Victorians*. London: Blackwell, 1987.
Reid, Loren. *Charles James Fox: A Man for the People*. Columbia, MO: University of Missouri Press, 1969.
Rhodes James, Robert. *Lord Randolph Churchill*. London: Weidenfeld and Nicolson, 1959.
———. *Churchill: A Study in Failure, 1900–1939*. Harmondsworth: Penguin, 1973.
Robbins, Keith. *John Bright*. London: Routledge & Kegan Paul, 1979.
Ross, Bob L. *A Pictorial Biography of C. H. Spurgeon*. Pasadena, TX: Pilgrim, 1974.
Russell, G. W. E. *Dr. Liddon*. London: Mowbray, 1905.
Russell, Lord John. *Memorials and Correspondence of Charles James Fox* (4 vols.). London, 1853–7.
Shannon, R. T. *Gladstone*, vol. 1. London: Hamilton, 1982.
———. *Gladstone: Heroic Minister, 1865–1898*. London: Penguin, 1999.

[Smith, Frederick W. F.], Earl of Birkenhead. *Frederick Edwin Earl of Birkenhead: The First Phase.* London: Butterworth, 1933.

Standley, Fred L. "Stopford Augustus Brooke: Studies Toward a Biography." Ph.D. diss. Northwestern University, 1964.

———. *Stopford Brooke.* New York: Twayne, 1972.

Stanhope, Earl. *Life of the Right Honourable William Pitt,* 3rd ed. (4 vols.). London, 1867.

Stansky, Peter. *Gladstone: A Progress in Politics.* Boston: Little, Brown, 1979.

Strachey, Lytton. *Eminent Victorians: Cardinal Manning, Florence Nightingale, Dr. Arnold, and General Gordon.* London: Chatto & Windus, 1918.

Taylor, H. A. *The Strange Case of Andrew Bonar Law.* London: Paul, [1932].

Tomline, George. *Memoirs of the Life of the Right Honourable William Pitt,* 4th ed. (3 vols.). London, 1822.

Trevelyan, George Macaulay. *The Life of John Bright.* Boston and New York: Houghton Mifflin, 1914.

Trevelyan, George Otto. *The Early History of Charles James Fox,* 3rd ed. London, 1881.

Trollope, Anthony. *The Life of Cicero* (2 vols.). London, 1880.

Walker-Smith, Derek and Edward Clarke. *The Life of Sir Edward Clarke.* London: Butterworth, 1939.

Walpole, Spencer. *The Life of Lord John Russell* (2 vols.). London, 1889.

B. BOOKS, ARTICLES, AND THESES

Abel-Smith, Brian and Robert Stevens. *Lawyers and the Courts: A Sociological Study of the English Legal System, 1750–1965.* London: Heinemann, 1967.

———. *In Search of Justice: Society and the Legal System.* London: Lane, 1968.

Adams, Pauline. *Somerville for Women: An Oxford College, 1879–1993.* Oxford: Oxford University Press, 1996.

Allen, Peter. *The Cambridge Apostles: The Early Years.* Cambridge: Cambridge University Press, 1978.

Altholz, Joseph L. *The Religious Press in Britain, 1760–1900.* Westport, CT: Greenwood, 1989.

Anderson, Olive. "Women Preachers in Mid-Victorian Britain: Some Reflexions on Feminism, Popular Religion and Social Change." *The Historical Journal* 12, no. 3 (1969): 467–84.

Andrew, Donna T. *London Debating Societies, 1776–1799.* London: London Record Society, 1994.

Arnstein, Walter L. "Queen Victoria Opens Parliament: The Disinvention of Tradition." *Historical Research* 63, no. 151 (1990): 178–94

———. "Queen Victoria's Speeches from the Throne: A New Look." In *Government and Institutions in the Post-1832 United Kingdom.* Alan O'Day, ed. Lewiston: Mellen, 1995.

Arthurs, H. W. "Special Courts, Special Law: Legal Pluralism in Nineteenth Century England." In *Law Economy and Society, 1750–1914: Essays in the History of English Law.* G. R. Rubin and David Sugarman, eds. Abingdon: Professional Books, 1984.

Aspinall, A. "The Reporting and Publishing of the House of Commons' Debates,

1771–1834." In *Essays Presented to Sir Lewis Namier.* Richard Pares and A. J. P. Taylor, eds. London: Macmillan, 1956.

Atkinson, J. Maxwell and Paul Drew. *Order in Court: The Organisation of Verbal Interaction in Judicial Settings.* Atlantic Highlands, NJ: Humanities Press, 1979.

Austin, John. *The Province of Jurisprudence Determined* and *The Uses of the Study of Jurisprudence.* London, 1832.

"Bagehot: The Golden Age of the Commons." *The Economist,* January 10, 1998, p. 50.

Bailey, Gemma, ed. *Lady Margaret Hall: A Short History.* London: Oxford University Press, 1923.

Bahlman, Dudley W. R. "The Queen, Mr. Gladstone, and Church Patronage." *Victorian Studies* 3, no. 4 (1960): 349–80.

Baker, J. H. "History of the Gowns Worn at the English Bar." *Costume,* no. 9 (1975), pp. 15–21.

———. *An Introduction to English Legal History,* 2nd ed. London: Butterworths, 1979.

Barish, Jonas. *The Antitheatrical Prejudice.* Berkeley: University of California Press, 1981.

Bebbington, D. W. "Gladstone and the Nonconformists: A Religious Affinity in Politics." *Studies in Church History* 12. Oxford: Blackwell, 1975.

Belchem, John. "1848: Feargus O'Connor and the Collapse of the Mass Platform." In *The Chartist Experience: Studies in Working-Class Radicalism and Culture, 1830–60.* James Epstein and Dorothy Thompson, eds. London: Macmillan, 1982.

———. *Popular Radicalism in Nineteenth-Century Britain.* New York: St Martin's, 1996.

——— and James Epstein. "The Nineteenth-Century Gentleman Leader Revisited." *Social History* 22, no. 2 (1997): 174–93.

Bentham, Jeremy. *The Works of Jeremy Bentham* (11 vols.). John Browring, ed. Edinburgh, 1843–46.

Bentley, Michael. *Politics Without Democracy: Great Britain, 1815–1914. Perception and Preoccupation in British Government.* Oxford: Blackwell, 1985.

Best, G. F. A. *Temporal Pillars: Queen Anne's Bounty, the Ecclesiastical Commission, and the Church of England.* Cambridge: Cambridge University Press, 1964.

———. "Evangelicalism and the Victorians." In *The Victorian Crisis of Faith.* Anthony Symondson, ed. London: SPCK, 1970.

Biagini, Eugenio F. "Marshall's 1873 'Lectures to Women.'" *Quaderni di Storia dell'Economica Politica* 9, nos. 2–3 (1991): 335–54.

———. *Liberty, Retrenchment and Reform: Popular Liberalism in the Age of Gladstone, 1860–1880.* Cambridge: Cambridge University Press, 1992.

Bishop, T. J. H. and Rupert Wilkinson. *Winchester and the Public School Elite: A Statistical Analysis.* London: Faber and Faber, 1967.

Bisset, Andrew. *Notes on the Anti-Corn Law Struggle.* London, 1884.

Blaikie, William Garden. *The Preachers of Scotland from the Sixth to the Nineteenth Century.* Edinburgh, 1888.

Blake, Robert. *Disraeli and Gladstone: The Leslie Stephen Lecture, 1969.* Cambridge: Cambridge University Press, 1969.

Bradley, Ian. *The Call To Seriousness: The Evangelical Impact on the Victorians.* London: Cape, 1976.

Brastow, Lewis O. *Representative Modern Preachers.* London: Macmillan, 1905.

Brett, Peter. "Political Dinners in Early Nineteenth-Century Britain: Platform, Meeting-Place and Battleground." *History* 81, no. 264: 527–52.

Briggs, Asa. *Victorian Cities.* New York: Harper & Row, 1965.

———. *The Birth of Broadcasting.* Oxford: Oxford University Press, 1995.

Brown, Callum G. *Religion and Society in Scotland Since 1707.* Edinburgh: Edinburgh University Press, 1997.

Brownlee, David. *The Law Courts: The Architecture of George Edmund Street.* New York: Architectural History Foundation, and Cambridge, MA: MIT Press, 1984.

Burritt, Elihu. *Walks in the Black Country and its Green Border-Land.* London, 1865.

Butler, Perry. *Gladstone: Church, State, and Tractarianism. A Study of His Religious Ideas and Attitudes, 1809–1959.* Oxford: Clarendon, 1982.

Cannadine, David. *Lords and Landlords: The Aristocracy and the Towns, 1774–1967.* Leicester: Leicester University Press, 1980

———. "The Transformation of Civic Ritual in Modern Britain: The Colchester Oyster Feast." *Past & Present* 94 (1982): 107–30.

———. "Introduction." *Blood, Toil, Tears and Sweat: The Speeches of Winston Churchill.* David Cannadine, ed. Boston: Houghton Mifflin, 1989.

———. *The Decline and Fall of the British Aristocracy.* New Haven: Yale University Press, 1990.

Cannon, John. *Aristocratic Century: The Peerage of Eighteenth-Century England.* Cambridge: Cambridge University Press, 1984.

Carlen, Pat. "The Staging of Magistrates' Justice." *The British Journal of Criminology* 16, no. 1 (1976): 48–55.

———. *Magistrates' Justice.* London: Robertson, 1976.

Chadwick, Owen. *The Victorian Church* (2 vols). Oxford: Oxford University Press, 1966–70.

Cheyne, A. C. *Studies in Scottish Church History.* Edinburgh: Clark, 1999.

Christie, Ian R. *British 'Non-Élite' MPs, 1715–1820.* Oxford: Clarendon, 1995.

Clark, G. S. R. Kitson. "The Romantic Element—1830–1850." In *Studies in Social History: A Tribute to G. M. Trevelyan.* John Harold Plumb, ed. London: Longmans Green, 1955.

———. *The Making of Victorian England.* New York: Athenaeum, 1966.

Clarke, M. L. *Classical Education in Britain, 1500–1900.* Cambridge: Cambridge University Press, 1959.

Cmiel, Kenneth. *Democratic Eloquence: The Fight Over Popular Speech in Nineteenth-Century America.* New York: Morrow, 1990.

Cocks, Raymond. *Foundations of the Modern Bar.* London: Sweet & Maxwell, 1983.

Coffey, John. "Democracy and Popular Religion: Moody and Sankey's Mission to Britain, 1873–1875." In *Citizenship and Community: Liberals, Radicals and Collective Identities in the British Isles, 1865–1931.* Eugenio F. Biagini, ed. Cambridge: Cambridge University Press, 1996.

Colley, Linda. *Britons: Forging the Nation, 1707–1837.* New Haven: Yale University Press, 1992.

Collini, Stefan. *Public Moralists: Political Thought and Intellectual Life in Britain, 1850–1930.* Oxford: Clarendon, 1991.

Collins, Philip. *Dickens and Crime,* 2nd ed. London: Macmillan, 1965.

Cook, Sir Edward. "The Classics in Daily Life." *More Literary Recreations.* London: Macmillan, 1919.

Cookson, J. E. *Lord Liverpool's Administration: The Crucial Years, 1815–22.* Hamden, CT: Archon, 1975.

Cornford, J. P. "The Parliamentary Foundations of the Hotel Cecil." In *Ideas and Institutions of Victorian Britain: Essays in Honour of George Kitson Clark.* Robert Robson, ed. London: Bell, 1967.

Cornish, W. R. and G. de N. Clark. *Law and Society in England, 1750–1950.* London: Sweet & Maxwell, 1989.

Cox, Edward W. *The Advocate: His Training, Practice, Rights, and Duties.* London, 1852.

Cradock, Percy. *Recollections of the Cambridge Union, 1815–1939.* Cambridge: Bowes & Bowes, 1953.

Craig, Robert. *A History of Oratory in Parliament, 1213–1913.* London: Heath, Cranton & Ousley, [1913].

Cunningham, Colin. *Victorian and Edwardian Town Halls.* London: Routledge & Kegan Paul, 1981.

Currie, Robert, Alan Gilbert, and Lee Horsley. *Churches and Churchgoers: Patterns of Church Growth in the British Isles Since 1700.* Oxford: Clarendon, 1977.

Curthoys, M. C. "The Careers of Oxford Men." In *The History of the University of Oxford,* vol. 6, *Nineteenth Century Oxford, Part 1.* M. G. Brock and M. C. Curthoys, eds. Oxford: Clarendon, 1997.

Curzon of Kedleston, [George Nathaniel] Earl. *Modern Parliamentary Eloquence: The Rede Lecture Delivered Before the University of Cambridge, November 6, 1913.* London: Macmillan, 1913.

———. *Subjects of the Day: Being a Collection of Speeches and Writings.* Desmond M. Chapman-Hudson, ed. London: George Allen & Unwin, 1915.

Davies, C. Maurice. *Unorthodox London: Or, Phases in the Religious Life of the Metropolis,* 2nd. ed. London, 1876.

Davies, Horton. *Worship and Theology in England,* vol. 4, *From Newman to Martineau, 1850–1900.* Princeton: Princeton University Press, 1962.

Davies, J. G. "The Role of a Cathedral in the Past." In *Cathedral & Mission.* Gilbert Cope, ed. Birmingham: University of Birmingham Institute for the Study of Worship and Religious Architecture, [1969].

Douthwaite, William Ralph. *Gray's Inn: Its History and Associations, Compiled from Original and Unpublished Documents.* London, 1886.

Du Cann, Richard. *The Art of the Advocate.* Harmondsworth: Penguin, 1964.

Duman, Daniel. *The English and Colonial Bars in the Nineteenth Century.* London: Croom Helm, 1983.

Edwards, J. Ll. J. *The Law Officers of the Crown.* London: Sweet & Maxwell, 1964.

Eliot, Simon. *Some Patterns and Trends in British Publishing, 1800–1919.* London: The Bibliographical Society, 1994.

Elliott-Binns, L. E. *Religion in the Victorian Era.* London: Lutterworth, 1936.

Engel, Matthew. *Tickle the Public: 100 Years of the Popular Press.* London: Gollancz, 1996.

Englander, David. "The Word and the World: Evangelicalism in the Victorian City." In *Re-*

ligion in Victorian Britain, vol. 2, *Controversies*. Gerald Parsons, ed. Manchester: Manchester University Press, 1988.

Ferguson, Robert A. *Law and Letters in American Culture*. Cambridge, MA: Harvard University Press, 1984.

Fields, Wayne. *Union of Words: A History of Presidential Eloquence*. New York: Free Press, 1996.

Fitzsimons, Reymund. *The Charles Dickens Show: An Account of His Public Readings, 1858–1870*. London: Bles, 1970.

Forsyth, William. *Hortensius: or, the Advocate. An Historical Essay*. London, 1849.

Fowler, J. T. "The Durham Union Society." *Durham University Journal* 20 (1912): 204–7.

Friedberg, Aaron L. *The Weary Titan: Britain and the Experience of Relative Decline, 1895–1905*. Princeton: Princeton University Press, 1988.

Gardner, Alice. *A Short History of Newnham College Cambridge*. Cambridge: Bowes & Bowes, 1921.

Gash, Norman. "Peel and the Party System, 1830–50." *Transactions of the Royal Historical Society*, 5th Series, 1 (1950): 47–69.

———. *Politics in the Age of Peel: A Study in the Technique of Parliamentary Representation, 1830–1850*. London: Longmans, 1953.

Gay, Peter. *The Bourgeois Experience: Victoria to Freud*: vol. 1, *Education of the Senses*. Oxford: Oxford University Press, 1984.

Gilbert, Alan D. *Religion and Society in Industrial England: Church, Chapel, and Social Change, 1740–1914*. London: Longman, 1976.

———. *The Making of Post-Christian Britain: A History of the Secularization of Modern Society*. London: Longman, 1980.

Goodbody, John. "The *Star*: Its Role in the Rise of the New Journalism." In *Papers for the Millions: The New Journalism in Britain, 1850s to 1914*. Joel H. Wiener, ed. New York: Greenwood, 1988.

Graves, Robert and Alan Hodge. *The Long Week-End: A Social History of Great Britain, 1918–1939*, 2nd ed. New York: Norton, 1963.

Gray, W. Forbes. "Chalmers and Gladstone: An Unrecorded Episode." *Records of the Scottish Church History Society* 10, (1948): 8–17.

Griffin, Penny, ed. *St Hugh's: One Hundred Years of Women's Education in Oxford*. London: Macmillan, 1986.

Guttsman, W. L. *The British Political Elite*. New York: Basic, 1963.

Habermas, Jürgen. *The Structural Transformation of the Public Sphere: An Inquiry into a Category of Bourgeois Society*. Thomas Burger, tr. Cambridge, MA: MIT Press, 1989.

Hamer, D. A. "Gladstone: The Making of a Political Myth." *Victorian Studies* 22, no. 1 (1978): 29–50.

Hamilton, Mary Agnes. *Newnham: An Informal Biography*. London: Faber and Faber, 1936.

Harbinger, Richard. "Trial by Drama." *Judicature* 55, no. 3 (1971): 122–28.

Harding, Alan. *A Social History of English Law*. Gloucester, MA: Smith, 1973.

Hare, David. *Asking Around: Background to the David Hare Trilogy*. Lyn Haill, ed. London: Faber and Faber, 1993.

Harrison, Brian. *Peaceable Kingdom: Stability and Change in Modern Britain*. Oxford: Clarendon, 1982.

Heffernan, Richard and Mike Marqusee. *Defeat from the Jaws of Victory: Inside Kinnock's Labour Party.* London: Verso, 1992.

Hempton, D. N. "Bickersteth, Bishop of Ripon: The Episcopate of a Mid-Victorian Evangelical." In *Religion in Victorian Britain,* vol. 4, *Interpretations.* Gerald Parsons, ed. Manchester: Manchester University Press, 1988.

Hennock, E. P. *Fit and Proper Persons: Ideal and Reality in Nineteenth-Century Urban Government.* London: Arnold, 1973.

Hewitt, Martin, ed. *Platform, Pulpit, Rhetoric.* Leeds Centre Working Papers in Victorian Studies, vol. 3 (2000).

Holdsworth, Sir William. *A History of English Law,* vol. 15. A. L. Goodhart and H. G. Hanbury, eds. London: Methuen, 1966.

Holley, Darrell. *Churchill's Literary Allusions: An Index to the Education of a Soldier, Statesman, and Litterateur.* Jefferson, NC: McFarland, 1987.

Hollis, Christopher. *The Oxford Union.* London: Evans, 1965.

Hollis, Patricia. *Ladies Elect: Women in English Local Government, 1865–1914.* Oxford: Clarendon, 1987.

Hooper, W. Eden. *The History of Newgate and the Old Bailey.* London: Underwood, 1935.

Hostettler, John. *The Politics of Criminal Law Reform in the Nineteenth Century.* Chichester: Rose, 1992.

Hutchins, Francis G. *The Illusion of Permanence: British Imperialism in India.* Princeton: Princeton University Press, 1967.

Hutchison, Keith. *The Decline and Fall of British Capitalism.* New York: Scribner, 1950.

Huxley, Thomas H. "Universities: Actual and Ideal" (1874). *Science and Education.* New York, 1895.

Jenkins, Roy. *The Chancellors.* London: Macmillan, 1998.

Jenkyns, Richard. *The Victorians and Ancient Greece.* Cambridge, MA: Harvard University Press, 1980.

———. *Dignity and Decadence: Victorian Art and the Classical Inheritance.* London: HarperCollins, 1991.

Jephson, Henry L. *The Platform: Its Rise and Progress* (2 vols.). London, 1892.

Jones, Gareth Stedman. *Languages of Class: Studies in English Working Class History, 1832–1982.* Cambridge: Cambridge University Press, 1983.

Jones, Ieuan Gwynedd. *Mid-Victorian Wales.* Cardiff: University of Wales Press, 1992.

Jones, Owen. *Some of the Great Preachers of Wales.* London, 1885.

Joyce, Patrick. *Visions of the People: Industrial England and the Question of Class.* Cambridge: Cambridge University Press, 1991.

———. *Democratic Subjects: The Self and the Social in Nineteenth-Century England.* Cambridge: Cambridge University Press, 1994.

Judd, Gerritt P., IV. *Members of Parliament, 1734–1832.* New Haven: Yale University Press, 1955.

Kenyon, Frederic George. *Comparison of Ancient and Modern Political Oratory. The Chancellor's Essay, 1889.* Oxford, 1889.

Kinnard, Joseph. "G. E. Street, the Law Courts, and the 'Seventies." In *Victorian Architecture.* Peter Ferriday, ed. London: Cape, 1963.

Koss, Stephen. *The Rise and Fall of the Political Press in Britain*: vol.1, *The Nineteenth Century.* London: Hamilton, 1981.

Langford, John Alfred. *Modern Birmingham and its Institutions, a Chronicle of Local Events from 1841 to 1871* (2 vols.). Birmingham, [1873–77].

Langford, Paul. *Public Life and the Propertied Englishman, 1686–1798.* Oxford: Clarendon, 1991.

———. *Englishness Identified: Manners and Character, 1650–1850.* Oxford: Oxford University Press.

Landale, James. "Never Mind the Quality of Speeches—Feel the Brevity." *The Times*, April 1, 1999, p. 33.

Laqueur, Thomas W. "Crowds, Carnival and the State in English Executions, 1604–1868." In *The First Modern Society: Essays in English History in Honour of Lawrence Stone.* A. L. Beier, David Cannadine, and James M. Rosenheim, eds. Cambridge: Cambridge University Press, 1989.

Law, William. *Our Hansard, or the True Mirror of Parliament.* London: Pittman, 1950.

Lee, Alan J. *The Origins of the Popular Press in England, 1855–1914.* London: Croom Helm, 1976.

Lemmings, David. *Gentlemen and Barristers: The Inns of Court and the English Bar, 1680–1730.* Oxford: Clarendon, 1990.

Lewis, J. R. *The Victorian Bar.* London: Hale, 1982.

Lytton, Edward Bulwer. *England and the English.* 1833. Standish Meacham, ed. Chicago: University of Chicago Press, 1970.

Macaulay, Thomas Babington. *Critical and Historical Essays Contributed to* The Edinburgh Review (2 vols.). London, 1856.

[———.] *The Works of Lord Macaulay Complete* (8 vols.). Lady Trevelyan, ed. London, 1871.

MacDonagh, Michael. *The Reporters' Gallery.* London: Hodder and Stoughton, [1913].

Manchester, A. H. *Sources of English Legal History: Law, History, and Society in England and Wales, 1750–1950.* London: Butterworths, 1984.

Marsh, P. T. *The Victorian Church in Decline: Archbishop Tait and the Church of England, 1868–1882.* London: Routledge, 1969.

———. *The Discipline of Popular Government: Lord Salisbury's Domestic Statecraft, 1881–1902.* Hassocks: Harvester, 1978.

Matthew, H. C. G. "Rhetoric and Politics in Great Britain, 1860–1950." In *Politics and Social Change in Britain: Essays Presented to A. F. Thompson.* P. J. Waller, ed. Hassocks: Harvester, 1987.

———, ed. *The Nineteenth Century.* Oxford: Oxford University Press, 2000.

Maugham, [Frederic Herbert] Lord. *The Tichborne Case.* London: Hodder & Stoughton, 1936.

McCord, Norman. *The Anti-Corn Law League.* London: Allen and Unwin, 1958.

McCurdy, Frances Lea. *Stump, Bar, and Pulpit: Speechmaking on the Missouri Frontier.* Columbia, MO: University of Missouri Press, 1969.

McKibbin, Ross. *The Ideologies of Class: Social Relations in Britain, 1880–1950.* Oxford: Clarendon, 1990.

———. *Classes and Cultures: England 1918–1951.* Oxford: Oxford University Press, 1998.

McLeod, Hugh. *Religion and Society in England, 1850–1914*. New York: St. Martin's, 1996.

McMaster, R. D. "Chaffanbrass for the Defence: Trollope and the Old Bailey Tradition." In *Trollope and the Law*. London: Macmillan, 1986.

McWilliam, Rohan "Radicalism and Popular Culture: The Tichborne Case and the Politics of 'Fair Play', 1867–1886." In *Currents of Radicalism: Popular Radicalism, Organised Labour and Party Politics in Britain, 1850–1914*. Eugenio F. Biagini and Alastair J. Reid, eds. Cambridge: Cambridge University Press, 1991.

Meisel, Joseph S. "Public Speech and the Culture of Public Life in the Age of Gladstone." Ph.D. diss. Columbia University, 1999.

———. "Embodying Oratory in Nineteenth-Century Britain: Space, Print, Organizations, Speakers, and Audiences." Unpublished paper delivered at the Leeds Centre for Victorian Studies, Trinity and All Saints College, University of Leeds, March 2000.

———. "Words by the Numbers: A Quantitative Analysis and Comparison of the Oratorical Careers of William Ewart Gladstone and Winston Spencer Churchill." *Historical Research*, vol. 73, no. 182 (2000), pp. 262–95.

———. "The Word in Man: Gladstone and the Great Preachers." In *The Gladstone Umbrella*. Peter Francis, ed. Hawarden: Monad, 2001.

Melikan, R. A. "Mr Attorney General and the Politicians." *The Historical Journal* 40, no. 1 (1997): 41–69.

Mellinkoff, David. *The Conscience of a Lawyer*. St. Paul, MN: West, 1973.

Morgan, J. Vyrnwy. *The Church in Wales in the Light of History: A Historical and Philosophical Study*. London: Chapman & Hall, 1918.

Morrah, Herbert Arthur. *The Oxford Union, 1823–1923*. London: Cassell, 1923.

Morris, A. J. A. *The Scaremongers: The Advocacy of War and Rearmament, 1896–1914*. London: Routledge & Kegan Paul, 1984.

Morrison, John and Philip Leith. *The Barrister's World, and the Nature of Law*. Milton Keynes: Open University Press, 1992.

Mugglestone, Lynda. *'Talking Proper': The Rise of Accent of Social Symbol*. Oxford: Clarendon, 1995.

Musolf, Karen J. *From Plymouth to Parliament: A Rhetorical Analysis of Nancy Astor's 1919 Campaign*. New York: St. Martin's Press, 1999.

Neel, Bege Bowers. "Lawyers on Trial: Attitudes Toward the Lawyer's Use and Abuse of Rhetoric in Nineteenth-Century England." Ph.D. diss. University of Tennessee, Knoxville, 1984.

Obelkevich, James. *Religion and Rural Society: South Lindsey, 1825–1875*. Oxford: Clarendon, 1976.

Ogilvie, R. M. *Latin and Greek: A History of the Influence of the Classics on English Life from 1600 to 1918*. Hamden, CT: Archon, 1964.

O'Gorman, Frank. "Campaign Rituals and Ceremonies: The Social Meaning of Elections in England, 1780–1860." *Past & Present* 135 (May 1992): 79–115.

Oliver, Robert T. *The Influence of Rhetoric in the Shaping of Great Britain*. Newark, DE: University of Delaware Press, 1986.

———. *Public Speaking in the Reshaping of Great Britain*. Newark, DE: University of Delaware Press, 1987.

Ong, Walter J. *Orality and Literacy: The Technologizing of the Word.* London: Routledge, 1989.

Ostrogorski, M. *Democracy and the Organization of Political Parties* (2 vols.). Frederick Clarke, tr. London: Macmillan, 1922.

Palmer, D. J. *The Rise of English Studies: An Account of the Study of English Language and Literature from its Origins to the Makings of the Oxford English School.* London: Oxford University Press, 1965.

Parker, Graham. "The Prisoner in the Box—The Making of the Criminal Evidence Act, 1898." In *Law and Social Change in British History: Papers Presented to the Bristol Legal History Conference, 14–17 July 1981.* J. A. Guy and H. G. Beale, eds. London: Royal Historical Society, 1984.

Parris, Matthew. "Political Sketch: Howard Finds Eloquence No Asset in the Credibility Game." *The Times,* March 3, 1999, p. 4.

Parry, Edward Abbott. *The Drama of the Law.* London: Unwin, 1924.

Parry, Jonathan. *The Rise and Fall of Liberal Government in Victorian Britain.* New Haven: Yale University Press, 1993.

Peel, Michael. "The Lost Voice of Public Speaking." *Financial Times,* January 10–11, 1998, p. xxii.

Perkin, Harold. *The Origin of Modern English Society.* Routledge & Kegan Paul, 1969.

Pickering, Paul A. and Alex Tyrrell. *The People's Bread: A History of the Anti-Corn Law League.* London: Continuum, 2000.

Pinto-Duschinsky, Michael. *The Political Thought of Lord Salisbury, 1854–68.* London: Constable, 1967.

"Political Orators and Writers of Pamphlets." In *The Cambridge History of English Literature,* vol. 14, *The Nineteenth Century III.* A. W. Ward and A. R. Waller, eds. Cambridge: Cambridge University Press, 1917.

Port, M. H., ed. *The Houses of Parliament.* New Haven: Yale University Press, 1976.

———. *Six Hundred New Churches: A Study of the Church Building Commission, 1818–1856, and its Church Building Activities.* London: SPCK, 1961.

Pue, William Wesley Thomas. "The Making of the English Bar: Metasomatism in the Nineteenth Century." D. Jur. thesis. York University (Canada), 1989.

Quarrie, P. "The Christ Church Collection Books." In *The History of the University of Oxford,* vol. 5: *The Eighteenth Century.* L. S. Sutherland and L. G. Mitchell, eds. Oxford: Clarendon, 1986.

Quinault, Roland. "John Bright and Joseph Chamberlain." *The Historical Journal* 28, no. 3 (1985): 623–46.

———. "Westminster and the Victorian Constitution." *Transactions of the Royal Historical Society,* 6th Series 2 (1992): 79–104.

Ray, Charles. *A Marvelous Ministry: The Story of C. H. Spurgeon's Sermons, 1855–1905.* London: Passmore and Alabaster, 1905.

Reid, Loren. "Gladstone's Essay on Public Speaking." *The Quarterly Journal of Speech* 39, no. 3 (1953): 265–72.

Robbins, Keith. *Nineteenth-Century Britain: Integration and Diversity. The Ford Lectures Delivered in the University of Oxford, 1986–1987.* Oxford: Clarendon, 1988.

Roe, Michael. *Kenealy and the Tichborne Cause: A Study in Mid-Victorian Populism.* Carlton: Melbourne University Press, 1974.

Rothblatt, Sheldon. "The Student Sub-culture and the Examination System in Early 19th Century Oxbridge." In *The University and Society*, vol. 1. Lawrence Stone, ed. Princeton: Princeton University Press, 1974.

Rowley, Andrew Swann. "Professions, Class and Society: Solicitors in 19th Century Birmingham." Ph.D. diss. University of Aston, Birmingham, 1988.

Sanderson, Michael. *From Irving to Olivier: A Social History of the Acting Profession in England, 1880–1983*. London: Athlone, 1984.

Saunders, William. *The New Parliament, 1880*. London, [1880].

Scott, Patrick. "The Business of Belief: The Emergence of 'Religious' Publishing." *Studies in Church History* 10. Oxford: Blackwell, 1973.

Shannon, R. T. *Gladstone and the Bulgarian Agitation, 1876*, 2nd ed. Hassocks: Harvester, 1975.

———. "Midlothian: 100 Years After." In *Gladstone, Politics and Religion: A Collection of Founder's Day Lectures Delivered at St. Deiniol's Library, Hawarden, 1967–83*. Peter J. Jagger, ed. London: Macmillan, 1985.

———. *The Age of Salisbury, 1881–1902: Unionism and Empire*. London: Longman, 1996.

Slee, Peter R. H. *Learning and a Liberal Education: The Study of Modern History in the Universities of Oxford, Cambridge, and Manchester, 1800–1914*. Manchester: Manchester University Press, 1986.

Smalley, Donald A., ed. *Trollope: The Critical Heritage*. London: Routledge & Kegan Paul, 1969.

Smith, E. A. *The House of Lords in British Politics and Society, 1815–1911*. London: Longman, 1992.

[Smith, F. E.] Viscount Birkenhead. "Oxford Union Society." *Points of View*, vol. 1. London: Hodder and Stoughton, [1923].

[———.] Earl of Birkenhead. "Eloquence." *Law Life and Letters*, vol. 2. New York: Doran, 1972.

Smith, Mark. *Religion in Industrial Society: Oldham and Saddleworth, 1740–1865*. Oxford: Clarendon, 1994.

Soffer, Reba N. *Discipline and Power: The University, History, and the Making of the English Elite, 1870–1930*. Stanford: Stanford University Press, 1994.

Stansky, Peter. *On or About December 1910: Early Bloomsbury and Its Intimate World*. Cambridge, MA: Harvard University Press, 1996.

Steadman, A. M. M. *Oxford: Its Life and Schools*. London, 1887.

Stephen, James Fitzjames. *A General View of the Criminal Law of England*, 2nd ed. London, 1890.

———. *A History of the Criminal Law of England* (3 vols.). London, 1893.

Stirling, James. "Advocacy and Acting." *Verdict* 2, no. 1 (1966): 7–9.

Stone, Lawrence. "The Size and Composition of the Oxford Student Body 1580–1910." In *The University and Society*, vol. 1. Lawrence Stone, ed. Princeton: Princeton University Press, 1974.

Stray, Christopher. *Classics Transformed: Schools, Universities, and Society in England, 1830–1960*. Oxford: Clarendon, 1998.

Svaglic, Martin J. "Classical Rhetoric and Victorian Prose." In *The Art of Victorian Prose*. George Levine and William Madden, eds. London: Oxford University Press, 1968.

Sydney, Sir Philip. *A Defence of Poetry* (1595). J. A. van Dorsten, ed. London: Oxford University Press, 1966.

Taylor, A. J. P. *The Trouble Makers: Dissent Over Foreign Policy, 1792–1939*. 1957. London: Panther, 1969.

———. *English History, 1914–1945*. Oxford: Oxford University Press, 1965.

Taylor, Antony. "Palmerston and Radicalism, 1847–1865." *Journal of British Studies* 33, no. 2 (1994): 157–79.

Taylor, Katherine Fischer. *In the Theater of Criminal Justice: The Palais de Justice in Second Empire Paris*. Princeton: Princeton University Press, 1993.

Thomas, Keith. "The Place of Laughter in Tudor and Stuart England." *The Times Literary Supplement*, January 21, 1977, pp. 77–81.

Thomas, P. D. G. *The House of Commons in the Eighteenth Century*. Oxford: Clarendon, 1971.

Thompson, E. P. *Customs in Common*. London: Penguin, 1993.

Tilly, Charles. *Popular Contention in Great Britain, 1758–1834*. Cambridge, MA: Harvard University Press, 1995.

Turner, Frank Miller. *The Greek Heritage in Victorian Britain*. New Haven: Yale University Press, 1981.

———. *Contesting Cultural Authority: Essays on Victorian Intellectual Life*. Cambridge: Cambridge University Press, 1993.

Valenze, Deborah M. *Prophetic Sons and Daughters: Female Preaching and Popular Religion in Industrial England*. Princeton: Princeton University Press, 1985.

Vance, Norman. *The Victorians and Ancient Rome*. Oxford: Blackwell, 1997.

Vernon, James. *Politics and the People: A Study in English Political Culture, c. 1815–1867*. Cambridge: Cambridge University Press, 1993.

Vince, C. A. "Latin Poets in the British Parliament." *The Classical Review* 46, no. 3 (1932): 97–104.

Vincent, John. *The Formation of the British Liberal Party, 1857–1868*, 2nd ed. Hassocks: Harvester, 1976.

Waller, P. J. "Democracy and Dialect, Speech and Class." In *Politics and Social Change in Britain: Essays Presented to A. F. Thompson*. P. J. Waller, ed. Hassocks: Harvester, 1987.

Walter, David. *The Oxford Union: Playground of Power*. London: Macdonald, 1984.

Watson, George. *The English Ideology: Studies in the Language of Victorian Politics*. London: Allen Lane, 1973.

Weber, Max. "Politics as a Vocation" (1919). *From Max Weber: Essays in Sociology*. H. H. Gerth and C. Wright Mills, eds. New York: Oxford University Press, 1958.

Weiner, Martin J. *English Culture and the Decline of the Industrial Spirit, 1850–1980*. Cambridge: Cambridge University Press, 1981.

Whiteley, William Henry. "The Social Composition of the House of Commons, 1868–1885." Ph.D. diss. Cornell University, 1960.

Whorlow, H. *The Provincial Newspaper Society, 1836–1886*. London, 1886.

Wickham, Glynne. "Gladstone, Oratory and the Theatre." In *Gladstone*. Peter J. Jagger, ed. London: Hambledon, 1998.

Williams, Raymond. *Culture and Society, 1780–1950*. London: Chatto & Windus, 1958.

Wills, Garry. *Lincoln at Gettysburg: The Words that Remade America*. New York: Simon & Schuster, 1992.

Winstanley, D. A. *Early Victorian Cambridge.* Cambridge: Cambridge University Press, 1940.

Winter, Alison. *Mesmerized: Powers of Mind in Victorian Britain.* Chicago: University of Chicago Press, 1998.

Woodruff, Douglas. *The Tichborne Claimant: A Victorian Mystery.* New York: Farrar, Strauss, and Cudahy, 1957.

Wooley, S. F. "The Personnel of the Parliament of 1833." *English Historical Review* 53, no. 210 (1938): 240–62.

Woolf, Virginia. "This is the House of Commons" (1932). *The London Scene: Five Essays by Virginia Woolf.* London: Hogarth, 1982.

C. REFERENCE WORKS

Boase, Frederick. *Modern English Biography* (6 vols). Truro, 1892–1921.

Cook, Chris and Brendan Keith. *British Historical Facts, 1830–1900.* London: Macmillan, 1975.

The Dictionary of National Biography, and supplements.

Foster, Joseph. *Alumni Oxonienses: The Members of the University of Oxford, 1715–1886: Their Parentage, Birthplace, and Year of Birth, with a Record of Their Degrees* (4 vols). London, 1887–8.

———. *Men-at-the-Bar: A Biographical Hand-List of the Members of the Various Inns of Court, Including Her Majesty's Judges, etc.* London, 1885.

The History of Parliament: The House of Commons, 1660–1690 (3 vols). Basil Duke Henning, ed. London: Secker & Warburg, 1983.

The History of Parliament: The House of Commons, 1754–1790 (3 vols.). Lewis Namier and John Brooke, eds. London: HMSO, 1964.

The History of Parliament: The House of Commons, 1790–1820 (5 vols.). R. G. Thorne, ed. London: Secker & Warburg, 1986.

Mitchell, B. R. *British Historical Statistics.* Cambridge: Cambridge University Press, 1988.

Venn, J. A. *Alumni Cantabrigienses: A Biographical List of All Known Students, Graduates and Holders of Office at the University of Cambridge from the Earliest Times to 1900. Part II: 1752–1900* (6 vols). Cambridge: Cambridge University Press, 1940–54.

Wilding, Norman and Philip Laundy. *An Encyclopædia of Parliament*, 4th ed. New York: St. Martin's Press, 1971.

Woolrych, Humphrey William. *Lives of Eminent Serjeants-at-Law of the English Bar* (2 vols.). London, 1869.

INDEX

A Note on Names and Titles:

Persons bearing aristocratic titles and those whose names or titles changed during the period covered by this book are indexed under their most frequently occurring appellations (for example, Disraeli not Beaconsfield; Palmerston not Temple; Hartington not Cavendish or Devonshire). Cross–references are supplied in most cases.

Aberdeen, George Hamilton Gordon, Earl of (1784–1860), 87, 223
Albert, Prince Consort (1819–61), 10
Albert Edward, Prince of Wales (1841–1910), 11, 205
Allon, Henry (1818–92), 130, 164
America, 57; *see also* United States
Ampthill, Odo Russell, Baron (1829–84), 294*n*27
Anti–Corn Law League, 237–38
  creation of Free Trade Hall 255
  and Midlothian campaigns, 244, 245
  role of oratory, 272, 332*n*51
  religious influence, 240
anti-slavery and anti–slave-trade movements, 237
Arnold, Matthew (1822–88), 11, 135
Arnold, Thomas (1759–1842), 67
Asquith, Herbert Henry (1852–1928), 220, 282
  classical knowledge, 83, 103
  Oxford Union, 41, 296*n*66
  and wireless, 288
Asquith, Raymond (1878–1916), 26, 295*n*48, 296*n*64
Astor, Nancy (1879–1964), 3, 336*n*150
Attorney General—*see* law officers
audiences for public speaking, 2
  "civic strangers," 267, 278
  demands upon, 276
  London as great supplier of, 9
  platform speeches, 180, 251, 258–62, 264, 274, 276
  for preaching, 147–48, 162
  transport, 278
  trials, 167–68, 170, 179–80, 188, 205, 206, 207
  women, 260, 337*n*179
Austin, John (1790–1859), 322*n*73

Bagehot, Walter (1826–77), 2
Bagot, William (1728–89), 58
Baldwin, Stanley (1867–1947), 93, 103
  plain speaking style, 284
  and wireless, 288–89

Balfour, Arthur James (1848–1930), 103, 251, 271, 282
Ballantine, William (1812–87), 191–92
Ballot Act (1872), 225, 248, 273
Bancroft, George Pleydell (1868–1956), 196, 198–99, 202
Bancroft, Marie Wilton (1839–1921), 184, 198, 201
Bancroft, Squire (1841–1926), 198, 201
Baptists, 125
 church-building, 112
 ministers, 108, 109
  see also Spurgeon
bar
 adaptation to external challenges, 172
 privileges, 172
 criticism of, 170, 172–173, 186–95
 professionalization, 172, 221
 scandals, 173, 187–189
 self–discipline, 173, 189, 221
  see also barrister–MPs, barristers, Inns of Court
Barnard, Edward (1717–81), 56
Barré, Isaac (1726–1802), 59
barrister-MPs, 7, 72, 79, 207–19, 220
 age of, 209, 327*n*172
 career patterns and advancement, 209–10, 211–12, 219
 lack of oratorical success in Commons, 213–18
 numbers, 170, 208, 282, 327*n*167, 327*n*169
 reputation, 210, 212–14, 219, 328*n*194
 social background and status, 195, 209
 as speakers, 212–19, 220
  see also law officers
barristers
 briefless, 171–72, 209
 compared to actors, 195–96
 compared to parliamentary speakers, 328*n*189
 concern over immorality of advocacy, 186–95
 education, 65, 182–83
 friendships with actors, 201–2
 increasing role in court, 172, 173, 174
 limited opportunities for speech-making, 173–74
 monopoly of a few, 171, 197
 nature of oratory, 181–83
 oratorical training (or lack thereof), 170, 183–85
 prejudices against, 191, 196, 213–14, 215, 323*n*93
 professional orators, 169
 right of address in court, 169
 robes, 195, 324*n*109
 size of practicing bar, 170–71
 social background and status, 183, 195, 203–4, 220–21
 speeches, 168, 205, 276
 theatrical experience, 183–84, 199–201, 202–3
  see also bar, barrister–MPs
Barry, Charles (1795–1860), 70
Bassett, Arthur Tilney, 241
BBC, 288–89
Beaconsfield—*see* Disraeli.
Beaconsfieldism, 244, 253
Beauchamp, Frederick Lygon, Earl (1830–91), 11
Beerbohm, Max, (1872–1956), 287
Belloc, Hilaire (1870–1953), 21, 22–23, 33
Benson, Edward White (1829–96), 145
Bentham, Jeremy (1748–1832), 186, 194
Berlin, Isaiah (1909–97), 290
Besant, Annie (1874–1933), 150
Bevan, Aneurin (1897–1960), 283
Bible, 91, 99, 133, 308*n*182
Bickersteth, Robert (1816–84), Bishop of Ripon, 115
Bingley Hall, Birmingham, 255–56, 262, 263, 266
Birkenhead, Frederick Edwin Smith, Earl of (1827–1930), 282
 eulogy for Gladstone, 31–32, 296*n*64
 Oxford Union, 19, 21, 22–23, 26–27, 29, 31–32, 33
 parliamentary speaker, 220
Birmingham, 9

oratorical second city, 249
see also Bingley Hall, Birmingham and Edgbaston Debating Society, Bright, Chamberlain, Dale, Dawson
Birmingham and Edgbaston Debating Society, 46–47, 249
Blake, Robert, Baron, 96, 97
Blomfield, Charles James (1786–1857), Bishop of London, 115
Bolingbroke, Henry St. John, Viscount, 53
Bonar Law, Andrew (1858–1923), 48–49
Bovill, William (1814–73), 218
Bowen, George Ferguson (1821–99), 41
Bradlaugh, Charles (1833–91), 150
Bright, John (1811–89), 79, 102
and Anti–Corn Law League, 237–38
biography by G. M. Trevelyan, 98
compared to Disraeli, 92, 99–100
compared to Macaulay, 313*n*18
compared to Spurgeon, 135–36, 313*n*18
earnestness, 136
extra-parliamentary speeches, 224, 238, 246, 265, 266, 269
influence on Chamberlian, 239, 249
MP for Birmingham, 46, 249, 256
non-classical, 90–91, 92, 99–100
oratorical education, 89
perceived honesty, 195
Quaker background, 240
quotations in speeches, 61, 90–91
religious quality in speeches, 267, 272
reporting of speeches, 269, 272
reputation as speaker, 90
style of speaking, 90
Tribune of the English People, 92, 135–36.
Brooke, Stopford Augustus (1832–1916), 145–48
Bedford Chapel debating society, 148
Bulgarian atrocities agitation, 154
and Gladstone, 151, 154, 155, 158–59, 160, 161
Brougham and Vaux, Henry Peter, Baron (1778–1868), 20, 187
campaign at Liverpool (1812), 226
defense of Queen Caroline, 190
on advocate's duty, 190–91
Brown, Florence Ada (1860–1958), 297*n*94
Browning, Robert (1812–99), 61
Bruce—*see* Elgin
Bryce, James (1838–1922), 209
Bulgarian atrocities agitation, 153–54, 240–241, 243, 244, 257, 273
Buller, Charles (1806–48), 96
Burke, Edmund (1729–97), 53–54, 58
extra-parliamentary speeches, 227, 229
parliamentary "dinner bell", 53, 229
published speeches, 53–54, 229
Butler, Samuel (1774–1839), 67
Byron, George Gordon, Baron (1788–1824), 61, 91

cabinet, social composition, 63
Cairns, Hugh (1819–85), 213
Cambridge, George William Frederick, Duke of (1819–1904), 168
Cambridge Union Society, 6–7, 184, 277
benefits of experience, 25–26
buildings, 15–16, 27–28
debates, 18–19
founding and early years, 11, 15
influence of Apostles, 15, 24
presidents and officers, 18, 20–21, 32–42, 296*n*66
publication of speeches, 22
rules and procedures, 21
social character, 17–18
style of speeches, 23–24
and other university debating societies, 24
women admitted, 42
Campbell, John (1779–1861), 167–68
Canning, George (1770–1827), 13–14, 84, 263, 296*n*58
and Edward Irving, 124
compared to Peel, 81
extra-parliamentary speeches, 229–31
on limits of first speaking, 304*n*109
published speeches, 230–31, 232

Carlyle, Thomas (1795–1881), 223, 224
Carpenter, William Boyd (1841–1918), 164
Carson, Edward (1854–35), 205
cathedrals, 119–22, 164, 276; *see also* St. Paul's Cathedral, Westminster Abbey
Catholic Relief bill (1829), 79
Catholics, 108, 109, 147
Cavendish—*see* Hartington
Cecil, Lady Gwendolen (1860–1945), 245, 249
Cecil—*see* Salisbury
censorship—*see* Defence of the Realm Act
Central Criminal Court (Old Bailey), 167, 174, 217, 287
Chalmers, Thomas (1780–1847), 122–24, 156
Chamberlain, Austen (1863–1937), 249
Chamberlain, Joseph (1836–1914), 280
  Birmingham and Edgbaston Debating Society, 47, 249
  compared to Chatham, 249
  extra-parliamentary speeches, 246–47, 248, 249–51, 252, 253, 256, 264–65, 270, 272–73
  lack of classical knowledge, 84
  influence of Bright, 239, 249
  National Education League, 239, 240
  on Midlothian campaigns, 244
  political fractures, 250
  Radical/Unauthorized Programme, 250–51
  reporting of speeches, 270, 271, 284
Chamberlain, Neville (1869–1940), 288–89
Chartism, 110, 236–37, 238
Chatham, William Pitt, Earl of [the "Elder Pitt"] (1708–78), 14, 53, 54, 81, 249
Chatterton, Thomas (1752–70), 91
Church Building Act (1818), 109
Church Building Commission, 109–10, 111, 112, 309*n*15
Church Building Society, 109–10, 111
Church Homiletical Society, 118–19, 277
Church of England, 7
  church-building and extension, 109–10, 115
  clergy, 108
  efforts to improve quality of preaching, 7, 114–22
  expands reach in new ways, 110–11
  limits on worship outside a church abolished (1855), 120, 128–29
  partitioning of parishes made easier (1843), 110
  see also Blomfield, Bickersteth, cathedrals, Liddon, Milman, Shaftesbury, Tait, Trench
Church of Ireland, disestablishment, 71, 88, 91, 217, 242
Church of Scotland
  church-building, 112
  ministers, 108
  see also Disruption of 1843
church-building, 109–12, 164, 276, 277, 309*n*15
Churchill, Jennie (1854–1921), 261–62, 267
Churchill, Randolph, Lord (1849–95), 51
  Dartford Programme, 252
  extra-parliamentary speeches, 245, 247, 249, 251–53, 257, 260, 261, 263–64, 265, 267, 271, 272–73, 277
  Gladstone a favorite target, 251–52
  Oxford Union, 25
  on political press, 268–69
  reporting of speeches, 271
  Tory Democracy, 252, 273
Churchill, Winston S. (1874–1965), 103, 105, 285
  oratorical education, 51–52, 53, 70, 71
  oratorical style, 51, 281
  study in failure, 284
Cicero, 12, 14, 52, 59, 67
  biography by A. Trollope, 192–93
  compares law to the stage, 196
  quoted, 79–80, 94–95
City Temple, London, 146, 148, 165, 274
civic celebrations, 181, 278–79
Clarendon Commission, 33, 66–67
Clarke, Edward (1841–1931), 185, 211, 212, 213, 282
Clifford, John (1836–1923), 164

Clough, Blanche Athena (1861–1960), 43, 45
Cobbett, William (1763–1835), 77
Cobden, Richard (1804–65), 61, 89, 238, 239, 244
Cockburn, Alexander (1802–80), 40
 on advocate's duty, 190–91
 law officer, 167–69, 216, 218
 Palmer trial, 167–69, 204
 parliamentary speaker, 215–16
 trial of Tichborne Claimant, 205
Coleridge, John Duke (1820–94), 11, 13, 40, 89–90
 law officer, 212, 218
 parliamentary speaker, 215, 216–17
 trial of Tichborne Claimant, 205–7
Coleridge, John Taylor (1790–1876), 66
College Historical Society, Dublin, 24
Common Law Procedure Act (1854), 175
communications, 277–78; *see also* BBC, railway, roads, press and printing, telegraphy, television, wireless
Congregationalists, 108–9, 128, 131, 134, 164; *see also* Dale, Parker
Conservative principles, 232, 233, 234, 235
Cooper—*see* Shaftesbury
Corn Importation bill (1846), 93
Corn Laws, 19, 26, 76, 89, 232, 233, 237–38, 272
Counsel for Prisoners Act (1836), 174, 175, 187, 217
County Courts, 176, 217
 County Courts Act (1846), 280, 321*n*55
 solicitors as advocates in, 320*n*34
  see also legislation, County Courts Act (1846)
courthouses and courtrooms, 1, 177–79, 205, 276, 277
 increasing number and wider distribution of, 169
 as performance space, 196
  see also Central Criminal Court, County Courts, Manchester Assize Courts, Royal Courts of Justice, Victoria Law Courts
Cox, Edward (1809–79), 184, 189–90
Criminal Evidence Act (1898), 197, 287
Criminal Procedure Amendment Act (1865), 175
Cromwell, Oliver, 53
Cross, Richard (1823–1914), 40, 247
Cruppi, Jean (1855–1933), 196, 326*n*162
Crystal Palace, 129, 235, 256, 259
Cuddesdon College, 138, 139, 142
Curzon of Kedleston, George Nathaniel, Earl (1859–1925), 282
 on appeal of Gladstone and Bright, 267
 on barrister–MPs, 214
 on decline of Latin quotations in House of Commons, 61
 on W. Churchill, 52
 on Disraeli, 97
 on 18th century politicians, 105
 on Eton Society, 13
 on extra-parliamentary speeches, 245–46
 on golden age of parliamentary oratory, 81

Dale, R. W. (1829–95), 164, 240, 249
Davidson, John Thain (1833–1904), 164
Dawson, George (1821–76), 125, 127, 249
Dean and Chapter Act (1840), 119; *see also* cathedrals
debating societies, 181, 276, 277, 289
 Bedford Chapel, 148
 collegiate, 12, 13–14, 15
 educational opportunity through public speech, 49
 18th century, 11
 essay clubs, 14
 legal, 7, 49, 184–85, 321*n*55, 321*n*56, 321*n*57
 political clubs, 47
 in provincial towns, 46, 277, 279–80
 at provincial universities, 46
 public school, 6, 12–13, 28, 84, 184
 reporting of speeches, 280
 serious recreation, 49

debating societies (*continued*)
sharp practice clubs, 43, 45
for solicitors, 321*n*55
university, 6–7, 70, 183
Welsh, 279–80
women's colleges, 42–46
see also Cambridge Union Society, Durham University Debating Society, Durham Union Society, Edinburgh Union Society, Eton Society, Historical Society Dublin, local parliaments, Oxford Union Society, political clubs, Rochdale Literary and Philosophical Society, United Debating Society Oxford
Defence of the Realm Act (1914), 285
Demosthenes, 14, 52, 61
Derby, 15th Earl of—*see* Stanley.
Derby, Edward George Stanley, 14th Earl of (1799–1869), 168, 234, 256, 260
Devonshire—*see* Hartington
Dickens, Charles (1812–70), 1, 61
Courvoisier trial, 323*n*95, 324*n*121
on law and lawyers, 191–92
parliamentary reporter, 303*n*95
public readings, 191–92
Dictionary of National Biography, 25–26, 37–40, 47
Dilke, Charles (1843–1911), 98
Disraeli, Benjamin, Earl of Beaconsfield (1804–81), 7, 79, 89, 91, 213, 216
budget of 1852, 86, 223
classical knowledge, 92–93, 103
education, 92–93
English quotations, 95
extra-parliamentary speeches, 235, 255, 256, 259, 263
foreign policies protested, 240, 244
and Gladstone, 10, 85, 103, 213, 251–52
Latin quotations and phrases, 60–61, 93–95, 98, 103, 104, 307*n*169
legal background, 183
maiden speech, 96–97
man of opposition, 97
monument erected by Victoria, 275
new–style politician, 99
on reporting of debates, 77
and Peel, 80, 93–95, 97, 255
phrase–maker, 98
style, 56, 95–97, 98, 104
and Tait, 310*n*38
Wilde compared to, 97
see also Beaconsfieldism
Disruption of 1843, 108, 112, 124
Don Pacifico affair, 102–3, 181, 215–16
Dufferin and Ava, Fredrick Blackwood, Marquis of (1835–1911), 41
Durham Union Society, 295*n*38
Durham University Debating Society, 24
Dykes, J. Oswald (1835–1912), 164

Eastern Question, 76, 154–55, 243
Ecclesiastical Commission, 309*n*15
Ecclesiastical Titles bill (1851), 84, 91
ecumenicism, 113–14, 163, 286
Edinburgh Union Society, 24
Education Act (1870), 239
Edward VII—*see* Albert Edward, Prince of Wales
elections
electoral culture, 225–26, 227
local customs, 330*n*13
uncontested, 226
see also general elections
electoral franchise, 6, 8, 221, 225, 274, 226, 248, 285; *see also* general elections Reform Acts, Reform bills, Reform debates
Elgin, James Bruce, Earl of (1811–63), 37, 41
Eliot, George (1819–80), 1, 43
Middlemarch, 225
on Spurgeon, 130, 133
Empire, 9, 14, 57, 243, 251, 283
Escott, T. H. S. (1844–1924), 64
Eton Society ("Pop"), 12–13, 28, 84, 184
Evangelical Alliance, 134
evangelical movement, 107, 133, 136–37, 150, 162, 278

Evans's Tavern, 202
Everett, William (1839–1910), 23–24
Exchange Telegraph, 270
executions, 169, 197
Exeter Hall, London, 120, 128–29
extra-parliamentary speech-making—*see* platform

Fabian Society, 273–74
Farrar, Frederic William (1831–1903), 145–48, 164
Fawcett, Henry (1833–84), 27–28
Forensic Society, 184, 277, 321*n*56, 321*n*57
Forsyth, William (1812–99), 182
Fox, Charles James (1749–1806), 12, 14, 62, 69, 72, 74, 77, 79, 81, 104, 199
  classical quotations, 58
  cultivation, 56
  English quotations, 58–59
  extra-parliamentary speeches, 228–29
  man of opposition, 56–57, 97, 103
  orator, 56–57, 59, 300*n*20
  oratorical education, 56
  and Pitt, 54, 56–57
  published speeches, 58–59, 230, 232
Fox, Henry—*see* Holland
Fraser, Donald (1826–92), 164
Free Church of Scotland, 124
  church–building, 112
  ministers, 108
    see also Disruption of 1843
Free Trade, 233, 255, 283
Free Trade Hall, Manchester, 234, 235, 237, 238, 241, 242, 255, 259, 281
Fry, Charles Burgess (1872–1956), 294*n*27

Garbett, Cyril Foster (1875–1955), 32
Garrett, Charles (1823–1900), 164
Garrick Club, 202
general elections
  1868, 242, 269
  1874, 242
  1880, 246, 269
  1885, 248, 251, 259, 269
  1886, 248
  1918, 285
Gilbert, William Schwenck (1836–1911), 171–72, 184, 192
Gladstone, Catherine (1812–1900), 260–61
Gladstone, Helen (1849–1925), 45
Gladstone, William Ewart (1809–98), 7, 10, 14, 45, 52, 79, 89, 239, 280, 282
  and Brooke, 151, 154, 155, 158–59, 160, 161
  budget speeches, 83, 86–87, 181, 283
  Bulgarian atrocities agitation, 240
  and Canning, 229, 241
  and Chalmers, 156
  Chancellor of the Exchequer, 40–41, 78, 83, 86–87, 91–92, 100–102, 113, 218, 223, 241, 268, 283
  and classics, 29, 84, 86, 91, 93, 99
  connoisseur of preaching, 155–56
  criticized, 10, 235, 244, 247, 251–52
  death, 31–32, 284, 296*n*64
  demagogue, 87, 220, 244, 248
  and Disraeli, 10, 85, 103, 213, 251–52
  Don Pacifico affair, 102–103, 216
  education, 13, 83, 99
  Eton, 8–9, 13, 84
  Eton Society ("Pop"), 13, 84
  evangelicalism, 150
  extra-parliamentary speeches, 88, 158, 160, 223–24, 234, 240–45, 246, 248, 257, 258, 259, 262, 263, 264, 265–66,269–70, 270–72, 278
  and Hallam, 15
  influence of preachers on use of platform, 160
  interest in rhetoric and oratory, 8–9, 241
  and E. Irving, 155–56
  and H. Irving, 203–4, 326*n*151
  Latin quotations, 84–86, 99, 100–102, 305*n*125, 305*n*130
  legal training, 183
  legislator, 76, 86–88
  and Liddon, 151–57, 160, 161
  lifts stamp and paper duties, 78, 113, 241, 268, 277

Gladstone, William Ewart (*continued*)
Lloyd George on, 283
mesmeric power, 264, 272
Midlothian campaigns (1879 and 1880), 8, 160, 161, 243–45, 247, 258, 260–61, 266, 269, 271, 272, 273
MP for Oxford University, 29–30, 295*n*54
on Manchester Assize Court, 177
on parliamentary reporting, 303*n*95
oratorical dominance of House of Commons, 83, 86, 283
oratorical innovations in Parliament, 83
Oxford Union, 27–32, 84, 85
and Parker, 151–57, 160, 161
and Peel, 83, 241
perceived honesty, 195
physical strain of speech-making, 263, 276
and Pitt, 83, 86–88
and great preachers, 150–62, 267
preaching, 156
reading, 304*n*116
regional accent, 81
religious nationality, 150
reporting of speeches, 241, 269–72, 285
retirement, 248
rhetorical leadership, 281
sense of divine mission, 161
sense of right timing, 273
speeches as commodity, 271, 284
speeches in House of Commons, 51, 100–102, 214, 276
speeches on Ireland, 87–88
and Spurgeon, 151–58, 160, 161–62, 316*n*182
unmuzzled, 30, 242
Virgilian duel with Lowe, 100–2
works by, 8–9, 83
Gladstone, William Henry (1840–91), 157
Godley, John Arthur, Baron Kilbracken (1847–1932), 87, 261
Gorst, John Eldon (1835–1916), 24–25, 211
Goschen, George Joachim (1831–1907), 41, 246
Granville, George Leveson-Gower, Earl (1815–91), 242
Gray, Thomas (1716–71), 306*n*149
Great Depression, 273
Grenville, William, Baron (1759–1834), 299*n*14
Greville, Charles (1794–1865), 313*n*18
Grey, Charles, Earl (1764–1845), 20, 168, 263
Guizot, François (1787–1874), 81
Gully, William, Viscount Selby (1835–1909), 20, 41
Guthrie, Thomas (1803–73), 125–26

Habermas, Jürgen, 5
Hallam, Arthur (1811–33), 15, 24
Halsbury, Hardinge Stanley Giffard, Earl of (1823–1921), 185
Hamilton, Walter Ker (1808–69), Bishop of Salisbury, 138
Harcourt, William Vernon (1827–1904)
at Cambridge Union, 18–19, 40
imitates Disraeli, 98
extra-parliamentary speeches, 246
law officer, 211
parliamentary speaker, 217
Hardwicke Society, 184–85, 221, 277
Harrison, Frederic (1831–1923), 185
Harrowby, Dudley Ryder, Earl of (1762–1847), 299*n*14
Hartington, Spencer Compton Cavendish, Lord (1833–1908), 84, 246, 248
Hayward, Abraham (1801–84), 64
Heath, Edward, 41
heckling, 149, 181, 259, 274
Herschell, Farrer, Baron (1837–99), 185
Hitler, Adolf, 284
Holland, Henry Fox, Baron (1705–74), 12, 56
Home Rule, 71, 76, 84, 88, 154–55, 185, 210, 211, 213, 228, 248, 251, 280
debated in Cambridge and Oxford Unions, 24–25
debated in Newnham College Political Society, 45

Homer, 29, 66, 67, 83
Hooper, Geraldine (1841–79), 149, 165
Horace, 61, 66, 67
quoted, 58, 93–94
translations by Pitt and Gladstone, 83
House of Commons, 56, 179, 233
changing nature of business and legislation, 76, 81, 86–88, 213, 215, 276
emotionalism and violence in 18th century, 57
English quotations in speeches, 58–59, 61, 80, 90–91, 95
Latin quotations in speeches, 55, 57–61, 79–80, 84–86, 93–95, 98, 100–102, 103, 305*n*125, 305*n*130, 307*n*169
legendary status of 18th century, 57
limitations of MPs, 59
model for debating societies, 7, 20, 44–45, 48–49, 277, 289
physical structure, 70–71
reporters' gallery, 77–78
spectators, 180
see also barrister–MPs, Members of Parliament, New Palace of Westminster, parliamentary oratory
House of Lords, 8, 108, 116, 211, 299*n*8
Howard, Michael, 328*n*194
Hughes, Hugh Price (1874–1902), 164
Hunt, Henry "Orator" (1773–1835), 41, 236
hustings, 8
definition, 225
nature of speeches, 225–28, 230, 233
rituals and traditions surrounding, 225–26
Huxley, Thomas Henry (1825–95) , 150, 152, 186

Inns of Court, 170, 172, 173, 179, 183, 184, 185, 190–91, 195, 199, 203, 208–9, 287
Ireland, 9, 243, 251, 253, 285
Irish Land bill (1870), 88
union with United Kingdom, 14, 57, 70
see also Home Rule
Irving, Edward (1792–1834), 122, 124, 155–56
Irving, Henry (1838–1905), 198, 203–4, 326*n*151
Irving, Henry B. (1870–1919), 189, 287
Isaacs, Rufus (1860–1935), 220

James, Edwin (1812–82), 167, 189, 199–200, 325*n*131
James, Henry (1828–1911), 185, 211, 216
Jenkins, Edward (1838–1910), 98
Jephson, Henry L. (fl. 1870), 224, 263, 272
Jervis, John (1802–56), 212
Jonson, Ben, 91
Joyce, Patrick, 4–5
Judge and Jury Society, 184, 202–3, 204; *see also* Nicholson
judges, 180, 182
Judicature Acts (1873 and 1875), 177, 185
Juries Act (1825), 180
juries, 180, 182
Juvenal, 61, 67

Keble, John (1792–1866), 137, 138
Keeley, Mary Anne (c. 1805–1899), 201
Keeley, Robert (1773–1869), 201
Kelly, Fitzroy (1796–1880), 189, 215
Kemble, Charles (1775–1854), 325*n*131
Kendal, Margaret (1849–1935), 201
Kendal, William (1843–1917), 201
Kenealey, Edward (1819–80), 189
Kenyon, Frederic George (1863–1952), 61–62
Kilbracken—*see* Godley
Kimberley, John Wodehouse, Earl of (1826–1902), 215
Kingsley, Charles (1819–75), 119–20
Kinnock, Neil, 283

Labouchère, Henry (1831–1912), 161
Labour party, 283
law
assize circuits, 171, 172, 173, 180
judicial calendar, 171
legal education, 173, 183, 221

law (*continued*)
morality of advocacy, 7, 186–95
as oratorical theater, 7, 195–98, 204–7, 280, 281
quarter sessions, 173
see also barristers, barrister–MPs, courthouses and courtrooms, Inns of Court, law officers, law reforms, legal oratory
law and lawyers, in literature, 191–95, 323*n*93
law officers, 210–12
in court, 329*n*205
duties, 218–19
legal work, 210
remuneration, 212
speeches, 213, 215–18, 219
see also barrister–MPs
law reforms, 7, 169, 172, 173–77, 180, 221, 276
appellate system, 174, 177, 185, 186, 211
capital offences reduced, 186, 197
convergence of common law and equity practices, 177
courtroom procedure, 186, 207, 219–20
special jurisdictions eliminated, 176
legal oratory, 168, 169–70, 181–83
becomes less free-wheeling, 219–21
classical models, 182
domain expanded, 173–77
melodramatic, 199–200
training, 7, 49, 181–85, 321*n*55, 321*n*56, 321*n*57
20th century, 287
Lenin, Vladimir I., 284
Leopold, Duke of Albany, 11
Liberal party
decline of, 282
fracturing, 248
role of platform and press, 224
Liberalism, connection with public speech, 282
Liddon, Henry Parry (1829–90)
Canon of St. Paul's Cathedral, 138, 140–42
earnestness, 145
education and early career, 137–38
evangelical influences, 136–37
compared to Farrar, 145–46
and Gladstone, 151–57, 160, 161
non-evangelical preaching star, 136
Oxford Movement, 137, 138–39
Oxford Union, 137, 314*n*128
perceived honesty, 195
physical strain of preaching, 138–39, 142
popularity, 127, 136, 141–42, 145, 149, 163, 164, 244, 279, 286
preaching and sermons, 138–45
resists Rome, 137
compared to Spurgeon, 137, 143–44, 312*n*86
Lincoln, Henry Pelham-Clinton, Lord (1811–1864), 29; *see also* Newcastle
Liverpool, Robert Jenkinson, Earl of (1770–1828), 109
Livy, 67
Lloyd George, David (1863–1945), 282, 284
courtroom orator, 280, 281
debating societies, 280, 281
demagogue, 281
extra-parliamentary speeches, 280,281, 285
on Gladstone, 283
influence of preaching on, 126, 279, 281
parliamentary speaker, 220, 281
"People's Budget," 86
pulpit experience, 279, 281
rhetorical leadership, 281, 282
sermon–taster, 279
upbringing and education, 279–80
on wireless, 289
local government, 46, 177
local parliaments, 7, 44, 48–49, 277, 289
Lockwood, Francis (1846–1897), 201, 325*n*135
London, 9
club and tavern life, 202

concentration of popular preachers, 127, 163, 165
diocese, 115–16
tourists, 127, 129, 131, 141–42, 163
Lowe, Robert (1811–1892), 11, 37, 41
Adullamites, 91, 242
Vigilian duel with Gladstone, 100–2
Lucretius, 86, 305*n*126
Lucy, Henry (1843–1924)
on Bright, 90
on Chamberlain, 249–50
on Disraeli, 97
on Harcourt, 217
Lygon—*see* Beauchamp
Lyndhurst, John Singleton Copley, Baron (1772–1863), 174
Lytton, Edward Bulwer (1803–73), 82

Macaulay, Thomas Babington, Baron (1800–59), 98, 305*n*125
Bright compared to, 313*n*18
on parliamentary government, 51
on press as fourth estate, 77
MacDonald, James Ramsay (1866–1937), 284
extra-parliamentary speeches, 285
member of local parliament, 48–49
on wireless, 288–89
Maclaren, Alexander (1826–1910), 164
Macready, William (1745–1829), 198
Macready, William Charles (1793–1873), 198, 201
Magee, William Connor (1821–1891), Bishop of Peterborough, later Archbishop of York, 164
Manchester Assize Court, 16, 177
Manchester
Bright at, 238–39
R. Churchill at, 267
Disraeli at, 235
Gladstone at, 223–24, 241, 242, 329*n*3
Palmerston at, 234
"Peterloo," 236, 255
see also Free Trade Hall, Manchester Assize Court
Manning, Henry Edward (1809–1892), 11, 37, 164
Marriage to a Deceased Wife's Sister bill (1866), 217
mass politics, 5, 274
Matthew, H. C. G., 6, 224–25, 296*n*60
Maurice, Frederick Denison (1805–72), 163
McTaggart, John Ellis (1866–1925), 23
Members of Parliament, 170
contributions to debates, 72–76, 303*n*90
education, 64–70, 71
increasingly public function, 276
Irish, 73, 74
more businesslike, 74–75
social composition, 60–63, 65, 71, 75, 89, 282
voting behavior, 73–74
see also barrister–MPs, House of Commons, New Palace of Westminster, parliamentary oratory
Merchant Tailors' Hall, London, 231–32, 234, 260
Methodists, 110
church–building, 111–12
ministers, 108, 148–49
see also Punshon, Wesley, Whitefield
Metropolitan Tabernacle, London, 127, 129, 141, 165, 281, 289; *see also* Spurgeon
Midlothian campaigns (1879 and 1880), 8, 160, 161, 243–45, 247, 258, 260–61, 266, 269, 271, 272, 273
Mill, John Stuart (1806–73), 152, 322*n*73
Milman, Henry Hart (1791–1868), Dean of St. Paul's, 120, 121
Milton, John, 54, 84, 91, 95
Moody, Dwight L. (1837–99), 160
Moots, 185
morality and public life, 103–4, 186–95
Morley, John (1838–1923), 3–4
on Burke, 53–54
and Gladstone, 28–29, 83
Oxford Union, 25
Morris, William (1834–96), 148

Mosley, Oswald (1896–1980), 285, 289
Municipal Corporations Act (1835), 46, 177
Musolf, Karen, 3
Mussolini, Benito, 284

Napoleon III, plot to assassinate, 200
National Association of Local Parliaments, 48
National Education League, 239, 240
National Secular Society, 150
Newcastle, Henry Pelham–Clinton, 4th Duke of (1785–1851), 29; *see also* Lincoln
New Forensic Society, 321*n*57
Newman, John Henry (1801–90), 138, 164
New Palace of Westminster, 70–71, 179
newspapers—*see* press and printing
Nicholson, "Baron" Renton (1809–1861), 184, 202–4; *see also* Judge and Jury Society
Nonconformity, 107, 108, 114, 117–18, 128, 134, 135, 136, 162, 165
  in Birmingham, 125
  and Bulgarian atrocities agitation, 153–54, 240
  and Gladstone, 152–54
  and National Education League, 240
  places of worship, 110–12, 120, 129
  in Wales, 126, 279
    see also Baptists, Congregationalists, Methodists, preachers and preaching, Salvation Army, Unitarians
Normanby, Constantine Phipps, Marquis of (1797–1866), 40
Northcote, Stafford (1827–1904), 246, 247

O'Brien, William (1803–64), 297*n*70
O'Connell, Daniel (1775–1847), 96
O'Connor, Feargus (1794–1855), 236
O'Connor, T. P. (1848–1929), 283
O'Gorman, Frank, 225–26
Old Bailey—*see* Central Criminal Court
Oliver, Robert T., 3
Ong, Walter, 5
Orton, Arthur—*see* trials, Tichborne Claimant
Ostrogorski, Moesi (1854–1919), 224
Oxford Movement, 136, 137, 138–39
Oxford Union Society, 6–7, 216, 277, 288
  amenities, 17
  and Asquith, 41, 296*n*66
  benefits of experience, 25–26
  buildings, 16–17
  debates, 19–20, 21
  fiftieth anniversary jubilee, 11, 30–31, 293*n*1, 295*n*57, 296*n*58, 314*n*128
  founding and early years, 11, 16
  and Gladstone, 27–32, 84, 85
  library, 17
  and Liddon, 314*n*128
  "nursery of statesmen," 12
  and other debating societies, 27–28, 24
  presidents and officers, 18, 20–21, 32–42, 294*n*27, 296*n*66
  publication of speeches, 22
  rules and procedures, 19, 21
  and Salisbury, 247, 296*n*66
  social character, 17–18
  style of speeches, 22–23
  women admitted, 42

Palmer, Roundell, Earl of Selborne (1812–1895)
  classical education, 66–67
  law officer, 212, 213
  Oxford Union, 11, 30, 37, 40, 42
  parliamentary speaker, 215, 220
Palmerston, Henry John Temple, Viscount (1784–1865), 14, 20, 30, 181, 215–16
  Don Pacifico affair, 102–103, 215–16
  ecclesiastical appointments, 115, 153, 310*n*38
  extra-parliamentary speeches, 233–34, 242, 331*n*35
Pankhurst, Emmeline (1858–1928), 285
Parker, Joseph (1830–1902), 279
  and Gladstone, 151–57, 160, 161
  preaching, 145–48, 163, 164

parliamentary oratory, 1, 5–6, 14
18th century "golden age," 7, 52–60, 73, 79, 81
19th century preoccupation with, 52
and aristocratic constitution, 19, 61–62, 73, 283
belief in decline of, 19, 52, 60
as branch of literature, 52
compared to legal speech, 194
debates, 181, 276
grandeur, 52
tradition of eloquence, 51
see also House of Commons, House of Lords, Members of Parliament, New Palace of Westminster
Pearse, Mark Guy (1842–1930), 164
Peel, Sir Robert (1788–1850), 20, 23, 89, 183, 218
Bulwer Lytton on, 82
and Canning, 81
and church–building, 110, 309*n*15
and Disraeli, 80, 93–95, 97, 255
education, 79, 99
English quotations, 80, 99
extra-parliamentary speeches, 231–32, 233, 254, 260, 263
Latin quotations, 79–80, 95, 99, 305*n*125
middle–class origins, 79, 81, 82
published speeches, 80, 232, 304*n*103
quality of speeches and oratorical reputation, 80–81, 82
reforms, 197
regional accent, 81
Tamworth Manifesto, 231
virtuous statesman, 82–83
Penny Pulpit, 114, 130, 141, 277
Phillips, Charles (c. 1787–1859), 187–88, 191, 220, 323*n*93
Pitt (the Elder)—*see* Chatham
Pitt, William ["the Younger"] (1759–1806), 14, 69, 74, 77, 79, 82, 89, 229
and Fox, 54, 56–57
and Gladstone, 83, 86–88
budget speeches, 86–87
classical knowledge, 54, 83, 92, 299*n*14
English quotations, 58–59
Latin quotations, 55–56, 58, 59–60, 92
maiden speech, 54–55, 96
man of government, 56–57, 103
oratorical education, 54
published speeches, 58–59, 230, 232
reputation as a speaker, 54–55, 62, 72, 81, 84, 296*n*58
speech on the slave trade (1792), 55–56, 59–60
speeches on Ireland, 87–88
platform, 76, 88, 181, 290
audibility and visibility of speakers, 262, 276
audiences, 180, 251, 258–62, 264, 274, 276
"battle of the platforms," 245–53
compared to other kinds of oratory, 195, 253–54
crowd conditions, 266–67
decline, 284
definition, 224, 225
effects on hearers, 264–65
early experiments by leading politicians, 228–35
heckling, 259
indoor venues, 237, 254–57, 276
"middle–class" protests, 332*n*48
out-of-doors, 257–58, 277, 335*n*128
physical and mental strain of speaking, 263–64
printing of speeches, 269
radical mass protest movements, 8, 228, 278, 235–41
religious appeal, 8, 240, 244, 267
ticketing and admission, 259
types of events, 258–62
use by leading politicians, 7–8, 223, 224, 246
women, 260–62, 337*n*179
see also Anti–Corn Law League, Bulgarian atrocities agitation, Chartism, Midlothian campaigns, National Education League

political parties, national organizations, 8, 47, 54, 74, 226, 227, 248, 268–69, 285
Pollock, Jonathan Frederick (1783–1870), 183, 218
Pollock, William Frederick (1815–1888), 183, 201
Pope, Alexander, 59
population, growth and urbanization, 276
Post Office, 270, 288
Potter, Beatrice (1858–1943), 264–65
Powell, John Enoch (1912–98), 103
preachers and preaching, 170, 278
  audiences, 180, 258–62, 264, 274, 276
  compared to other kinds of oratory, 181, 194–95
  influence on broader political culture, 7, 8, 159–62, 240, 267
  number of preachers, 108–9
  number of sermons in 1880s, 107
  out-of-doors, 115, 116, 129, 149, 165, 254, 277
  physical strain of, 124, 139, 142, 149
  popularity, 7, 107–8, 163–64, 265, 267, 278, 286
  secularity in consumption of preaching, 162–63, 165, 286
  20th century, 285–86
  Wales, 126, 279
    see also Nonconformity, religion, secularization, sermon–tasting
press and printing, 5, 6, 224, 225, 277, 278, 288
  courtroom reporting, 113, 180, 287
  Gladstone lifts duties affecting, 78, 113, 180, 241, 268, 277
  growth of, 78, 180, 268
  legal, 188
  new journalism, 287, 288
  news agencies, 78, 270
  parliamentary reporting, 62, 77–78
  platform speeches, 113, 241–42, 269–72
  political influence, 268, 277
  religious, 112–14, 123, 131–32, 148, 310*n*28
  trade in great men's speeches, 270–71, 273, 284
    see also Exchange Telegraph, Press Association
Press Association, 270, 284
Primrose—*see* Rosebery
professions
  organizations, 8, 278
  "rise" of, 186
public halls, 165, 254–57, 277; *see also* Bingley Hall, Crystal Palace, Exeter Hall, Free Trade Hall, Merchant Tailors' Hall, Metropolitan Tabernacle
public life
  culture of, 279
  relationship with public speech, 276, 277, 279
  term comes in to currency in 18th century, 301*n*54
public schools, 33, 64–67, 84, 92, 198; *see also* Clarendon Commission
public speaking
  as manifestation of Victorian energy, 276
  diminished influence in 20th century, 282
  historical study of, 2–5
  production and consumption of, 276–77, 282
Pugin, Augustus Welby (1812–52), 70
Punshon, William Morley (1824–81), 145–48
Pusey, Edward B. (1800–1882), 136, 137, 138

radicalism
  assimilation into Liberal mainstream, 236–37
  protest movements, 235–41
railways, 76, 127, 172, 263, 277–78, 288
recording technology, 5
Reform Acts
  1832, 20, 28–29, 60, 61, 62–63, 64, 85, 231

1867, 63, 64, 75, 226
1884, 62, 63, 76, 250, 259, 281
effects (or lack thereof) on background of MPs, 60–65, 75
Reform bill (1866), 85, 88, 91, 100, 216, 242, 238–39, 242
Reform debates, 230, 233, 236, 269
Reform League, 239
religion
influence in platform movements, 240, 244
publications, 112–14, 310*n*28
religious census of 1851, 107, 111
sermons on wireless, 289
transformation of worship, 7
see also preachers and preaching, secularization, sermon–tasting, worship
roads, macadamized, 127
Robbins, Keith, 9
Robertson, Frederick William (1816–1853), 124–25, 148
Rochdale Literary and Philosophical Society, 46, 89
Roebuck, Disney (1819–85), 201
Rosebery, Archibald Philip Primrose, Earl of (1847–1929), 13, 271
Royal Courts of Justice, London, 178–79
Russell, Charles, Baron Russell of Killowen (1832–1900), 185, 201–2
Russell, John, Lord (1792–1878), 14, 23, 72, 84, 93, 96, 263, 299*n*14, 305*n*124
extra-parliamentary speeches, 232–33
Russell, William, Lord, 187

St. Paul's Cathedral, 119–20, 127, 140–42, 279
St. Peter's Field, Manchester, demonstration (1819), 236, 255
Salisbury, Robert Arthur Talbot Gascoyne–Cecil, Marquis of (1830–1903), 11, 211
extra-parliamentary speeches, 245, 246, 247–48, 249, 253, 256, 335*n*113
Oxford Union, 247, 296*n*66
Salvation Army, 109, 112, 147, 244
Sankey, Ira D., 160
"Saxon" idiom
advised for barristers, 182
in architecture, 71
Bright, 90, 135, 136
Spurgeon, 135, 136
Scotland, 9, 14, 70
secularization, 7, 289
masked by popularity of preaching, 162–63, 286
Selborne—*see* Palmer
sermon-tasting, 163, 286, 290
Sex Disqualification (Removal) Act (1919), 318*n*9
Shaftesbury, Anthony Ashley Cooper, Earl of (1801–1885), 128–29
Shakespeare, William, 54, 59, 91, 102
Shaw, George Bernard (1856–1950), 148, 274
Shee, William (1804–1868), 167–69, 188, 204
Sheridan, Richard Brinsley (1751–1816), 59, 82, 89, 199
Simon, John (1873–1954), 282, 296*n*64
Oxford Union, 22, 25, 26, 29, 31
parliamentary speaker, 220
Smiles, Samuel (1812–1904), 274
Smith, F. E.—*see* Birkenhead
Smith, W. H. (1825–1891), 246
Smith, Willliam (1856–1909), Archbishop of Sidney, 41
Soane, John (1753–1837), 178
Social Democratic Federation, 273–74
Solicitor General—*see* law officers
solicitors
as advocates, 176, 280, 281, 320*n*34
debating societies, 321*n*55
space in relation to oratory, 6, 164, 273; *see also* cathedrals, church–building, courthouses and courtrooms, New Palace of Westminster, public halls, platform, worship
Spa Fields, mass meetings at, 236, 237
Speakers' Corner, 273

speeches and speech-making
  civic rituals, 278–79
  comparisons, 181, 194–95, 253–54, 275–76, 328*n*189
  dedication ceremonies, 278
  entertainment value, 127, 150, 163, 265, 274, 289–90
  as historical sources, 2
  importance of, 1–2
  literary and professional societies, 278
  in novels, 1–2, 192–94, 225
  physical strain of, 124, 139, 142, 149, 263–64, 276
  prevalence, 2, 8–9, 278–79, 290
  public and semi–public occasions, 278
  public lectures, 191–92, 278
  published, 5–6, 58–59, 62, 77–78, 80, 112–14, 180, 230–32, 241–42, 269–73, 284, 304*n*301, 310*n*28
  types, 8–9
    see also audiences for public speaking, debating societies, legal oratory, parliamentary oratory, platform, preachers and preaching, public speaking, trials
Spenser, Edmund, 91, 95
sports, 265, 290, 294*n*27
Spurgeon, Charles Haddon (1834–1892), 289
  Arnold on, 135
  audiences, 129, 130–31
  and Bright, 135–36, 313*n*118
  Eliot on, 130, 133
  and Gladstone, 151–58, 160, 161–62, 316*n*182
  Hooper compared to, 149
  compared to Liddon, 137, 143–44, 312*n*86
  New Park Street, 128
  Pastor's College, 130
  perceived honesty, 195
  popularity, 127, 128–31, 134–36, 145, 163, 164, 279, 286, 312*n*87
  preaching and sermons, 128–31, 133, 135, 136
  publication of sermons, 130–32
  "Saxon" speech, 135, 136
  theological views, 133, 152
  tragedy at Surrey Gardens Music Hall, 129, 266
  upbringing and education, 128
Stanhope, Philip Henry, Earl (1805–1875), 11, 55–56
Stanley, Arthur Penrhyn, (1815–81) Dean of Westminster Abbey, 163
Stanley, Edward Henry, Lord [15th Earl of Derby] (1826–93), 73–74, 102,105, 212, 213, 305*n*130
Stanley—*see* Derby
Stedman Jones, Gareth, 4–5
Stephen, James Fitzjames (1829–1894)
  on the bar, 182, 189, 194
  compares English and French trials, 197
  on the Palmer trial, 167, 168
  public moralist, 186, 220
Stephen, Leslie (1832–1904), 295*n*42
Strachey, Lytton (1880–1932), 10, 114
Street, George Edmund (1824–81), 179
suffragettes, 262, 285

Tacitus, 299*n*14
Tait, Archibald Campbell (1811–1882)
  appointed Bishop of London, 114–15, 310*n*38
  Archbishop of Canterbury, 116, 138, 310*n*38
  cathedral services, 119–22, 142
  earnestness, 116
  Oxford Union, 11, 37, 41
  oratory, 115–16
  organizes services in public halls, 120, 128–29
  promotes improvement in preaching, 116–18, 162
Talfourd, Francis (1828–62), 201, 203
Talfourd, Thomas Noon (1795–1854), 201
Taylor, A. J. P., 289
Taylor, Katherine Fischer, 196
Telegraph Act (1868), 270

telegraphy, 278, 288
television, 284
Temple—*see* Palmerston
Tennyson, Alfred Lord (1809–92), 61
Terence, 307*n*162
Thackeray, William Makepeace (1811–63), 1
theater, 8, 198–204, 290
Thesiger, Frederick (1794–1878), 214
Thompson, Edward P., 196
Thucydides, 299*n*14
Trelawny, Sir John (1816–85), 105
Trench, Richard Chenevix (1807–1886), Dean of Westminster Abbey, 41, 120, 121
Trevelyan, George Macaulay (1876–1962), 98–99, 103
Trevelyan, George Otto (1838–1928), 98, 104, 217
trials
  audiences, 167–68, 170, 179–80, 188, 205, 206, 207
  contest of opposing counsel, 197–98
  compared to drama, 197–98, 204–7, 324*n*115
  declining number of criminal trials in superior courts, 175–76
  specific trials discussed or mentioned:
    Bernard (1858), 200
    Courvoisier (1840), 187–88, 189, 192, 193, 323*n*93, 323*n*95, 324*n*121
    Hopwood (1855), 216
    Hastings (1788–95), 57, 82
    Mannings (1849), 199–200
    Palmer (1856), 167–69, 188, 204, 207, 216
    Queen Caroline (1820), 190
    Tawell (1845), 189
    Tichborne (1871–72), 204–7
    Wilde (1895), 205
Trollope, Anthony (1815–1882), 1
  law and lawyers, 192–94, 209–10
  on speaking in Parliament, 96
  popularity of works, 192, 194
truthfulness, Victorian obsession with, 186, 195

Unitarians, 108, 125
United States
  Civil War, 233, 238
  rhetorical culture of, 292*n*15
  Spurgeon's continued importance, 312*n*87
  see also America
universities, Scottish, 65, 68
University of Cambridge
  Apostles, 15, 24
  classical education, 67, 68, 69
  honors examinations, 34–35
  revived law curriculum, 173
  social background of students, 64–65
  women admitted, 42
    see also Cambridge Union Society, debating societies, women's colleges
University of London, 68
University of Oxford
  classical curriculum, 67–68, 69
  Gladstone MP for, 29–30
  revived law curriculum, 173
  social background of students, 64–65
  tradition of silence for parliamentary candidates, 30, 333*n*70
  women admitted, 42
    see also debating societies, women's colleges, Oxford Union Society, United Debating Society Oxford
University Tests bill (1866), 216

Verney, Richard Greville, Lord Willoughby de Broke (1869–1923), 227
Vernon, James, 225–26
Victoria Law Courts, Birmingham, 177
Victoria, Queen (1819–1901), 10, 140, 203–4, 275, 283, 310*n*38
Vincent, John, 224
Virgil, 59, 61, 66, 67, 68, 84, 307*n*162
  quoted, 55–56, 84–85, 100–102, 305*n*124, 305*n*130

Wales, 9, 14
debating societies, 279–80
preaching culture, 126, 279
Walpole, Horace (1717–97), 53
Walpole, Spencer (1806–98), 40
wars
American Civil War, 233, 238
Crimean War, 167
French Revolutionary and Napoleonic wars, 54, 57
Seven Years War, 57
World War I, 282, 285, 286
Waterhouse, Alfred (1830–1905), 16, 177
Watson, Joshua (1771–1855), 109
Webb, Beatrice—*see* Potter
Webb, Sidney (1859–1947), 148
Weber, Max (1864–1920), 244
Wesley, John (1703–91), 122, 165, 267
Westminster Abbey, 82, 120
Brooke preaches at, 159
Farrar as Canon at, 145–46
White, William (1807–82), 71
Whitefield, George (1714–70), 122, 267
Wilberforce, Samuel (1805–73), Bishop of Oxford, 37, 164
debates Huxley, 150
and Liddon, 139
Wilde, Oscar (1854–1900), 205
compared to Disraeli, 97
cross–examined by Carson, 205
Wilde, Thomas, Lord Truro (1782–1885), 199
Wilkins, Charles (c. 1802–1857), 167, 199–200, 220, 325*n*128, 325*n*131
Wilkite demonstrations, 235
Williams, Ivy (1877–1966), 43
Williams, Montagu (1835–1892), 182, 201, 202, 262, 264
Willoughby de Broke—*see* Verney
Wilton, Marie—*see* Bancroft
wireless, 288–89, 290
Wodehouse, P. G. (1881–1925), 285–86
women, 10
at the bar, 43, 318*n*9
in elected office, 46, 239
at platform events, 260–62, 337*n*179
as preachers, 148–49
see also suffragettes
Woolf, Virginia (1882–1941), 284, 290
worship
experience of transformed in 19th century, 107, 162
limits on Anglican worship outside a church abolished (1855), 120, 128–29
spaces for, 109–12, 119–22, 164–65
see also preachers and preaching, secularization, sermon–tasting, religion
Wraxall, Nathaniel (1751–1831), 59